DEFINING DOCUMENTS
IN WORLD HISTORY

The Middle Ages
(476-1500)

DEFINING DOCUMENTS
IN WORLD HISTORY

The Middle Ages
(476-1500)

Editor

Michael Shally-Jensen, PhD

SALEM PRESS
A Division of EBSCO Information Services
Ipswich, Massachusetts

GREY HOUSE PUBLISHING

Publisher's Cataloging-In-Publication Data

Publisher's Cataloging-In-Publication Data
(Prepared by The Donohue Group, Inc.)

The Middle Ages : (476-1500) / editor, Michael Shally-Jensen, PhD. --
  [First edition].

    pages : illustrations ; cm. -- (Defining documents in world history)

  Edition statement supplied by publisher.
  Includes bibliographical references and index.
  ISBN: 978-1-61925-773-3 (hardcover)

  1. Middle Ages--Sources. 2. Civilization, Medieval--Sources. 3. Church history--Middle Ages, 600-1500--Sources.
I. Shally-Jensen, Michael.

D113 .M53 2015
909.07

FIRST PRINTING
PRINTED IN THE UNITED STATES OF AMERICA

Table of Contents

Byzantium and Western Europe in the Early Middle Ages

The Catholic Church and its Vicissitudes

England and France

THE NEAR EAST AND BEYOND

PHILOSOPHY, RELIGION, AND SCIENCE

APPENDIXES

Publisher's Note

Defining Documents in American History series, produced by Salem Press, consists of a collection of essays on important historical documents by a diverse range of writers on a broad range of subjects in American history. This established series offers a dozen titles ranging from Colonial America to Post War 1940s.

This volume, *Defining Documents in World History: Middle Ages,* broadens the scope of the series to include world history. *Middle Ages* surveys key writing and documents produced from 476 to 1500, and includes a number of maps to help the reader understand the state of the world during this period. The material is organized under five broad categories:

- Byzantium and Western Europe in the Early Middle Ages
- The Catholic Church and its Vicissitudes
- England and France
- The Near East and Beyond
- Philosophy, Religion, and Science

Historical documents provide a compelling view of ancient world history. Designed for high school and college students, the aim of the series is to advance historical document studies as an important activity in learning about history.

Essay Format

Middle Ages contains 40 primary source documents – many in their entirety. Each document is supported by a critical essay, written by historians and teachers, that includes a Summary Overview, Defining Moment, Author Biography, Document Analysis, and Essential Themes. Readers will appreciate the diversity of the collected texts, including journals, letters, speeches, political and religious sermons, laws, government reports, and trial notes, among other genres. An important feature of each essay is a close reading of the primary source that develops evidence of broader themes, such as the author's rhetorical purpose, social or class position, point of view, and other relevant issues. In addition, essays are organized by section themes, listed above, highlighting major issues of the period, many of which extend across eras and continue to shape life as we know it around the world. Each section begins with a brief introduction that defines questions and problems underlying the subjects in the historical documents. A brief glossary included at the end of each document highlights keywords important in the study of the primary source. Each essay also includes a Bibliography and Additional Reading section for further research.

Appendixes
- **Chronological List** arranges all documents by year.
- **Web Resources** is an annotated list of web sites that offer valuable supplemental resources.
- **Bibliography** lists helpful articles and books for further study.

Contributors

Salem Press would like to extend its appreciation to all involved in the development and production of this work. The essays have been written and signed by scholars of history, humanities, and other disciplines related to the essay's topics. Without these expert contributions, a project of this nature would not be possible. A full list of contributor's names and affiliations appears in the front matter of this volume.

Editor's Introduction

The Middle Ages is a period in European history falling between the classical age (ancient history) and the emergence of the Renaissance in the 15th century. Humanists of the Renaissance, in fact, were the first to employ the term "middle ages"—along with its synonym, "Dark Ages"— to describe the era that immediately preceded their own. That era was thought to have been something of a dark period in history because of its legacy of barbarism, ignorance (or scantiness of learning), superstition, and ecclesiastical crudity (under the Crusades, etc.). Alternatively, it was viewed as a kind of transition between the great achievements of the classical era and the later developments of the Renaissance—hence the notion of a "middle time." Not that any of these characterizations holds up completely in light of the objective historical evidence—every era, after all, seems to have its own forms of barbarism and ignorance. But such is how the Renaissance scholars viewed the matter, and the designation stuck (although the term "dark ages" is no longer used).

The start of the Middle Ages is traditionally assigned the date of 476, when the last Roman emperor in the West, Romulus Augustulus, was deposed by the German chief Odoacer. Although that event brought an end to the Western Roman Empire, the empire in the east, based in Constantinople (Istanbul), survived as the Christianized Byzantine Empire. The ancient world did not end abruptly in 476 but rather declined gradually from the 3d century through the 7th century. By "declined" one means that longstanding institutions and systems of thought and governance were overturned and not necessarily replaced with institutions or systems of comparable stature or durability. Even so, the Middle Ages is the time when the Roman Catholic Church came to the fore throughout Europe, as the "pagan" beliefs of the earlier Roman era and the ensuing "barbarian" invasions gave way to Christian doctrine and a well organized clerical order. By the 5th century the bishop of Rome, known as the pope, was recognized as the head of the church. The Byzantine, or Eastern Orthodox Church took a different path.

The end date of the Middle Ages is a little fuzzier, in the scheme of things. It stands amid the transition to the Renaissance in 15th century. It is generally understood that in Italy, where the first effects of Renaissance culture were felt, the Middle Ages had come to an end by the late 14th century. In the rest of Europe, on the other hand, it took another century before the Middle Ages had faded, yielding to a new Age of Discovery. By both convention and convenience, then, one can safely date the end of the Middle Ages in Europe at around 1500.

The Early Middle Ages

With the Roman Empire in sharp decline by the 4th century, various Germanic tribes, having already infiltrated the empire, began a migration through much of Europe. The Visigoths (or Vesi), for example, moved into the Danube River valley and then south to Italy. From there, likely in response to Hunnic invasions from the east, they migrated southwest to Gaul (France) and Iberia (Spain and Portugal). There they founded a Visigothic kingdom, which existed between 415 and 711, when Moorish invaders from North Africa disunited it. The Visigoths were replaced in the east by the Ostrogoths, who, under King Theodoric, conquered Italy and Sicily. With the death of Theodoric in 526, his kingdom collapsed, leaving the Lombards (or Langobards) to build a kingdom in northern Italy while the Byzantine emperor Justinian reestablished imperial rule in southern Italy and Sicily. Another Germanic tribe, the Vandals, ravaged Gaul, entered Spain, and extended their reach into northern Africa, where they established a kingdom. The latter kingdom disrupted Mediterranean shipping and pillaged widely until Justinian retook North Africa in the 6th century.

In Gaul, beginning in the late 5th century, the Franks moved in from the Rhine River region. Under their chief, Clovis (reigned 481-511), the Franks conquered other Germanic tribes and came to occupy most of Gaul. Clovis accepted Christianity and obtained the support of the pope for himself and his people. The move laid the foundation of the Merovingian kingdom, which existed until 751.

In Britain at the start of the Middle Ages, the Romans were expelled by the Angles and Saxons, two Germanic tribes that eventually mingled (hence Anglo-Saxon) and coexisted, not always peacefully, with the native Celtic peoples. Eventually, the Anglo-Saxons came to occupy most of Britain—Wales and northern Scotland excepted. By the 7th century, England consisted of seven Anglo-Saxon kingdoms. Most of these later succumbed to Viking invasions from the north. Only the kingdom of Wessex, under Alfred the Great (reigned 871-899), remained unconquered. Indeed, subsequent Wessexian leaders expanded their control into the rest of England, creating an Anglo-Saxon kingdom that survived into the 11th century. The conquest of England by Norman invaders from across the channel took place in 1066.

Meanwhile, another legacy of the "dark ages" was the rise of Catholicism (Christianity) along with the abandonment of Latin and Greek literatures, which were thought, now, pagan. Only a few of the clergy retained Latin, and Greek scholarship became a very limited activity. Boethius (480-522) wrote a treatise, *The Consolation of Philosophy*, while jailed under Theodoric and awaiting execution for treason. Gregory of Tours (538-594) wrote his *History of the Franks* in corrupted Latin and with little evidence. Isidore of Seville (c. 560-636) compiled a questionable summary of all knowledge to date. In contrast, Bede the Venerable (673-735), a Northumbrian monk, prepared a useful *Ecclesiastical History of the English People*.

The most significant figure of the early Middle Ages, though, was Charlemagne (Latin, Carolus; c. 742-814), creator or the Carolingian Empire, which covered most of western Europe. Charlemagne introduced a well functioning system of central and local administration, oversaw a uniform system of justice, strove to build a general economy, and helped to reform the church and religious education. In 800 he was crowned in Rome as emperor by Pope Leo III, thus inaugurating what later was called the Holy Roman Empire. Under Charlemagne, Latin study and religious education were preserved and further developed. Yet, a series of Viking and Arab attacks brought disarray toward the end of his reign. By 887 the Carolingian empire was gone, and within a hundred years Europe was a mosaic of competing feudal states. Feudalism, with its fiefdoms, lords, knights, and vassals, became the prevailing system through the end of the 13th century. The church, too, became feudal in nature, with bishops and abbots receiving fiefs in return for services rendered, including military services. Not even a revived Holy Roman Empire, on a smaller scale, under Otto the Great (reigned 936-972), could tame the evident turbulence in European politics and culture during this era. Although merchant and craft guilds, along with development of a middle or bourgeois class, contributed to a stable economic environment and the rise of large towns and cities, there continued to be enormous inequalities and injustices throughout the region, along with corruption and ecclesiastical intrigue—just as there was, in equal measure, the cultivation of chivalry, or a code of conduct pertaining to knighthood and courtly interactions.

With the Investiture Controversy, a struggle for power took place between the German emperor Henry IV (reigned 1056-1106) and Pope Gregory VII (reigned 1073-1085). Gregory's victory in 1077 weakened lay rulers' control over the church. Yet, similar confrontations erupted in later years, most notably one in England between Thomas Becket, archbishop of Canterbury, and King Henry II. The struggle ended with Becket's murder in 1170 and a newly strengthened king. During this period, too, the church sought to extend its control militarily by means of the Crusades. It encouraged the bringing of its dogmas and doctrines to the heathens and infidels of the world (i.e., pagans and non-Christians). The First Crusade (1096-1099) targeted Turks in Asia Minor and the Levant and largely achieved its ends. Later Crusades, however, proved less successful—though during the Fourth Crusade (1201-1202) Constantinople was taken from the Byzantine emperors.

The High Middle Ages

Between 1100 and 1300, medieval civilization in Europe reached its height. Relatively stable states, headed by kings, developed, along with strong institutions. There were new, more efficient economies and financial organizations. The church reached its peak in power and authority. Intellectual and artistic activities were such that scholars have variously applied the terms "renewal," "revival," or even "renaissance" (with a small "r") to the period.

The English kings, whose power was almost absolute by the late 12th century, established an efficient central administration made up of an exchequer and a court contingent consisting of highly effective individuals. To confront major questions of the day, kings could assemble a council of court officials and leading magnates, although the final decision was the king's along to make. The reign (1199-1216) of King John was marked by controversy. Locked in a struggle with Pope Innocent III, unpopular with the magnates for losing English possessions to France, and known to flaunt laws and civil procedures, John faced an aristocratic revolt in 1215 and was obliged to grant concessions to the barons of the realm in the form of a written document known as Magna Carta. The document affirmed that the king was subject to the law, a premise central to the form of government known as constitutional monarchy. By the late 13th century, an assembly, or parliament, was in place, giving voice to lords and commoners.

In France, Germany, and Italy, meanwhile, different developments took place. France varied in its institutions by region. French kings, more so than the English, consolidated their power by pitting one region against the other. The French kings also retained absolute authority under the principle of the divine right of kings, which made them essentially vehicles of god. German kings, in contrast, remained relatively weak owing to the Investiture Controversy and to their failed attempts at controlling northern Italy. With few effective rulers, various princes assumed authority and made Germany into a patchwork of principalities, which remained central there into the 19th century. Italy, on the other hand, was convulsed by struggles between the German kings and the papacy, both of whom sought authority over it. With neither side achieving a decisive, lasting victory, what remained in Italy were independent city-states such as Venice and Florence. Similar city-states, or emergent states based on stable cities, were present in Spain, Portugal, and elsewhere. In such locations, capitalism took hold and flourished along with arts and letters.

Despite some heresies and challenges to its authority, the church stood triumphant in the 12th and 13th centuries. Crusades were ordered by the pope, kings were often humbled by ecclesiastical expressions of power, and church doctrine itself was occasionally adjusted to ensure its continuing supremacy over secular life. Even so, variations from the norm could and did occur—such as the establishment of the Franciscan friars, devoted to austerity and assisting the poor, by Francis of Assisi in 1209. Other specialized religious orders arose at this time, as well. Through it all, papal government remained exceptionally efficient and continued to accrue to the church a wealth of valuable holdings.

The Late Middle Ages

Except in northern Italy, by the late 13th century economic growth had halted and a lengthy cycle of stagnation took root, causing considerable social strife. There were peasant revolts in England, France, and the Netherlands. Worse, the Plague, or Black Death, cut through European society between 1348 and 1350, killing nearly a quarter of the population. In consequence, seignorialism, or the manor system on which

feudal society was based, began to unravel. Peasants were released or claimed their freedom, as landholders could no longer sustain their enterprises. The middle class became ever stronger in light of the budding shift from manorial forms to capitalist (mercantile) forms of economic activity. Kings now sometimes aligned themselves with the commoners over the aristocracy in order to gain advantage. Such a broad-based alliance between ruler and ruled spelled the end of the feudal state and the rise of the nation state.

Thus, by the 14th century a variety of medieval patterns were being replaced by newer ones. In central Europe, the emerging Habsburg dynasty increased its power by acquiring the Low Countries (Netherlands) through the marriage of archduke Maximilian of Austria to the daughter of the Burgundian duke Charles the Bold. In Burgundy itself, lying between Germany and France and separate from either, a remarkable culture developed, rivaling that of England and France. Eventually, Spain too would become a Habsburg possession through another opportunistic marriage, and Spanish culture would flourish.

Meanwhile, for over one hundred years between 1337 and 1453, France and England would be at war (the Hundred Years' War). It began with a claim by Edward III that he was heir to the French crown and would recapture English possessions lost to France. Despite English combat successes at Crécy (1346) and Poitiers (1356), the war drew out into an endless series of skirmishes and retaliations. The French court was dealing with its own internal factional conflict at the time, thus weakening its military efforts. In England, a string of weak kings left the English magnates largely in charge of political and legal affairs. Only when Joan of Arc (1412-1431), a peasant girl from Lorraine, sought to rally French forces at the Siege of Orléans (1428-1429), was a turning point reached and England was forced to give up its continental claims. And, yet, immediately after the Hundred Years' War, England faced a civil war, the War of the Roses (1453-1485), brought on by a dispute over the crown between rival families from York and Lancaster. The war ended when Henry Tudor defeated and killed the Yorkist king, Richard III.

Italy during this period was likewise marked by political and military maneuvering, as various small states aligned and realigned themselves under a shifting array of princes and mercenaries. Milan was seized by Francesco Sforza in 1450; Florence fell under the sway of the Medici family; the Papal States were wracked by dissension and struggle; and Sicily went to the house of Aragon while southern Italy went to the Angevins. The Catholic Church, too, became notably unsettled, with Pope Clement V (reigned 1305-1314) and his successors taking up residence in Avignon (France) rather than in Rome. With Gregory XI, the papacy returned to Rome, in 1377, and yet the following year saw the eruption of a great schism whereby different claimants at different times and places declared themselves pope. The schism ended only in 1417, by which time the church had already suffered a great decline in prestige. Events during that long rivalry, and lingering criticisms afterward, laid the foundation for the rise of a new religious vision, one that eventually would take the form of the Protestant Reformation as set out by Martin Luther. By then, a new age was in the making.

Michael Shally-Jensen, PhD

Bibliography and Additional Reading

Bennett, Judith. *Medieval Europe: A Short History.* New York: McGraw Hill, 2010.

Fried, Johannes. *The Middle Ages.* Cambridge, MA: Belknap Press, 2015.

Frugoni, Chiara. *A Day in a Medieval City.* Chicago: University of Chicago Press, 2005.

Herlihy, David V., ed. *Medieval Culture and Society.* Prospect Heights, IL: Waveland Press, 1993.

Jordan William Chester. *Europe in the High Middle Ages.* New York: Viking, 2001.

Lyon, Bryce D., ed. *The High Middle Ages.* New York: Free Press, 1984.

Contributors

William E. Burns, PhD
Georgetown University

Steven L. Danver, PhD
Walden University

Tracey DiLascio, JD
Framingham, MA

Bethany Groff, MA
Historic New England

Laurence W. Mazzeno, PhD
Norfolk, Virginia

Lee Tunstall, PhD
Calgary, Alberta, Canada

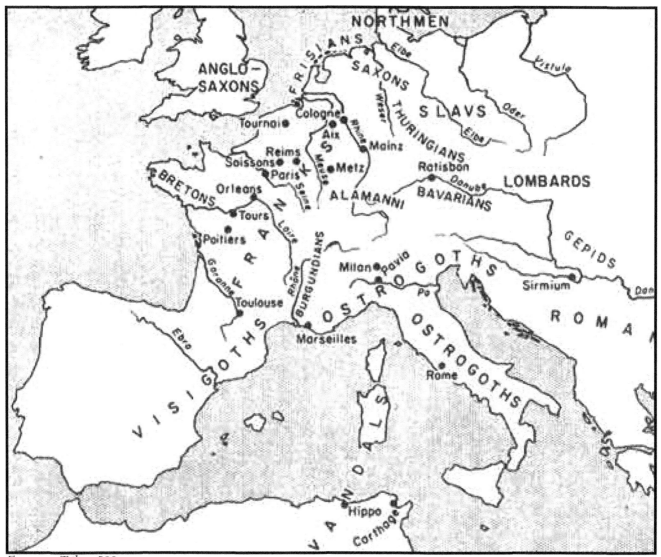

European Tribes, 500

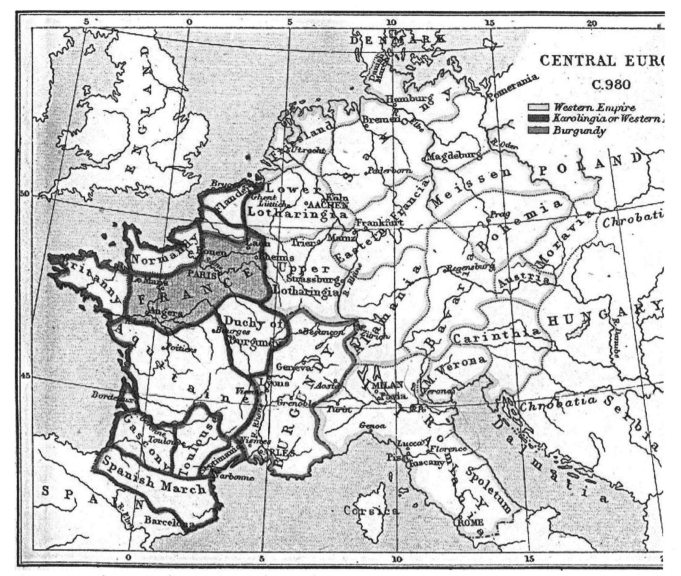

Europe, c. 980, showing Carolingian Empire and Burgundy

The Holy Roman Empire, c. 1000

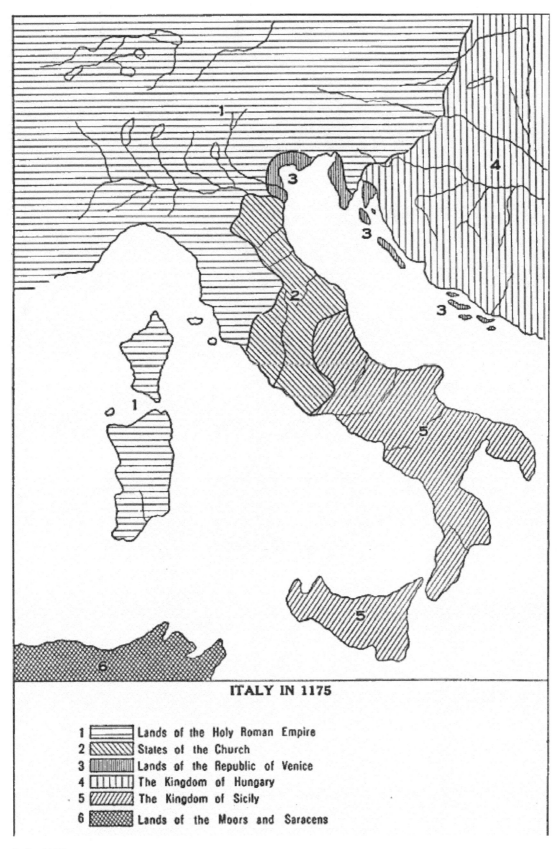

ITALY IN 1175

1 Lands of the Holy Roman Empire
2 States of the Church
3 Lands of the Republic of Venice
4 The Kingdom of Hungary
5 The Kingdom of Sicily
6 Lands of the Moors and Saracens

Italy, 1175

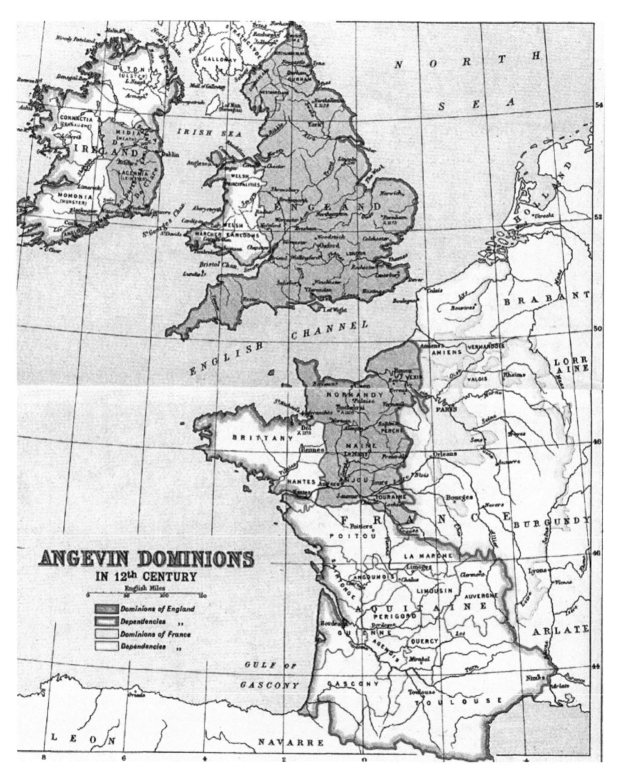

England and France, 12th Century

DEFINING DOCUMENTS
IN WORLD HISTORY

The Middle Ages
(476-1500)

BYZANTIUM AND WESTERN EUROPE IN THE EARLY MIDDLE AGES

The Byzantine Empire was the successor to the Roman Empire, or rather to the eastern half of the Roman Empire. The western half struggled from at least the year 320, when Constantine the Great rose to power and shifted the capital from Rome to Constantinople. By 476, the start of the Middle Ages, the western empire was no more, having fallen to Germanic tribes from the north. In the east, however, the state thrived under a variety of Christianized emperors. Emperors were considered to have been chosen by god, and a complex court system evolved to protect and promote the person of the emperor. Part of the emperor's role was to preside over the Orthodox Church and to serve as the guardian of orthodoxy. A detailed set of laws, codified by Emperor Justinian in the 6th century, governed daily affairs and gave rise to a substantial bureaucracy. The ability to tax provincial estates and other subjects of the empire provided much of the state's revenues.

In western Europe during the early Middle Ages no comparable grand empire existed. Instead, a collection of smaller kingdoms arose, most of them tied to powerful individuals rather than to any overarching institution or ideal. The Frankish king Clovis I ascended to the throne in 481, and the Franks adopted Roman Christianity in 500. The Visigoths, ultimately settling in Iberia, practiced Arian Christianity, a non-trinitarian form of belief—until in 589, when they adopted Catholicism. The Angles and Saxons invaded Britain in 450 and eventually established a number of small kingdoms there. Roman Catholicism took hold in England in 664. Laws were established and agreements with outside rulers were instituted to maintain peace and order, not always successfully. The kingdom of Wessex, in particular, overseen at its height by Alfred the Great (reigned 871-899), was a model Anglo-Saxon realm—although even it faced challenges from Danish raiders. Few areas during the early Middle Ages were not subject to military challenges.

The greatest of the European empires at this time was the one founded by Charlemagne (reigned 800-814). His Carolingian Empire (so called because of his Latin name, Carolus) was centered in northern Gaul (France), and he extended its boundaries to parts of Italy and northeastern Spain. His followers spread Roman Christianity to other parts of Europe, laying the foundation of the Holy Roman Empire (from 962), a somewhat decentralized system of principalities, duchies, lesser kingdoms and other governing powers that persisted, in spirit if not always in empirical substance, into the early modern era.

■ Codex Justinianus: Children of the Unfree

Date: ca. 530
Geographic Region: Byzantine Empire
Author: Justinian I

Summary Overview

The Byzantine (Eastern Roman) emperor Justinian I ruled from 527 until 565 CE and had a major impact on the empire's social and political structure. Shortly after his ascension, he began work on his most ambitious project, a revised collection of Roman civil law known as the *Corpus Juris Civilis* (*Body of Civil Law*; also known as the *Codex Justinianus,* or *Code of Justinian*). It brought together analysis of past laws and legal opinions and adapted these according to Justinian's wishes. The resulting section known as the *Codex Constitutionum* went through all laws issued by previous emperors, negated those that were obsolete or that Justinian considered unjust, and updated others.

The selection "Children of the Unfree" deals with the law regarding the inheritance of social status among the lowest classes of society. The empire at the time had a complex system of unfree people, with slaves at the bottom and *adscripticii* (land-bonded serfs) just above. Justinian changed previous tradition to state that any children born of a union between any members of these unfree people would inherit the status of the mother. It established that slaves and *adscripticii* were legally equal.

Defining Moment

When Justinian rose to power as an adviser to his uncle, Emperor Justin I, in 518, the Roman Empire was divided. The Western Empire had crumbled under invasions of Germanic tribes. The Eastern Empire remained more stable, with the city of Constantinople serving as the capital for the Byzantine rulers, including the Justinian dynasty. Justinian seems to have had a hand in the selection of his elderly uncle Justin as emperor after his predecessor, Emperor Anastasius, died without naming a successor. Some sources suggest Justinian ruled with his uncle, and as Justin became increasingly erratic, Justinian's power increased. In 527, Justin officially appointed Justinian as coemperor, and after his

uncle died that same year, Justinian took on full leadership of the Byzantine Empire. His main goal quickly became to restore the empire to its previous heights by reconquering former Roman territories and strengthening his government's power.

Justinian was a man of extraordinary ambition and energy. He also had a talent for promoting capable men, whatever their social status. His vision would significantly shape not only the territory of the empire, but its entire social structure through legal, political, religious, and cultural policies. First came military action, as Justinian and his generals turned to the problem of the Germanic tribes that had been attacking the borders of the empire and demanding tributes. Wars were also fought on the eastern front against the Persian Empire. Successful conquests would eventually expand Byzantine power to its greatest reach, encompassing most of the Mediterranean, and Justinian reorganized the government to better administer the empire's territory. Justinian also overcame domestic revolts and championed Orthodox Christianity, opposing rival branches of Christianity as well as paganism. Major efforts were undertaken in the arts and architecture, including the construction of the Hagia Sophia church in Constantinople.

Another focus of Justinian's ambition was the revision of the entire body of Roman law. Early in his reign, he assembled a council of legal scholars who pored over existing laws and eliminated those that were redundant or obsolete. This was not universally popular among the aristocracy in the empire, already displeased that Justinian had circumvented traditional families and appointed many commoners to top administrative and military positions. Justinian's belief that his will was law also weakened the influence of the Senate, and his authoritarian approach was unpopular. However, his reforms were enacted despite his controversial standing and codified in the *Codex Justinianus*. The final legal

3

doctrine ensured the survival of Roman law in history, as it was preserved in the empire and then spread through Europe in the Middle Ages.

Author Biography and Document Information

Emperor Justinian I, also known as Justinian the Great, was born as Petrus Sabbatius around 482 CE in Dardania, a province of the Roman Empire in the Balkans (present-day Macedonia). He was adopted by his uncle Justin, then in the Byzantine imperial guard. When Justin became emperor in 518, Justinian was his closest adviser before becoming official coemperor in 527 and sole ruler later that year. He married the courtesan Theodora despite her low social class, and she proved

instrumental to his reign. Justinian successfully expanded the Byzantine Empire to its greatest extent and undertook a comprehensive revision of Roman law. He died in 565 in Constantinople and is considered a saint by Eastern Orthodox Christians.

Justinian's collection of legal works is the *Corpus Jurus Civilis*. It was compiled from 529 to 565 and divided into four sections: the *Codex Constitutionum,* the *Digesta* (or *Pandectae*), the *Institutiones*, and the *Novellae Constitutiones post Codicem*. The *Codex Constitutionum*, from which the extract "Children of the Unfree" is taken, was released around 529 and revised in 534. It was developed by a commission of legal scholars led by the jurist Tribonian.

HISTORICAL DOCUMENT

In marriages between those of unfree status, when within that category the parents were of different social classes, the children followed the condition of the mother. For all practical purposes slaves and *adscripticii* were equal before the law.

XI.48.xxi. Lest there be any further doubt, if any one is descended from a bondwoman and a slave or *adscripticius* and a female slave, who is (and this might be worse fortune) either of bond or of servile rank, we decree that those things which were provided in former laws for such offspring, born of bondwoman and freeman, shall be

left in their present state, and the offspring procreated from such connection shall be of bond status. But if any one were born either of a slave and a bondwoman or of a female slave and a bondman, he should follow the condition of his mother and be of such condition as she was, either slave or bondwoman; which rule has hitherto been observed only in cases of marriage between free and servile. For what difference is evident between slaves and *adscripticii* when both are placed in the *potestas* of a lord and he is able to manumit a slave with his goods and to expel from his dominion an *adscripticius* with land?

GLOSSARY

adscripticii: (plural form of *adscripticus*) the free, but landless workers who were recorded on the census records under the name of the owner of the land on which they worked and lived

manumit: to set free

potestas: legal power over another

servile: held in servitude; relating to slaves

Document Analysis

The question of how to manage social status, including that of slaves, vexed lawmakers throughout Roman history and carried into the Byzantine era. In this section, Justinian specifically addresses the issue of determining the social status of children born to those marrying across classes at the bottom of the spectrum.

Many separate categories of unfree people exist, but Justinian focuses on outright slaves (the lowest class) and *adscripticii* (serfs who are bonded to the land but not technically enslaved). Above them all are free Roman citizens, whose rights are more clearly defined and protected by other laws. Justinian's text seeks to clarify and simplify the law regarding the status of the offspring of couples who have married across these social categories.

Justinian explains that in previous laws there was consensus that the offspring of a freeman and a slave woman or bondwoman would follow the condition of the mother and be slave or bonded rather than free, and he declares that this rule will remain. However, there had been disagreement on whether the children of a slave man and a bondwoman, or alternately a bondman and a slave woman, would be a slave or not. Justinian establishes once and for all that the principle that applies between free men and slave women applies here as well. The condition of the mother determines the condition of the child.

Significantly, Justinian justifies this decision by explaining his view that slaves and *adscripticii* are essentially equal when it comes to the practical nature of landowners' power over unfree people. "What difference is evident between slaves and *adscripticii* when both are placed in the potestas of a lord?" he asks, perhaps to allay the fears of lords who would prefer children be slaves rather than *adscripticii*. Though he does not change the existing social order, Justinian recognizes that these two classes are legal equivalents. This ruling is a good example of Justinian's attempts to streamline and clarify conflicting legal opinions with his *Codex Justinianus*.

Essential Themes

Though this passage sought only to clarify the status of the offspring of unfree couples, it is just one of several sections of the *Codex Justinianus* devoted to clarifying issues of slavery and freedom, highlighting the importance of the subject. Elsewhere in the code, Justinian addressed other questions regarding whether children were free or enslaved under certain circumstances, including if a child were conceived while the mother was free, then subsequently enslaved. His ruling was that if at any time in her pregnancy the mother was free, the child would be free as well. Justinian's laws tended toward the rational and logical, and he was not afraid of offending or alienating the aristocracy by reducing their access to slaves. This contributed to his unpopularity with the traditional Byzantine elite. However, the writing also shows how vital and accepted slavery and other forms of social stratification were in Byzantine society, even after the widespread adoption of Christianity.

Justinian's text here and throughout the codex illustrate his efforts to simplify a complicated legal system. Years of imperial decrees had created a convoluted, often contradicting patchwork of civil law; recognizing the importance of jurisprudence to government power, Justinian sought to clarify everything in one collection. Although it is not known how strong an impact the codex had upon its release, the work survived and eventually had a profound influence on legal thought in the Western world. It would become a cornerstone for many modern aspects of Western legal systems.

—*Bethany Groff, MA*

Bibliography and Additional Reading:

Brooks, Sarah. "The Byzantine State under Justinian I (Justinian the Great)." *Heilbrunn Timeline of Art History*. Metropolitan Museum of Art, 2000. Web. 13 Mar. 2015.

Evans, James Allan. *The Emperor Justinian and the Byzantine Empire*. Westport: Greenwood, 2005. Print.

Grabar, André. *The Golden Age of Justinian: From the Death of Theodosius to the Rise of Islam*. New York: Odyssey, 1967. Print.

■ Novella 146: On Jews

Date: 553
Geographic Region: Constantinople (present-day Turkey)
Author: Justinian I

Summary Overview

Judaism could be found in every corner of the Roman Empire in its first centuries. The polytheistic Romans were tolerant of the Jews, as they generally allowed existing religions to continue in conquered territories, so long as they did not interfere with the worship of Roman gods. By the time of Emperor Justinian I, in the sixth century, however, the Eastern Roman Empire (or the Byzantine Empire, as the remaining eastern half of the empire is known to history) was Christian, and the Jews faced increasing restrictions on their lives and religious practice. This is exemplified by Justinian's laws restricting the way that Jewish texts could be read and also legislating what Jewish beliefs were and were not permissible. Justinian saw himself as the ultimate authority on Christian Orthodoxy in his empire, and he thought it appropriate to impose a Christian perspective on Jewish religious practices as well. Novella 146 concerns restrictions on how Jewish religious texts can be read and interpreted. This is one of many laws pertaining to the Jews of the Byzantine Empire issued by Justinian.

Defining Moment

Justinian ruled as emperor from 527 until 565 (he had been the de facto coruler since 518). Shortly after his ascension, he assembled a commission of legal scholars to begin work on his most ambitious project, the *Corpus juris civilis* (body of civil law). This was not a new legal code. Rather, it brought together analysis of past laws and legal opinions, and adapted these according to Justinian's wishes. The resulting *Codex constitutionum* (now known as the *Codex Justinianus*), went through all the laws issued by centuries of previous emperors, negated the laws that were obsolete or that Justinian considered unjust, and adapted the language to reflect present circumstances. Later in his reign, Justinian added to his code of laws with the *Novellae constitutiones* (new laws) issued after the second edition of the

Codex Justinianus in 534. These *Novellae*, some one hundred sixty of them, reveal the attention paid by Justinian to every aspect of law in the empire, including his attention to the status and rights of Jewish people and his attempts to introduce Christian principals into the legal system.

The legal standing of the Jewish people was unique in the history of the Roman Empire. While most religions in the empire were polytheistic, and thus absorbed elements of Roman religious belief, the Jewish faith was monotheistic; therefore, the Jews in the empire were exempted from the requirement that they worship the Roman gods. In 330, Emperor Constantine I moved the capital of the empire from Rome to Byzantium, renaming it Constantinople. Shortly thereafter, Christianity became the official religion of the empire, and many other religions, including Christian heresies and the "pagan" polytheistic religions, were forbidden. The Jews, who had been made Roman citizens in 212, were allowed to maintain their citizenship and practice their religious beliefs, including circumcision, so long as they paid a special tax.

As Christianity continued to establish itself in the empire, restrictions on non-Christians increased. By 425, Jewish men were barred from civil service, military positions, and all other public offices, with the exception of tax collection. They were prohibited from purchasing Christian slaves, though they could inherit them. The building of new synagogues was prohibited, one of several efforts to check the spread of Judaism. In the fifth century, these restrictions were erratically enforced, as rulers occupied themselves with more pressing matters. Justinian, however, had the energy and will to enforce Christian Orthodoxy, and he included significant legislation regarding Jews in his exhaustive code of laws. Under Justinian, Christian slaves could no longer be owned by Jews, and those who defied this law could be executed. This was an enormous economic hardship in a society that relied heavily on slave labor. In addition, he ordered that synagogues could be converted to churches, and he outlawed all non-Christian places of worship in Egypt and North Africa. The restriction dealt with in Novella 146 was the right of the government to legislate religious issues within Judaism—in this case, the language in which the Pentateuch (the first five books of the Hebrew Bible) could be read, the portions of the scriptures that were forbidden, and the beliefs that must be held (or at least could not be refuted).

Author Biography

Justinian (Petrus Sabbatius) was born around 482 in Dardania, a province of the Roman Empire in the Balkans (around present-day Macedonia). He was adopted by his uncle Justin, then in the imperial guard, and later the Byzantine emperor. Justinian was educated in Constantinople, and so was well-versed in Roman law and history. When Justin became emperor in 518, Justinian was his closest adviser and served as a virtual regent before becoming official co-emperor in 527 because of Justin's increasing senility. When Justin died later that year, Justinian became sole ruler. Justinian had no children and adopted his nephew. His marriage to Theodora, a commoner and former courtesan, was allowed only because Justin had repealed a ban on aristocratic men marrying lower-class women. Justinian is best known for his comprehensive revision of Roman law and his successful attempts with the help of his two generals, Narses and Belisarius, to regain territory lost to the empire, including Italy, Spain, and North Africa. Justinian died in 565, in Constantinople. He is venerated as a saint by Eastern Orthodox Christians.

HISTORICAL DOCUMENT

8.ii.553. Nov.146. Justinian to Areobindas, P.P.

A Permission granted to the Hebrews to read the Sacred Scriptures according to Tradition, in Greek, Latin or any other Language, and an Order to expel from their community those who do not believe in the judgment, the Resurrection, and the Creation of Angels.

Preface.

Necessity dictates that when the Hebrews listen to their sacred texts they should not confine themselves to the meaning of the letter, but should also devote their attention to those sacred prophecies which are hidden from them, and which announce the mighty Lord and Saviour Jesus Christ. And though, by surrendering themselves to senseless interpretations, they still err from the true doctrine, yet, learning that they disagree among themselves, we have not permitted this disagreement to continue without a ruling on our part. From their own complaints which have been brought to us, we have understood that some only speak Hebrew, and wish to use it for the sacred books, and others think that a Greek translation should be added, and that they have been disputing about this for a long time. Being apprised of the matter at issue, we

give judgment in favour of those who wish to use Greek also for the reading of the sacred scriptures, or any other tongue which in any district allows the hearers better to understand the text.

Ch. I.

We therefore sanction that, wherever there is a Hebrew congregation, those who wish it may, in their synagogues, read the sacred books to those who are present in Greek, or even Latin, or any other tongue. For the language changes in different places, and the reading changes with it, so that all present may understand, and live and act according to what they hear. Thus there shall be no opportunity for their interpreters, who make use only of the Hebrew, to corrupt it in any way they like, since the ignorance of the public conceals their depravity. We make this proviso that those who use Greek shall use the text of the seventy interpreters, which is the most accurate translation, and the one most highly approved, since it happened that the translators, divided into two groups, and working in different places, all produced exactly the same text.

i. Moreover who can fail to admire those men, who, writing long before the saving revelation of our mighty

Lord and Saviour Jesus Christ, yet as though they saw its coming with their eyes completed the translation of the sacred books as if the prophetic grace was illuminating them. This therefore they shall primarily use, but that we may not seem to be forbidding all other texts we allow the use of that of Aquila, though he was not of their people, and his translation differs not slightly from that of the Septuagint.

ii. But the Mishnah, or as they call it the second tradition, we prohibit entirely. For it is not part of the sacred books, nor is it handed down by divine inspiration through the prophets, but the handiwork of man, speaking only of earthly things, and having nothing of the divine in it. But let them read the holy words themselves, rejecting the commentaries, and not concealing what is said in the sacred writings, and disregarding the vain writings which do not form a part of them, which have been devised by them themselves for the destruction of the simple. By these instructions we ensure that no one shall be penalised or prohibited who reads the Greek or any other language. And their elders, Archiphericitae and presbyters, and those called magistrates, shall not by any machinations or anathemas have power to refuse this right, unless by chance they wish to suffer corporal punishment and the confiscation of their goods, before they yield to our will and to the commands which are better and clearer to God which we enjoin.

Ch.II.

If any among them seek to introduce impious vanities, denying the resurrection or the judgment, or the work of God, or that angels are part of creation, we require them everywhere to be expelled forthwith; that no backslider raise his impious voice to contradict the evident purpose of God. Those who utter such sentiments shall be put to death, and thereby the Jewish people shall be purged of the errors which they introduced.

Ch. III.

We pray that when they hear the reading of the books in one or the other language, they may guard themselves against the depravity of the interpreters, and, not clinging to the literal words, come to the point of the matter, and perceive their diviner meaning, so that they may start afresh to learn the better way, and may cease to stray vainly, and to err in that which is most essential, we mean hope in God. For this reason we have opened the door for the reading of the scriptures in every language, that all may henceforth receive its teaching, and become fitter for learning better things. For it is acknowledged that he, who is nourished upon the sacred scriptures and has little need of direction, is much readier to discern the truth, and to choose the better path, than he who understands nothing of them, but clings to the name of his faith alone, and is held by it as by a sacred anchor, and believes that what can be called heresy in its purest form is divine teaching.

Epilogue.

This is our sacred will and pleasure, and your Excellency and your present colleague and your staff shall see that it is carried out, and shall not allow the Hebrews to contravene it. Those who resist it or try to put any obstruction in its way, shall first suffer corporal punishment, and then be compelled to live in exile, forfeiting also their property, that they flaunt not their impudence against God and the empire. You shall also circulate our law to the provincial governors, that they learning its contents may enforce it in their several cities, knowing that it is to be strictly carried out under pain of our displeasure.

GLOSSARY

Aquila: Aquila of Sinope, second-century CE translator of the Pentateuch into Greek

Mishnah: a collection of Jewish laws passed down through oral tradition and transcribed in the second century CE

Septuagint: earliest translation of the Pentateuch into Greek, dating to perhaps the second century BCE; literally, "the Seventy" (Latin, referring to the number of scholars alleged to have completed it)

Document Analysis

This novella laid out some of the religious beliefs and practices permitted to Jews by Emperor Justinian. Though there had been significant civic and public restrictions on the rights of Jews in the Roman Empire, this legislation is notable for specifically controlling beliefs and teachings within Judaism.

The text begins with the claim that it is written in response to a Jewish controversy and at their request. It declares that the reading of the "sacred texts," the Pentateuch, could be in languages other than Hebrew, so that its hearers everywhere could understand it. Justinian's intent here was not to spread the Jewish faith more widely. In fact, the opposite was true: if people heard the sacred texts in a language they could understand, Justinian reasoned that they would be more likely to recognize "sacred prophecies which are hidden from them, and which announce the mighty Lord and Savior Jesus Christ." If the Pentateuch were read only in Hebrew, its interpretation could be skewed, and Jewish religious authorities could "corrupt it in any way they like, since the ignorance of the public conceals their depravity." Justinian believed that since the prophecies in these first books of the Bible were clearly pointing to the coming of Jesus Christ, if the people were allowed to understand them in their own language, they could then also see the "prophetic grace . . . illuminating" the writers of these books. This part of the decree also bans the Mishnah, a consolidation of Jewish oral tradition committed to writing in the second century CE. Justinian dismissed this foundational text of rabbinical literature as the work of men rather than inspired by God; these were "vain writings" devised for "the destruction of the simple."

Another part of the decree provides that any person denying the "resurrection or the judgment, or the work of God, or that angels are part of creation" should be exiled or killed, since such teachings "contradict the evident purpose of God." The emperor thus had become the enforcer of God's will, as this document makes clear. Justinian sought to enforce a Christian Orthodoxy in his empire, and while not banning Judaism outright, he sought to remove what he saw as obstacles to Jews' perception of the reality of Christ as the coming of the Jewish messiah, foretold in their own scriptures. Novella 146 is to be circulated and enforced, and those not following it are to be severely punished; it is to be "strictly carried out under pain of our displeasure."

Essential Themes

This novella set out Justinian's view that the real use of allowing Judaism to survive was in the service of Christianity. Since the Pentateuch contained prophecies that the Christians believed led people to Jesus, they were allowed as being divinely inspired. Other Jewish laws and teachings were prohibited, as they were only the works of misguided men. It was crucial, therefore, that people should understand the sacred, divinely inspired texts in their own language, as the reading of them exclusively in Hebrew left room for the interpreter to mislead his listeners. Jewish teachings could not dent the primary tenets of Christianity—the resurrection of Christ, God's final judgment, and the existence of angels. The Roman (Byzantine) emperor was the final arbiter of what was allowed in the Christian faith. He was also the last word on what could be taught among the Jews.

—*Bethany Groff, MA*

Bibliography and Additional Reading

Fine, Steven, ed. *Sacred Realm: The Emergence of the Synagogue in the Ancient World*. New York: Oxford UP, 1996. Print.

Grabar, André. *The Golden Age of Justinian: From the Death of Theodosius to the Rise of Islam*. New York: Odyssey, 1967. Print.

Law, Timothy Michael, and Alison Salvesen, eds. *Greek Scripture and the Rabbis*. Leuven: Peeters, 2012. Print.

■ Excerpt from the Visigothic Code

Date: ca. 642 CE
Geographic Region: Spain
Author: King Chindaswinth

Summary Overview

During the late fourth century CE, threat of invasion by the Huns of central Asia pushed the Visigoths, a Germanic tribe, west into Roman territory. Clashes with the Romans led to further western migration, until around 418, when the Visigoths finally settled in Spain and southern France. Over the next three centuries, they established a kingdom, adopted Christianity and other Roman customs, and created written codes of law.

The Visigothic Code was established by King Chindaswinth near the beginning of his reign in 642. It covered many areas of substantive law, including property ownership, inheritance, marriage rules, and contract law. Book I, Title 2 discussed the principles that should govern the creation of laws and identified the important role of justice and equity. The code also stated its applicability to all individuals living in Visigothic territory, regardless of whether the person was considered Visigothic or Roman.

Defining Moment

The Visigoths were a Germanic tribe that originated in northern Europe and settled in eastern Europe west of the Black Sea, near present-day Romania. To the east of the Visigoths were the Ostrogoths; to the west and north were the Franks, Angles, and Saxons. The Rhine and Danube rivers separated the Romans and these Germanic tribes, although the borders were somewhat flexible: the Romans often traded in German territory, and Germans sometimes entered Roman territory as slaves.

By the third century, the Roman Empire had declined significantly. In hopes of maintaining some control over the farthest reaches of their territory, the Romans invited the German tribes to settle on vacated lands near the Rhine and Danube Rivers. Many Germans even served in the Roman Legion as friends of the empire. Soon, however, the Visigoths were driven forcefully farther west by an invasion of the Huns, a nomadic central Asian tribe that fought on horseback. The Huns fought and conquered the Ostrogoths during the 370s. Fearing they would be next, the Visigoths formally requested permission to resettle in Roman territory on friendly terms.

Permission was granted, and in 376, the entire tribe of Visigoths crossed the Danube River to resettle on Roman land. But despite having official approval for their presence, upon their arrival, they were subjected to poor treatment by corrupt Roman officials. Eventually the Visigoths rebelled against their Roman rulers. Roman emperor Valens and his army attempted to subdue the Visigoths during the Battle of Adrianople in 378, but failed. Valens's successor, Emperor Theodosius I, maintained an uneasy peace with the Visigoths through governorships and diplomacy until his death in 395. However, when mistreatment resumed, the tribe invaded Italy and sacked Rome in 410.

The Visigoths continued to march west across Europe during the early fifth century, alternately fighting against and aligning themselves with the Romans whenever it proved beneficial to their interests. In 418, Western Roman emperor Honorius granted the tribe land in southwestern Gaul (present-day southern France) to thank them for helping in a military campaign, and the Visigoths created a permanent settlement.

The Visigoths eventually expanded their kingdom across the Pyrenees mountain range and into Spain by pushing the Vandals, another Germanic tribe, out of the Iberian Peninsula and into northern Africa. Throughout the next three centuries, the Visigoths mingled with the locals. They adopted many of the Roman customs that existed in Spain before their invasion, including Nicene Christianity (which became Catholicism). Despite later fragmentation and invasion attempts, the Visigothic kingdom lasted from the early fifth century until the Muslim conquest in the beginning of the eighth century.

Author Biography and Document Information
Chindaswinth was born around 563 in the Visigothic kingdom of Hispania. In 642, at the age of seventy-nine, he led a rebellion to usurp the throne and became king. To secure his new position, he infamously executed hundreds of nobles, banished numerous others from the kingdom, and established harsh penalties for anyone entertaining the notion of another rebellion.

Ironically, Chindaswinth's actions led the kingdom into a peaceful period. In the 640s, he began work on the Visigothic Code, a comprehensive collection of laws that covered many different categories of civil matters and built upon earlier versions of Visigothic law. He continued to refine the code throughout his reign.

In 649, Chindaswinth crowned his son Recceswinth as "co-king" in attempt to establish a hereditary monarchy. Historians believe that Recceswinth actually led the kingdom from 649 on, and it was he who eventually completed the Visigothic Code in 654.

HISTORICAL DOCUMENT

Book I: Concerning Legal Agencies
Title 2: The Law

I. What the Lawmaker Should Observe in Framing the Laws.
In all legislation the law should be fully and explicitly set forth, that perfection, and not partiality, may be secured. For, in the formation of the laws, not the sophisms of argument, but the virtue of justice should ever prevail. And here is required not what may be prompted by controversy, but what energy and vigor demand; for the violation of morals is not to be coerced by the forms of speech, but restrained by the moderation of virtue.

II. What the Law Is.
The law is the rival of divinity; the oracle of religion; the source of instruction; the artificer of right; the guardian and promoter of good morals; the rudder of the state; the messenger of justice; the mistress of life; the soul of the body politic.

III. What the Law Does.
The law rules every order of the state, and every condition of man; it governs wives and husbands; youth and age: the learned and the ignorant, the polished and the rude. It aims to provide the highest degree of safety for both prince and people, and, in renown and excellence, it is as conspicuous as the noon-day sun.

IV. What the Law Should Be.
The law should be plain, and not lead any citizen to commit error or fraud. It should be suitable to the place and the time, according to the character and custom of the state; prescribing justice and equity; consistent, honorable, worthy, useful, and necessary; and it should be carefully noted whether its provisions are framed rather for the convenience, than for the injury, of the public; so that it may be determined whether it sufficiently provides for the administration of justice; whether or not it appears to be contrary to religion, and whether it defends the right, and may be observed without detriment to any one.

GLOSSARY

conspicuous: highly obvious; in poor taste

equity: fairness or even-handedness in justice

partiality: favoritism or bias

sophism: any false argument; fallacy

Document Analysis

Book I, Title 2 of the Visigothic Code contains guiding principles as to how and why laws are to be established within the kingdom. Its opening section states that "the law should be fully and explicitly set forth," such that "the virtue of justice should ever prevail." The second section describes the law as "the rival of divinity." It is to be a source of instruction on how to behave, a "guardian and promoter of good morals," and a "messenger of justice."

The third section states that the law applies to everyone in the kingdom, regardless of gender, age, education level, or status. It also "aims to provide the highest degree of safety for both prince and people." Together, these establish that laws should be universally applicable and also provide universal protection.

Section 4 describes more specifically what the law should be. It states that laws should be straightforward and "plain," such that they are easy to interpret and do not "lead any citizen to commit error or fraud." Laws should be based on the "character and custom of the state" and be just and equitable. The code again emphasizes that the law should provide for the "administration of justice." Careful consideration should be given to whether the law "appears to be contrary to religion" and "may be observed without detriment to any one."

The code further explains that laws are made to restrain "human wickedness" through "fear of their execution." In order to keep the innocent safe, laws are needed to steer criminals away from temptation through fear of punishment for wrongdoing.

Finally, the code describes how law allows for triumph over "enemies." The code explains that conquest is more likely to be successful when the people of the kingdom feel "prosperous and secure, through the influence of peace and order" at home. It says that experience demonstrates that justice "overwhelms the enemy" because citizens unite in conquests, thereby leading to victory. It further states that a leader's success "will be more conspicuous when a reputation for justice accompanies him." The code concludes by reasoning that a ruler who provides justice for his kingdom and is victorious over his enemies achieves a "celestial kingdom" upon his death, thereby "increas[ing] his glory."

Essential Themes

Prior to settling in Spain, the Visigoths lacked a comprehensive written code of law. Feuds were settled by trial, which required sworn witnesses. If no witnesses were available, the accused was subjected to "trial by ordeal." For example, the accused would be required to walk blindfolded and barefoot across a floor covered in pieces of red-hot metal; if the person successfully avoided the metal, he or she was innocent. If not, he or she was guilty. While some of these methods persisted even after settlement, the establishment of written laws demonstrated a significant step toward a more uniform legal system.

One important, but debated, theme of the Visigothic Code is expressed indirectly in this portion of the document. Some historians believe that prior to King Chindaswinth's version of the code, different laws applied to individuals living within the kingdom, depending on their ethnic identity. The codes established by prior Visigothic monarchs, including Euric, Alaric II, and Leovigild, contained different provisions applicable to Visigoths and Romans, and these older codes separately addressed disputes that involved both Visigothic and Roman parties.

Other historians disagree with this interpretation and believe that prior codes distinguished between Visigoths and Romans because of territorial boundaries, rather than because of their ethnic identities. These historians suggest these separate laws might have been an artifact from when the Visigoths lived in—and later ruled over—territory that belonged to the Romans. But in either case, King Chindawinth's code departed significantly from prior documents because it clearly stated its applicability to all subjects within the territory that he considered part of his kingdom—regardless of ethnicity, place of origin, or loyalties.

The Visigothic Code underwent several revisions after its initial adoption, including a significant enlargement by King Chindaswinth's son, Recceswinth, once he ruled independent of his father. The code remained largely in effect long after the Visigothic kingdom itself disappeared: significant portions of the code still applied following the issue of the Usatges of Barcelona in Catalonia from 1131 to 1162 and even after Alfonso X the Wise issued the *Siete Partidas* in Castile between 1251 and 1265. Historians report that the code was still considered to be in effect in some areas as late as the fourteenth century.

—*Tracey M. DiLascio, JD*

Bibliography

Brummett, Palmira J., et al. *Civilizations Past and Present.* Vol. 1. 11th ed. London: Longman, 2005. Print.

Carr, Raymond, ed. Spain: A History. Oxford. Oxford UP, 2000. Print.

Collins, Roger. *Visigothic Spain, 409–711.* Hoboken: Wiley, 2008. Print.

James, Edward, ed. *Visigothic Spain: New Approaches.* Oxford: Oxford UP, 1980. Print.

Lear, Floyd Seyward. "The Public Law of the Visigothic Code." *Speculum: A Journal of Medieval Studies* 26.1 (1951): 1–23. Print.

Scott, S. P., ed. "The Visigothic Code (Forum Judicum)." *Library of Iberian Resources Online.* U of Central Arkansas, 2015. Web. 2 Apr. 2015.

The Farmer's Law, from Byzantium

Date: ca. 700
Geographic Region: Anatolia (present-day Turkey)
Author: Leo III
Translator: Walter Ashburner

Summary Overview

The Byzantine Empire in the eighth century had been weakened by plague, invasion, and internal conflict, and relations between the state and the agricultural heartland changed significantly during this time. Though the capital of Constantinople had long been the political and administrative heart of the empire, like most ancient and medieval societies, the empire was primarily agrarian and depended on its farmers for food and tax revenue. In the previous century, huge sections of the empire had been reorganized as "themes" (in Greek, *themata*), state-owned land that was farmed by soldiers in return for hereditary military service. As these themes were independent of the traditional landowning aristocracy, they provided money directly to the state. Many soldier-farmers were granted land outright, a significant change from the earlier system where people were tied permanently to the land of a large estate. As reliance on the loyalty and support of the aristocracy waned, the government looked directly to its small agrarian landowners for taxes and made them collectively responsible for payments. Promulgated sometime around the early eighth century, the Farmer's Law assumed that most of the inhabitants of a village were freeholders, and it set up protections for private property. Though scholars debate the date of this document, many believe that it was written during the reign of the Byzantine emperor Leo III (r. 717–741).

Defining Moment

Roman law (the law of the Byzantine or Eastern Roman Empire) provided for a fairly rigid social hierarchy. There were slaves, coloni (singular "colonus," tenant farmers), and *adscripticii* (singular *adscripticus*, or serfs, who were tied to the land, but not technically enslaved). Above them all were citizens, whose rights were clearly defined and protected by law. The distinction between these categories was often blurred, though citizens at one end and slaves at the other had clearly defined roles.

In the seventh century, the Byzantine Empire was threatened by plague and invasion, and its coffers were drained by costly wars. Under Emperor Heraclius, four military districts or themes were set up to provide a buffer against Muslim invasion from the east. Soldiers were given farmland in exchange for hereditary military service, and they were responsible for the cost of their own supplies. Under this arrangement, the government had a citizen army, the soldiers had land, and the empire had protection from invasion. This allotment of land to individuals was a middle ground between the large estates, with their slaves and *adscripticii*, and the coloni, who were also bound to the land, but liable for their own taxes. Byzantine rulers realized that their most reliable tax base, and those most motivated to contribute to the state's coffers, were small landowners not tied in perpetuity to land, but able to work it for their own benefit. Many military families in the themes were given land outright, and villages were grouped together and taxed collectively. These Byzantine farmers owned their land, but the organization of the agrarian economy was still far from a modern concept of private property. Since communities were responsible for taxes as a unit, a significant amount of energy went into determining how to treat abandoned land, which, under Roman law, remained the property of its original owner and on which taxes were still owed. Both the community and the individual had rights to the land, and there was also land held in common. The example of a mill is instructive. If a mill was constructed on common land, the community should pay the builder, and share in its use. If a mill was constructed on private land, it was not required to be shared with anyone. Communities were inspected and assessed periodically for tax purposes, but these inspections came at irregular intervals, and multiple generations could pass without an assessment. It was incumbent on communities to manage the day-to-day land and tax issues that arose, and the Farmers Law provided the executive power that community leaders needed to regulate land divisions and enforce property rights under this economic configuration.

Author Biography

Leo III (born Konon), founder of the Isaurian dynasty, was born around 675 in a province of Syria that is today part of Turkey. As a young man, Konon entered the service of the Byzantine emperor Justinian II, and he was appointed by the subsequent Emperor Anastasius II as the commander of the Anatolian theme, the largest theme in Asia Minor. When Anastasius was deposed, Konon and another theme commander refused to recognize the new emperor, Theodosius III. They marched on Constantinople in 717, seized the throne, and Konon became emperor as Leo III. Leo is known for his defeat of a Muslim siege of Constantinople, in which he employed Greek fire, a highly flammable petroleum mix, to fend off an attack by sea. Leo brought order to the fragmented Byzantine Empire, as his strategic alliances and clever negotiations with neighboring powers bore fruit. He reorganized the themes into smaller, more efficient units, and he broadened the tax base by inspecting land holdings in the empire. Leo was also known for legal reforms, particularly those dealing with family, property, and military law. He also enforced a prohibition on the worship of icons, or images of holy men and women, a position (known as iconoclasm) that was deeply unpopular with some in the church leadership. Leo III died in 741 and was succeeded by his son, Constantine V.

HISTORICAL DOCUMENT

After the attacks by Persians, Arabs and Slavs, there is some indication that the great landed estates of late antiquity gave way, in the Byzantine heartland of Anatolia, to a system of free peasant farms. These peasants paid taxes to the state and enabled a functional local army to operate throughout the empire. Although this might be overemphasized, the contrast with western Europe is outstanding. In the west the "state" as a function of society either disappeared or shrank to insignificant proportions and distinctions between public and private power were minimal. In Byzantium, by contrast, the state maintained its distinctive identity. The lives of Byzantine peasants are not entirely invisible to us: we can see them in hagiographical material, such as the *Life of St. Theodore of Sykeon*, as well as in legal sources. Here are extracts from the 7th–8th century Farmer's Law, which regulated the behavior of free peasants.

The Farmer who is working his own field must be just and must not encroach on his neighbor's furrows. If a farmer persists in encroaching and dock's a neighboring lot—if he did this in plowing time, he loses his plowing; if it was in sowing time that he made his encroachment, he loses his seed and his husbandry and his crop—the farmer who encroached.

If a farmer without his landowner's cognizance enters and plows or sows let him not receive either wages for his plowing or the crop for his sowing—no, not even the seed that has been cast.

If two farmers agree with the other before two or three witnesses to exchange lands and they agree for all time, let their determination and their exchange remain firm and secure and unassailable.

If two farmers, A and B, agree to exchange their lands for the season of sowing and A draws back, then, if the seed was cast, they may not draw back; but if the seed was not cast they may draw back; but if A did not plow while B did, A also shall plow.

If two farmers exchange lands either for a season or for all time and one plot is found deficient as compared with the other, and this was not their agreement, let him who has more give an equivalent in land to him who has less; but if this was their agreement, let them give nothing in addition.

If a farmer who has a claim on a field enters against the sower's will and reaps, then, if he had a just claim, let him take nothing from it; but if his claim was baseless, let him provide twice over the crops that were reaped.

If two territories contend about a boundary or a field, let the judges consider it and they shall decide in favor of the territory which had thee longer possession; but if there is an ancient landmark, let the ancient determination remain unassailed.

If a division wronged people in their lots or lands, let them have license to undo the division.

If a farmer on shares reaps without the grantor's consent and robs him of his sheaves, as a thief shall he be deprived of all his crop.

A share holder's portion is nine bundles, the grantor's one: he who divides outside these limits is accursed.

If a man takes land from an Indigent farmer and agrees to plow only and to divide, let their agreement prevail; if they also agreed on sowing, let it prevail according to their agreement.

If a farmer takes from some indigent farmer, his vineyard to work on a half share and does not prune it as is filling and dig it and fence it and dig it over, let him receive nothing from the produce....

If a farmer takes over the farming of a vineyard or piece of land and agrees with the owner and takes earnest-money and starts and then draws back and gives it up, let him give the just value of the field and let the owner have the field.

If a farmer enters and works another farmer's woodland, for three years he shall take its profits for himself and then give the land back again to its owner.

If a farmer who is too poor to work his own vineyard takes flight and goes abroad, let those from whom claims are made by the public treasury gather in the grapes, and the farmer if he returns shall not be entitled to mulct them in the wine.

If a farmer who runs away from his own field pays every year the extraordinary taxes of the public treasury, let those who gather in the grapes and occupy the field be mulcted twofold.

Concerning Herdsmen. If a neat herd in the morning receives an ox front a farmer and mixes it with the herd, and it happens that the ox is destroyed by a wolf, let him explain the accident to its master and he himself shall go harmless.

If a herdsman who has received an ox loses it and on the same day on which the ox was lost does not give notice to the master of the ox that "I kept sight of the ox up to this or that point, but what is become of it I do not know," let him not go harmless, but, if he gave notice, let him go harmless.

If a herdsman receives an ox from a farmer in the morning and goes off and the ox gets separated front the mass of oxen and goes off and goes into cultivated plots or vineyards and does harm, let him not lose his wages, but let him make good the harm done.

If a herdsman in the morning receives all ox from a farmer and the ox disappears, let him swear in the Lord's name that he has not himself played foul and at he had no part in the loss of the ox and let him go harmless.

If a guardian of fruit is found stealing in the place which he guards, let him lose his wages and be well beaten.

If a hired shepherd is found milking his flock without the owner's knowledge and selling them, let him be beaten and lose his wages.

If a man is found stealing another's straw, he shall restore it twice over.

If a man takes an ox or an ass or any beast without its owner's knowledge and goes off on business, let him give its hire twice over; and if it dies on the road, he shall give two for one, whatever it may be....

If a man steals all ox or an ass and is convicted, he shall be whipped and give it twice over and all its gain.

If while a mail is trying to steal one ox from a herd, the herd is put to flight and eaten by wild beasts, let him be blinded.

If a man finds an ox in a wood and kills it, and takes the carcass let his hand be cut off.

If a slave kills one ox or ass or ram in a wood, his master shall make it good.

If a slave, while trying to steal by night, drives the sheep away from the flock in chasing them out of the fold, and they are lost or eaten by wild beasts, let him be hanged as a murderer.

If a man is found in a granary stealing corn, let him receive in the first place a hundred lashes, and make good the damage to the owner; if he is convicted a second time, let him pay twofold damages for his theft; if a third time, let him be blinded.

If a man at night steals wine from a jar or from a vat or out of a butt, let him suffer the same penalty as is written in the chapter above.

If people have a deficient measure of corn and wine and do not follow the ancient tradition of their fathers but out of covetousness have unjust measures contrary to those that are appointed, let them be beaten for their impiety.

If a man delivers cattle to a slave for pasture without his master's knowledge and the slave sells them or otherwise damages them, let the slave and his master go harmless. Where a man destroys another's beast on any pretense, when he is recognized, let him indemnify its owner.

If a man harvests his lot before his neighbor's lots have been harvested and he brings in his beasts and does harm to his neighbors, let him receive thirty lashes and make good the damage to the party injured.

If a man gathers in the fruits of his vineyard arid while the fruits of some lots are still ungathered brings in his beasts, let him receive thirty lashes and make good the damage to the party injured.

If a man lawlessly, when he has a suit with another, cuts his vines or any other tree, let his hand be cut off.

If a man who is dwelling in a district ascertains that a piece of common ground is suitable for the erection of a mill and appropriates it and then, after the completion of the building, if the commonalty of the district complain of the owner of the building as having appropriated common ground, let them give him all the expenditure that's due to him for the completion of the building and let them share it in common with its builder.

If after the land of the district has been divided, a man finds in his own lot a place which is suitable for the erection of a mill and sets about it, the farmers of the other lots are not entitled to say anything about the mill.

If the water which comes to the mill leaves dry cultivated plots or vineyards, let him make the damage good; if not, let the mill be idle.

If the owners of the cultivated plots are not willing that the water go through their plots, let them be entitled to prevent it.

GLOSSARY

mulct: to impose a fine.

unassailed: not attacked or criticized

Document Analysis

While it acknowledges and regulates the behavior of slaves and hired landless workers (such as herdsmen), the Farmers Law is intended for free, landowning peasants. It deals with private property, such as livestock and produce, and also with communal use of land. There are significant regulations concerning stealing and negligence that results in lost property. These laws are set up to govern a community that honors both communal responsibilities, such as tax payment, and private enterprise. In several cases, the needs of the community seem to be trumped by the rights of landowners, as in the case of the building of a mill.

According to the law, if a man builds a mill on land that is determined to be held in common, the community can pay him for the cost of building the structure, and then all will be entitled to use it. However, if he builds a mill on his own land, he can use it for his own benefit, and his neighbors "are not entitled to say anything about the mill." If his mill redirects water from other properties, and those farmers suffer as a result, the mill owner should pay them for their losses, or he may not use his mill. If neighbors do not want water for the mill running across their land, they can prevent it.

Laws against stealing and regulations regarding compensation for negligence are also indicative of a legal intent to protect private property. Slaves are still present in this world, however, and any theft or negligence on their part is the responsibility of their masters, unless the damage is egregious: "If a slave, while trying to steal by night, drives the sheep away from the flock in chasing them out of the fold, and they are lost or eaten by wild beasts, let him be hanged as a murderer." In an agrarian society, the loss of livestock could mean the difference between life and death, so punishment for killing animals or ruining crops could be severe.

Land use is also highly regulated, as the tax revenue for the community depends on all farming their allotted land. When land was abandoned, and other community members took it over, in order to pay taxes, the landowner had a limited amount of time to pay it back or forfeit the land. Unfair distribution of land could be challenged in court.

Essential Themes

The Farmers Law illuminated a system or property law that was both communal and private, with obligations and rights accruing to both individual landowners and the community as a whole. The rights of property owners were protected in a way that was relatively new in Roman law, and peasants were obligated to the state, rather than to the owners of large estates as in the past. These laws also governed how owners of land could settle issues that arose between them. The laws provided a framework for settling disputes over everything from the unfair distribution of land to a stolen sheep or damage to crops. This document privileged property rights and provided significant penalties for property stolen outright or lost through negligence.

—Bethany Groff, MA

Bibliography and Additional Reading

Cavallo, Guglielmo. *The Byzantines.* Chicago: U of Chicago P, 1997. Print.

Davis, Jennifer R. & Michael McCormick, eds. *The Long Morning of Medieval Europe: New Directions in Early Medieval Studies.* Burlington: Ashgate, 2008. Print.

Gorecki, Danuta M. "The Heraclian Land Tax Reform: Objectives and Consequences." *Byzantine Studies 4* (1977): 127–46. Print.

Laiou, Angeliki E. & Cécile Morrisson. *The Byzantine Economy.* New York: Cambridge UP, 2007. Print.

■ The Laws of Alfred, Guthrum, and Edward the Elder

Date: ca. 886
Geographic Region: Great Britain
Authors: Alfred; Guthrum; Edward the Elder

Summary Overview

From the 790s until the 880s, the Anglo-Saxon kingdoms in Great Britain were under near-constant invasion by Vikings from Denmark, Norway, and Sweden. The battle and negotiation tactics of King Alfred of Wessex were instrumental in recovering much of the Anglo-Saxon territory from the Vikings.

Around 886, following the creation of a peace and land partition treaty, King Alfred and King Guthrum of Denmark established a series of laws that applied to the both the Anglo-Saxon and Danish kingdoms in Great Britain; these laws were periodically updated, including by Alfred's successor, his son Edward the Elder. Many of the laws codified elements of Christianity, such as the requirement to rest on Sunday, and allowed for the banishment of "witches" and "adulteresses." Violators generally paid a fine to the government and were also subjected to some type of punishment by the church. The laws also define the oaths to be recited in various situations, including oaths of accusation, innocence, and affirming the credibility of a witness.

Defining Moment

During the eighth century, seven independent Anglo-Saxon kingdoms existed on the island of Great Britain, covering much of what is today England: Wessex, East Anglia, Kent, Mercia, Essex, Sussex, and Northumbria. Beginning around the 790s, Vikings from Denmark, Norway, and Sweden raided the coasts and inland waterways of Great Britain, sometimes establishing permanent settlements. Over the course of the ninth century, the raids turned into full-scale invasions, and during the 860s and 870s most of Great Britain's kingdoms were overcome by Viking invasions.

The British had been introduced to Christianity during the Roman occupation, as early as the third century. During the fifth century, the pagan Angles and Saxons invaded and settled the islands, but were eventually converted to Christianity. The Vikings brought yet another pagan invasion to the British Isles, worshiping gods such as Odin, Thor, and Frey.

In 870, Danish Vikings attacked Wessex, which by then was one of the last remaining independent kingdoms on the island. Led by Alfred and his older brother, King Aethelred, the Wessex forces fought and successfully halted the invasion. But within a few years, the fighting resumed. When King Aethelred died in 871, Alfred took the throne. He eventually negotiated a peace treaty with the Vikings, who agreed to leave Wessex alone, but continued to occupy and rule over the northern and eastern part of the island.

Despite the treaty, in 877, Guthrum, ruler of the Danish-controlled territories of Great Britain, led yet another raid on Wessex. By this time, Wessex was the only remaining independent Anglo-Saxon kingdom in Great Britain. This time the raid was successful, and the Vikings drove Alfred into hiding in the Somerset tidal marshlands. There, he built a fortress to gather refugees fleeing from Wessex, Somerset, Wiltshire, and Hampshire. Together, they returned to Wessex in 878 and defeated the Viking army in the Battle of Edington. Thanks to this victory, Alfred was able to negotiate the Peace of Wedmore and regain control over much of his previous territory.

In 886, Alfred negotiated a partition treaty, wherein northern and eastern England remained under the control of the Vikings, in an area that later came to be known as the Danelaw, and west Mercia and Kent joined Wessex under Alfred's reign. He reorganized his kingdom's defenses to protect against future raids and sought to improve literacy and education as a way to help England recover from years of Viking invasion.

Around this time, Alfred and Guthrum also established laws to govern the entire region, including both the English- and Danish-controlled kingdoms. The exact date of the writing is disputed, but most historians place its creation sometime between 880 and 890.

The laws drew heavily from the rules of the Christian church, and the oaths were all to be made in the name of the Christian god. This marked a significant change for the pagan Vikings.

Author Biography and Document Information

Alfred was born in the county of Berkshire, England, in 849, as the fifth son of Aethelwulf, king of the West Saxons (Wessex). After his father's death, three of Alfred's older brothers inherited the throne in succession. Alfred fought alongside his brothers to protect the kingdom, and he became king himself in 871, at the age of twenty-one. At the time, Wessex was one of the last remaining Anglo-Saxon kingdoms not controlled by the Vikings.

For nearly twenty years, Alfred struggled to maintain his kingdom's independence. Around 886, he successfully negotiated a treaty with the Vikings to reclaim territory in southern and western England. His efforts to improve literacy and revive Anglo-Saxon traditions helped reestablish his kingdom's dominance in the wake of the invasions. By the time of his death in 899,

he had consolidated many of the Anglo-Saxon kingdoms under his leadership from Wessex and set the stage for future leaders to eventually unite all of Great Britain. He was succeeded by his son Edward the Elder, who ruled Wessex until his death in 924, capturing yet more land from the Danes during his reign.

Two sets of agreements between the Anglo-Saxons and the Danes have been found in the historical record from around this time, one commonly called the Laws of Alfred and Guthrum and the other initially referred to by historians as the Laws of Edward and Guthrum. However, as Edward took the throne following his father's death in 899 and Guthrum is believed to have died around 890, historians speculate that Edward may have made his agreements with Guthrum's successor or successors, whose identities are unclear; other scholars believe these later agreements were not even made by Edward, but by one of his successors. The text presented here was reproduced in volume four of *The Library of Original Sources*, published in 1901 and edited by Oliver J. Thatcher.

HISTORICAL DOCUMENT

These are the dooms which King Alfred and King Guthrum chose. And this is the ordinance also which King Alfred and King Guthrum, and afterwards King Edward and King Guthrum, chose and ordained, when the English and Danes fully took to peace and to friendship; and the witan also, who were afterwards, oft and unseldom that same renewed and increased with good.

This is the first which they ordained: that they would love one God, and zealously renounce every kind of heathendom. And they established worldly rules also for these reasons, that they knew that else they might not many control, nor would many men else submit to divine bot as they should: and the worldly bot they established in common to Christ and the king, wheresoever a man would not lawfully submit to divine bot, by direction of the bishops.

1. And this then is the first which they ordained: that church-grith within the walls, and the king's hand-grith, stand equally inviolate.

2. If any one violate Christianity, or reverence heathenism, by word or by work, let him pay as well wer, as wite or lah-slit, according as the deed may be.

3. And if a man in orders steal, or fight, or forswear, or fornicate, let him make bot for it according as the deed may be, as well by wer, as by wite or by lah-slit; and, above all things, make bot before God as the canon teaches, and find borh thereof, or yield to prison. And if a mass-priest misdirect the people about a festival or about a fast, let him pay thirty shillings among the English, and among the Danes three half-marks. If a priest fetch not the chrism at the right term, or refuse baptism to him who has need thereof, let him pay wite among the English, and among the Danes lah-slit; that is, twelve ores.

Of incestuous persons.

4. And concerning incestuous persons, the witan have ordained that the king shall have the upper, and the bishop the nether, unless bot be made before God and

before the world, according as the deed may be; so as the bishop may teach. If two brothers or near kinsmen commit fornication with the same woman, let them make bot very strictly, in such wise as it may be allowed, as well by wer, as by wite or by lah-slit, according as the deed may be. If a man in orders fordo himself with capital crime, let him be seized and held to the bishop's doom.

5. If a man guilty of death desire confession, let it never be denied him. And all God's dues let every one zealously further, by God's mercy, and by the wites which the witan have annexed thereto.

6. If any one withhold tithes, let him pay lah-slit among the Danes, wite among the English. If any one withhold Rom-feoh, let him pay lah-slit among the Danes, wite among the English. If any one discharge not light-scot, let him pay lah-slit among the Danes, wite among the English. If any one give not plough-alms, let him pay lah-slit among the Danes, wite among the English. If any one deny any divine dues, let him pay lah-slit among the Danes, wite among the English. As if he fight and wound any one, let him be liable in his wer. If he fell a man to death, let him then be an outlaw, and let every one of those seize him with hearm who desire right. And if he so do that any one kill him, for that he resisted God's law or the kings, if that be proved true, let him lie uncompensated.

Of workings on a festival-day.

7. If any one engage in Sunday marketing, let him forfeit the chattel, and twelve ores among the Danes, and thirty shillings among the English. If a freeman work on a festival-day, let him forfeit his freedom, or pay wite or lah-slit. Let a theow-man suffer in his hide or hide-gild. If a lord oblige his theow to work on a festival-day, let him pay lah-slit within the Danish law, and wite among the English.

Of feasts.

8. If a freeman break a lawful feast, let him pay wite or lahslit. If a theowman do so, let him suffer in his hide or hide-gild.

Of ordeals and oaths.

9. Ordeal and oaths are forbidden on festival-days and lawful fast-days; and he who shall break that, let him pay lah-slit among the Danes, and wite among the English. If it can be so ordered, no one condemned should ever be executed on the Sunday festival, but be secured and held till the festival be gone by.

10. If a limb-maimed man who has been condemned or forsaken, and he after that live three days then any one who is willing to take care of sore and soul may help him, with the bishop's leave.

Of witches, diviners, perjurers, etc.

11. If witches or diviners, perjurers or morth-workers, or foul, defiled, notorious adulteresses, be found anywhere within the land; let them be driven from the country, and the people cleansed, or let them totally perish within the country, unless they desist, and the more deeply make bot.

Of ecclesiastics and foreigners.

12. If any one wrong an ecclesiastic or a foreigner, through any means, as to money or as to life, then shall the king or the eorl there in the land, and the bishop of the people, be unto him in the place of a kinsman and of a protector, unless he have another; and let bot be strictly made, according as the deed may be, to Christ and to the king, as it is fitting; or let him avenge the deeds very deeply who is king among the people.

How a twelve-hynde man shall be paid for.

13. A twelve-hynde man's wer is twelve hundred shillings. A two-hynde man's wer is two hundred shillings. If any one be slain, let him be paid for according to his birth. And it is right that the slayer, after he has given wed for the wer, find, in addition, wer-borh according as shall thereto belong; that is, to a twelve-hynde's wer-borh, eight of the paternal kins and four of the maternal kin. When that is done, then let the king's mund be established, that is, that they all of either kindred, with their hands in common upon one weapon, engage to the mediator that the king's mund shall stand. In twenty-one days from that day let 120 shillings be paid asheals-fang at a twelve-hynde's wer. Heals-fang belongs to no

kinsman, except to those who are within the degrees of blood. In twenty-one days from that day that the heals-fang is paid, let the manbot be paid; in twenty-one days from this, the fight-wite; in twenty-one days from this, the frum-gyld of the wer; and so forth, till it be fully paid, within the time that the witan have appointed. After this they must depart with love, if they desire to have full friendship. All men shall do with regard to the wer of a ceorl that which belongs to his condition, like as we have said about a twelve-hynde man.

Of Oaths.
Thus shall a man swear fealty oaths.
1. By the Lord, before whom this relic is holy, I will be to ____ faithful and true, and love all that he loves, and shun all that he shuns, according to God's law, and according to the world s principles, and never, by will nor by force, by word nor by work, do ought of what is loathful to him; on condition that he keep me as I am willing to deserve, and all that fulfil that our agreement was, when I to him submitted and chose his will.

Thus shall a man swear when he has discovered his property and brings it in process.

2. By the Lord, before whom this relic is holy, so I my suit prosecute with full folk-right, without fraud and without deceit, and without any guile, as was stolen from me the cattle ____ that I claim, and that I have attached with ____.

The other's oath with whom a man discovers his cattle.

3. By the Lord, I was not at rede nor at deed, neither counsellor nor doer, where were unlawfully led away ____'s cattle. But as I cattle have, so did I lawfully obtain it. And: as I vouch it to warranty, so did he sell it to me into whose hand I now set it. And: as I cattle have, so did it come to my own property and so it by folk-right my own possession is, and my rearing.

The oath of him who discovers his property that he does it not either for hatred or for envy.

4. By the Lord, I accuse not ____ either for hatred or for envy, or for unlawful lust of gain; nor know I anything soother; but as my informant to me said, and I myself in sooth believe, that he was the thief of my property.

The other's oath that he is guiltless.

5. By the Lord, I am guiltless, both in deed and counsel, and of the charge of which ____ accuses me.

His companion's oath who stands with him.

6. By the Lord, the oath is clean and unperjured which ____ has sworn.

Oath if a man finds his property unsound after he has bought it.

7. In the name of Almighty God, you did engage to me sound and clean that which you sold to me, and full security against afterclaim, on the witness of ____, who then was with us two.

How he shall swear who stands with another in witness.

8. In the name of Almighty God, as I here for ____ in true witness stand, unbidden and unbought, so I with my eyes over-saw, and with my ears over-heard, that which I with him say.

Oath that he knew not of foulness or fraud.

9. In the name of Almighty God, I knew not, in the things about which you sued, foulness or fraud, or infirmity or blemish, up to that day's-tide that I sold it to you: but it was both sound and clean, without any kind of fraud.

10. In the name of the living God, as I money demand, so have I lack of that which ____ promised me when I mine to him sold.

Denial.
11. In the name of the living God, I owe not to ____ sceatt or shilling, or penny or penny's worth; but I have discharged to him all that I owe him, so far as our verbal contracts were at first.

Of the oath and degree-bot of men in orders.
12. A mass-priest's oath, and a secular thane's, are in English law reckoned of equal value; and by reason of

the seven church-degrees that the mass-priest, through the grace of God, has acquired, he is worthy of thane-right.

Of the Mercian oath.

13. A twelve-hynde man's oath stands for six ceorls oaths: because, if a man should avenge a twelve-hynde man, he will be fully avenged on six ceorls, and his wer-gild will be six ceorls' wer-gilds. Bequeathed it and died, he who it owned, with full folk-right, so as it his elders, with money and with life, lawfully got, and let and left, in power of him, whom they well gifted. And so it have, as he it gave, who had it to give, without fraud and unforbidden; and I will possess it, as my own property, that that I have; and ne'er for thee design, nor plot nor ploughland, nor turf nor toft, nor furrow nor foot-mark, nor land nor lea-sowe, nor fresh nor marsh, nor rough nor plain, by wood nor field, by land nor by strand, by weald nor by water, but that will maintain, the while that I live; for there is no man alive, who ever heard that any one made plaint against, or summoned him at the hundred, or anywhere at gemot, in market-place, or among church-folk, the while that he lived. Sackless he was in life, be he in the grave, so as he may. Do as I teach: be you with yours, and leave me with mine: I covet not yours, nor laeth nor land, nor sac nor socn: nor need you mine; nor design I to you anything.

GLOSSARY

borh: a security or pledge

bot: a penalty or requirement to make atonement, regulated by the church

ceorl: a freeman of the lowest class, churl, countryman

chattel: any movable personal property; a slave

frum-gyld: a first payment or compensation, especially concerning the repayment of the wer

-grith: protection or asylum for a limited period of time, either by the church or the crown

lah-slit: a breach or violation of the law; this term is believed to combine the Saxon word for law (lah) and Danish word for breach (slit)

morth-workers: worshipers of the dead, also murderers

mund: protection, brideprice

sceatt: a silver Anglo-Saxon coin, sometimes including a small amount of gold (seventh and eighth centuries)

theow/theow-man/theowman: a servant or slave

twelve-hynde man: a nobleman in Anglo-Saxon law

wer: a monetary penalty paid for injuring or killing another person

wer-borh: security for the payment of the wer

witan: to wit, know, have knowledge; the members of the national council or witenagemot

wite: a fine for committing a crime, regulated by (and often payable to) the secular government

Document Analysis

The opening paragraphs of the laws (referred to as "dooms") of Alfred, Guthrum, and Edward the Elder note that, at the time of their writing, the English and Danes "fully took to peace and to friendship." They establish the supremacy of Christianity across the entire realm and require of all citizens that "they would love one God, and zealously renounce every kind of heathendom," or paganism.

The first law explicitly states that the rules of both the church and the government "stand equally inviolate" and, therefore, carry equal weight. The second law requires a fine to be paid should any person "violate Christianity, or reverence heathenism, by word or by work." The third law addresses legal violations by members of the religious order, requiring them to pay a fine to the government as well as make atonement through the church.

The laws then address several specific violations. For example, if a man wounds another man in a fight, he must pay in penalty the monetary equivalent of the value of the man's injury. If he kills the man, he becomes "an outlaw" and may be subjected to vigilante justice on the part of those who "desire right." If he is killed while resisting the law of God or the kings, there will be no penalty to his killer.

The "festival-day," or Sunday Sabbath, must be respected. If a lord requires his men to work on a Sunday, he must pay a fine. The penalties are harsher for other classes of individuals: Anyone engaged in "Sunday marketing" must "forfeit the chattel" and cannot keep the benefit of his sale. If a freeman is caught working on a Sunday and cannot pay the required fine, he must "forfeit his freedom." Similarly, legal matters such as trials by ordeal or oaths cannot be conducted on Sundays. Likewise, executions are forbidden on Sundays. Anyone who violates this requirement must pay a fine. Additionally, any "witches or diviners, perjurers or morth-workers [murderers], or foul, defiled, notorious adulteresses" can be driven from the kingdom and left to die in the countryside unless they make penance to the church.

The last section of the laws contains a series of oaths for use in legal trials. These include oaths for accusing someone of stealing property, asserting one's innocence in a crime, confirming the truth of another's statement, and denying knowledge of fraud. Each of these is an oath before God and begins with phrases such as, "In the name of Almighty God," or, "By the Lord."

Essential Themes

After being subjected to centuries of Viking raids, the English were eager to "civilize" the Danish "heathens" by converting them to Christianity. Upon negotiation of the initial peace treaty, Guthrum was successfully converted, and the laws created by Alfred and Guthrum largely codified behavior that was required or encouraged by the Christian church. The opening paragraphs of the laws even explicitly required that all citizens "love one God" and renounce "heathendom." Its oaths cover a variety of legal circumstances and required the speaker to swear to his testimony before the Christian god.

Similarly, the laws established the dual importance of the church and the government within the kingdom. The first provision of the laws explicitly stated that the rules of the church and the government carry equal weight. For example, a monetary fine serves as punishment for withholding tithes (donations) from the church or "Rom-feoh" (similar to taxes) from the government. Additionally, in many instances, violation of a law resulted in both a civil and a religious penalty. For example, if anyone in the kingdom wrongs "an ecclesiastic or a foreigner," that person must make atonement "to Christ and to the king, as it is fitting." Even the oaths reinforced this idea: although trials were generally government matters, the required oaths were all sworn to before the Christian god.

Among the interesting features of this collection of laws is that they were written to apply to two groups of people, the English and the Danes, under two separate rulers. However, the laws distinguish between the two groups. For example, should a priest "misdirect the people about a festival or about a fast," his penalty is thirty shillings if he is English or three half-marks if he is Danish. Historians generally believe the laws applied equally and carried comparable penalties regardless of ethnicity; that is, thirty shillings and three half-marks are thought to have been a roughly equal penalty in their respective territories. Historians believe the primary reason for the difference was territorial rather than discriminatory, since even though the same set of laws applied, England and the Danes were technically two separate kingdoms with different currencies and legal systems.

—*Tracey M. DiLascio, JD*

Bibliography and Further Reading

"Alfred First King of the English, 'Known as the Great.'" *England and English History.* EnglandAndEnglish-History.com, 2012. Web. 12 May 2015.

"Alfred 'The Great' (r. 871–899)." *The British Monarchy.* Royal Household, n.d. Web. 12 May 2015.

Gobbitt, Thom. "Treaty of Alfred and Guthrum." *Early English Laws.* University of London, n.d. Web. 12 May 2015.

Thorpe, Benjamin. *Ancient Laws and Institutes of England: Comprising Laws Enacted under the Anglo-Saxon Kings from Aethelbirht to Cnut.* Cambridge: Cambridge UP, 1840. Print.

■ The Laws of King Alfred

Date: ca. 890
Geographic Region: Wessex (present-day southern England)
Author: Alfred of Wessex

Summary Overview

King Alfred of Wessex spent the early years of his reign defending his Anglo-Saxon kingdom against Viking invaders. After a decisive battle in 878 at Edington, Alfred made peace with the Viking king Guthrum and turned his attention to protecting his territory with fortified towns as well as promoting literacy and order among his people. Decades of Viking raids had emptied the monasteries, traditional centers of learning, of their libraries, and shifting boundaries and unstable rulers had led to overlapping, sometimes contradictory laws. A significant part of this process was the establishment of a legal code that brought together Alfred's own laws with those of other kings and neighboring kingdoms. Like Justinian I in the Byzantine Empire, the Doom Book (*Domboc* or Law Book) of Alfred consolidated existing law, eliminated obsolete or contradictory laws, and also served as a rich history of his reign. Like most Germanic law, the Anglo-Saxon laws were based on the principal of compensation rather than revenge and family as well as individual responsibility.

Defining Moment

Vikings from Scandinavia raided the British Isles from the end of the eighth century. These incursions began as sporadic coastal attacks, targeting monasteries and churches specifically for their wealth, and destroying most of their libraries in the process. Vikings used fast, shallow-draft vessels that were very effective on the coast and navigable rivers of the British Isles. As their successes grew, they began to winter in captured territory, eventually forming permanent settlements. By 866, the Vikings had established their capital at York and moved south and west, attacking the kingdoms of East Anglia, Mercia, and Wessex.

Alfred was fifth in line for the kingdom of Wessex. His father died, followed by his older brothers, until there were only two remaining sons—Alfred and his brother, Ethelred. Around 866, Ethelred had succeed-

ed their brothers to the throne. The years that followed were occupied with unsuccessful attempts to repel the so-called Great Heathen Army from the neighboring kingdom of Mercia. In 870, the Vikings invaded Wessex, and the following year, Ethelred died, leaving Alfred as the ruler of a besieged kingdom. After a significant loss in May 871, Alfred paid a large tribute, which convinced the Vikings to withdraw in the fall to winter quarters in London. For the next five years, they turned their attention to other parts of England. In 876, under a new Viking king, Guthrum, the attacks began anew. Two years later, Guthrum defeated Alfred and forced him to hide with his few remaining men in a swamp fortress.

Alfred rallied his troops, reformed his army, and marched to a decisive victory against Guthrum at the Battle of Edington that same year. One of his terms of surrender for the Vikings was that Guthrum convert to Christianity, with Alfred as his godfather. England was divided into two kingdoms; East Anglia, known after as the Danelaw, and West Anglia, united under Alfred. Though sporadic Viking raids continued for all of his reign, Alfred had settled the most immediate threat to his kingdom and turned his considerable energy to building defensible towns along his borders, promoting literacy, and amassing a comprehensive legal code. This legal code compiled laws of Mercia and Kent along with his own laws to form an inclusive set of laws in the Germanic tradition. These laws illustrated Alfred's religious devotion (most of his Doom Book is dedicated to recording biblical laws and adjusting them to fit an Anglo-Saxon kingdom) and set payments for lost property and injury or death.

Author Biography

King Alfred of Wessex was born in Oxfordshire in 849. He was the fourth son of the West Saxon king Aethelwulf, and each of his older brothers was appointed to succeed to the kingship in turn, rather than in a linear inheritance, a system that ensured a mature king during a time when the country was under constant threat of attack from the Vikings. Alfred may have been sent to Rome to study as a child. In any case, he was well educated and encouraged literacy during his reign. When Alfred became king in 871, after his father and brothers had died, Wessex was the only Anglo-Saxon kingdom that had not been overrun by the Vikings. After seven years of fighting, Alfred won a decisive victory in 878 and made peace with the Danish king. Alfred established a series of fortified towns across his kingdom and instituted a standing army that served in rotation. Alfred also established a legal code, based on the laws of preceding kings and his own laws, and by the time he died in 899, he had consolidated territorial gains that would eventually lead to the unification of Anglo-Saxon England.

HISTORICAL DOCUMENT

The Lord spoke these words to Moses, and thus said: "I am the Lord your God. I led you out of the land of the Egyptians, and of their bondage."

Of oaths and of weds.
1. At the first we teach, that it is most needful that every man warily keep his oath and his wed. If any one be constrained to either of these wrongfully, either to treason against his lord, or to any unlawful aid; then it is juster to belie than to fulfil. But if he pledge himself to that which it is lawful to fulfil, and in that belie himself, let him submissively deliver up his weapon and his goods to the keeping of his friends, and be in prison forty days in a king's tun; let him there suffer whatever the bishop may prescribe to him; and let his kinsmen feed him, if he himself have no food. If he have no kinsmen, or have no food, let the king's reeve feed him. If he must be forced to this, and he otherwise will not, if they bind him, let him forfeit his weapons and his property. If he be slain, let him lie uncompensated. If he flee thereout before the time, and he be taken, let him be in prison forty days, as he should before have been. But if he escape, let him be held a fugitive, and be excommunicate of all Christ's churches. If, however, there be another man's borh, let him make bot for the borhbryce, as the law may direct him, and the wedbryce, as his confessor may prescribe to him.

Of churchsocns
2. If any one, for whatever crime, seek any of the mynsterhams to which the king's feorm is incident, or other freehired which is worthy of reverence, let him have a space of three days to protect himself, unless he be willing to come to terms. If during this space, any one harm him by blow, or by bond, or wound him, let him make bot for each of these according to regular usage, as well with wer as with wite: and to the brotherhood one hundred and twenty shillings, as bot for the churchfrith: and let him not have forlongen his own.

Of borhbryce
3. If any one break the king's borh, let him make bot for the plaint, as the law shall direct him; and for the borhbryce with five pounds of maerra pence. For an archbishop's borhbryce, or his mundbyrd, let him make bot with three pounds: for any other bishop's or an earldormans borhbryce, or mundbyrd, let him make bot with two pounds.

Of plotting against a lord.
4. If any one plot against the king's life, of himself, or by harbouring of exiles, or of his men; let him be liable with his life and in all that he has; or let him prove himself according to his lord's wer.

Of churchfryth
5. We also ordain to every church which has been hallowed by a bishop, this fryth: if a fahman flee to or reach one, that for seven days no one drag him out. But if anyone do so, let him be liable in the king's mundbyrd and the churchfryth; more if he there commit more wrong, if, despite of hunger, he can live; unless he fight his way out. If the brethren have further need of their church, let them keep him in another house, and let not that have more doors than the church. Let the churchealdor take care that during this term no one give him food. If he

himself be willing to deliver up his weapons to his foes, let them keep him thirty days, and then let them give notice of him to his kinsmen. It is also churchfryth: if any man seek a church for any of those offences, which had not been before revealed, and there confess himself ill God's name, be it half forgiven. He who steals on Sunday, or at Yule, or at Easter, or on Holy Thursday, and on Rogation days; for each of these we will that the bot be twofold, as during Lent-fast.

Of stealing in a church.
6. If any one thieve aught in a church, let him pay the angylde, and the wite, such as shall belong to theangylde; and let the hand be struck off with which he did it. If he will redeem the hand, and that be allowed him, let him pay as may belong to his wer.

In case a man fight in the king's hall.
7. If any one fight in the king's hall, or draw his weapon, and he be taken; be it in the king's doom, either death, or life, as he may be willing to grant him. If he escape, and be taken again, let him pay for himself according to his wergeld, and make bot for the offence, as well wer as wite, according as he may have wrought.

Of fornication with a nun.
8. If any one carry off a nun from a minster, without the king's or the bishop's leave, let him pay a hundred and twenty shillings, half to the king, half to the bishop and to the church-hlaford who owns the nun. If she live longer than he who carried her off, let her not have aught of his property. If she bear a child, let not that have of the property more than the mother. If any one slay her child, let him pay to the king the maternal kindred's share; to the paternal kindred let their share be given. . . .

Of those men who lend their weapons for man-slaying.
19. If any one lend his weapon to another that he may kill some one therewith, they may join together if they will in the wer. If they will not join together, let him who lent the weapon pay of the wer a third part, and of the wite a third part. If he be willing to justify himself, that he knew of no ill-design in the loan; that he may do. If a sword-polisher receive another man's weapon to fur-

bish, or a smith a man's material, let them both return it sound as either of them may have before received it: unless either of them had before agreed that he should not hold it angylde. . . .

Of confession of debt.
22. If any one at the folk-mote make declaration of a debt, and afterwards wish to withdraw it, let him charge it on a righter person, if he can; if he cannot, let him forfeit his angylde [and take possession of the wite.] . . .

Of kinless men.
27. If a man, kinless of paternal relatives, fight, and slay a man, and then if he have maternal relatives, let them pay a third of the wer; his guild-brethren a third part; for a third let him flee. If he have no maternal relatives, let his guild-brethren pay half, for half let him flee.

Of slaying a man thus circumstanced.
28. If a man kill a man thus circumstanced, if he have no relatives, let half be paid to the king; half to his guild-brethren.

Of hloth-slaying of a two-hynde man.
29. If any one with a hloth slay an unoffending twyhynde man, let him who acknowledges the death-blow paywer and wite; and let every one who was of the party pay thirty shillings as hloth-bot.

Of a six-hynde man.
30. If it be a six-hynde man, let every man pay sixty shillings as hloth-bot; and the slayer, wer and full wite.

Of a twelve-hynde man.
31. If he be a twelve-hynde man, let each of them pay one hundred and twenty shillings; and the slayer, werand wite. If a hloth do this, and afterwards will deny it on oath, let them all be accused, and let them then all pay the wer in common; and all, one wite, such as shall belong to the wer.

Of those who commit folk-leasing.
32. If a man commit folk-leasing, and it be fixed upon him, with no lighter thing let him make bot than that his tongue be cut out; which must not be redeemed at

any cheaper rate than it is estimated at according to hiswer. . . .

Of a holdgetael.

37. If a man from one holdgetael wish to seek a lord in another holdgetael, let him do it with the knowledge of the ealdorman whom he before followed in his shire. If he do it without his knowledge, let him who entertains him as his man pay 120 shillings as wite; let him, however, deal the half to the king in the shire where he before followed, half in that into which he comes. If he has done anything wrong where he before was, let him makebot for it who has their received him as his man; and to the king 120 shillings as wite.

In case a man fight before an ealdorman in the gemot.

38. If a man fight before a king's ealdorman in the gemot, let him make bot with wer and wite as it may be right; and before this 120 shillings to the ealdorman as wite. If he disturb the folkmote by drawing his weapon, one hundred and twenty shillings to the ealdorman as wite. If aught of this happen before a king's ealdorman's junior, or a king's priest, thirty shillings as wite.

Of fighting in a ceorlish man's flet.

39. If any one fight in a ceorlish man's flet, with six shillings let him make bot to the ceorl. If he draw his weapon and fight not, let it be half of that. If, however, either of these happen to a six-hynde man, let it increase threefoldly, according to the ceorlish bot to a twelve-hynde man, twofoldly, according to the six-hynde's bot.

Of burh-bryce.

40. The king's burh-bryce shall be 120 shillings. An archbishop's, ninety shillings. Any other bishop's, and an ealdorman's, sixty shillings. A twelve-hynde man's, thirty shillings. A six-hynde man's, fifteen shillings. A ceorl's edorbryce, five shillings. If aught of this happen when the fyrd is out, or in Lent fast, let the bot be twofold. If any one in Lent put down holy law among the people without leave, let him make bot with 120 shillings.

Of boc-lands.

41. The man who has boc-land, and which his kindred left him, then ordain we that he must not give it from hismaeg-burg, if tere be writing or witness that it was forbidden by those men who at first acquired it, and by those who gave it to him, that he should do so; and then let that be declared in the presence of the king and of the bishop, before his kinsmen.

Of feuds.

42. We also command: that the man who knows his foe be homesitting fight not before he demand justice of him. If he have such power that he can beset his foe, and besiege him within, let him keep him within for seven days, and attack him not, if he will remain within. And, then, after seven days, if he will surrender, and deliver up his weapons, let him be kept safe for thirty days, and let notice of him be given to his kinsmen and his friends. If, however, he flee to a church, then let it be according to the sanctity of the church; as we have before said above. But if he have not sufficient power to besiege him within, let him ride to the ealdorman, and beg aid of him. If he will not aid him, let him ride to the king before he fights. In like manner also, if a man come upon his foe, and he did not before know him to be homestaying; if he be willing to deliver up his weapons, let him be kept for thirty days, and let notice of him be given to his friends; if he will not deliver up his weapons, then he may attack him. If he be willing to surrender, and to deliver up his weapons, and any one after that attack him, let him pay as well wer as wound, as he may do, and wite, and let him have forfeited his maegship. We also declare, that with his lord a man may fight orwige, if any one attack the lord: thus may the lord fight for his man. After the same wise, a man may fight with his born kinsman, if a man attack him wrongfully, except against his lord; that we do not allow. And a man may fight orwige, if he find another with his lawful wife, within closed doors, or under one covering, or with his lawfully-born daughter, or with his lawfully-born sister, or with his mother, who was given to his father as his lawful wife.

Of the celebration of mass-days.

43. To all freemen let these days be given, but not to theow-men and esne-workmen: twelve days at Yule,

and the day on which Christ overcame the devil, and the commemoration day of St. Gregory, and seven days before Easter and seven days after, and one day at St. Peter's tide and St. Paul's, and in harvest the whole week before St. Mary-mass, and one day at the celebration of All-Hallows and the four Wednesdays in the four ember weeks. To all theow-men be given, to those whom it may be most desirable to give, whatever any man shall give them in God's name, or they at any of their moments may deserve.

GLOSSARY

borhbryce/burh-bryce: a breaking of a pledge

bot: payment or compensation, often as a fine

ceorl: a kind of freeman of the lowest traditional order

hloth: a gang or band of men

maegship: family relationship

reeve: an administrative officer of a town or district

twy-hynde man: an individual whose value is two hundred shillings

weds: pledges given as security

Document Analysis

This selection of King Alfred's laws was embedded in a much larger collection of laws compiled from the records of his predecessors and extrapolated from biblical law, illustrated by the introductory sentences, a biblical admonition to Moses: "I am the Lord your God. I led you out of the land of the Egyptians, and of their bondage." It is possible that Alfred assumed that his readers would equate the flight of God's people from Egypt with their liberation from the Vikings. In any case, the remainder of this selection deals primarily with offenses against other men, not against God.

A fundamental principle of these laws is the responsibility of a man to keep his word. Failure to do so meant imprisonment. The law, however, held a man's responsibility to be loyal to his lord to be superior to his responsibility to keep an oath. Therefore, if an oath would force a man to commit treason, he was not obligated to fulfill it. This is one of the only situations where imprisonment is indicated. Loyalty is reinforced as the primary responsibility of men through the assignment of the death penalty to treachery against a lord.

Most of the stated laws assign values to be paid if damages to property or people occur. They also illustrate the responsibilities of kinship to the Anglo-Saxons. "If a man, kinless of paternal relatives, fight, and slay a man, and then if he have maternal relatives, let them pay a third of the wer; his guild-brethren a third part; for a third let him flee. If he have no maternal relatives, let his guild-brethren pay half, for half let him flee." In other words, a man's kin network, or in extreme cases, his guild, were responsible for paying part of his fine ("wer," the monetary value of the man killed). The cost of theft, bodily harm, and even slaying, was meted out according to the status of the person harmed.

The regulations around feuds are also illustrative, as the ability to settle a dispute remained with individual people who felt that they had been wronged. These rules are complicated, but illustrate the formalities surrounding feuds. If a man who has a feud with another found him at home, he had to demand that he make it right and could not fight him for seven days if he stayed inside. Likewise, he could not fight him if he gave up his weapons, but then could hold him for thirty days. A man could fight for his lord and vice versa without it constituting a feud, and the same rule applied for any man whom he finds insulting his wife, daughter, sister, or mother.

This selection concludes with a list of holidays provided for freemen. Serfs do not fare so well, however, as they are only entitled to "whatever any man shall give them in God's name, or they at any of their moments may deserve."

Essential Themes

The laws of Alfred illustrate several foundational principals of Anglo-Saxon culture and Germanic law. These legal codes helped to set a precedent for instituting legislation comprehensively connected to and representative of cultural identity.

First, loyalty to one's lord in a highly regimented social hierarchy was paramount. Failure to protect a lord, or treachery against one, was punishable by death, in a society where most crimes were settled with payment. Second, the concept of payment as punishment, rather than physical revenge, is typical of Germanic law. Even killing could be settled with a payment, though the amount varied according to the status of the person

harmed. Third, kinship relations were so important as to require shared responsibility for crimes committed by a member. Maternal and paternal relatives were required to pay portions of the money owed to the family of a person harmed.

—*Bethany Groff, MA*

Bibliography and Additional Reading

Albert, Edoardo & Katie Tucker. *In Search of Alfred the Great: The King, the Grave, the Legend.* Stroud: Amberley, 2014. Print.

Preston, Todd. *King Alfred's Book of Laws: A Study of the Domboc and Its Influence on English Identity, with a Complete Translation.* Jefferson: McFarland, 2012. Print.

Wormald, Patrick. *The Making of English Law: King Alfred to the Twelfth Century; Legislation and Its Limits.* Vol 1. Malden: Blackwell, 1999. Print.

The Catholic Church and Its Vicissitudes

The Catholic Church was, without question, the most important institution in medieval Europe. It provided to its subjects not only spiritual solace and eternal salvation but also a level of protection from harm and a ready system of justice—the same variety of things that secular rulers provided, and more. The church often mediated between feuding kingdoms, and it promoted learning and the arts. It was, in that sense, the shared cultural experience for virtually all Europeans. Religion informed all aspects of medieval life, from birth to death, and most people put their faith in god over any secular authority.

At the same time, the church demanded something back from ordinary people. Besides participation in the sacraments and regular attendance at Mass, one could expect to pay to the church a fixed portion of one's annual income in cash or a comparable amount in kind. Parish priests generally knew their parishioners and ensured their conformance in order to guard them against sin and safeguard their place in heaven. However, church clergy were never completely free from corruption and greed, and they sometimes exploited parishioners' good will. Church leaders could also be overzealous in various ways, as evidenced, above all, by the Crusades.

The First Crusade, authorized by Pope Urban II in 1095, was initially a response to a request for military aid from a fellow Christian leader, the Byzantine emperor Alexios Komnenos. Seljuk Turks had been threatening the empire and moving through the Holy Lands, and Alexios appealed for volunteers to help turn them back. The pope, however, transformed the simple appeal into a grand opportunity for an armed pilgrimage, hoping to convert or otherwise dispense with the non-Christians in the region. He sent a force far in excess of what was needed for the routing of the Turks. The First Crusade, consisting of several armies led by feudal princes from different regions of Europe, was largely successful in its aims. New Christian states were established in the Levant (at Jerusalem and Antioch, for example), and a subsequent wave of migrants from the West helped sustain them. In contrast, later Crusades proved far less successful, with even Jerusalem falling (again) to foreign hands.

■ Four Documents from the Investiture Controversy

Date: ca. 1075; 1076; 1122
Geographic Region: Rome; Holy Roman Empire (present-day Italy and Germany)
Author: Pope Gregory VII; Henry IV; Pope Calixtus II; Henry V

Summary Overview

The Investiture Controversy was a series of conflicts centered on the authority of the Roman pope in medieval Europe. This conflict dominated the relationship between Western European rulers and the church from about 1073 to the Concordat of Worms, which settled the matter in 1122. At the heart of the conflict was whether ultimate authority for the selection and install- ment (or investiture) of bishops and other church lead- ers rested primarily with the pope or with the ruler. Also at issue was whether the pope had the right to depose the leader of the Holy Roman Empire, then encom- passing much of modern-day Italy and Germany. Pope Gregory VII, an outspoken reformist pope, brought the issue to a head with his December 1075 letter to Holy Roman Emperor Henry IV, in which he threatened the emperor with excommunication and deposition if he did not accept papal reforms. The conflict that fol- lowed engulfed Europe, as rulers sought to maintain their authority over church leaders, and the pope and other reformers sought to strengthen the authority of the church.

Defining Moment

The practices of clerical marriage, simony (the purchas- ing of religious positions), and lay investiture (the ap- pointing and investment of bishops by secular rulers), were attacked in the eleventh and twelfth centuries by Pope Gregory VII and like-minded church officials. It was the issue of lay investiture, however, that caused the greatest conflict, as it threatened the power of mon- archies all over Europe.

Lay investiture was the practice of secular rulers "investing" church officials with the symbols of their spiritual offices, a process that established the church official's first loyalty to the crown, rather than the pope. In practice, church offices were often given as rewards to supporters of the ruler, who typically believed that he stood next after God in spiritual authority. In the centuries after the collapse of the Roman Empire in the fifth century, European churches had become dis- tant from papal authority, with the rulers in Christian lands assuming the role of head of the church. Bish- ops were "invested" by the king, and then confirmed by their church superior. Bishops and other church lead- ers had enormous power and wealth in medieval Eu- rope, with control over vast areas of land. If the right of investiture was taken away, and local religious leaders' primary loyalty was to the pope, it spelled a significant reduction in the authority of the king. Plus, if simony were brought to an end, rulers would lose a significant source of revenue.

A conflict over the appointment of the archbishop of Milan brought the issue of lay investiture to a head. In 1068, under the previous pope, two archbishops had been confirmed—one by the pope, and one by the bish- ops of Lombard at the behest of Henry IV. In 1073, facing war at home and unable to resolve the issue, Henry IV asked the new pope, Gregory VII, to settle the matter. Gregory acted by forbidding lay investiture, a pronouncement that Henry IV accepted for two years until, fresh from military victory, he decided once again that he would make his court chaplain the archbishop of Milan. Pope Gregory responded with a stern warning in early 1075, advising Henry IV that he was in viola- tion of an agreement that he was bound to respect and reminding him of the supremacy of papal authority. In a fit of anger, in January 1076, Henry IV issued a let- ter demanding that the pope step down and had his bishops refuse to obey Gregory. Gregory responded by excommunicating Henry IV, effectively stripping him of his spiritual authority to rule. The bishops who had opposed the pope then hastily recanted and recognized the authority of the church. Faced with opposition from the nobility, Henry IV asked the pope's forgiveness, and they were briefly reconciled.

Over the next three years, Pope Gregory banned lay investiture in all of Europe, bringing him into conflict with the rulers of England and France as well; the reconciliation with Henry IV was short-lived. The empire devolved into civil war, with the princes allied with the pope electing another king in opposition to Henry, and in 1080, Henry appointed another pope (known as an antipope), Clement III. In 1084, Henry invaded Rome, and Gregory eventually fled to Salerno, where he died in 1085.

Subsequent popes continued to struggle with the issue of lay investiture, until the issue was finally settled in a series of agreements, or concordats. The last of these, the Concordat of Worms, finally eliminated lay investiture in the Holy Roman Empire, but allowed for the emperor to settle disputed elections and to invest bishops with the symbols of their allegiance to the ruler. They were invested with the symbols of their spiritual authority by a representative of the pope.

Author Biography

Pope Gregory VII was born as Hildebrand Bonizi, also known as Hildebrand of Sovana, in present-day Tuscany, Italy, around 1020. When he was a young man, he was sent to Rome to study and was taught by some of the most learned men at the papal court. He traveled through religious communities in France and present-day Germany and seems to have become a monk around 1046. In 1049, Hildebrand returned to Rome with the new pope, Leo IX, and served as a papal administrator and representative, eventually becoming archdeacon. When Pope Alexander II died in 1073, Hildebrand was the popular choice as his successor, and cheering crowds demanded that he be made pope. The cardinals confirmed this choice, and he took the papal name of Gregory VII. He was an energetic reformer, dedicated to the consolidation of the power of the church and the elimination of secular interference in church appointments. He also believed in the right of popes to depose the Holy Roman emperor (the first Christian emperor of Rome, Constantine, had been anointed by a pope), and these beliefs led to conflicts with the rulers of Europe, particularly Emperor Henry IV. As a result of this conflict, Gregory VII was exiled to the city of Salerno, in southern Italy, where he died on May 25, 1085. He was declared a saint in 1728.

HISTORICAL DOCUMENT

DICTATUS PAPAE

1. That the Roman church was established by God alone.

2. That the Roman pontiff alone is rightly called universal.

3. That he alone has the power to depose and reinstate bishops.

4. That his legate, even if he be of lower ecclesiastical rank, presides over bishops in council, and has the power to give sentence of deposition against them.

5. That the pope has the power to depose those who are absent.

6. That, among other things, we ought not to remain in the same house with those whom he has excommunicated.

7. That he alone has the right, according to the necessity of the occasion, to make new laws, to create new bishoprics....

8. That he alone may use the imperial insignia.

9. That all princes shall kiss the foot of the pope alone.

10. That his name alone is to be recited in the churches.

11. That the name applied to him belongs to him alone.

12. That he has the power to depose emperors.

13. That he has the right to transfer bishops from one see to another when it becomes necessary.

14. That he has the right to ordain as a cleric anyone from any part of the church whatsoever.

15. That anyone ordained by him may rule over another church....

16. That no general synod may be called without his order.

17. That no action of a synod and no book shall be regarded as canonical without his authority.

18. That his decree can be annulled by no one, and that he can annul the decrees of anyone.

19. That he can be judged by no one.

20. That no one shall dare to condemn a person who has appealed to the Apostolic See.

21. That the important cases of any church whatsoever shall be referred to the Roman Church.

22. That the Roman Church has never erred and will never err to all eternity, according to the testimony of the holy scriptures.

23. That the Roman pontiff who has been canonically ordained is made holy by the merits of St. Peter....

24. That by his command or permission subjects may accuse their rulers.

25. That he can depose and reinstate bishops without the calling of a synod.

26. That no one can be regarded as catholic who does not agree with the Roman Church.

27. That he has the power to absolve subjects from their oath of fidelity to wicked rulers.

Letter of Henry IV to Gregory VII,
January 24, 1076

Henry, king not by usurpation, but by the holy ordination of God, to Hildebrand, not pope, but false monk.

This is the salutation which you deserve, for you have never held any office in the Church without making it a source of confusion and a curse to Christian men instead of an honor and a blessing. To mention only the most obvious cases out of many, you have not only dared to touch the Lord's anointed, the archbishops, bishops, and priests; but you have scorned them and abused them, as if they were ignorant servants not fit to know what their master was doing. This you have done to gain favor with the vulgar crowd. You have declared that the bishops know nothing and that you know everything; but if you have such great wisdom you have used it not to build but to destroy. Therefore we believe that St. Gregory, whose name you have presumed to take, had you in mind when he said: "The heart of the prelate is puffed up by the abundance of subjects, and he thinks himself more powerful than all others." All this we have endured because of our respect for the papal office, but you have mistaken our humility for fear, and have dared to make an attack upon the royal and imperial authority which we have received from God. You have even threatened to take it away, as if we had received it from you, and as if the empire and kingdom were in your disposal and not in the disposal of God.

Our Lord Jesus Christ has called us to the government of the empire, but he never called you to the rule of the Church. This is the way you have gained advancement in the Church: through craft you have obtained wealth; through wealth you have obtained favor; through favor, the power of the sword; and through the power of the sword, the papal seat, which is the seat of peace; and then from the seat of peace you have expelled peace. For you have incited subjects to rebel against their prelates by teaching them to despise the bishops, their rightful rulers.

You have given to laymen the authority over priests, whereby they condemn and depose those whom the bishops have put over them to teach them. You have attacked me, who, unworthy as I am, have yet been anointed to rule among the anointed of God, and who, according to the teaching of the fathers, can be judged by no one save God alone, and can be deposed for no crime except infidelity. For the holy fathers in the time of the apostate Julian did not presume to pronounce sentence of deposition against him, but left him to be judged and condemned by God.

St. Peter himself said: "Fear God, honor the king" [1 Pet. 2:17]. But you, who fear not God, have dishonored me, whom He has established. St. Paul, who said that even an angel from heaven should be accursed who taught any other than the true doctrine, did not make an exception in your favor, to permit you to teach false doctrines. For he says: "But though we, or an angel from heaven, preach any other gospel unto you than that which we have preached unto you, let him be accursed" [Gal. 1:8]. Come down, then, from that apostolic seat which you have obtained by violence; for you have been declared accursed by St. Paul for your false doctrines and have been condemned by us and our bishops for your evil rule. Let another ascend the throne of St. Peter, one who will not use religion as a cloak of violence, but will teach the life-giving doctrine of that prince of apostles. I, Henry, king by the grace of God, with all my bishops, say unto you: "Come down, come down, and be accursed through all the ages."

Gregory VII's First Excommunication and Deposition of Henry IV

St. Peter, prince of the apostles, incline your ear to me, I beseech you, and hear me, your servant, whom you have nourished from my infancy and have delivered from my enemies who hate me for my fidelity to you. You are my witness, as are also my mistress, the mother of God, and St. Paul your brother, and all the other saints, that your holy Roman church called me to its government against my own will, and that I did not gain your throne by violence; that I would rather have ended my days in exile than have obtained your place by fraud or for worldly ambition. It is not by my efforts, but by your grace, that I am set to rule over the Christian world which was specially entrusted to you by Christ. It is by your grace and as your representative that God has given to me the power to bind and to loose in heaven and in earth.

Confident of my integrity and authority, I now declare in the name of omnipotent God, the Father, Son, and Holy Spirit, that Henry, son of the emperor Henry, is deprived of his kingdom of Germany and Italy; I do this by your authority and in defense of the honor of your church, because he has rebelled against it. He who attempts to destroy the honor of the Church should be deprived of such honor as he may have held. He has refused to obey as a Christian should, he has not returned to God from whom he had wandered, he has had dealings with excommunicated persons, he has done many iniquities, he has despised the warnings which, as you are witness, I sent to him for his salvation, he has cut himself off from your Church, and has attempted to rend it asunder; therefore, by your authority, I place him under the curse. It is in your name that I curse him, that all people may know that you are Peter, and upon your rock the Son of the living God has built his Church, and the gates of hell shall not prevail against it.

The Concordat of Worms

The Oath of Calixtus II
Calixtus, Bishop, servant of the servants of God, to his beloved son, Henry, by the grace of God emperor of the Romans, Augustus.

We hereby grant that in Germany the elections of the bishops and abbots who hold directly from the crown shall be held in your presence, such elections to be conducted canonically and without simony or other illegality. In the case of disputed elections you shall have the right to decide between the parties, after consulting with the archbishop of the province and his fellow-bishops. You shall confer the regalia of the office upon the bishop or abbot elect by the scepter, and this shall be done freely without exacting any payment from him; the bishop or abbot elect on his part shall perform all the duties that go with the holding of the regalia.

In other parts of the empire the bishops shall receive the regalia from you in the same manner within six months of their consecration, and shall in like manner perform all the duties that go with them. The undoubted rights of the Roman Church, however, are not to be regarded as prejudiced by this concession. If at any time you shall have occasion to complain of the carrying out of these provisions, I will undertake to satisfy your grievances as far as shall be consistent with my office. Finally, I hereby make a true and lasting peace with you and with all of your followers, including those who supported you in the recent controversy.

The Oath of Henry V
In the name of the holy and undivided Trinity.

For the love of God and his holy church and of Pope Calixtus, and for the salvation of my soul, I, Henry, by the grace of God, emperor of the Romans, Augustus, hereby surrender to God and his apostles, Sts. Peter and Paul, and to the holy Catholic Church, all investiture by ring and staff. I agree that elections and consecrations shall be conducted canonically and shall be free from all interference. I surrender also the possessions and regalia of St. Peter which have been seized by me during this quarrel, or by my father in his lifetime, and which are now in my possession, and I promise to aid the Church to recover such as are held by any other persons. I restore also the possessions of all other churches and princes, clerical or secular, which have been taken away during the course of this quarrel, which I have, and promise to aid them to recover such as are held by any other persons.

Finally, I make true and lasting peace with Pope Calixtus and with the holy Roman Church and with all who are or have ever been of his party. I will aid the Roman Church whenever my help is asked, and will do justice in all matters in regard to which the Church may have occasion to make complaint.

GLOSSARY

bishopric: the area under a bishop's control, also known as a diocese

ecclesiastical: relating to the clergy or the church

iniquities: wicked acts, sins

legate: a representative of the pope who exercises authority on his behalf

prelate: an ecclesiastic of high order, such as an archbishop or bishop; a church dignitary

Roman pontiff: the pope of the church in Rome; in the Middle Ages, the head of all Christian churches in the West

see: the seat of authority of a bishop

simony: the sale of a church title or office

synod: a church council; a meeting of church leaders

Document Analysis

The documents in this selection begin with the *Dictatus papae*, a list of twenty-seven statements on the power of the pope, a document that appeared in the papers of Pope Gregory VII and is usually dated to 1075. The principles of this document form the central tenets of Gregory's papal reform agenda, based on the supremacy of the church over the authority of secular leaders. Along with general statements confirming the pope's authority are several specific statements regarding the exclusive right of the pope over bishops: "He alone has the power to depose and reinstate bishops. . . . He has the right to transfer bishops from one see to another when it becomes necessary. . . . He has the right to ordain as a cleric anyone from any part of the church whatsoever. . . . Anyone ordained by him may rule over another church." These statements, along with his declaration that he has the right to depose emperors, set the stage for the controversy that followed.

The next document is a 1076 letter from Holy Roman Emperor Henry IV, responding with anger to a letter from Gregory (not included here) advising Henry that Gregory could depose him. Henry denies that the pope has authority over him, calling him "not pope, but false monk," a reference to Pope Gregory VII's being declared pope by a crowd before he was confirmed by the cardinals. The letter is scathing, accusing the pope of encouraging people to rebel against their rightful rulers and proclaiming that Henry had been "anointed to rule among the anointed of God . . . [and] can be judged by no one save God alone, and can be deposed for no crime except infidelity." Though this letter clearly denied the legitimacy of this pope, it stopped short of disclaiming the papacy in general, claiming instead that Gregory VII was an imposter. Gregory responds to this attack in the third document, also dated 1076, announcing Henry's excommunication and declaring that Henry "is deprived of his kingdom of Germany and Italy."

The 1122 Concordat of Worms settled the issue of lay investiture decades later, when Pope Calixtus II and Emperor Henry V came to a compromise: the secular powers of bishops would be granted by the emperor, and their spiritual powers would be granted by the pope. The election of bishops (by other bishops on the pope's behalf) would take place in the emperor's presence, and the emperor had the power to decide contested elections. Henry V agreed that "elections and consecrations shall be conducted canonically and shall be free from all interference," including simony. Both parties agreed to a "true and lasting peace" with one another.

Essential Themes

The Investiture Controversy is a critical moment in the establishment of the power of the papacy. The loyalty of the bishops, significant landholders and nobles in their own right, was at stake in this controversy, and rulers fought hard to protect their authority. Reforming clerics, most notably Gregory VII, saw lay investiture as one of several ways that relations between church and state were violating the laws of God and fought to bring church leaders back under the authority of the papacy. The settlement that resulted from the Concordat of Worms significantly expanded the authority of the pope, while acknowledging church leaders as also being vassals of the secular ruler. Conflicts between the papacy and secular rulers did not end with the concordat, but it is regarded as a significant turning point in medieval history.

—*Bethany Groff, MA*

Bibliography and Additional Reading

Blumenthal, Ute-Renate. *The Investiture Controversy: Church and Monarchy from the Ninth to the Twelfth Century*. Philadelphia: U of Pennsylvania P, 1988. Print.

Fichtenau, Heinrich. *Living in the Tenth Century: Mentalities and Social Order*. Chicago: U of Chicago P, 1991. Print.

Miller, Maureen C. *Power and the Holy in the Age of the Investiture Conflict: A Brief History with Documents*. New York: Palgrave, 2005. Print.

■ A Truce of God, Decree of the Emperor Henry IV

Date: 1085
Geographic Region: Holy Roman Empire (present-day Italy and Germany)
Author: Emperor Henry IV

Summary Overview

The Truce of God was an attempt to curb violence and warfare in the Holy Roman Empire at a time when both medieval Europe lacked strong centralized governments and nobles with private armies frequently set upon one another and caused havoc. The Truce of God prohibited fighting from Thursday to Sunday, on holy and feast days, and during the seasons of Lent and Advent. It also included permanent prohibitions on violence against merchants, farm laborers at work, clergy, and women. This Truce of God is one of several that grew out of the larger Peace of God movement, an ecclesiastical effort to control violence and protect church property. Although not very effective, the movement was nonetheless a sign of the growing power of the church in Europe, which took over many of the roles traditionally held by secular rulers during a time marked by insecurity and lawlessness. The timing of this Truce of God is important, as it came when the Holy Roman emperor, Henry IV, was locked in a bitter conflict with Pope Gregory VII and with rebellious German nobles. His decree sought both to remind the people of Henry's devotion to their safety and to that of the church (though not the pope) and to quell some of the violent uprisings breaking out all over his empire.

Defining Moment

The Peace of God (Latin, *Pax Dei*) began in France at a time marked by instability and upheaval; the movement was informed by religious millennialism and supported by ancient pagan tradition. Evidence exists for the suspension of warfare in Germanic tribes and Roman cities during periods of the veneration of a specific god or goddess. The first written evidence of the Christian Peace of God appeared in several synods, or meetings of church officials, on and around 990. Church officials declared the peace to protect clergy, church lands, and noncombatants, such as women, children, and peasants. Punishments for violating the peace included ex-

ile and excommunication. These efforts were supported by bishops, who were themselves powerful nobles, and by the royal family of Aquitaine, the most powerful ruling house in France. As the year 1000 approached, a religious zeal was added to the Peace of God movement, as crowds gathered in anticipation of miraculous events at abbeys and cathedrals throughout Europe. This in turn strengthened the influence of the church as men at these gatherings swore renewed allegiance to the church and its saints. The Peace of God sought to bring heavenly order to earth through the intercession of the saints, and it was believed that the angels and saints were especially close to earth during the years approaching the millennium. At great religious estates, such as Cluny in France, warfare and violence was prohibited, nobles and clergy had sworn to uphold this peace, and travelers could expect a degree of protection not afforded in other parts of medieval Europe.

The Truce of God (Latin, *Treuga Dei*) was an outgrowth of the Peace of God movement that broadened its scope, as it moved from church-protected classes of people and areas of land to whole kingdoms, and eventually, for certain periods of time, through all of Christian Europe by order of the pope. One of the earliest instances of a Truce of God was in 1027, when a synod in the city of Elne in southern France, declared Sundays off limits for fighting, from Saturday night until Monday morning. By 1041, this prohibition had extended to encompass the other Christian holy days of the week. Thursday was holy, since it was the day when Christ ascended into heaven. Friday was the day that Christ was crucified. Lent and Advent, the weeks surrounding the birth and death of Christ, were also restricted. The penalty for violating these restrictions was excommunication and exile. The Truce of God was declared first in France, but spread to Italy and Germany, where the Henry VII declared it in 1085.

41

Author Biography

Henry IV was born in Saxony in 1050. He was the only son of Holy Roman Emperor Henry III and Agnes of Poitou. When Henry III died in 1056, Agnes served as regent for the young king for five years. In 1062, Henry was kidnapped in a coup led by Anno, the archbishop of Cologne, who proceeded to rule on Henry's behalf while sheltering and educating the boy. In 1065, at age fifteen, Henry assumed his duties as Holy Roman emperor. He inherited rebellious nobles, a quarrel with the Roman papacy, and scandal when, in 1068, he tried to divorce his queen, Bertha of Savoy. In 1075, Pope Gregory VII declared that only the church had the right to invest bishops with the power of their offices and that bishops therefore owed their allegiance foremost to the church. Henry strenuously objected, and on January 25, 1076, a group of church leaders summoned by Henry deposed the pope. Gregory VII responded by excommunicating and deposing Henry. By 1084, Henry marched into Rome and installed another pope, and Gregory died in exile the following year. Two of Henry's sons joined a group of rebellious princes in opposition to their father. In 1105, Henry was captured by his son Henry V and forced to abdicate. He escaped, but died soon after, on August 7, 1106.

HISTORICAL DOCUMENT

Decree of the Emperor Henry IV Concerning a Truce of God

Whereas in our times the holy church has been afflicted beyond measure by tribulations through having to join in suffering so many oppressions and dangers, we have so striven to aid it, with God's help, that the peace which we could not make lasting by reason of our sins, we should to some extent make binding by at least exempting certain days. In the year of the Lord's incarnation, 1085, in the 8th indiction, it was decreed by God's mediation, the clergy and people unanimously agreeing: that from the first day of the Advent of our Lord until the end of the day of the Epiphany, and from the beginning of Septuagesima until the 8th day after Pentecost, and throughout that whole day, and on every Thursday, Friday, Saturday, and Sunday, until sunrise on Monday, and on the day of the fast of the four seasons, and on the eve and the day itself of each of the apostles—moreover on every day canonically set apart, or in future to be set apart for fasting or for celebrating,—this decree of peace shall be observed. The purpose of it is that those who travel and those who remain at home may enjoy the greatest possible security, so that no one shall commit murder or arson, robbery or assault, no man shall injure another with a whip or a sword or any kind of weapon, and that no one, no matter on account of what wrong he shall be at feud, shall, from the Advent of our Lord to the 8th day after Epiphany, and from Septuagesima until the 8th day after Pentecost, presume to bear as weapons a shield, sword, or lance-or, in fact, the burden of any armour. Likewise on the other days—namely, on Sundays, Thursdays, Fridays, Saturdays, and on the eve and day of each of the apostles, and on every day canonically fixed, or to be fixed, for fasting or celebrating,—it is unlawful, except for those going a long distance, to carry arms; and even then under the condition that they injure no one in any way. If, during the space for which the peace has been declared, it shall be necessary for any one to go to another place where that peace isn't observed, he may bear arms; provided, nevertheless, that he harm no one unless he is attacked and has to defend himself. Moreover, when he returns, he shall lay aside his weapons again. If it shall happen that a castle is being besieged, the besiegers shall cease from the attack during the days included in the peace, unless they are attacked by the besieged, and are obliged to beat them back.

And lest this statute of peace be violated with impunity by any person, the following sentence was decreed by all present: If a freeman or a noble shall have violated it—that is, if he shall have committed murder, or shall have transgressed it in any other way,—he shall, without any payments or any friends being allowed to intervene, be expelled from within his boundaries, and his heirs may take his whole estate; and if he hold a fief, the lord to whom it belongs shall take it. But if, after his expulsion, his heirs shall be found to have given him any aid or support, and shall be convicted of it, the estate shall be taken from them and shall fall to the portion of the king. But if he wish to clear himself of the charges against him, he shall swear with 12 who are equally noble and free. If a slave kill a man he shall be beheaded; if he wound him he shall have his right hand cut off; if he have transgressed in any other way—by striking with his fist, or a stone, or a whip, or any thing else—he shall be flogged and shorn. But if the accused (slave) wish to prove his innocence, he shall purge himself by the ordeal of cold water: in such wise, however, that he himself, and no one in his place, be sent to the water. But if, fearing the sentence that has been passed against him, he shall have fled,—he shall be forever under the bane. And wherever he is heard to be, letters shall be sent there announcing that he is under the bane, and that no one may hold intercourse with him. The hands may not be cut off of boys who have not yet completed their 12th year; if boys, then, shall transgress this peace, they shall be punished with whipping only. It is not an infringement of the peace if any one order a delinquent, slave, or a scholar, or any one who is subject to him in any way, to be beaten with rods or with whips. It is an exception also to this statute of peace, if the emperor shall publicly order an expedition to be made to seek the enemies of the realm, or shall be pleased to hold a council to judge the enemies of justice. The peace is not violated if, while it continues, the duke, or other counts or bailiffs, or their substitutes hold courts, and lawfully exercise judgment over thieves and robbers, and other harmful persons. This imperial peace has been decreed chiefly for the security of all those who are at feud; but not to the end that, after the peace is over, they may dare to rob and plunder throughout the villages and homes. For the law and judgment that was in force against them before this peace was decreed shall be most diligently observed, so that they be restrained from iniquity; —for robbers and plunderers are excepted from this divine peace, and, in fact, from every peace. If any one strive to oppose this pious decree, so that he

will neither promise the peace to God nor observe it, no priest shall presume to sing a mass for him or to give heed to his salvation; if he be ill, no Christian shall presume to visit him, and, unless he come to his senses, he shall do without the Eucharist even at the end. If any one, either at the present time or among our posterity forever, shall presume to violate it, he is banned by us irrevocably. We decree that it rests not more in the power of the counts or centenars, or any official, than in that of the whole people in common, to inflict the above mentioned punishments on the violators of the holy peace. And let them most diligently be on their guard lest, in punishing, they show friendship or hatred, or do anything contrary to justice; let them not conceal the crimes of any one, but rather make them public. No one shall accept money for the redemption of those who shall have been found transgressing. Merchants on the road where they do business, rustics while labouring at rustic work—at ploughing, digging, reaping, and other similar occupations,—shall have peace every day. Women, moreover, and all those ordained to sacred orders, shall enjoy continual peace. In the churches, moreover, and in the cemeteries of the churches, let honour and reverence be paid to God; so that if a robber or thief flee thither he shall not at all be sieved, but shall be besieged there until, induced by hunger, he shall be compelled to surrender. If any one shall presume to furnish the culprit with means of defence, arms, victuals, or opportunity for flight, he shall be punished with the same penalty as the guilty man. We forbid under our bane, moreover, that any one in sacred orders, convicted of transgressing this peace, be punished with the punishments of laymen—he shall, instead, be handed over to the bishop. Where laymen are decapitated, clerks shall be degraded; where laymen are mutilated, clerks shall be suspended from their positions; and, by the consent of the laity, they shall be afflicted with frequent fasts and flagellations until they shall have atoned. Amen.

GLOSSARY

bane: a rule outlawing a banned person; banishment

canonically: by church law

centenar: a commander of one hundred infantry soldiers, especially during the Hundred Years' War

GLOSSARY CONTINUED

fief: a territory held on the condition that feudal obligations are met by the owner to his lord

indiction: (Middle English) an announcement

iniquity: gross injustice or wickedness; sin

ordeal of cold water: a medieval test of guilt or innocence; in most cases it was believed that, bound and cast into water, a guilty person would sink, and an innocent person would float

Septuagesima: the third Sunday before Lent

Document Analysis

Henry IV's declaration begins by acknowledging that, due to human sinfulness, complete peace is not possible, but that the rate of violence can perhaps be limited: "that the peace which we could not make lasting by reason of our sins, we should to some extent make binding by at least exempting certain days." The decree asserts further that it is a result of agreement among God, the emperor, the clergy, and the people. The goal of the truce is clearly stated: "that those who travel and those who remain at home may enjoy the greatest possible security"; it is later stated that the decree is "for the security of all those who are at feud." This gets at an important motivation for such decrees: ongoing bloody feuds between medieval lords—at times rising almost to the level of civil war—were a source of chronic unrest and mayhem at this time, and the general desire for order was great.

Thus, breaches of the peace—such as "murder or arson, robbery or assault," or even the brandishing of a weapon—are not allowed from Wednesday evening until Monday morning, and also prohibited during Lent and Advent, feast days, and any other day "canonically set aside." Exceptions are made for self-defense, or aiding the ruler in the defense of the realm. The penalties for violating these restrictions differ, depending on the status of the person in violation. Freemen or nobles violating the peace are to be exiled, and their lands taken by their heirs or their liege lord. Slaves, on the other hand, are to be beheaded for killing a man; they lose a hand for wounding someone; and they may be flogged for any lesser offense. Boys under the age of twelve are exempt from this rule and are to be beaten rather than maimed. Punishment of wrongdoing is excepted from the truce: masters retain the right to beat those in their charge, such as "a delinquent, slave, or a scholar," and normal criminal trial and punishment may proceed. The spiritual penalties for violators of the peace are also enumerated: "no priest shall presume to sing a mass for him . . . no Christian shall presume to visit him, and . . . he shall do without the Eucharist even at the end." Protected classes of people who should be secure from violence at all times—women, field workers, merchants, clergy—are also identified, and lesser punishments for clergy who violate the peace are set, to be meted out by their bishop rather than secular authorities.

Essential Themes

Henry's Truce of God combined the language of the earlier Peace of God decrees with time limits on fighting between nonprotected classes of people. Noncombatants and church lands were protected at all times, but this truce added days when fighting and the bearing of arms was banned and feuding prohibited, even if the feud was justified, on the majority of the days of the year. Punishments were both corporal and spiritual: exile and excommunication for landowners and beheading, maiming, and whipping for others. In a world where competing fiefdoms and feudal lords maintained private armies and fought endless battles for territory and titles, it also provided some legal framework for the maintenance of law and order, enforced, in this case, by both the secular ruler and the church.

Although the effect of this and other such decrees was limited, they were an important development in the history of Western legal tradition. As monarchical power over national polities was consolidated with the waning of the Middle Ages, the "Peace of God" backed up by the authority of the church came increasingly to be replaced by the "king's peace," backed up more effectively by the force of the secular ruler.

—*Bethany Groff, MA*

Bibliography and Additional Reading

Head, Thomas F., & Richard Allen Landes, eds. *The Peace of God: Social Violence and Religious Response in France around the Year 1000*. Ithaca: Cornell UP, 1992. Print.

Miller, Maureen C. *Power and the Holy in the Age of the Investiture Conflict: A Brief History with Documents*. New York: Palgrave, 2005. Print.

Robinson, I. S. *Henry IV of Germany, 1056–1106*. New York: Cambridge UP, 1999. Print.

■ The Crusaders in Mainz, May 27, 1096

Date: ca. 1140
Geographic Region: Holy Roman Empire (present-day Germany)
Author: Solomon bar Samson

Summary Overview

In 1095, Pope Urban II called for a crusade, an armed pilgrimage, to free Eastern Christians from the Muslim Seljuk Turks, who were attacking the Byzantine (Eastern) Christians in Anatolia, and to retake the city of Jerusalem, held by Muslims since the seventh century. Ultimately, it was this latter objective that fueled the religious zeal and motivated thousands of armed Christians to march across Europe to Constantinople and then on to Jerusalem. As they marched, following the traditional route to the Middle East that extended down the Rhine and the Danube Rivers, bands of crusaders, looking for supplies and motivated by greed and religious fervor, began to attack Jewish communities. By the time they reached the Rhineland, the crusaders were an unruly mob—and despite orders from the Holy Roman Emperor, Henry IV, and attempts to pay them off—crusaders entered German cities such as Speyer, Worms, and Mainz, rounded up the Jewish inhabitants, and either forced them to convert or killed them outright. In Mainz, despite seeking protection from the bishop and hiding in the abbey where sanctuary was traditionally provided, over one thousand Jews were killed.

Defining Moment

In November 1095, Pope Urban II addressed a large crowd of clergy and noblemen gathered for an official council in the town of Clermont, France. Representatives had been sent from the Byzantine emperor in Constantinople, asking his fellow Christians in Europe to help him defend against Muslims attacking his empire. To add to the immediacy of his request, he provided graphic testimony of violence against Christian pilgrims in Jerusalem. The lack of strong centralized governments in feudal Europe meant that there were numerous nobles with private armies of knights with little to do but feud and fight each other, and they were ripe for a mission. Knights who would help fight were promised both earthly and spiritual rewards: their lands would be held for them, and their sins would be forgiven. There were powerful reasons for others to join as well, as debts were suspended and land-bound serfs were allowed to travel. Through the next several months, knights set off for Constantinople and the Holy Land, joined by swelling groups of peasants and serfs.

Jewish people in European cities and towns lived in relative peace at this time. They were barred from some traditional employment, but were allowed to participate in some trades not permitted to Christians, such as money lending. They lived in self-contained communities and were regarded as mysterious, with real and perceived wealth. Traditional Christian distrust of the Jews was inflamed by the religious zeal in the armed mobs marching toward the Holy Land. Emicho of Flonheim, a German count (German lands were, at this time, part of the Holy Roman Empire), joined the Crusade, claiming Christ had appeared to him. He gathered an army, and thousands of French and German crusaders joined him. In May, his forces arrived in Speyer, a cathedral city with a powerful bishop, who sheltered the Jews of Speyer in his cathedral and then moved them to fortified cities in the countryside. Despite this protection, a number of Jews were killed. The group moved on to Worms, where the bishop was unable to protect the city's Jewish residents; on May 18, some eight hundred Jews were killed in Worms when they refused baptism. When Emicho's crusaders arrived outside Mainz on May 25, the Jewish community there sent out a gift of money, hoping to induce the crusaders to leave them alone. They also sought protection in the bishop's palace, which was defended by a militia of his guards and townspeople. The townspeople of Mainz (many of whom had business connections with Jews) and the bishop's men held off a first attack, but the ranks of the crusader mob swelled, and despite these efforts, the mob broke through the city's defenses on May 27. The bishop and his guard fled, and many townspeople joined the mob. The bishop's castle was overrun, and over one thousand Jewish men, women, and children were either killed by the crusaders or committed suicide. Emicho's army left Mainz and continued through the Rhine Valley and into Hungary, where the Hungarians decimated them in battle near present-day Bratislava; Emicho himself was killed in battle a short time later, never making it to the Holy Land.

Author Biography and Document Information

Solomon bar Samson is thought to be a contemporary of Rashi (Shlomo Yitzchaki), an influential rabbi and scholar living in Worms. Little else is known about his life. The Solomon bar Samson chronicles were recorded around 1140 and transcribed in the fifteenth century. They were rediscovered in the late nineteenth century.

HISTORICAL DOCUMENT

I.

It was on the third of Siwan.... at noon, that Emico the wicked, the enemy of the Jews, came with his whole army against the city gate, and the citizens opened it up for him. Emico a German noble, led a band of plundering German and French crusaders. Then the enemies of the Lord said to each other: 'look! They have opened up the gate for us. Now let us avenge the blood of 'the hanged one'."

The children of the holy covenant who were there, martyrs who feared the Most High, although they saw the great multitude, an army numerous as the sand on the shore of the sea, still clung to their Creator. Then young and old donned their armor and girded on their weapons and at their head was Rabbi Kalonymus ben Meshullam, the chief of the community. Yet because of the many troubles and the fasts which they had observed they had no strength to stand up against the enemy. Then came gangs and bands, sweeping through like a flood until Mayence was filled from end to end.

The foe Emico proclaimed in the hearing of the community that the enemy be driven from the city and be put to flight. Panic was great in the town. Each Jew in the inner court of the bishop girded on his weapons, and all moved towards the palace gate to fight the crusaders and the citizens. They fought each other up to the very gate, but the sins of the Jews brought it about that the enemy overcame them and took the gate.

The hand of the Lord was heavy against His people. All the Gentiles were gathered together against the Jews in the courtyard to blot out their name, and the strength of our people weakened when they saw the wicked Edomites overpowering them. The bishop's men, who had promised to help them, were the very first to flee, thus delivering the Jews into the hands of the enemy. They were indeed a poor support; even the bishop himself fled from his church for it was thought to kill him also because he had spoken good things of the Jews....

When the children of the covenant saw that the heavenly decree of death had been issued and that the enemy had conquered them and had entered the courtyard, then all of them—old men and young, virgins and children, servants and maids—cried out together to their Father in heaven and, weeping for themselves and for their lives, accepted as just the sentence of God. One to another they said: "Let us be strong and let us bear the yoke of the holy religion, for only in this world can the enemy kill us-and the easiest of the four deaths is by the sword. But we, our souls in paradise, shall continue to live eternally, in the great shining reflection."

With a whole heart and with a willing soul they when spoke: "After all it is not right to criticize the acts of God—blessed be He and blessed be His name—who has given to us His Torah and a command to put ourselves to death, to kill ourselves for the unity of His holy name. Happy are we if we do His will. Happy is anyone who is killed or slaughtered, who dies for the unity of His name so that he is ready to enter the World to Come, to dwell in the heavenly camp with the righteous—with Rabbi Akiba and his companions, the pillars of the universe, who were killed for His names sake. Not only this; but he exchanges the world of darkness for the world of light, the world of trouble for the world of joy, and the world that passes away for the world that lasts for all eternity. Then all of them, to a man, cried out with a loud voice: "Now we must delay no longer for the enemy are already upon us. Let us hasten and offer ourselves as a sacrifice to the Lord. Let him who has a knife examine it that it not be nicked, and let him come and slaughter us for the sanctification of the Only One, the Everlasting and then let him cut his own throat or plunge the knife into his own body."

As soon as the enemy came into the courtyard they found some of the very pious there with our brilliant master, Isaac ben Moses. He stretched out his neck, and his head they cut off first. The others, wrapped by their fringed praying-shawls, sat by themselves in the courtyard, eager to do the will of their Creator. They did not care to flee into the chamber to save themselves for this temporal life, but out of love they received upon themselves the sentence of God. The enemy showered stones and arrows upon them, but they did not care to flee, and [Esther 9:5] "with the stroke of the sword, and with slaughter, and destruction" the foe killed all of those whom they found there. When those in the chambers saw the deed of these righteous ones, how the enemy had already come upon them, they then cried out, all of them: "There is nothing better than for us to offer our lives as a sacrifice."

The women there girded their loins with strength and slew their sons and their daughters and then themselves. Many men, too, plucked up courage and killed their wives, their sons, their infants. The tender and delicate mother slaughtered the babe she had played with, all of them, men and women arose and slaughtered one another. The maidens and the young brides and grooms looked out of the Windows and in a loud voice cried: "Look and see, O our God, what we do for the sanctification of Thy great name in order not to exchange you for a hanged and crucified one...."

Thus were the precious children of Zion, the Jews of Mayence, tried with ten trials like Abraham, our father, and like Hananiah, Mishael, and Azariah [Daniel 3:21]. They tied their sons as Abraham tied Isaac his son, and they received upon themselves with a willing soul the yoke of the fear of God, the King of the Kings of Kings, the Holy One, blessed be He, rather than deny and exchange the religion of our King [Isaiah 14: 19] "an abhorred offshoot....' They stretched out their necks to the slaughter and they, delivered their pure souls to their Father in heaven. Righteous and pious women bared their throats to each other, offering to be sacrificed for the unity of the Name. A father turning to his son or brother, a brother to his sister, a woman to her son or daughter neighbor to a neighbor or a friend, a groom to a bride, a fiancé to fiancée, would kill and would be killed, and blood touched blood, The blood of the men mingled with their wives', the blood of the fathers with their children's, the blood of the brothers with the sisters, the blood of the teachers with their disciples', the blood of the grooms with their brides', the blood of the leaders with the cantors', the blood of the judges with their scribes', and the blood of infants and sucklings with their mothers'. For the unity of honored and awe-inspiring Name were they killed and slaughtered.

The ears of him who hears these things will tingle, for who ever heard anything like this? Inquire now and look about, was there ever such an abundant sacrifice as this since the days of the primeval Adam? Were there ever eleven hundred offerings on one day, each one of them like the sacrifice of Isaac, the son of Abraham?

For the sake of Isaac who was ready to be sacrificed on Mount Moriah, the world shook, as it is said [Isaiah 33:7]: "Behold their valiant ones cry without;" and [Jeremiah 4:28] "the heavens grow dark." Yet see what these martyrs did! Why did the heavens not grow dark and the stars not withdraw their brightness? Why did not the moon and the sun grow dark in their heavens when on one day, on the third of Siwan, on a Tuesday eleven hundred souls were killed and slaughtered, among them the many infants and sucklings who had not transgressed nor sinned, many poor, innocent souls?

Wilt Thou, despite this, still restrain Thyself, O Lord? For thy sake it was that these numberless souls were killed. Avenge quickly the blood of Thy servants which was spilt in our days and in our sight. Amen.

II. Rachel and Her Children

Now I shall recount and tell of the most unusual deeds that were done on that day by these righteous ones.... Who has ever seen anything like this? Who has ever heard of a deed like that which was performed by this righteous and pious woman, the young Rachel, the daughter of Rabbi Isaac ben Asher, the wife of Rabbi Judah? For she said to her friends: "I have four children. Do not spare even them, lest the Christians come, take them alive, and bring them up in their false religion. Through them, too, sanctify the name of the Holy God."

So one of her companions came and picked up a knife to slaughter her son. But when the mother of the children saw the knife, she let out a loud and bitter lament and she beat her face and breast, crying: Where are Thy mercies, O God?" In the bitterness of her soul she said to her friend: "Do not slay Isaac in the presence of his brother Aaron lest Aaron see his brother's death and run away." The woman then took the lad Isaac, who was small and very pretty, and she slaughtered him while the mother spread out her sleeves to receive the blood, catching it in her garment instead of a basin. When the child Aaron saw that his brother Isaac was slain, he screamed again and again: "Mother, mother, do not butcher me," and ran and hid under a chest.

She had two daughters also who still lived at home, Bella and Matrona, beautiful young girls, the children of her husband Rabbi Judah. The girls took the knife and sharpened it themselves that it should not be nicked. Then the woman bared their necks and sacrificed them to the Lord God of Hosts who has commanded us not to change His pure religion but to be perfect with Him, as it is written [Deuteronomy 18:13]: "Perfect shall you be with the Lord your God."

When this righteous woman had made an end of sacrificing her three children to their Creator, she then raised her voice and called out to her son Aaron: "Aaron, where are you? You also I will not spare nor will I have any mercy." Then she dragged him out by his foot from under the chest where he had hidden himself, and she sacrificed him before God, the high and exalted. She put her children next to her body, two on each side, covering them with her two sleeves, and there they lay struggling in the agony of death. When the enemy seized the room they found her sitting and wailing over them "Show us the money that is under your sleeves," they said to her. But when it was the slaughtered children they saw, they struck her and killed her, upon her children, and her spirit flew away and her soul found peace at last. To her applied the Biblical verse [Hosea 10:14]: "The mother was dashed in pieces with her children." . . .

When the father saw the death of his four beautiful, lovely children, he cried aloud, weeping and wailing, and threw him upon the sword in his hand so that his bowels came out, and wallowed in blood on the road together with the dying who were convulsed, rolling in their life's blood. The enemy killed all that who were left in the room and then stripped them naked; [Lamentations 1:11] "See, O Lord, and behold, how abject I am become." Then the crusaders began to give thanks in the name of "the hanged one" because they had done what they wanted with all those in the room of the bishop so that not a soul escaped.

GLOSSARY

Edomites: traditional enemies of the Jewish people; descendants of Esau, an Old Testament figure

four deaths: in Judaism, the four acceptable capital punishments: stoning, strangulation, decapitation, and burning.

hanged one, the: a pejorative term for Jesus Christ (a reference to his crucifixion)

Rabbi Akiba: Jewish scholar and martyr killed by the Romans in the second century CE

Siwan: also Sivan, a month in the Hebrew calendar

Document Analysis

This selection is part of a longer history of the attacks on the Jewish people of the Rhineland at the beginning of the Crusades. It opens after a first attack against Mainz (Mayence) is repelled, with the citizens opening the city gates rather than continuing to resist. The Jewish people gathered under their rabbi to fight, but they were weak from devotional fasting they had undergone in hopes of averting an attack. The city was soon filled by gangs of crusaders. In this account, Emicho is assigned personal responsibility for issuing the order to drive the Jews from the city. The Jews took refuge under the protection of the bishop and his men, who are accused of doing little to protect them: "They were indeed a poor support." When the bishop himself fled, it became clear to the Jewish people gathered there that they were all to be killed.

The chronicler identifies the sinfulness of the Jews as the reason they were overwhelmed, and describes them as receiving a "heavenly decree of death," which they "accepted as just," so great was their faith in God. Throughout this ordeal, Samson describes the group calling on the examples of previous martyrs such as Rabbi Akiba, killed by the Romans, to give themselves courage. Rather than be killed by their attackers, the Jews decided instead to "put ourselves to death, to kill ourselves for the unity of His holy name." When the attackers broke through into the courtyard of the bishop's palace, the senior leaders of the community allowed themselves to be killed. Those who observed this knew that it was their time as well. The remainder of the selection is a description of how the Jewish people of Mainz killed themselves and each other, after first sharpening their knives so they would be ritualistically pure. Families killed each other, in the name of God. A particularly poignant example is set by a rabbi's wife, Rachel, who is described killing her four children and then allowing herself to be killed. Though Samson makes the argument that this sacrifice is for the glory of God, he also pleads for God to "avenge quickly the blood of thy servants," so many of whom chose to die rather than give up their faith.

Essential Themes

The primary theme of this selection is the horrific slaughter of Jewish communities in the Rhineland by the armed mobs that made up the bulk of the First Crusade. Solomon bar Samson's chronicle recounted this episode as both a slaughter of innocents and a sacrifice that received God's people into paradise. Many of the Jews chose to kill themselves and their families rather than be killed by the invaders. It is one of the more famous incidents in Jewish history to which mass suicide is attested, and it led to revisions of the strict Judaic prohibition on suicide. It is also a graphic example of how many crusaders turned the call for a military intervention on religious grounds into an excuse for lawless violence. The attacks on the Jewish communities in the Rhineland took place while they were under the protection of church leaders and violated strict orders from secular and church authorities.

—*Bethany Groff, MA*

Bibliography and Additional Reading

Chazan, Robert. *In the Year 1096: The First Crusade and the Jews.* Philadelphia: Jewish Publication Soc., 1996. Print.

Claster, Jill N. *Sacred Violence: The European Crusades to the Middle East, 1095–1396.* Toronto: U of Toronto P, 2009. Print.

Peters, Edward. *The First Crusade: The Chronicle of Fulcher of Chartres and Other Source Materials.* Philadelphia: U of Pennsylvania P, 2011. Print.

Excerpt from "The Capture of Jerusalem"

Date: 1099
Geographic Region: Jerusalem (present-day Israel)
Author: Fulcher of Chartres

Summary Overview

In November 1095, Pope Urban II addressed a large crowd of clergy and noblemen gathered for an official council in the town of Clermont, France. Representatives had been sent from the Byzantine emperor in Constantinople to ask his fellow Christians of Europe to help him defend against Muslim Turks attacking his empire. To add to the immediacy of his request, he provided graphic testimony of violence against Christian pilgrims in Jerusalem. During this time, because of the lack of a strong royal authority, there were numerous nobles with private armies of knights who were ripe for a mission. Knights who would help fight were promised secular and spiritual protection: their lands would be held for them, and their sins would be forgiven. In 1096, knights set off for Constantinople and the Holy Land, determined to recapture Jerusalem. In June 1099, the crusaders arrived in Jerusalem and laid siege. They succeeded in scaling the walls on June 14 and sacked the city, putting its inhabitants, including those they had been sent to protect, to death. Fulcher (Fulk) of Chartres was a French priest traveling with the crusaders, and he chronicled the siege of the city and ensuing slaughter.

Defining Moment

The first people to respond to Pope Urban II's call for a crusade, or armed pilgrimage, were mobs of undisciplined peasants, following lesser nobles and charismatic priests toward Constantinople and murdering and pillaging as they went. Pope Urban II had issued a call to free Eastern Christians from Muslim Seljuk (Seljuq) Turks. The latter were attacking the Christians in Anatolia and had captured the city of Jerusalem, which had been held by Muslims since the seventh century. Reportedly, Christian pilgrims were being mistreated at holy sites and kept from visiting some entirely. In addition to the "Peasant Crusade" (also known as the "People's Crusade"), a second "Princes' Crusade"

was formed by lords with experienced knights and infantry. By the spring of 1097, this crusader army—led by Godfrey of Bouillon; Raymond IV, Count of Toulouse; Robert II, Count of Flanders; and Bohemond of Otranto—had crossed into present-day Turkey and gathered outside Constantinople. The Byzantine emperor Alexios demanded, and received, an oath that any lands recaptured from the Turks would be returned to him, and he ferried the quarrelsome knights across the Bosporus as quickly as possible.

The crusader army was joined by the small remnant of peasants who had survived the march to Constantinople under Peter the Hermit, and they marched on the city of Nicea, which had been taken by the Turks. They then defeated a much larger army of Turks at Dorylaeum. Their next conquest was the well-fortified port city of Antioch, which survived a sustained siege as the crusaders fought off Turkish relief armies. In June 1098, a Turkish traitor opened the Bridge Gate, and the all but Antioch's citadel was taken. The Christian knights massacred civilians and soldiers alike and repulsed a large Turkish force sent to regain the city. After the Antioch citadel surrendered to the crusaders, they stayed in the city for months, replenishing their supplies, terrorizing what remained of the populace, and preparing for the siege of Jerusalem. They departed from Antioch in January 1099.

On June 7, 1099, the invading army reached Jerusalem and found it well defended. The city had been retaken by the Fatimids, Muslims of North Africa who had expelled the Turks. The Fatimids offered generous terms to the invaders, but the Christian invaders were intent on forcing the city to surrender completely. When the crusaders realized how difficult the siege would be, they built ladders to enter the city, a tactic that proved ineffective. Next, they built siege towers, and finally, on July 15, soldiers breached the walls of Jerusalem. The Christian soldiers slaughtered men, women, and children, and they ended Muslim control of Jerusalem until 1517, when the city was taken by Ottoman Turks. The leaders of the crusade set up kingdoms around Jerusalem, failing to return the land to the Byzantine emperor as promised.

Author Biography

Fulcher of Chartres was born in France around 1059. He was trained for the priesthood, and in 1096, he accompanied his liege lord, Stephen of Blois, to Constantinople via Bulgaria. In Constantinople, he became the chaplain of Baldwin of Boulogne (later Baldwin I of Edessa), accompanying him to Jerusalem in 1099. Baldwin I became king of Jerusalem in 1100. Fulcher remained in Jerusalem for the rest of his life, chronicling the siege that captured the city and other events there until his death in or around 1127.

HISTORICAL DOCUMENT

Chapter 27: The Siege of the City of Jerusalem

On the seventh of June the Franks besieged Jerusalem. The city is located in a mountainous region, which is lacking in rivers, woods, and springs, except the Fountain of Siloam, where there is plenty of water, but it empties forth only at certain intervals. This fountain empties into the valley, at the foot of Mount Zion, and flows into the course of the brook of Kedron, which, during the winter, flows through the valley of Jehosaphat. There are many cisterns, which furnish abundant water within the city. When filled by the winter rains and well cared for, they offer both men and beasts an unfailing supply at all times. Moreover, the city is laid out most beautifully, and cannot be criticized for too great length or as being disproportionately narrow. On the west is the tower of David, which is flanked on both sides by the broad wall of the city. The lower half of the wall is solid masonry, of square stones and mortar, sealed with molten lead. So strong is this wall that, if fifteen or twenty men should be well supplied with provisions, they would never be taken by any army. . . .

When the Franks saw how difficult it would be to take the city, the leaders ordered scaling ladders to be made, hoping that by a brave assault it might be possible to surmount the walls by means of ladders and thus take the city, God helping. So the ladders were made, and on the day following the seventh, in the early morning, the leaders ordered the attack, and, with the trumpets sounding, a splendid assault was made on the city from all sides. The attack lasted till the sixth hour, but it was discovered that the city could not be entered by the use of ladders, which were few in number, and sadly we ceased the attack.

Then a council was held, and it was ordered that siege machines should be constructed by the artisans, so that by moving them close to the wall we might accomplish our purpose, with the aid of God. This was done. . . .

. . .When the tower had been put together and had been covered with hides, it was moved nearer to the wall. Then knights, few in number, but brave, at the sound of the trumpet, took their places in the tower and began to shoot stones and arrows. The Saracens defended themselves vigorously, and, with slings, very skilfully hurled back burning firebrands, which had been dipped in oil and fresh fat. Many on both sides, fighting in this manner, often found themselves in the presence of death.

. . . On the following day the work again began at the sound of the trumpet, and to such purpose that the rams, by continual pounding, made a hole through one part of the wall. The Saracens suspended two beams before the opening, supporting them by ropes, so that by piling stones behind them they would make an obstacle to the rams. However, what they did for their own protection became, through the providence of God, the cause of their own destruction. For, when the tower was moved nearer to the wall, the ropes that supported the beams were cut; from these same beams the Franks constructed a bridge, which they cleverly extended from the tower to the wall. About this time one of the towers in the stone wall began to burn, for the men who worked our machines had been hurling firebrands upon it until the wooden beams within it caught fire. The flames and smoke soon became so bad that none of the defenders of this part of the wall were able to remain near this place. At the noon hour on Friday, with trumpets sounding, amid great commotion and shouting "God help us," the Franks entered the city. When the pagans saw one standard planted on the wall, they were completely demoralized, and all their former boldness vanished, and they turned to flee through the narrow streets of the city. Those who were already in rapid flight began to flee more rapidly.

Count Raymond and his men, who were attacking the wall on the other side, did not yet know of all this, until they saw the Saracens leap from the wall in front of them. Forthwith, they joyfully rushed into the city to pursue and kill the nefarious enemies, as their comrades

were already doing. Some Saracens, Arabs, and Ethiopians took refuge in the tower of David, others fled to the temples of the Lord and of Solomon. A great fight took place in the court and porch of the temples, where they were unable to escape from our gladiators. Many fled to the roof of the temple of Solomon, and were shot with arrows, so that they fell to the ground dead. In this temple almost ten thousand were killed. Indeed, if you had been there you would have seen our feet colored to our ankles with the blood of the slain. But what more shall I relate? None of them were left alive; neither women nor children were spared.

GLOSSARY

Franks: the Germanic peoples of Gaul (France); although crusaders came from across Western Europe, they were assumed to be French

Saracens: a general term for Muslims

Document Analysis

This selection provides a detailed report of the siege and capture of Jerusalem from the vantage point of a warrior priest who is both at the center of the action and privy to the plans of the siege's leaders. Fulcher begins by describing the landscape around the city, an important element in an extended siege. He identifies sources of water and natural features and obstacles. He then turns his attention to the defenses of the city. He notes the thickness of the walls and the ability of the city to be held "if fifteen or twenty men should be well supplied with provisions." Fulcher devotes considerable attention to describing the siege towers from which knights could shoot arrows and firebrands (flaming pieces of wood). The crusaders finally succeeded in setting a tower on the wall on fire and were able to breach the city's defenses. Fulcher makes a point of noting that the city was breached on a Friday, the day of the crucifixion of Jesus. From Fulcher's perspective, this, along with the hasty retreat of the city's defenders once the wall was breached, provides additional proof of the rightness of their cause.

Fulcher's description of the attack makes clear that the crusaders were advancing from multiple points. When Raymond of Toulouse and his men saw that the Muslim defenders jumping from the wall, they entered the city from another point. "Forthwith, they joyfully rushed into the city to pursue and kill the nefarious enemies, as their comrades were already doing." Once the crusaders breached the wall, they carried out the slaughter of the "Saracens, Arabs, and Ethiopians." Even inhabitants of the city who took refuge in temples and other sacred places were killed. Fulcher takes evident glee in describing the blood running in the street, until "our feet colored to our ankles with the blood of the slain," and no man, woman, or child was left alive.

Essential Themes

The fighters of the First Crusade achieved their goal of recapturing Jerusalem in 1099 during the siege described in this piece. Fulcher of Chartres, a chaplain who traveled on the crusade with Baldwin, described many elements of the siege, from the natural features of the region to the way that the crusaders approached the siege. The excerpt also notes the slaughter of civilians during capture of Jerusalem, one of many instances of such tactics during the First Crusade. Fulcher took evident delight in describing the killing of the inhabitants of the city.

—*Bethany Groff, MA*

Bibliography and Additional Reading

Bredero, Adriaan. *Christendom and Christianity in the Middle Ages.* Grand Rapids: Eerdmans, 1987. Print.

Claster, Jill N. *Sacred Violence: The European Crusades to the Middle East, 1095–1396.* Toronto: U of Toronto P, 2009. Digital file.

Peters, Edward. *The First Crusade: "The Chronicle of Fulcher of Chartres" and Other Source Materials.* 2nd ed. Philadelphia: U of Pennsylvania P, 1998. The Middle Ages Ser. Print.

Tyerman, Christopher. *God's War: A New History of the Crusades.* Cambridge: Belknap P of Harvard UP, 2006. Print.

Excerpt from *Historia Constantinopolitana*

Date: ca. 1204
Geographic Region: Constantinople (present-day Turkey)
Author: Gunther of Pairis

Summary Overview

Gunther of Pairis was a Cistercian monk who wrote an account of the Fourth Crusade (1202–04) based on the testimony of Martin, the abbot of Pairis, an abbey in northeastern France. Pope Innocent III had called the Fourth Crusade for the purpose of returning Jerusalem, lost in 1187 to Saladin (a Muslim sultan), to Christian control. The Third Crusade (1189–92) had both failed to recapture Jerusalem and heightened tensions between Roman Christian Europe and the Byzantine Empire. The leaders of the Fourth Crusade made an arrangement with the leaders of Venice to provide for the massive undertaking of transporting their men and horses to Egypt; however, the crusaders were ultimately unable to pay the Venetians. Instead, they agreed to help the cause of Alexios IV Angelos, the son of the recently deposed Byzantine emperor Isaac II Angelos. In return, Alexios promised to pay their debts and the costs of the crusade to the Holy Land. After besieging Constantinople, Alexios IV was able to take the throne, but he was killed in a coup in 1204. The crusaders then attacked Constantinople, and amid widespread looting, many of its religious relics were stolen. Gunther of Pairis wrote an account of the looting of religious relics by his abbot, Martin of Pairis.

Defining Moment

When Pope Innocent III ascended to the papacy in 1198, he immediately called for a crusade to take back the city of Jerusalem from Saladin, the Ayyubid sultan. Jerusalem had been captured in 1099 during the First Crusade but had returned to Muslim control in 1187. The year 1198 was an inauspicious time for a pan-European endeavor, however, as England and France were at war, German states were fighting among themselves and with the pope, and other conflicts occupied the attention of Europe's fighting men. Support built for a Fourth Crusade over the following years, as charismatic preachers and noblemen joined the cause and began to gather support.

In 1200, leaders of the crusade traveled to Venice to negotiate for transport and supplies. They persuaded the Venetians to spend a year building a massive fleet to attack Egypt, the heart of the Ayyubid Empire. The contract would provide transportation for more than thirty thousand crusaders. By the spring of 1202, however, only twelve thousand crusaders had materialized; they could pay less than half the money they owed the Venetians, who refused to transport them until paid in full. Historians debate whether an attack on the Byzantine Empire was always part of the plan for some of the crusaders; nonetheless, when the Venetians proposed that the crusaders attack the Byzantine port city of Zara to help pay their debt, the crusaders agreed. Zara fell in November 1202. Meanwhile, Isaac II Angelos, the Byzantine emperor, had been deposed and blinded by his brother. Alexios IV Angelos, the son of Isaac II Angelos, offered the crusaders an extraordinary deal: if they helped him retake the Byzantine throne, he would offer them two hundred thousand silver marks and knights to help capture and hold Jerusalem. He also promised that the Byzantine Church would be put under the authority of the pope. The crusader army in Zara agreed and marched on Constantinople, arriving outside the city in June 1203.

Constantinople was besieged for most of July. The crusaders made significant gains, despite being vastly outnumbered. After a failed counterattack, Emperor Alexios III Angelos, uncle of Alexios IV, the prince for whom that the crusaders were fighting, fled the city. The leaders of Constantinople reinstalled Isaac II as emperor, leaving the crusaders without either a cause or payment for their efforts. They demanded that Alexios IV be crowned as coruler and that they be paid. Alexios IV was crowned with his father on August 1. Isaac II died in January 1204, and Alexios was deposed, imprisoned, and strangled in February. The crusaders demanded that their contract with Alexios be honored. When the new emperor refused, they attacked the city. By April 13, 1204, the crusaders had control of the entire city and burned and looted it for three days. Byzantine churches were desecrated, and their religious art and relics were stolen. The Venetians were paid off, and the Latin Empire of Constantinople was established. Pope Innocent III, who had ordered the initial crusade, was displeased with the violence against fellow Christians, and the actions of the crusaders solidified the rift between the Byzantine and Roman churches; animosity between them would continue for centuries.

Author Biography and Document Information

Gunther of Pairis was a Cistercian monk at the Alsatian abbey of Pairis. Little is known about his life, but he is thought to have been born around 1150 and died around 1220. He was a learned man—a teacher in the monastery school and tutor to the royal family. After Abbot Martin of Pairis returned from the Fourth Crusade, Gunther recorded his experiences in the *Historia Constantinopolitana*. This manuscript was copied in the fourteenth century by monks in Germany, and Gunther's writing also appeared in collections of religious texts in the fifteenth and sixteenth centuries. It was rediscovered in the nineteenth century and reprinted in Latin. The original text does not survive.

HISTORICAL DOCUMENT

While the victors were rapidly plundering the conquered city, which was theirs by right of conquest, the abbot Martin began to cogitate about his own share of the booty, and lest he alone should remain empty-handed, while all the others became rich, he resolved to seize upon plunder with his own sacred bands. But, since he thought it not meet to handle any booty of worldly things with those sacred hands, he began to plan how he might secure some portion of the relics of the saints, of which he knew there was a great quantity in the city.

Accordingly, having a presentiment of some great result, he took with him one of his two chaplains and went to a church which was held in great reverence because in it the mother of the most famous emperor Manuel had a noble grave, which seemed of importance to the Greeks, but ours held for naught. There a very great amount of money brought in from all the surrounding country was stored, and also precious relics which the vain hope of security had caused them to bring in from the neighboring churches and monasteries. Those whom the Greeks had driven out, had told us of this before the capture of the city. When many pilgrims broke into this church and some were eagerly engaged in stealing gold and silver, others precious stones, Martin, thinking it unbecoming to commit sacrilege except in a holy cause, sought a more retired spot where the very sanctity of the place seemed to promise that what he desired might be found.

There he found an aged man of agreeable countenance, having a long and hoary beard, a priest, but very unlike our priests in his dress. Thinking him a layman, the abbot, though inwardly calm, threatened him with a very ferocious voice, saying—"Come, perfidious old man, show me the most powerful relics you have, or you shall die immediately." The latter, terrified by the sound rather than the words, since be heard but did not understand what was said, and knowing that Martin could not speak Greek, began in the *Romana lingua*, of which he knew a little, to entreat Martin and by soft words to turn away the latter's wrath, which in truth did not exist. In reply, the abbot succeeded in getting out a few words of the same language, sufficient to make the old man understand what he wanted. The latter, observing Martin's face and dress, and thinking it more tolerable that a religious man should handle the sacred relics with fear and reverence, than that worldly men should, perchance, pollute them with their worldly hands, opened a chest bound with iron and showed the desired treasure, which was more grateful and pleasing to Martin than all the royal wealth of Greece. The abbot hastily and eagerly thrust in both hands and working quickly, filled with the fruits of the sacrilege both his own and his chaplain's bosom. He wisely concealed what seemed the most valuable and departed without opposition.

Moreover what and how worthy of veneration those relics which the holy robber appropriated were, is told more fully at the end of this work. When he was hastening to his vessel, so stuffed full, if I may use the expression, those who knew and loved him, saw him from their ships as they were themselves hastening to the booty, and inquired joyfully whether he had stolen anything, or with what he was loaded down as he walked. With a joy-ful countenance, as always, with pleasant words he said: "We have done well." To which they replied: "Thanks be to God."

GLOSSARY

cogitate: to think upon or about

Greeks: the crusader term for Byzantines

Manuel: Manuel I Komnenos, Byzantine emperor from 1118 to 1180

relics: objects or body parts of a saint, revered in the Christian tradition

Romana lingua: the language of Rome

Document Analysis

This selection explains how holy relics—objects or remains of body parts associated with saints—were taken during the looting of Constantinople by Martin of Pairis. The passage serves as both a justification of the removal of these relics and a recounting of the way they were taken. Martin is clearly conflicted about looting the city, but feels justified because the relics are from a church outside the protection of the papacy. He was afraid that, having worked so hard to conquer the city, he would be left out of the plunder, but "he thought it not meet to handle any booty of worldly things with those sacred hands, he began to plan how he might secure some portion of the relics of the saints." These holy relics are potentially more valuable than art or even treasure, as they will ensure the prestige and security of the monastery in which they are housed, not to mention their potential spiritual benefits.

Martin breaks into a church of questionable importance to him, but one revered by the Byzantines. It was thought to be a safe place for the treasure from other churches in the countryside. Other crusaders also pillaged its goods. Martin believes that a church should be violated only for good reason, however, "thinking it unbecoming to commit sacrilege except in a holy cause." He seeks a quieter place where relics were more likely to be found. Martin finds a priest, and since the latter is dressed very differently than a European priest, he threatens to kill him if he does not give up the relics. Despite a language barrier, the Byzantine priest understands what Martin wants and believes that the relics would be better handled by another priest than by the pillaging crusaders. Thus, Martin has an excuse to take the relics: he is saving them from a worse fate. "The abbot hastily and eagerly thrust in both hands and working quickly, filled with the fruits of the sacrilege both his own and his chaplain's bosom. He wisely concealed what seemed the most valuable and departed without opposition." When Martin returns to the ship, laden with these relics, and the company's prizes are revealed, the group praises God.

Essential Themes

This selection records the removal of sacred relics from the city of Constantinople during the Fourth Crusade. Gunther of Pairis recorded the experience of the abbot of his order, Martin. Though he considered Constantinople a fair conquest, Martin was ambivalent about looting riches from the churches of the city. He also did not feel that he should be looting secular goods, given his position as a spiritual leader. This passage justifies the taking of these relics: at least they were given the respect of being handled by a religious leader. The sack of the city solidified the schism in the Roman and Byzantine churches, as the pope failed to protect fellow Christians, and the people of the city, even its clergy, were subjected to all manner of brutality.

—Bethany Groff, MA

Bibliography and Additional Reading

Angold, Michael. *The Fourth Crusade: Event and Context.* New York: Longman, 2003. Print.

Perry, David M. *Sacred Plunder: Venice and the Aftermath of the Fourth Crusade.* Philadelphia: U of Pennsylvania P, 2015. Print.

Swietek, Francis R. "Gunther of Pairis and the Historia Constantinopolitana." *Speculum* 53.1 (1978): 49–79. *Humanities and Social Sciences Index Retrospective: 1907–1984* (H.W. Wilson). Web. 14 May 2015.

■ Statute in Favor of the Princes

Date: ca. 1231
Geographic Region: Germany
Author: Frederick II
Translators: Oliver J. Thatcher, Edgar H. McNeal

Summary Overview

The Statute in Favor of Princes (published in Latin as the *Statutum in favorem principum*) was issued by Holy Roman emperor Frederick II through his son Henry VII, who was ruling as the king of Germany, which formed the largest portion of the Holy Roman Empire. Frederick II was embroiled in conflicts across his empire during his reign—most notably with the popes. From infancy, Frederick was king of Germany, Italy, Burgundy, and Sicily. He was crowned Holy Roman emperor in 1220. His territory in Italy and Sicily surrounded the Papal States, and his most enduring conflicts were with a succession of popes. Though he was excommunicated four times from the church, his relationship with the five popes that held office during his reign was complicated. In fact, it was Pope Innocent III who supported his claim to the throne of Germany in 1212, with the understanding that he would not simultaneously hold the title of king of Germany and king of Sicily. Frederick used his son Henry as a proxy to hold one title (king of Germany) on his behalf, while he held the other title (king of Sicily). In 1231, Henry VII made significant concessions to the German princes on his father's behalf in the Statute in Favor of the Princes, in order to assure their support in Frederick's conflict with the papacy.

Defining Moment

The reign of Frederick II was defined by his conflict with the papacy over control of Italy, and this can be traced back to his grandfather and father's inability to secure a solid block of support in northern Italy. Henry VI, the Holy Roman emperor from 1191 to 1197, had attempted to consolidate his control of Italy from the south by marrying Constance, heiress of Sicily. When Henry VI died suddenly, his three-year-old son Frederick became a pawn of the pope and German princes,

along with a host of other enterprising barons. Pope Innocent III, who was appointed Frederick's guardian upon Constance's death a year later, crowned rival Otto of Brunswick as Holy Roman emperor in 1209, after he promised not to oppose papal authority in Italy. Once crowned, however, Otto lost no time in reestablishing his authority throughout the empire. He reclaimed papal lands as his fiefs and demanded that Frederick appear and do homage for lands that he held. When Frederick did not appear, Otto declared that his lands were forfeited. Otto marched on Rome and attempted to invade Sicily, which was under the protection of Innocent III.

Otto was excommunicated by the pope in 1211, and his adventuring in Italy had alienated him from the German princes. Pope Innocent III and King Phillip II of France encouraged an election in Germany that named Frederick king of Germany. After years of fighting, Otto was defeated in 1214. Frederick returned to Italy to be crowned emperor by the pope in 1220 and arranged for his son Henry to be named king of Germany the same year, thus ensuring that Frederick would maintain control over both Sicily and Germany, though he had promised the pope he would not hold both titles.

The papacy was bent on expanding its territory in Italy, from which it received taxes, dues, troops, and protection. Frederick was equally committed to regaining control of Italy, arguing that the church should return to its vow of poverty and leave worldly rule to the emperor. Frederick II put his Sicilian house in order, setting up administrative structures that efficiently managed the collection of taxes and duties on commercial goods; thus enriched with the wealth of Sicily, he concentrated his efforts on controlling Italy from the north through the semi-independent states of Lombardy. In order to concentrate his efforts on regaining control of Italy, Frederick II needed to placate the princes of Germany. In 1231, through Henry, he granted the princes sweeping authority in his Statute in Favor of Princes. In the statute, he gave concessions that allowed the German princes near-autonomy over their principalities. This turned them into virtually independent states, ensuring that a united, central government would not thrive in Germany until the nineteenth century.

Author Biography and Document Information

Frederick II was born on December 26, 1194, in Jesi, Ancona, then part of the Papal States in central Italy. He was the son of Constance—heir to the Norman kingdom of Sicily—and of Holy Roman emperor Henry VI. Frederick was elected the king of Germany as an infant. When his father died unexpectedly in 1197, Frederick's mother renounced his claim to the German throne and took him back to Sicily, where he was crowned king. His mother died shortly thereafter, and he was raised under the auspices of various tutors and guardians, including Pope Innocent III. Frederick took control of Germany at age fourteen, defeated his rival Otto IV, and in 1220, was crowned Frederick II, Holy Roman emperor. Frederick's court in Sicily was known for its brilliance and opulence. Frederick II spoke numerous languages and was a patron of poets and musicians. He also authored a distinctive guide to falconry and was an accomplished hunter and horseman. His contemporaries called him the "wonder of the world." Frederick negotiated the return of the city of Jerusalem from the sultan of Egypt, and crowned himself its king in 1229. Frederick came into conflict with all five popes whose reigns coincided with his. He died in 1250 and was buried in Sicily in the Cathedral of Palermo.

HISTORICAL DOCUMENT

In the name of the holy and undivided Trinity, Frederick II, by divine mercy emperor of the Romans, Augustus, king of Jerusalem, king of Sicily.

1. No new castles or cities shall be erected by us or by anyone else to the prejudice of the princes.
2. New markets shall not be allowed to interfere with the interests of former ones.
3. No one shall be compelled to attend any market against his will.
4. Travellers should not be compelled to leave the old highways, unless they desire to do so.
5. We will not exercise jurisdiction within the ban-mile of our cities.
6. Each prince shall possess and exercise in peace according to the customs of the land the liberties, jurisdiction, and authority over counties and hundreds, which are in his own possession or are held as fiefs from him.
7. Centgrafs shall receive their office from the prince or from the person who holds the land as a fief.
8. The location of the hundred court shall not be changed without the consent of the lord.
9. No nobleman shall be amenable to the hundred court.
10. The citizens who are known as phalburgii shall be expelled from the cities.
11. Payments of wine, money, grain, and other rents, which free peasants have formerly agreed to pay, are here by remitted, and shall not be collected henceforth.
12. The serfs of princes, nobles, ministerials, and churches shall not be admitted to our cities.
13. Land and fiefs of princes, nobles, ministerials, and churches, which have been seized by our cities, shall be restored and shall never again be taken.
14. The right of the princes to furnish safe-conduct within the lands they hold as fiefs from us shall not be infringed by us or by anyone else.
15. Inhabitants of our cities shall not be compelled by our judges to restore any possessions which they may have received from others before they moved there.
16. Notorious, condemned, and proscribed persons shall not be admitted to our cities; if they have been, they shall be driven out.

17. We will never cause any money to be coined in the land of any of the princes which shall be injurious to his coinage.

18. The jurisdiction of our cities shall not extend beyond their boundaries, unless we possess special jurisdiction in the region.

19. In our cities the plaintiff shall bring suit in the court of the accused.

20. Lands or property which are held as fiefs shall not be pawned without the consent of the lord from whom they are held.

21. No one shall be compelled to aid in the fortifying of cities unless he is legally bound to render that service.

22. Inhabitants of our cities who hold lands outside shall pay to their lords or advocates the regular dues and services, and they shall not be burdened with unjust exactions.

23. If serfs, freemen subject to advocates, or vassals of any lord, shall dwell within any of our cities, they shall not be prevented by our officials from going to their lords.

GLOSSARY

ban-mile: the area outside of city walls where the authority of the city was in force

centgrafs: minor German nobility, a type of count

fiefs: lands held in exchange for feudal services

hundred: a geographic subdivision; part of a county

phalburgii: people or groups living outside a city but who had political rights within it

Document Analysis

Existing from the tenth through the early nineteenth century, the Holy Roman Empire was made up of a large and diverse collection of political entities throughout central Europe, including hundreds of lands ruled directly by nobles (princes) with a high degree of autonomy who were constantly negotiating and sometimes fighting over their relationship with the emperor. In addition to these princely lands, there were certain important cities ruled directly by the emperor, known as imperial cities. This selection from the Statute in Favor of the Princes clarifies the relationship between these imperial cities and the princely lands surrounding them, returning to the German princes many privileges previously reserved for the king or emperor.

Most of these privileges involve control of money and land. For example, Frederick allows the princes to mint their own currency, manage their own toll roads, and collect payments from free peasants that had previously been made to the emperor. The authority of the imperial cities is scaled back, with their laws not to extend beyond the city walls, and princely land seized by the cities is to be returned. The emperor also promises not to build any new castles or defenses without permission of the princes, or require that they help to fortify existing cities.

These restrictions on the authority of the emperor reduced his sphere of influence in the governing of the empire. Where before Germany had been on a path to consolidation within the empire, individual princes now had the ability to secure their borders, coin their own money, charge tolls, and control the minor nobility in their principalities.

Essential Themes

This selection from the Statute in Favor of Princes released the German princes from many of their feudal duties and responsibilities to the Holy Roman emperor. This spelled the end of the development of a unified nation-state in Germany until the nineteenth century. Emperor Frederick II, desperate to avoid wasting his energy and resources in conflicts with quarrelsome German princes, made concessions that gave them greater control over their principalities at the expense of the unity of the empire. Germany was not unlike other European countries in the thirteenth century—it was a collection of states loosely held together by a complex web of feudal allegiances. In other European nations, however, powerful monarchies were consolidating their territory one province at a time, while in Germany, the feudal network of nearly autonomous states would continue for centuries, until the unification of Germany in the nineteenth century. This statute is an example of how far Frederick II was willing to go to placate the German princes so he could focus on consolidating his power in Italy.

—*Bethany Groff, MA*

Bibliography and Additional Reading

Abulafia, David. *Frederick II: A Medieval Emperor.* Oxford: Oxford UP, 1998. Print.

Coy, Jason Philip, Benjamin Marschke, & David Warren Sabean. *The Holy Roman Empire, Reconsidered.* New York: Berghahn, 2010. Print.

Kantorowicz, Ernst Hartwig. *The King's Two Bodies: A Study in Mediaeval Political Theology.* Princeton, NJ: Princeton UP, 1957. Print.

Report from China

Date: 1305
Author: John of Monte Corvino
Geographic Region: China
Translator: Henry Yule

Summary Overview

This document is a letter from the Franciscan missionary John of Monte Corvino to the church in Europe reporting on the success of his mission to Asia, particularly Mongol-ruled China, and pleading for assistance to follow up on what he had already begun. As an early European visitor to far eastern Asia, his account of his travels across the continent is a valuable window into cross-cultural contact in the Middle Ages. Although John had not managed to convert the Mongol ruler himself, he painted a picture of a thriving mission, with a church built and many converts. His enthusiasm and demonstrated success was key to early efforts to establish Western Christianity in China, and his translations and surviving letters would have a lasting influence.

Defining Moment

The establishment of the Mongol Empire in the thirteenth century following the conquests of Genghis Khan (1162–1227) and his successors opened up the possibility of ongoing communication between Europe and East Asia; the unification of the vast space from Poland to Korea under Mongol authority made it possible for Europeans to visit China in significant numbers for the first time. The two groups who took the most advantage of this new possibility were merchants, such as the famous Venetian Marco Polo, and Christian missionaries. The Mongol rulers, or khans, were known for their relative religious toleration, and some European Catholics saw the Mongols both as potential converts and allies against Muslims in the Holy Land. Even beyond the hopes of alliance, conversion of the Great Khan, thought to be the world's richest and most powerful ruler, would be an enormous win for the Catholic Church. Catholic missionary approaches to the khans began in the mid-thirteenth century.

By the end of the thirteenth century, the geopolitical situation for European rulers had grown urgent. Acre, the last crusader state in the Middle East, had fallen to the Muslim Mamluks in 1291, and the Christian world was increasingly on the defensive. The possibility of an alliance with the Mongols was attractive to Christian leaders fearing a new Muslim offensive. The Mongol Empire was administratively subdivided into four khanates. Europeans had the most direct contact with the Ilkhanate of Persia, an occasional ally of the crusaders against the Mamluks of Egypt, but the central Mongol authorities were the "great khans" of the East, who were also emperors of China.

The thirteenth century also saw the establishment and growth of new religious orders known collectively as friars. The earliest friar was Francis of Assisi, and the friars like John of Monte Corvino who followed in his tradition were known as Franciscans or Friars Minor. Less tied to a particular place than monks (who took up fixed residence in monasteries), friars were mobile and particularly oriented to preaching and conversion. The orders of friars, working under papal direction, were the spearhead of the Christian mission to the East. The Franciscans dominated the mission to China. Unlike Marco Polo and other merchant visitors to China, whose business was trade, missionary friars like John of Monte Corvino could plan to spend the rest of their lives there.

Author Biography and Document Information

John of Monte Corvino, also known as Giovanni da Montecorvino, was born in Italy around 1247 and by 1272 had joined the Franciscan order. He acquired extensive experience dealing with the non-Catholic peoples of the Eastern Mediterranean. In 1289, he was sent by Pope Nicholas IV on a mission to the Mongol rulers of Persia and China. From the Middle East he traveled to India, where he stayed over a year and helped establish the first Catholic mission on the subcontinent. It was not until 1294 that he finally reached China. Much of the opposition he faced in China came not from non-Christians, but from the Nestorian Christians who had a long history in Asia and viewed John as a rival. In 1308, John was consecrated as the archbishop of Peking and patriarch of the Orient. He continued to promote Christianity in China until his death in Peking (later Beijing) around 1328. Although his original letters are not preserved, early copies are found in a Latin chronicle at the National Library of France in Paris.

HISTORICAL DOCUMENT

I, Friar John of Monte Corvino, of the order of Minor Friars, departed from Tauris, a city of the Persians, in the year of the Lord 1291, and proceeded to India. And I remained in the country of India, wherein stands the church of St. Thomas the Apostle, for thirteen months, and in that region baptized in different places about one hundred persons. The companion of my journey was Friar Nicholas of Pistoia, of the order of Preachers, who died there, and was buried in the church aforesaid.

I proceeded on my further journey and made my way to Cathay, the realm of the Emperor of the Tartars who is called the Grand Cham. To him I presented the letter of our lord the Pope, and invited him to adopt the Catholic Faith of our Lord Jesus Christ, but he had grown too old in idolatry. However he bestows many kindnesses upon the Christians, and these two years past I am abiding with him. . . . In this mission I abode alone and without any associate for eleven years; but it is now going on for two years since I was joined by Friar Arnold, a German of the province of Cologne.

I have built a church in the city of Cambaliech, in which the king has his chief residence. This I completed six years ago; and I have built a bell-tower to it, and put three bells in it. I have baptized there, as well as I can estimate, up to this time some 6000 persons; and if those charges against me of which I have spoken had not been made, I should have baptized more than 30,000. And I am often still engaged in baptizing.

Also I have gradually bought one hundred and fifty boys, the children of pagan parents, and of ages varying from seven to eleven, who had never learned any religion. These boys I have baptized, and I have taught them Greek and Latin after our manner. Also I have written out Psalters for them, with thirty Hymnaries and two Breviaries. By help of these, eleven of the boys already know our service, and form a choir and take their weekly turn of duty as they do in convents, whether I am there or not. Many of the boys are also employed in writing out Psalters and other things suitable. His Majesty the Emperor moreover delights much to hear them chanting. I have the bells rung at all the canonical hours, and with my congregation of babes and sucklings I perform divine service, and the chanting we do by ear because I have no service book with the notes.

Indeed if I had had but two or three comrades to aid me 'tis possible that the Emperor Cham would have been baptized by this time! I ask then for such brethren to come, if any are willing to come, such I mean as will make it their great business to lead exemplary lives. . . .

As for the road hither I may tell you that the way through the land of the Goths, subject to the Emperor of the Northern Tartars, is the shortest and safest; and by it the friars might come, along with the letter-carriers, in five or six months. The other route again is very long and very dangerous, involving two sea-voyages; . . . But, on the other hand, the first-mentioned route has not been open for a considerable time, on account of wars that have been going on.

It is twelve years since I have had any news of the Papal court, or of our Order, or of the state of affairs generally in the west. . . .

I have myself grown old and grey, more with toil and trouble than with years; for I am not more than fifty-eight. I have got a competent knowledge of the language and character which is most generally used by the Tartars. And I have already translated into that language and character the New Testament and the Psalter, and have caused them to be written out in the fairest penmanship they have; and so by writing, reading, and preaching, I bear open and public testimony to the Law of Christ. . . .

As far as I ever saw or heard tell, I do not believe that any king or prince in the world can be compared to his majesty the Cbam in respect of the extent of his dominions, the vastness of their population, or the amount of his wealth. Here I stop.

Dated at the city of Cambalec in the kingdom of Cathay, in the year of the Lord 1305, and on the 8th day of January.

GLOSSARY

breviaries: books containing all the daily psalms, hymns, prayers, and lessons necessary for worship

Cambaliech: the capital of China and the Mongol Empire; modern Beijing; also spelled Cambalec or Khanbaliq

idolatry: the religious worship of idols

Order of Preachers: Dominican Friars

psalters: psalms

Tartars: an ethnic group within the Mongol Empire, often used interchangeably with "Mongol" by Europeans

Document Analysis

This document is a missionary report, and as such it combines optimism about the conversions John has already made, reasons why he has not attained some of his goals, and hopes for more support. First he relates the story of his travels beginning in Persia in 1291. He mentions his time in India and the conversions he made there before continuing on to Cathay, as China was commonly identified by Europeans at this time. Significantly, he also discusses the different routes between Europe and the Far East, noting the varying lengths, difficulties, and closures due to wars.

Most of the letter explains his progress in China, including the failure to convert the Mongol khan (the "Grand Cham") himself. The conversion of a ruler was frequently followed by the conversion of an entire country, as had been the case in many states in Europe during the early Middle Ages. The "idolatry" to which John refers in discussing the khan is probably Buddhism, which Temür Khan, the emperor at the time, and other great khans were known to favor. Medieval Christian Europeans had no conception of Buddhism as a distinct religious tradition and tended to lump all religions other than Christianity, Judaism, and Islam together as "idolatry."

However, even if the khan has not become a Christian, there is still room for optimism in that he has per-mitted John's mission to go forward and even favored Christianity in some ways. This may well have been a reflection of the broad Mongol policy of tolerating numerous religions instead of advancing one as the official religion. John recounts his achievements in making converts and establishing Christian institutions in China. He talks about baptisms and the building of churches. He has taken advantage of slave markets to purchase young boys, raise them as Christians, and organize them into a choir. John has also begun the work of translating the Bible into the native language, probably Uighur, the written language of the Mongol elite, beginning with the New Testament and the Psalms. He has also carried out some of the rituals that were vital to the conception of the Christian life in the Middle Ages, such as the ringing of bells.

John worked alone for eleven years before being joined by one other Western missionary, and the primary goal of his letter is to ask for additional help. So eager is he that even after acknowledging the intransigent idolatry of the great khan, he raises the possibility of converting him if the church were able to send more missionaries. However, these new missionaries must be dedicated and willing to "lead exemplary lives."

Essential Themes

John's letter succeeded in its immediate goal of winning more support from Rome. In 1308, Franciscans sent by the pope consecrated John archbishop of Peking and patriarch of the Orient. John continued to expand the Catholic presence in China until his death around 1328, and his legacy remained influential in the region for years after. However, the Mongol Empire was already declining by the early fourteenth century, and the direct access between Europe and China that made John's mission possible would become more difficult in the decades after his letter.

The Ilkhanate between Europe and China began to grow more Islamic in character and politically weaker, and the possibility of a European-Mongol alliance against the Muslim states of the Middle East receded. The territory of the khans grew unfriendly to Christian missionaries, particularly after the disintegration of Mongol rule in Persia after 1335, and no longer offered a gateway to the East. The native Chinese Ming dynasty that succeeded the Mongol Yuan dynasty in 1368 would also be far more hostile to foreigners and their religions than the Mongols of John's time. The accession of the Ming, a dynasty that strongly emphasized Chinese tradition in the wake of the expulsion of the Mongol invaders was followed by persecution of Christians and other foreign religions.

The Catholic Church in China that John and his successors had led disappeared without a trace shortly after the Ming accession. No more missionaries would be sent and the hope of converting the emperor or all of China would be abandoned until the establishment of the sea route around Africa to China in the sixteenth century saw a revival of the Catholic mission. However, the legend of the wealth and power of the Chinese emperor would live on for centuries and provide a motivation for both Columbus's voyages across the Atlantic and Vasco da Gama's voyage around Africa.

—*William E. Burns, PhD*

Bibliography and Additional Reading

Dawson, Christopher, ed. *The Mongol Mission: Narratives and Letters of the Franciscan Missionaries in Mongolia and China in the Thirteenth and Fourteenth Centuries.* New York, Sheed, 1955. Print.

Jackson, Peter. *The Mongols and the West: 1221–1410.* New York: Routledge, 2014. Print.

Robson, Michael J. P. *The Franciscans in the Middle Ages.* Woodbridge: Boydell, 2009. Print.

Yule, Henry, ed. *Cathay and the Way Thither.* London: Hakluyt Soc., 1914. Print.

■ Letter to Gregory XI

Date: ca. 1377
Author: Catherine of Siena
Geographic Region: Italy

Summary Overview

This is one of a series of letters in which the Dominican tertiary and theologian Catherine of Siena urges Pope Gregory XI to reform the Catholic Church, end his war with Florence and the Tuscan League (the War of the Eight Saints), and launch a new crusade to the Holy Land. The language is frank and informal, and expresses Catherine's disappointment with the behavior of the pope so far in his pontificate. However, Catherine respects his office and hopes that he will improve in the future. If he is incapable of improvement, she suggests, it would be best for both the church and his own spirit if he resigned the office. Throughout the letter, she claims not to speak with her own authority, but to be expressing the will of God.

Defining Moment

The papacy was at a low point in its prestige in the mid-fourteenth century. The period when the popes lived in the southern French city of Avignon, from 1309 to 1377, gave the papacy a reputation for corruption and subservience to the French monarchy. The pontificate of Gregory XI, a Frenchman like all the Avignon popes, was the last of the "Avignon Captivity." The pope returned to Rome in 1377 (the probable date of Catherine's letter), but it was not clear if this relocation was to be permanent or a temporary measure aimed at resolving the military and political crisis of the Papal States at the time. (Like many Italians, Catherine had ardently supported the return of the papacy to Rome, although the issue is not addressed in this letter.) The Black Death, which had reached Europe the same year Catherine was born, further called into question the leadership of the Church, which had failed to avert the wrath of God manifested in such a striking way.

After the 1291 Muslim capture of Acre, the last crusader-held city in the Middle East, the position of the Christians in the eastern Mediterranean continued to deteriorate, as the Byzantine Empire and the Christian states of the Balkans retreated before the advance of the Ottoman Turks as far as the borders of Hungary. Although the Christians won some confrontations, the overall failure of Christian Europe to effectively oppose the Ottoman advance was frequently ascribed to the disunity of European rulers and the failure of papal leadership. Two nations that had contributed to earlier crusading forces, the English and the French, spent much of the second half of the century battling one another in the disastrous Hundred Years' War (1337–1453), making the organization of a crusading army particularly difficult. The identification of the Avignon papacy with France added to the difficulty of forming a united Christian army.

Siena during Catherine's time was riven by struggles between noble and popular factions and various leading families for control of the city, sometimes erupting into violence. In this aspect, Siena was a microcosm of Italy itself. The absence of the popes from Italy and the governing of the Papal States by French officials with a poor understanding of the region led to a massive revolt, in which the rebels allied with the city of Florence outside the Papal States. The war in the Papal States was suppressed with great brutality, and the conflict led to a war between the papacy and Florence, the War of the Eight Saints (1375–78).

Author Biography

Catherine was born on March 25, 1347, to a middle-class family in the town of Siena, then an independent republic and later part of Tuscany, Italy. Her religious vocation appeared early in life, as she claimed to have received a vision of Jesus blessing her as a small child. She had difficulties with her family due to her refusal to marry, or, alternatively, become a nun. She ended by joining the tertiary order of the Dominicans, a group of lay men and women under pious and penitential vows. Catherine entered a life of strict self-denial, far beyond what was required of a tertiary, refusing to speak except in confession and sleeping for a half-hour every two days. This ended in late adolescence when she received a vision in which Christ married her. Catherine, whose spirituality was frequently expressed through the body, also claimed that God had removed her heart and replaced it with his own heart.

As Catherine's fame grew, she gathered around herself a group of disciples, beginning with older women of the Sienese elite. She continued to attract clergy and young men of the Sienese upper classes. She also became involved in Italian politics, promoting the cause of peace through the diversion of military force into a crusade and the return of the papacy from Avignon to Rome by Gregory XI.

Catherine's letters, dictated rather than written, were gathered, edited, and compiled by her disciples after her death in 1380.

HISTORICAL DOCUMENT

TO GREGORY XI
In the Name of Jesus Christ crucified and of sweet Mary:

Most holy and sweet father, your poor unworthy daughter Catherine in Christ sweet Jesus, commends herself to you in His precious Blood: with desire to see you a manly man, free from any fear or fleshly love toward yourself, or toward any creature related to you in the flesh; since I perceive in the sweet Presence of God that nothing so hinders your holy, good desire and so serves to hinder the honour of God and the exaltation and reform of Holy Church, as this. Therefore, my soul desires with immeasurable love that God by His infinite mercy may take from you all passion and lukewarmness of heart, and re-form you another man, by forming in you anew a burning and ardent desire; for in no other way could you fulfil the will of God and the desire of His servants. Alas, alas, sweetest "Babbo" mine, pardon my presumption in what I have said to you and am saying; I am constrained by the Sweet Primal Truth to say it. His will, father, is this, and thus demands of you. It demands that you execute justice on the abundance of many iniquities committed by those who are fed and pastured in the garden of Holy Church; declaring that brutes should not be fed with the food of men. Since He has given you authority and you have assumed it, you should use your virtue and power: and if you are not willing to use it, it would be better for you to resign what you have assumed; more honour to God and health to your soul would it be.

Another demand that His will makes is this: He wills that you make peace with all Tuscany, with which you are at strife; securing from all your wicked sons who have rebelled against you whatever is possible to secure without war—but punishing them as a father ought to punish a son who has wronged him. Moreover, the sweet goodness of God demands from you that you give full authority to those who ask you to make ready for the Holy Crusade—that thing which appears impossible to you, and possible to the sweet goodness of God, who has ordained it, and wills that so it be. Beware, as you hold your life dear, that you commit no negligence in this, nor treat as jests the works of the Holy Spirit, which are demanded from you because you can do them. If you want justice, you can execute it. You can have peace, withdrawing from the perverse pomps and delights of the world, preserving only the honour of God and the due of Holy Church. Authority also you have to give peace to those who ask you for it. Then, since you are not poor but rich—you who bear in your hand the keys of Heaven, to whom you open it is open, and to whom you shut it is shut—if you do not do this, you would be rebuked by God. I, if I were in your place, should fear lest divine judgment come upon me. Therefore I beg you most gently on behalf of Christ crucified to be obedient to the will of God, for I know that you want and desire no other thing than to do His will, that this sharp rebuke fall not upon you: "Cursed be thou, for the time and the strength entrusted to thee thou hast not used." I believe, father, by the goodness of God, and also taking hope from your holiness, that you will so act that this will not fall upon you.

I say no more. Pardon me, pardon me; for the great love which I bear to your salvation, and my great grief when I see the contrary, makes me speak so. Willingly would I have said it to your own person, fully to unburden my conscience. When it shall please your Holiness that I come to you, I will come willingly. So do that I may not appeal to Christ crucified from you; for to no other can I appeal, for there is no greater on earth. Remain in the holy and sweet grace of God. I ask you humbly for your benediction. Sweet Jesus, Jesus Love

GLOSSARY

iniquities: a gross injustice or wickedness, sin

Document Analysis

The letter strikes a balance among Catherine's disappointment in Gregory XI, her acknowledgement of the authority of his office, and her hopes that he will do better in the future. Catherine's concerns are twofold: both the welfare of the Church and the welfare of Gregory's own soul. Tonally, the letter is intimate, even addressing Gregory by the affectionate diminutive "Babbo." The opening reference to the blood of Christ is characteristic of Catherine, who frequently refers in her writings to the sacredness of the blood.

The specific suggestions that Catherine makes are that Gregory make a generous peace with the people of Tuscany who have supported the rebels against him and that he launch a new crusade, both causes that Catherine had been promoting for a long time. Catherine does not attempt to defend the cause of the Tuscans, but suggests that Gregory treat them as a loving father treats an erring son—she is appealing for mercy in order to avoid war. The complementary goals of making peace among Christians and waging war against the enemies of Christianity is common in crusade literature, and Catherine and many others saw the diversion of military power to a crusade as a cure for the wars that plagued Italy. Since a crusade could only be called by the pope, she argues, this is something within Gregory's control.

Throughout the letter, Catherine speaks not of what she wants Gregory to do, but what God wants. Her respect for the office of the pope is reflected in her reference to the "keys of Heaven" controlled by Gregory, as well as her statement that any appeal to an authority higher than Gregory can only be to Christ, since there is no higher authority on Earth. Catherine's stress on Gregory's power is related to what she sees as a principal problem of his pontificate: timidity. By reminding him of both the power and responsibility of his office, Catherine hopes to spur him to action. Even though the cause of the crusade may seem to Gregory "impossible," Catherine reminds him that it is very possible to God. Catherine's confidence is evident, as she bluntly states that if Gregory is not willing to put his power to use, he should resign as pope.

Essential Themes

The War of the Eight Saints ended in 1378, shortly after Gregory's death. The papacy permanently returned to Rome in 1378, when Pope Urban VI was elected as Gregory's successor, but its troubles had scarcely begun. Urban proved an unpopular pope, and a rival line of antipopes continued at Avignon. Catherine strongly supported Urban, whom she viewed as the only legitimate pope, but grief over the schism and the failure of Urban's papacy may have hastened her death in 1380.

For decades afterward, Europe was religiously divided between the popes in Rome and Avignon. Urban sought some of the same reforms that Catherine supported, but his harsh and dictatorial manner meant that his efforts were mostly in vain. Catherine's cries for reform would continue to echo down the decades, but the next major reform of the Catholic Church and the papacy would not occur until the sixteenth century. Catherine's crusading effort was also a failure. There would not be another major crusade from Europe until 1396, and that would lead to the disastrous defeat of the crusading army at the hands of the Turks in the Battle of Nicopolis.

Catherine was canonized in 1461. In 1970, she was named a doctor of the church by Pope Paul VI, a title given only to the greatest of Catholic theologians who have led saintly lives along with making great contributions to Catholic thought. She has also been named a patron saint of Italy and a patron saint of Europe. Her feast day is April 29, the anniversary of her death.

—*William E. Burns, PhD*

Bibliography and Additional Reading

Catherine of Siena. *The Letters of St. Catherine of Siena.* Trans. Susan Noffke. Tempe: Arizona Ctr. for Medieval and Early Renaissance Studies, 2012. Medieval & Renaissance Texts & Studies Ser. Print.

Curtayne, Alice. *Saint Catherine of Siena.* Devon: Augustine, 1981. Print.

Raymond of Capua. *The Life of St. Catherine of Siena: The Classic on Her Life and Accomplishments as Recorded by Her Spiritual Director.* Charlotte: Tan, 2011. Print.

Thibault, Paul R. *Pope Gregory XI: The Failure of Tradition.* Lanham: UP of America, 1986. Print.

ENGLAND AND FRANCE

In myriad ways, the histories of England and France were intertwined during the Middle Ages. While the commoners in each country spoke varieties of English and French, respectively, the high-ranking nobles and kings, in the years after 1066, spoke an Anglo-Norman dialect linked to northern France. In the later Middle Ages, French proper tended to be used over English. The landed gentry of England could claim various fiefs in France, and English possessions there were a source of both comfort and trouble over the centuries. Both countries' systems of government and legal institutions shared deep affinities. And, yet, there were profound differences and animosities, as well, which frequently came to the surface. This occurred most notably during the Hundred Years' War (1337-1453).

From the 12th century, the territorial designs of the Angevin, or Plantagenet dynasty in England (members of the House of Anjou) resulted in an expansion of territory in the British Isles. Parts of Ireland and Wales were conquered, but the kingdom of Scotland remained undefeated. The Angevins numbered among their rulers some of the most beloved and hated of the English kings, and the dynasty as a whole maintained a rivalry with the Capetian kings of France.

Under the Capetians, France became an efficiently organized, centrally governed political power. The dynasty ruled France from 987 to 1328, and during much of their rule France could boast an economic and social stability that was virtually unmatched elsewhere. Disagreements over English possessions within France, however, led to the Hundred Years' war between the two countries. Open hostility existed between the two nations from the mid-1330s, and during the ensuing war several regions changed hands fairly regularly, depending on the tides of military success and failure. Ultimately, French armies, partly as a result of the passions of Joan of Arc, proved victorious.

■ The Assize of Clarendon

Date: 1166
Country: England
Author: Henry II

Summary Overview

Henry II became king of England in the aftermath of a prolonged civil war between his mother, Matilda, and her cousin, Stephen. The Crusades left many estates in limbo without their lords and knights. Soldiers hired by warring factions wandered through England stealing and pillaging, and local feuds erupted between families caught up in land disputes. Legal authority had broken down, as property had been given first to supporters of one side, then another. Henry II worked hard to consolidate his authority, first tackling the semiautonomous church estates that recognized the authority of the pope over the king, and then establishing the assizes, or periodic courts whose authority was derived from the crown.

The Assize of Clarendon was an effort to return the country to the rule of law, and it established an early form of grand jury. The system used respected men who were to bring before the king's justices any person accused of robbery or murder, or anyone suspected of harboring them. The Assize of Clarendon removed judicial authority from local barons and church courts and established the jury system that would become a foundational element in English common law.

Defining Moment

When Henry II became king, England had survived a tumultuous period known as the Anarchy, a civil war in which Henry himself had played a part. The strife began when Henry I's only son died at sea in 1120. In 1127, Henry I named his only living legitimate child, Matilda, as his new heir. This was not a popular choice, as she had married Geoffrey of Anjou, who had quarreled with the king. She was also a woman, which put her at an immediate disadvantage in any dynastic contest.

Henry I's nephew, Stephen, son of his sister Adela, who had been raised in Henry's court, felt that he had the strongest claim to the throne. After Henry I died in 1135, despite having taken an earlier oath to Matilda, Stephen crossed the English Channel and seized the throne. Though Stephen was initially a popular king, he lost the support of many key English nobles and bishops. When Matilda invaded in 1139 with the help of her half-brother Robert of Gloucester, she defeated Stephen after a long campaign and captured him at Lincoln, England, in 1141.

Matilda proved as unpopular as Stephen, however, and she also failed to win over the nobility that could have ensured her success. Stephen's army continued to fight while he languished, and months later, Stephen was freed in a prisoner swap and returned to his place on the throne. Matilda consolidated her position in the southwest of England, and Stephen in the southeast, and the two rivals picked away at each other until the death of Robert of Gloucester in October 1147. Matilda left England the following spring, leaving her son Henry to fight for her crown.

The future Henry II made several military expeditions to England, but he also failed to gain the support of the nobility. Worn down by decades of instability, the aristocracy refused to fight for either side, but forced a compromise whereby Stephen would rule, but name Henry as his heir. Stephen died in 1154, and Henry became king of England.

Henry began working to shore up the position of the degraded monarchy. While Matilda and Stephen were fighting, the nobility and the church had gained significant power. To counter this, Henry established (or revived, in cases where feudal authority existed but had not been exercised) the most thorough administrative structure of any kingdom in Europe. Henry made good use of his councilors, chief among them Thomas Becket, with whom he later famously quarreled, and reasserted his authority over the nobility. He reformed the exchequer, the agency into which taxes flowed, and asserted the king's authority over the English church.

His reform of the legal system and establishment of procedure for criminal law, outlined in the Assize of Clarendon, reasserted the authority of the crown to uphold and enforce the law. Juries of respected men presented those accused of major crimes to the king's circuit justices, an early version of the grand jury. In addition, Henry II set up courts to determine inheritance and land rights, all under the authority of the king.

Author Biography and Document Information

Henry II was born in Le Mans, in present-day France, in 1133. He was the son of Matilda, daughter of Henry I, who engaged in a war with her cousin Stephen for the English throne. Henry was well educated, partly in England under the care of his uncle, Robert of Gloucester, and also in Anjou, where he studied with several well-known academics. As a young man, Henry led several small-scale attacks on his cousin Stephen, but it was not until after his marriage in 1151 to the powerful heiress Eleanor of Aquitaine that he turned his full attention to the English crown.

In 1153, after securing his continental lands, Henry returned to England. After fighting for a year, Stephen and Henry concluded a peace agreement that gave Henry the crown when Stephen died. Henry became king in 1154 and reigned for over thirty-four years. He is remembered for expanding the kingdom's territory, reforming the administrative system, and founding the Plantagenet dynasty. He died in 1189 in the midst of another familial conflict over the English crown—this one between his sons.

HISTORICAL DOCUMENT

1. In the first place the aforesaid king Henry, by thee counsel of all his barons, for the preservation of peace and the observing of justice, has decreed that an inquest shall be made throughout the separate counties, and throughout the separate hundreds, through twelve of the more lawful men of the hundred, and through four of the more lawful men of each township, upon oath that they will speak the truth: whether in their hundred or in their township there be any man who, since the lord king has been king, has been charged or published as being a robber or murderer or thief; or any one who is a harbourer of robbers or murderers or thieves. And the Justices shall make this inquest by themselves, and the sheriffs by themselves.

2. And he who shall be found through the oath of the aforesaid persons to have been charged or published as being a robber, or murderer, or thief, or a receiver of them, since the lord king has been king, shall be taken and shall go to the ordeal of water, and shall swear that he was not a robber or murderer or thief or receiver of them since the lord king has been king, to the extent of five shillings as far as he knows.

3. And if the lord of him who has been taken, or his steward or his vassals, shall, as his sureties, demand him back within three days after he has been taken, he him-self, and his chattels, shall be remanded under surety until he shall have done his law.

4. And when a robber or murderer or thief, or harbourers of them, shall be taken on the aforesaid oath, if the Justices shall not be about to come quickly enough into that county where they have been taken, the sheriffs shall send word to the nearest Justice through some intelligent man, that they have taken such men; and the Justices shall send back word to the sheriffs where they wish those men to be brought before them: and the sheriffs shall bring them before the Justices. And with them they shall bring, from the hundred or township where they were taken, two lawful men to bear record on the part of the county and hundred as to why they were taken; and there, before the Justice, they shall do their law.

5. And in the case of those who shall be taken on the aforesaid oath of this Assize, no one shall have court or justice or chattels save the king himself in his own court, before his own Justices; and the lord king shall have all their chattels. But in the case of those who shall be taken otherwise than through this oath, it shall be as it ordinarily is and ought to be.

6. And the sheriffs who take them shall lead them before the Justice without other summons than they have from him. And when the robbers or murderers or thieves, or receivers of them, who shall be taken through

the oath or otherwise, are given over to the sheriffs, they also shall receive them straightway without delay.

7. And, in the different counties where there are no jails, such shall be made in the burgh or in some castle of the king from the money of the king and from his woods if they be near, or from some other neighbouring woods, by view of the servants of the king; to this end, that the sheriffs may keep in them those who shall be taken by the servitors who are accustomed to do this, and through their servants.

8. The lord king wills also that all shall come to the county courts to take this oath; so that no one shall remain away, on account of any privilege that he has, or of a court or soc that he may have, from coming to take this oath

9. And let there be no one, within his castle or without his castle, nor even in the honour of Wallingford, who shall forbid the sheriffs to enter into his court or his land to take the view of frankpledge; and let all be under pledges: and let them be sent before the sheriffs under free pledge.

10. And, in the cities or Burroughs, let no one have men or receive them in his home or his land or his soc whom he will not take in hand to present before the Justice if they be required; or let them be in frankpledge.

11. And let there be none within a city or Burroughs or castle, or without it, nor also in the honour of Wallingford, who shall forbid the sheriffs to enter into their land or soc to take those who shall have been charged or published as being robbers or murderers or thieves, or harbourers of the same, or outlawed or accused with regard to the forest, but he (the king) commands that they shall aid them (the sheriffs) to take them (the robbers, etc.).

12. And if any one shall be taken who shall be possessed of robbed or stolen goods, if he be notorious and have evil testimony from the public, and have no warrant, he shall not have law. And if he be not notorious, on account of the goods in his possession, he shall go to the water.

13. And if any one shall confess before lawful men, or in the hundred court, concerning robbery, murder, or theft, or the harbouring of those committing them, and afterwards wish to deny it, he shall not have law.

14. The lord king wishes also that those who shall be tried and shall be absolved by the law, if they be of very bad testimony and are publicly and disgracefully defamed by the testimony of many and public men, shall forswear the lands of the king, so that within eight days they shall cross the sea unless the wind detains them; and, with the first wind which they shall have afterwards, they shall cross the sea; and they shall not return any more to England unless by the mercy of the lord king: and there, and if they return, they shall be outlawed; and if they return they shall be taken as outlaws.

15. And the lord king forbids that any waif, that is vagabond or unknown person, shall be entertained any where except in the burgh, and there he shall not be entertained more than a night, unless he become ill there, or his horse, so that he can show an evident essoin

16. And if he shall have been there more than one night, he shall be taken and held until his lord shall come to pledge him, or until he himself shall procure safe pledges; and he likewise shall be taken who shall have entertained him.

17. And if any sheriff shall send word to another sheriff that men have fled from his county into another county on account of robbery or murder or theft, or the harbouring of them, or for outlawry, or for a charge with regard to the forest of the king, he (the sheriff who is informed) shall capture them: and even if he learn it of himself or through others that such men have fled into his county, he shall take them and keep them in custody until he have safe pledges from them.

18. And all sheriffs shall cause a register to be kept of all fugitives who shall flee from their counties; and this they shalt do before the county assemblies; and they shall write down and carry their names to the Justices when first they shall come to them, so that they may be sought for throughout all England, and their chattels may be taken for the service of the king.

19. And the lord king wills that, from the time when the sheriffs shall receive the summonses of the itinerant Justices to appear before them with their counties, they shall assemble their counties and shall seek out all who have come anew into their counties since this assize; and they shall send them away under pledge that they will come before the Justices, or they shall keep them in custody until the Justices come to them, and then they shall bring them before the Justices.

20. The lord king forbids, moreover, that monks or canons or any religious house, receive any one of the petty people as monk or canon or brother, until they know of what testimony he is, unless he shall be sick unto death.

21. The lord lying forbids, moreover, that any one in all England receive in his land or his soc or the home under him any one of that sect of renegades who were excommunicated and branded at Oxford. And if any one receive them, he himself shall be at the mercy of the lord king; and the house in which they have been shall be carried without the town and burned. And each sheriff shall swear that he will observe this, and shall cause all his servitors to swear this, and the stewards of the barons, and all the knights and free tenants of the counties.

22. And the lord king wills that this assize shall be kept in his kingdom as long as it shall please him.

GLOSSARY

assize: a trial, either civil or criminal, held periodically in specific locations in England

burgh: a partially independent town

chattels: a slave; a movable article of personal property

essoin: a reason for not appearing in court

frankpledge: a system under which groups of freeman were responsible for each other's lawful behavior, or a member of such a group

hundred: a unit of local government based on one hundred freeholds

ordeal of water: medieval test of innocence, based on whether the accused floated or sank

Document Analysis

The Assize of Clarendon returns the enforcement of law, as well as the expenses and rewards of law, to the king, after a long period when the authority of barons or the clergy was more often used to settle criminal and civil cases. The Assize of Clarendon firmly states the supremacy of the king's court: "no one shall have court or justice or chattels save the king himself in his own court, before his own Justices; and the lord king shall have all their chattels." In other words, the king's justice prevails, and he can take the lands and goods of a guilty man. However, Henry II also makes clear the king's responsibility to his subjects. For example, he decrees that the king is responsible for the building and maintenance of prisons in those places that lack such facilities, and they shall be paid for and built "from the money of the king and from his woods if they be near."

Perhaps the most striking element of this document, and the one with the most lasting impact, is Henry's use of grand juries to bring charges against the accused. The Assize of Clarendon establishes a jury of twelve men in each hundred, and four in each town, which would investigate crimes in their district and report to the king's circuit judges any "robber or murderer or thief; or anyone who is a harbourer of robbers or murderers or thieves." Though the twelve "more lawful men" are not responsible for the sentence, they do have an impact on the accused. If the accused is found to be a person of ill repute, even if their trial by ordeal (specified as the ordeal of water) showed them to be innocent in that specific case, they are to be banished from the kingdom. If they return, they will be declared an outlaw.

The king's power to find and try criminals gives him far-reaching powers to search the homes and estates of all of his subjects, including churchmen and nobility. "And let there be none within a city or Burroughs or castle, or without it . . . who shall forbid the sheriffs to enter into their land." The church is also forbidden to allow anyone who may be a criminal to become a monk or canon. Sheltering heretics is also to be dealt with severely, and houses in which they were sheltered were to be burned. Taken together, these laws firmly establish the ultimate authority of the crown in the enforcement of criminal law.

Essential Themes

The Assize of Clarendon was intended to reestablish royal authority over the legal process in England on the heels of a time period when nobles and the church had asserted their authority. During previous years of civil war, the crown had failed to exercise its feudal authority, and in the chaos, robbery and violence went unchecked. When he assumed the crown in 1154, Henry II worked tirelessly to consolidate his realm (which included significant territory on the continent), reassert his authority, and establish administrative systems that supported it.

The Assize of Clarendon was one part of a pattern of reforms that Henry instituted to assert his power over nobles and the church, and though groundbreaking, it did not immediately change the entire justice system. However, along with later assizes, such as the Assize of Northhampton, it shifted power back to the king and his administration and marked the beginning of the transition to modern criminal-law procedure. In particular, its establishment of investigating juries would have long-term influence on English common law.

—*Bethany Groff, MA*

Bibliography and Additional Reading

Amt, Emilie. *The Accession of Henry II in England: Royal Government Restored, 1149–1159.* Woodbridge: Boydell, 1993. Print.

Bradbury, Jim. *Stephen and Matilda: The Civil War of 1139–53.* Charleston, SC: History Press, 2012. Print.

Turner, Ralph V. *Judges, Administrators, and the Common Law in Angevin England.* Rio Grande: Hambledon, 1994. Print.

Letter from Peter of Blois to Queen Eleanor of England

Date: 1173
Country: England
Author: Peter of Blois

Summary Overview

Eleanor of Aquitaine was the French-born queen of Henry II of England and one of the most influential European women of the Middle Ages. She and Henry were a dynamic and successful pair who produced eight children, many of whom would also become important figures in medieval Europe. However, they became increasingly estranged, and Eleanor eventually left England for Poitiers, in her own Duchy of Aquitaine, where she established a court known for its literature, music, and poetry. She received visiting monarchs and was able to achieve a degree of independence impossible in England.

By 1173, Henry had vastly extended his territory, invading Ireland and dealing with rebellions in Wales and in his territory on the continent. Eleanor joined with her three eldest sons in a revolt against their father. Though this letter from the French diplomat Peter of Blois implored her to return to her husband peacefully, she was arrested and imprisoned by Henry until his death in 1189.

Defining Moment

The marriage of Eleanor of Aquitaine and Henry of Anjou was one of the great dynastic matches in European history. Eleanor was a ruler in her own right and had inherited the Duchy of Aquitaine only to be spirited away to marry the heir to the French throne, Louis VII. She would be the queen consort of France for fifteen years, but did not find Louis a suitable match, and after she accompanied the king on a crusade in 1147, their relationship began to unravel. Eleanor asked publicly for an annulment, which was finally granted in 1152. Less than two months later, Eleanor married Henry, Count of Anjou and Duke of Normandy, who was eleven years her junior. Two years later, Henry became the king of England as well.

Eleanor and Henry had eight children. The eldest of Eleanor's surviving sons was known as Young Henry, the heir to the throne. He was ambitious, and even though his father had greatly enlarged their territory and had even gone so far as to crown Henry as the associate king, he had no real authority or land and grew bored and resentful. When the elder king made plans to give three castles in Young Henry's territory of Anjou to his younger brother, John, the young king left his father and went to the French court of his father-in-law (and his mother's first husband) in Paris, where enemies of the English king were plentiful. He may have travelled to Aquitaine, where his brothers Richard and Geoffrey were staying with their mother, or his brothers may have been summoned from England by their mother. In any case, it is clear that Eleanor supported the revolt of 1173, and with her help, Young Henry assembled a significant force.

The elder Henry had made enemies across Europe for his part in the slaying of the archbishop of Canterbury, Thomas Becket. Though the elder Henry was not directly implicated in the murder, he had fought with Becket over the limits of church authority, and it was rumored that he had ordered the killing. In addition, Young Henry was willing to promise land and titles from his own inheritance to nobles who would fight for him.

The rebellion did not succeed, however. Eleanor was captured by Henry II and taken back to England, where she lived as a prisoner for the next sixteen years. Young Henry and his brothers were defeated by their father and reconciled with him after eighteen months of fighting.

Author Biography

Peter of Blois was born in 1130 in Blois, in modern-day France. He was well-educated in history and the classics as a young man, studying with notable teachers in Tours and Paris, and later travelling to Bologna to study law. In 1167 he traveled to Sicily to tutor the young Sicilian king, William II. He returned to France once again, but immigrated to England by 1173 to assist the archbishop of Canterbury.

In England, Peter also became a diplomat for King Henry II, and helped to negotiate between the king, the pope, and other European heads of state, particularly Louis VII of France. Peter was a secretary to the king and an emissary to the pope during the 1173 revolt.

Though he urged Eleanor of Aquitaine to make peace with her husband, he later served her after the king's death. Peter held several important church positions in England, including archdeacon of Bath and London and dean of the college at Wolverhampton. He was a prodigious letter writer, and much of his correspondence survives. Peter died in 1203.

HISTORICAL DOCUMENT

To Aleanor, Queen of England.
From the Archbishop of Rouen & his Suffragens:

Greetings in the search for peace—

Marriage is a firm and indissoluble union. This is public knowledge and no Christian can take the liberty to ignore it. From the beginning biblical truth has verified that marriage once entered into cannot be separated. Truth cannot deceive: it says, "What God has joined let us not put asunder." Truly, whoever separates a married couple becomes a transgressor of the divine commandment.

So the woman is at fault who leaves her husband and fails to keep the trust of this social bond. When a married couple becomes one flesh, it is necessary that the union of bodies be accompanied by a unity and equality of spirit through mutual consent. A woman who is not under the headship of the husband violates the condition of nature, the mandate of the Apostle, and the law of Scripture: "The head of the woman is the man." She is created from him, she is united to him, and she is subject to his power.

We deplore publicly and regretfully that, while you are a most prudent woman, you have left your husband. The body tears at itself. The body did not sever itself from the head, but what is worse, you have opened the way for the lord king's, and your own, children to rise up against the father. Deservedly the prophet says, "The sons I have nurtured and raised, they now have spurned me." As another prophet calls to mind, "If only the final hour of our life would come and the earth's surface crack open so that we might not see this evil"!

We know that unless you return to your husband, you will be the cause of widespread disaster. While you alone are now the delinquent one, your actions will result in ruin for everyone in the kingdom. Therefore, illustrious queen, return to your husband and our king. In your reconciliation, peace will be restored from distress, and in your return, joy may return to all. If our pleadings do not move you to this, at least let the affliction of the people, the imminent pressure of the church and the desolation of the kingdom stir you. For either truth deceives, or "every kingdom divided against itself will be destroyed." Truly, this desolation cannot be stopped by the lord king but by his sons and their allies.

Against all women and out of childish counsel, you provoke disaster for the lord king, to whom powerful kings bow the neck. And so, before this matter reaches a bad end, you should return with your sons to your husband, whom you have promised to obey and live with. Turn back so that neither you nor your sons become suspect. We are certain that he will show you every possible kindness and the surest guarantee of safety.

I beg you, advise your sons to be obedient and respectful to their father. He has suffered many anxieties, offences and grievances. Yet, so that imprudence might not demolish and scatter good will (which is acquired at such toil!), we say these things to you, most pious queen, in the zeal of God and the disposition of sincere love.

Truly, you are our parishioner as much as your husband. We cannot fall short in justice: Either you will return to your husband, or we must call upon canon law and use ecclesiastical censures against you. We say this reluctantly, but unless you come back to your senses, with sorrow and tears, we will do so.

GLOSSARY

apostle: one of the twelve disciples of Jesus Christ; here the reference is to Paul

canon law: laws made by church leadership

ecclesiastical: relating to the clergy of the Christian church

Suffragens: suffragan bishops, assistants to senior bishops

Document Analysis

Peter of Blois's letter to Eleanor is intended to entice the queen back to her husband and encourage her to end the rebellion of her sons. Peter uses the language of traditional Christian marriage vows to remind Eleanor that she had agreed to obey her husband, and if she refused to do this, she was violating not only a promise she made to him, but the trust of the people she governed and ultimately the will of God.

Peter reminds Eleanor that marriage is indissoluble, and once entered into, it was not possible to separate from it. Eleanor is reminded that in the taking of wedding vows she and her husband had come together in "unity and equality of spirit," but with her husband as the head. The ideal of equality of spirit does not make husband and wife social equals in the eyes of the church, for "she is created from him, she is united to him, and she is subject to his power." Peter compares marriage to a body and argues that Eleanor's actions are tearing the body apart unnaturally. In addition, he claims that her separation from the king has inspired her sons' own rebellion against their father. He suggests that if she returns to the king, her sons will follow.

If the argument that marriage was indissoluble was not convincing enough to Eleanor and the argument that Henry was her and their sons' natural leader also failed to inspire obedience, Peter asks her to consider the impact on her people. He assures the rebel queen that "your actions will result in ruin for everyone in the kingdom." Surely even if she could not be made to obey her husband, the good of her kingdom and the will of God would be compelling enough to return her to Henry, Peter reasons. He carefully places the responsibility for the conflict on her; if she refuses to reconcile, there is nothing the king can do: "Truly, this desolation cannot be stopped by the lord king but by his sons and their allies."

The letter ends with a plea and a threat. The king has suffered enough from the loss of his wife and their sons, Peter argues. Eleanor needs to return herself and their sons to his affection, and they will be forgiven and their safety guaranteed. If she still refuses, however, "we must call upon canon law and use ecclesiastical censures against you." Peter underscores the fact that his side does not want to fight and hopes to still view Eleanor as a friend, but will be forced to take action in pursuit of justice if she does not repent.

Essential Themes

The main theme of this letter is the argument that Eleanor is obligated by her marriage vows, the teachings of the church, the will of God, and the good of her people to return to her husband. Peter provides insight into the church's views on women's place in society during the time period, as well as into diplomatic procedure. It is clear that Eleanor was powerful and respected, despite her actions that opposed the traditional power structure. Though she was threatened with physical harm and church censure, the arguments made in this letter were insufficient to sway her. If marriage was indissoluble, why had she been allowed an annulment from her first husband? If her husband was her head and she was subject to his authority, why had she been able to rule on her own terms so successfully?

Eleanor may have genuinely believed that her sons would be better rulers than her husband, and the country better off in their hands. It is also possible that she wanted revenge for Henry II's infidelities. Whatever the case, Peter of Blois failed in his mission to reunite the feuding monarchs. Eleanor went to join her sons in Paris, but was arrested on orders from Henry II and subsequently imprisoned. Even after the rebellion failed and the family was reconciled, she remained captive and was only freed after her husband's death. After her son

Richard was crowned king of England, Eleanor again became a highly influential political figure until her death in 1204.

—Bethany Groff, MA

Bibliography and Additional Reading

Cotts, John D. *The Clerical Dilemma: Peter of Blois and Literate Culture in the Twelfth Century.* Washington: Catholic U of America P, 2009. Print.

Kramer, Ann. *Eleanor of Aquitaine: The Queen Who Rode Off to Battle.* Washington: National Geographic, 2006. Print.

Seward, Desmond. *Eleanor of Aquitaine: The Mother Queen of the Middle Ages.* New York: Pegasus, 2014. Print.

Weir, Alison. *Eleanor of Aquitaine: By the Wrath of God, Queen of England.* London: Vintage, 2008. Print.

■ Excerpt from *Dialogue Concerning the Exchequer*

Date: ca. 1180
Country: England
Author: Richard FitzNeal (also known as Richard Fitz Nigel)

Summary Overview

Richard FitzNeal's *Dialogue Concerning the Exchequer* (*Dialogus de Scaccario*) served a number of important purposes in medieval England. First, it was a treatise on the running of the royal household. Even further, it was one of the first efforts to explain how the economic system of England functioned. Commentators through the centuries since it was written have noted the success of FitzNeal's efforts to explain his work as the royal treasurer. For anyone who could read and wanted to know, FitzNeal's *Dialogue* presented a full, clear description of the financial workings of the royal household and the English government. Focusing on the practical rather than theoretical aspects of the inner workings of government and finance, the work has long been the essential primary source for knowledge of how revenue was collected as well as about the people and procedures that allowed the government to function in the Middle Ages.

Defining Moment

During the late eleventh and early twelfth centuries, England began an effort to concentrate economic power in the hands of the royal household by systematizing the collection of taxes and the workings of government. By 1086, under orders from William I (William the Conqueror), a survey was taken regarding how much land and livestock each landholder in England possessed and how much it was worth. These values were recorded in what was known as the Domesday (or Doomsday) Book, and formed the basis for how much each landholder—a category that included both nobles and religious leaders and orders—owed in taxes.

The organization of the treasury department, known as the Exchequer, as the main means of funding the secular government in England began with Richard FitzNeal's granduncle, Roger of Salisbury. Roger had been a simple parish priest in English-controlled Normandy when a chance encounter with the future Henry

I led to his entering into the service of the new king. Although he remained a priest, becoming bishop of Salisbury, his financial and organizational skills revolutionized the royal government. He earned the complete trust of Henry I, accumulating so much power and authority that when Henry was leading his armies in Normandy, Roger ruled England in the king's absence. As taxes were being collected, it became apparent to Roger that the entire administrative system of the royal government needed to be revised.

Under Roger's direction, the administration of the king's household and the English government as a whole was redesigned. As a result of his power and influence with the king, Roger gained power and wealth for his own family, including his son Roger la Poer, his nephew Nigel of Ely, and his grandnephew, Richard FitzNeal. After Henry's death, Stephen of Blois came to the English throne, and Roger continued in office. After Henry II came to the throne in 1154, the family still had sufficient wealth and influence to allow Nigel to purchase an appointment for FitzNeal to the position of king's treasurer. Like his great uncle, FitzNeal held powerful positions in both the government and the church and proved to be a skilled administrator, earning the respect of Henry II.

Author Biography

Richard FitzNeal was born around 1130, the son of Nigel, bishop of Ely. Around 1158, Nigel paid King Henry II to appoint FitzNeal as his successor to the post of treasurer. As a result of his family's power and wealth, FitzNeal not only served as treasurer, but also as dean of Lincoln and, later, bishop of London, both powerful administrative positions within the Church of England. FitzNeal was loyal to Henry II and innovative in terms of accounting, serving for almost forty years. At the king's suggestion, he described his work in the *Dialogue Concerning the Exchequer* beginning around 1177. FitzNeal was replaced as treasurer in 1196 (though he continued as bishop of London) and died two years later.

HISTORICAL DOCUMENT

I. What the Exchequer is, and what is the reason of this name.

Disciple. What is the exchequer?

Master. The exchequer is a quadrangular surface about ten feet in length, five in breadth, placed before those who sit around it in the manner of a table, and all around it it has an edge about the height of one's four fingers, lest any thing placed upon it should fall off. There is placed over the top of the exchequer, moreover, a cloth bought at the Easter term, not an ordinary one but a black one marked with stripes, the stripes being distant from each other the space of a foot or the breadth of a hand. In the spaces moreover are counters placed according to their values; about these we shall speak below. Although, moreover, such a surface is called exchequer, nevertheless this name is so changed about that the court itself which sits when the exchequer does is called exchequer; so that if at any time through a decree any thing is established by common counsel, it is said to have been done at the exchequer of this or that year. As, moreover, one says today "at the exchequer," so one formerly said "at the tallies."

D. What is the reason of this name?

M. No truer one occurs to me at present than that it has a shape similar to that of a chess board.

D. Would the prudence of the ancients ever have called it so for its shape alone, when it might for a similar reason be called a table (tabularium)?

M. I was right in calling thee painstaking. There is another, but a more hidden reason. For just as, in a game of chess, there are certain grades of combatants and they proceed or stand still by certain laws or limitations, some presiding and others advancing: so, in this, some preside, some assist by reason of their office, and no one is free to exceed the fixed laws; as will be manifest from what is to follow. Moreover, as in chess the battle is fought between kings, so in this it is chiefly between two that the conflict takes place and the war is waged, the treasurer, namely, and the sheriff who sits there to render account; the others sitting by as judges, to see and to judge.

D. Will the accounts be received then by the treasurer, although there are many there who, by reason of their power, are greater.

M. That the treasurer ought to receive the account from the sheriff is manifest from this, that the same is required from him whenever it pleases the king: nor could that be required of him which he had not received. Some say nevertheless, that the treasurer and the chamberlains should be bounden alone for what is written in the rolls in the treasury, and that for this an account should be demanded of them. But it is believed with more truth that they should be responsible for the whole writing of the roll, as will be readily understood from what is to follow.

XVI. What is the Doomsday Book, and for what Purpose composed.

When that distinguished conqueror of England, a relative by blood of this same prelate, had subdued the utmost limits of the island to his rule, and had tamed the minds of the rebels by examples of terrible things, he decreed, lest a free opportunity of erring should again be given, that the people subject to him should submit to written custom and laws. The English laws, therefore being laid before him according to their triple distinction that is, Mercian law, Dane law, and West Saxon law, some he rejected; others, moreover, approving he added to them the transmarine laws of Neustria which seemed most efficacious for protecting the peace of the kingdom At length, lest anything should seem to be wanting to the sum of all his forethought, having taken counsel, he despatched from his side the most discreet men in circuit throughout the kingdom. By these men, in this way, a diligent description of the whole land was made with regard to its woods as well as its pastures and meadows, also its agriculture; and this description having been noted down in common words, it was collected into a book; in order, namely, that each one, content with his own right, should not with impunity usurp that of another. Moreover the survey is made by counties, by hundreds and by hides, the name of the king being marked at the very head, and then, in turn, the names of the other lords being placed according to the dignity of their standing; that is to say, those who are tenants in chief of the king. Moreover against the separate names thus arranged in order are placed numbers by means of which, below, in the course of the book itself, whatever concerns these persons is more easily found. This book is called by the natives Domesday; that is, by metaphor, the day of judgment, for just as a sentence of that strict and terrible last trial cannot possibly be eluded by any art of tergiversation: so when, in the kingdom, contention shall arise concerning those things that are there noted, when the book is appealed to its sentence can not be scorned or avoided with impunity. On this account we have named this book the hoof of dooms; not that, in it, a sentence is given concerning any doubtful matters that come up, but that from it, as from a judgment that has been given, it is not allowed in any way to depart.

GLOSSARY

prelate: an ecclesiastic of a high order; a church dignitary

tergiversation: an abandonment or reversal of faith; an avoidance of clear statement of belief

Document Analysis

The Dialogue Concerning the Exchequer takes the form of a dialogue between a disciple who asks a series of questions regarding the workings of the English government and a master who provides detailed answers. Some have called FitzNeal's work the first treatise on government of the Middle Ages, while others have viewed it as the most comprehensive work on accounting during the era. It is a unique explanation of the inner workings of royal finances, which had become a particular area of importance to fund the many wars of the era.

In these two excerpts, FitzNeal retells two stories told to him by those who came before him. First, he explains the origins of the Exchequer—the system of managing royal finances—which had originally been devised by his granduncle, Roger of Salisbury. Later, FitzNeal tells of the origins of the Domesday Book, which he claims had been told to him by "Henry, formerly bishop of Winchester" (Henry of Blois, William the Conqueror's grandson).

The first section, regarding the origins of the Exchequer, tells of the genesis of the term itself. He describes the special counting table, called an exchequer due to its cloth top resembling a chessboard, used by the treasurer and which lent its name to the department. The table is used to track the taxes owed in the realm, the amount that had been paid in, and the resulting balance. FitzNeal then tells of the system of collecting taxes, in which the treasurer engages in a "battle," which he likens to a game of chess, against each local sheriff presenting the account for the land value and income of their shire. The audit results in the yearly production of documents (later known as Pipe Rolls), which would then be sent back to the Exchequer.

The information contained in the Pipe Rolls was a more specific version of the earlier Domesday Book, which was the first census of land and income from the land, created at the request of William the Conqueror. FitzNeal explains that the name "Domesday" (otherwise rendered as "Doomsday") invokes the biblical Day of Judgment, implying that the financial determinations of the royal household are to be just as weighty and as much respected as the final word of God.

Essential Themes

The Dialogue Concerning the Exchequer described the prevailing method of accounting during the Middle Ages directly from the viewpoint of the treasurer and was written for a general audience. As a source on accounting and the mechanisms of government, historians, accountants, and political theorists have studied

FitzNeal's work for centuries. Additionally, the ritualistic nature of the early Exchequer gives a window into the historic development of bureaucracy. The process that FitzNeal describes was rather informal in its initial form and, yet, became highly institutionalized, with officials under FitzNeal serving the exchequer as their occupation.

In the near term, the *Dialogue Concerning the Exchequer* was important for a number of reasons. It served as a handbook for those who would follow FitzNeal, demonstrating an effective way to administer government taxes and finances. As such, it was the most advanced financial system in use in all of Western Europe. The exchequer system served its purpose for centuries. From a longer historical perspective, the charge and discharge system of accounting, which charged the local sheriffs with collecting all taxes and then allowed them to discharge themselves of the collected taxes at the exchequer, was important because it served as a model for the collection of taxes for other nations in Western Europe. It evolved into the model that would be used in England until the nineteenth century.

Though it was FitzNeal's work that would form the basis for the evolving nature of the Exchequer, FitzNeal is clear that his granduncle, Roger of Salisbury, deserves the credit for the innovation of the system, and that the Domesday Book would not have come to be had it not been for William the Conqueror. Both of these systems relied on the system of heritability, which saw the lands passed down within families, preserving the wealth for the noble class in England. Serving both as a window to the evolution of finances in the Middle Ages and a model that would continue to shape royal finances for hundreds of years, FitzNeal's *Dialogue* both recorded the history of the prior century and influenced much of the history of the centuries to come.

—*Steven L. Danver, PhD*

Bibliography and Additional Reading

Fleming, Robin. *Domesday Book and the Law: Society and Legal Custom in Early Medieval England.* New York: Cambridge UP, 2003. Print

Harris, Sara. "Ancestral Neologisms in Richard Fitz Nigel's Dialogue of the Exchequer." *Journal of Medieval History* 39.4 (2013): 416–30. Print.

Hollister, C. Warren & John W. Baldwin. "The Rise of Administrative Kingship: Henry I and Philip Augustus." *American Historical Review* 83.4 (1978): 867–905. Print.

Hudson, John. "Administration, Family and Perceptions of the Past in Late Twelfth-Century England: Richard FitzNigel and the Dialogue of the Exchequer." *The Perception of the Past in Twelfth-Century Europe.* Ed. Paul Magdalino. London: Hambledon, 1992. 75–98. Print.

Jones, Michael John. "The Dialogus de Scaccario (c. 1179): The First Western Book on Accounting?" *Abacus* 44.4 (2008): 443–74. Print.

Poole, Reginald L. *The Exchequer in the Twelfth Century: The Ford Lectures Delivered in the University of Oxford in Michaelmas Term, 1911.* Clark: Lawbook Exchange, 2006. Print.

■ On the Rules of Love and Chivalry

Date: ca. 1180
Country: France
Author: Andreas Capellanus
Translator: John Jay Parry

Summary Overview

Courtly love was a literary, social, and cultural movement of the High Middle Ages. It centered on the ideal lady—the object of slavish devotion—and had its origins in the poems and songs of troubadours. Troubadours were male lyric poets and poet-musicians who gained prominence in European courts beginning in the eleventh century and who most often sang about love and lovers. Troubadours' songs often praised the ladies of medieval courts and invented imaginative romantic scenarios between knights and ladies, with the woman always the center of the attention of the impassioned suitor. Devotion to courtly love gained prominence at the same time as veneration of the Virgin Mary, a relatively minor religious figure until the twelfth century; the worship of a beautiful, unattainable, virtuous lady was at the heart of both of these movements. The ideals of courtly love became most refined at the court of Eleanor of Aquitaine, Queen of England, who, after she separated from her husband Henry II, set up a royal household court in Poitiers, France, that became the center of courtly love, with its elaborate rules and manners. Andreas Capellanus, a courtier of Eleanor's daughter Marie, codified some of these rules and rituals in his book of advice for lovers.

Defining Moment

Courtly love first gained prominence in the complex milieu of court life in France, beginning around the time of the First Crusade at the end of the eleventh century. Powerful female rulers such as Eleanor of Aquitaine held court while their husbands went on a crusade or to fight for territory, and courtly love provided men and women in the court with diversion, pleasure, and rules for behavior. It also signaled a dramatic cultural shift in the attitude toward women in Europe in the twelfth century.

The literary roots of courtly love can be found in the songs and poems of the troubadours. Troubadours were travelling performers, initially from Spain, who became increasingly popular in the courts of France. Their subject matter was secular, and regional variations of their art flourished, though the poets sometimes drew on religious themes in praise of a woman's virtue. The poems of the troubadours spoke the language of feudalism, swearing allegiance to their ruling lady, and even referring to her as "my lord."

Courtly love was the highly structured expression of knightly devotion to an idealized woman. The devotion of a lover to his lady, usually a woman of higher status, mirrored the devotion of a vassal to his lord, promising slavish obedience and the gratification of her every desire. Elite women were praised not only for their physical beauty, but for their nobility, gentleness, and generosity. The act of loving a woman in this idealized way was seen as a form of personal growth for the lover, since his depth of feeling was refined as a result. Sexual gratification was not the point of courtly love, though it was in the mix. Women were expected to remain above the impassioned pleas of the lover, to be served and flattered, and to dole out such attention as was necessary to keep the passion alive. The important thing was the ennobling experience of being in love.

It is easy to see why courtly love appealed to the female-centered courts of crusading Europe. Women were firmly in control of this process, which emphasized gentle wooing and depth of feeling over sexual predation. Courtly love provided an outlet for romantic and sexual feeling in an environment in which women were worshipped and protected, rather than exploited.

Author Biography and Document Information

Andreas Capellanus, also known as Andrew the Chaplain, is believed to have been a court chaplain in the court of Marie, Countess of Champagne, daughter of Eleanor of Aquitaine. Little is known of his life, and this treatise on the nature of love is all that survives of his work. Scholars believe that this may have been written between 1184 and 1186, as there is a reference to the wealth of Hungarians, and at that time, Marie's sister was being courted by the Hungarian royal family. This book was initially written in Latin, and drew significantly on the Roman poet Ovid. The book was titled *De arte honeste amandi,* literally, *The Art of Honest Loving.* It was not until the nineteenth century that the book became known as *The Art of Courtly Love;* Victorian interest in medieval writing peaked at this time, and scholars came to see Capellanus's work as the foundational document for the cultural phenomenon of courtly love.

HISTORICAL DOCUMENT

Book Two: On the Rules of Love

1. Marriage is no real excuse for not loving.
2. He who is not jealous cannot love.
3. No one can be bound by a double love.
4. It is well known that love is always increasing or decreasing.
5. That which a lover takes against his will of his beloved has no relish.
6. Boys do not love until they arrive at the age of maturity.
7. When one lover dies, a widowhood of two years is required of the survivor.
8. No one should be deprived of love without the very best of reasons.
9. No one can love unless he is impelled by the persuasion of love.
10. Love is always a stranger in the home of avarice.
11. It is not proper to love any woman whom one should be ashamed to seek to marry.
12. A true lover does not desire to embrace in love anyone except his beloved.
13. When made public love rarely endures.
14. The easy attainment of love makes it of little value; difficulty of attainment makes it prized.
15. Every lover regularly turns pale in the presence of his beloved.
16. When a lover suddenly catches sight of his beloved his heart palpitates.
17. A new love puts to flight an old one.
18. Good character alone makes any man worthy of love.
19. If love diminishes, it quickly fails and rarely revives.
20. A man in love is always apprehensive.
21. Real jealousy always increases the feeling of love.
22. Jealousy, and therefore love, are increased when one suspects his beloved.
23. He whom the thought of love vexes, eats and sleeps very little.
24. Every act of a lover ends with in the thought of his beloved.
25. A true lover considers nothing good except what he thinks will please his beloved.
26. Love can deny nothing to love.
27. A lover can never have enough of the solaces of his beloved.
28. A slight presumption causes a lover to suspect his beloved.
29. A man who is vexed by too much passion usually does not love.
30. A true lover is constantly and without intermission possessed by the thought of his beloved.
31. Nothing forbids one woman being loved by two men or one man by two women.

GLOSSARY

avarice: obsession with attaining wealth

vexes: worries or distresses

Document Analysis

Capellanus's rules of love appear in a three-part book of advice to a young man named Walter who is upset by a romantic encounter. The rules list universal truths about love, and how to pursue the beloved. This selection begins with a rule that highlights the very functional purpose of marriage at this time, and the fact that marriage based on love was almost an alien concept: "Marriage is no real excuse for not loving." Marriage was important and so was love, but the two were not necessarily connected. Being married was, perhaps, not enough reason to avoid falling in love with someone else. After all, "no one should be deprived of love without the very best of reasons," and the purpose of marriage is not love, but procreation.

Capellanus's rules illuminate the clandestine and possessive nature of courtly love. Jealousy and love went hand in hand and increased or decreased together. A person could not love if they were not jealous, and the slightest perceived threat could cause apprehension. Since jealousy increased feelings of love, suspicion was a sign of devotion. Secrecy fueled the flame of courtly love, in part because these affairs were carried on between men and women who were often married to other people. Once exposed, "love rarely endures."

Another theme of courtly love was slavish, obsessive devotion to the object of love, and the purifying qualities of love. Lovers are to "turn pale" and their hearts palpitate at the sight of the beloved. They were unable to eat or sleep. Everything they did was for their lover, to the extent that "a true lover considers nothing good except what he thinks will please his beloved." It is necessary that the lover be of "good character," since love is a "stranger in the home of avarice."

Though devotion and obedience were crucial to courtly love, Capellanus also acknowledges that love is fickle, and once lost, is difficult to recover. It is always in flux, and a "new love puts to flight an old one." When love fades, it generally dies completely.

Most of Capellanus's rules are really characteristics of the kind of love that he endorsed; however, there are several rules on the list that restrict the behavior of lovers. Boys need to have reached maturity in order to truly love; if a man forces himself on a woman, that would not produce love; and lovers should not pursue a relationship with those whom they would be ashamed to marry. Lovers who die should be mourned like a spouse for two years before another relationship is pursued. Capellanus also promotes love between adults of different social ranks; generally a lower-ranking courtier or knight would pursue a married lady of higher rank. He discouraged rape and allowed adultery. These rules continued to define Western notions of love for centuries.

Essential Themes

This selection listed the primary characteristics of love among noble classes, which would later be called courtly love. It defined this love as clandestine and often adulterous, with jealousy and suspicion as signs that love was real. This love was all-consuming, with every word and action designed to please and woo the beloved. These rules also acknowledged the capriciousness of love, which could be lost to a new lover, and once lost, was almost never won back. Capellanus also defined love as being consensual. In a time when sexual violence was common, and rape and abduction were often featured in courtship, love could not be pursued with force. Though at least one of the partners in love, generally the woman, was married, this was not a good enough reason to avoid the pursuit, and indeed, the struggle to win over a reluctant partner inflamed the passions and heightened the experience of love.

—*Bethany Groff, MA*

Bibliography and Additional Reading:

Porter, Pamela. *Courtly Love in Medieval Manuscripts.* Toronto: U of Toronto P, 2003. Print.

Seward, Desmond. *Eleanor of Aquitaine: The Mother Queen of the Middle Ages.* New York: Pegasus, 1978. Print.

Wollock, Jennifer G. *Rethinking Chivalry and Courtly Love.* Santa Barbara: Praeger, 2011. Print.

■ Magna Carta

Date: 1215
Country: England
Author: King John; Archbishop Stephen Langton; et al.

Summary Overview

The Magna Carta ("Great Charter") was issued in June 1215 by King John of England to try to end a conflict with the church and a group of English barons that threatened to end John's reign. Though the Magna Carta dealt mostly with specific grievances of the barons, the document is significant because it includes the first articulation in medieval Europe of the principal of the rule of law. According to the document, everyone, including the king, was bound by law and had the right to justice under the law. As a peace treaty, the Magna Carta was a failure. After the agreement was first repudiated by King John and then renounced by the pope, war resumed in September 1215. The lasting legacy of the Magna Carta is its framework for a new relationship between monarchs and their subjects. The Magna Carta was altered and reissued several times in the thirteenth century and became part of English law in 1297. It is a foundational document of English law, and its declaration of the rights of the governed (originally only "freemen"—a small portion of the population) against arbitrary authority has influenced constitutional documents for centuries.

Defining Moment

When John became king of England in 1199, he inherited a nation with a significant administrative structure, based on his father Henry II's energetic revision of traditional laws and consolidation of his territory in Ireland, England, and France. John's reign was marked by heavy taxation, arbitrary seizure of land and property by the king, and the use of force to achieve the king's wishes. It was clear that John believed himself to be above the law. In 1202, war broke out with France, and despite early successes, by 1204, King John had lost most of his territory in northern France, including land inherited from his mother, Eleanor of Aquitaine. For the following decade, John mounted a series of expensive and ultimately futile expeditions to recover these

lands, draining the treasuries of England and then raising additional funds through taxes and scutage, a payment made to the king in lieu of military service. By 1214, King John was fighting in France with a mercenary army paid for by the English nobility. When this army was defeated at the Battle of Bouvines, the barons, already in rebellion against the king, began to plan for John's removal. King John's reign was also marked by conflict with the English church. He had rejected Stephen Langton as the archbishop of Canterbury and was excommunicated by Pope Innocent III in 1209, until, desperate for support against his rebel barons, he swore fealty to the pope and accepted Langton as archbishop.

In October 1214, King John returned from France to a kingdom in full-scale rebellion, its treasury drained, and its archbishop aligned with his enemies. In January 1215, he called a council to make peace with the rebel barons; he also may have been trying to buy time while waiting for letters of support from the pope. The barons insisted that the king should adhere to the charter made by Henry I in 1100, which had promised that England would not be "unjustly oppressed." King John refused to meet their demands. The rebel barons renounced their fealty to the king and marched on London, capturing it in May, along with the key cities of Lincoln and Exeter.

With the capital in rebel hands, King John had no choice but to meet with the barons. His letters of support from the pope had arrived a month earlier, but the barons paid little attention. In June 1215, Archbishop Langdon, who was sympathetic to the rebels, led negotiations at Runnymede, near Windsor on the Thames River. King John agreed to the demands of the barons on June 15, 1215, and on June 19, the barons renewed their fealty to the king. The charter later known as the Magna Carta was copied for distribution throughout the kingdom. Four copies of the 1215 Magna Carta survive, all of which are housed in England.

Author Biography and Document Information

King John was born in 1166, the youngest of five sons of Henry II and Eleanor of Aquitaine. He was not expected to rule, but when three of John's older brothers died as young men, and a fourth brother, Richard, became king in 1189, John became next in line for the throne. Despite John's leading an attempted coup while Richard was away on crusade, John became king in 1199. His nephew, Arthur, had been supported by Phillip II of France as a contender for the throne, and John's territory in France was contested throughout his reign. John further damaged his relationship with France when he annulled his first marriage in order to marry an heiress already betrothed to a French nobleman. King John's behavior cost him significant territory in France, and his efforts to reclaim those lands dragged on for years. His forays in France were paid for by harsh taxes and the enforcement of questionable feudal rights in England. His barons rebelled, forcing him to accept the charter later known as the Magna Carta. King John later repudiated the charter, and Pope Innocent III declared it void. War with the barons was renewed, but John died of dysentery in October 1216. He was succeeded by his son, Henry III, who renewed the Magna Carta several times. King John is buried in Worcester Cathedral.

HISTORICAL DOCUMENT

Preamble: John, by the grace of God, king of England, lord of Ireland, duke of Normandy and Aquitaine, and count of Anjou, to the archbishop, bishops, abbots, earls, barons, justiciaries, foresters, sheriffs, stewards, servants, and to all his bailiffs and liege subjects, greetings. Know that, having regard to God and for the salvation of our soul, and those of all our ancestors and heirs, and unto the honor of God and the advancement of his holy Church and for the rectifying of our realm, we have granted as underwritten by advice of our venerable fathers, Stephen, archbishop of Canterbury, primate of all England and cardinal of the holy Roman Church, Henry, archbishop of Dublin, William of London, Peter of Winchester, Jocelyn of Bath and Glastonbury, Hugh of Lincoln, Walter of Worcester, William of Coventry, Benedict of Rochester, bishops; of Master Pandulf, subdeacon and member of the household of our lord the Pope, of brother Aymeric (master of the Knights of the Temple in England), and of the illustrious men William Marshal, earl of Pembroke, William, earl of Salisbury, William, earl of Warenne, William, earl of Arundel, Alan of Galloway (constable of Scotland), Waren Fitz Gerold, Peter Fitz Herbert, Hubert De Burgh (seneschal of Poitou), Hugh de Neville, Matthew Fitz Herbert, Thomas Basset, Alan Basset, Philip d'Aubigny, Robert of Roppesley, John Marshal, John Fitz Hugh, and others, our liegemen.

1. In the first place we have granted to God, and by this our present charter confirmed for us and our heirs forever that the English Church shall be free, and shall have her rights entire, and her liberties inviolate; and we will that it be thus observed; which is apparent from this that the freedom of elections, which is reckoned most important and very essential to the English Church, we, of our pure and unconstrained will, did grant, and did by our charter confirm and did obtain the ratification of the same from our lord, Pope Innocent III, before the quarrel arose between us and our barons: and this we will observe, and our will is that it be observed in good faith by our heirs forever. We have also granted to all freemen of our kingdom, for us and our heirs forever, all the underwritten liberties, to be had and held by them and their heirs, of us and our heirs forever.

2. If any of our earls or barons, or others holding of us in chief by military service shall have died, and at the time of his death his heir shall be full of age and owe "relief", he shall have his inheritance by the old relief, to wit, the heir or heirs of an earl, for the whole barony of an earl by £100; the heir or heirs of a baron, £100 for a whole barony; the heir or heirs of a knight, 100s, at most, and whoever owes less let him give less, according to the ancient custom of fees.

3. If, however, the heir of any one of the aforesaid has been under age and in wardship, let him have his inheri-

tance without relief and without fine when he comes of age.

4. The guardian of the land of an heir who is thus under age, shall take from the land of the heir nothing but reasonable produce, reasonable customs, and reasonable services, and that without destruction or waste of men or goods; and if we have committed the wardship of the lands of any such minor to the sheriff, or to any other who is responsible to us for its issues, and he has made destruction or waster of what he holds in wardship, we will take of him amends, and the land shall be committed to two lawful and discreet men of that fee, who shall be responsible for the issues to us or to him to whom we shall assign them; and if we have given or sold the wardship of any such land to anyone and he has therein made destruction or waste, he shall lose that wardship, and it shall be transferred to two lawful and discreet men of that fief, who shall be responsible to us in like manner as aforesaid.

5. The guardian, moreover, so long as he has the wardship of the land, shall keep up the houses, parks, fishponds, stanks, mills, and other things pertaining to the land, out of the issues of the same land; and he shall restore to the heir, when he has come to full age, all his land, stocked with ploughs and wainage, according as the season of husbandry shall require, and the issues of the land can reasonable bear.

6. Heirs shall be married without disparagement, yet so that before the marriage takes place the nearest in blood to that heir shall have notice.

7. A widow, after the death of her husband, shall forthwith and without difficulty have her marriage portion and inheritance; nor shall she give anything for her dower, or for her marriage portion, or for the inheritance which her husband and she held on the day of the death of that husband; and she may remain in the house of her husband for forty days after his death, within which time her dower shall be assigned to her.

8. No widow shall be compelled to marry, so long as she prefers to live without a husband; provided always that she gives security not to marry without our consent, if she holds of us, or without the consent of the lord of whom she holds, if she holds of another.

9. Neither we nor our bailiffs will seize any land or rent for any debt, as long as the chattels of the debtor are sufficient to repay the debt; nor shall the sureties of the debtor be distrained so long as the principal debtor is able to satisfy the debt; and if the principal debtor shall fail to pay the debt, having nothing wherewith to pay it, then the sureties shall answer for the debt; and let them have the lands and rents of the debtor, if they desire them, until they are indemnified for the debt which they have paid for him, unless the principal debtor can show proof that he is discharged thereof as against the said sureties.

10. If one who has borrowed from the Jews any sum, great or small, die before that loan be repaid, the debt shall not bear interest while the heir is under age, of whomsoever he may hold; and if the debt fall into our hands, we will not take anything except the principal sum contained in the bond.

11. And if anyone die indebted to the Jews, his wife shall have her dower and pay nothing of that debt; and if any children of the deceased are left under age, necessaries shall be provided for them in keeping with the holding of the deceased; and out of the residue the debt shall be paid, reserving, however, service due to feudal lords; in like manner let it be done touching debts due to others than Jews.

12. No scutage not aid shall be imposed on our kingdom, unless by common counsel of our kingdom, except for ransoming our person, for making our eldest son a knight, and for once marrying our eldest daughter; and for these there shall not be levied more than a reasonable aid. In like manner it shall be done concerning aids from the city of London.

13. And the city of London shall have all it ancient liberties and free customs, as well by land as by water; furthermore, we decree and grant that all other cities, boroughs, towns, and ports shall have all their liberties and free customs.

14. And for obtaining the common counsel of the kingdom anent the assessing of an aid (except in the three cases aforesaid) or of a scutage, we will cause to be summoned the archbishops, bishops, abbots, earls, and greater barons, severally by our letters; and we will moveover cause to be summoned generally, through our sheriffs and bailiffs, and others who hold of us in chief, for a fixed date, namely, after the expiry of at least forty days, and at a fixed place; and in all letters of such summons we will specify the reason of the summons. And

when the summons has thus been made, the business shall proceed on the day appointed, according to the counsel of such as are present, although not all who were summoned have come.

15. We will not for the future grant to anyone license to take an aid from his own free tenants, except to ransom his person, to make his eldest son a knight, and once to marry his eldest daughter; and on each of these occasions there shall be levied only a reasonable aid.

16. No one shall be distrained for performance of greater service for a knight's fee, or for any other free tenement, than is due therefrom.

17. Common pleas shall not follow our court, but shall be held in some fixed place.

18. Inquests of novel disseisin, of mort d'ancestor, and of darrein presentment shall not be held elsewhere than in their own county courts, and that in manner following; We, or, if we should be out of the realm, our chief justiciar, will send two justiciaries through every county four times a year, who shall alone with four knights of the county chosen by the county, hold the said assizes in the county court, on the day and in the place of meeting of that court.

19. And if any of the said assizes cannot be taken on the day of the county court, let there remain of the knights and freeholders, who were present at the county court on that day, as many as may be required for the efficient making of judgments, according as the business be more or less.

20. A freeman shall not be amerced for a slight offense, except in accordance with the degree of the offense; and for a grave offense he shall be amerced in accordance with the gravity of the offense, yet saving always his "contentment"; and a merchant in the same way, saving his "merchandise"; and a villein shall be amerced in the same way, saving his "wainage" if they have fallen into our mercy: and none of the aforesaid amercements shall be imposed except by the oath of honest men of the neighborhood.

21. Earls and barons shall not be amerced except through their peers, and only in accordance with the degree of the offense.

22. A clerk shall not be amerced in respect of his lay holding except after the manner of the others aforesaid;

further, he shall not be amerced in accordance with the extent of his ecclesiastical benefice.

23. No village or individual shall be compelled to make bridges at river banks, except those who from of old were legally bound to do so.

24. No sheriff, constable, coroners, or others of our bailiffs, shall hold pleas of our Crown.

25. All counties, hundred, wapentakes, and trithings (except our demesne manors) shall remain at the old rents, and without any additional payment.

26. If anyone holding of us a lay fief shall die, and our sheriff or bailiff shall exhibit our letters patent of summons for a debt which the deceased owed us, it shall be lawful for our sheriff or bailiff to attach and enroll the chattels of the deceased, found upon the lay fief, to the value of that debt, at the sight of law worthy men, provided always that nothing whatever be thence removed until the debt which is evident shall be fully paid to us; and the residue shall be left to the executors to fulfill the will of the deceased; and if there be nothing due from him to us, all the chattels shall go to the deceased, saving to his wife and children their reasonable shares.

27. If any freeman shall die intestate, his chattels shall be distributed by the hands of his nearest kinsfolk and friends, under supervision of the Church, saving to every one the debts which the deceased owed to him.

28. No constable or other bailiff of ours shall take corn or other provisions from anyone without immediately tendering money therefor, unless he can have postponement thereof by permission of the seller.

29. No constable shall compel any knight to give money in lieu of castle-guard, when he is willing to perform it in his own person, or (if he himself cannot do it from any reasonable cause) then by another responsible man. Further, if we have led or sent him upon military service, he shall be relieved from guard in proportion to the time during which he has been on service because of us.

30. No sheriff or bailiff of ours, or other person, shall take the horses or carts of any freeman for transport duty, against the will of the said freeman.

31. Neither we nor our bailiffs shall take, for our castles or for any other work of ours, wood which is not ours, against the will of the owner of that wood.

32. We will not retain beyond one year and one day, the lands those who have been convicted of felony, and the lands shall thereafter be handed over to the lords of the fiefs.

33. All kydells for the future shall be removed altogether from Thames and Medway, and throughout all England, except upon the seashore.

34. The writ which is called praecipe shall not for the future be issued to anyone, regarding any tenement whereby a freeman may lose his court.

35. Let there be one measure of wine throughout our whole realm; and one measure of ale; and one measure of corn, to wit, "the London quarter"; and one width of cloth (whether dyed, or russet, or "halberget"), to wit, two ells within the selvedges; of weights also let it be as of measures.

36. Nothing in future shall be given or taken for a writ of inquisition of life or limbs, but freely it shall be granted, and never denied.

37. If anyone holds of us by fee-farm, either by socage or by burage, or of any other land by knight's service, we will not (by reason of that fee-farm, socage, or burage), have the wardship of the heir, or of such land of his as if of the fief of that other; nor shall we have wardship of that fee-farm, socage, or burgage, unless such fee-farm owes knight's service. We will not by reason of any small serjeancy which anyone may hold of us by the service of rendering to us knives, arrows, or the like, have wardship of his heir or of the land which he holds of another lord by knight's service.

38. No bailiff for the future shall, upon his own unsupported complaint, put anyone to his "law", without credible witnesses brought for this purposes.

39. No freemen shall be taken or imprisoned or disseised or exiled or in any way destroyed, nor will we go upon him nor send upon him, except by the lawful judgment of his peers or by the law of the land.

40. To no one will we sell, to no one will we refuse or delay, right or justice.

41. All merchants shall have safe and secure exit from England, and entry to England, with the right to tarry there and to move about as well by land as by water, for buying and selling by the ancient and right customs, quit from all evil tolls, except (in time of war) such merchants as are of the land at war with us. And if such are found in our land at the beginning of the war, they shall be detained, without injury to their bodies or goods, until information be received by us, or by our chief justiciar, how the merchants of our land found in the land at war with us are treated; and if our men are safe there, the others shall be safe in our land.

42. It shall be lawful in future for anyone (excepting always those imprisoned or outlawed in accordance with the law of the kingdom, and natives of any country at war with us, and merchants, who shall be treated as if above provided) to leave our kingdom and to return, safe and secure by land and water, except for a short period in time of war, on grounds of public policy- reserving always the allegiance due to us.

43. If anyone holding of some escheat (such as the honor of Wallingford, Nottingham, Boulogne, Lancaster, or of other escheats which are in our hands and are baronies) shall die, his heir shall give no other relief, and perform no other service to us than he would have done to the baron if that barony had been in the baron's hand; and we shall hold it in the same manner in which the baron held it.

44. Men who dwell without the forest need not henceforth come before our justiciaries of the forest upon a general summons, unless they are in plea, or sureties of one or more, who are attached for the forest.

45. We will appoint as justices, constables, sheriffs, or bailiffs only such as know the law of the realm and mean to observe it well.

46. All barons who have founded abbeys, concerning which they hold charters from the kings of England, or of which they have long continued possession, shall have the wardship of them, when vacant, as they ought to have.

47. All forests that have been made such in our time shall forthwith be disafforsted; and a similar course shall be followed with regard to river banks that have been placed "in defense" by us in our time.

48. All evil customs connected with forests and warrens, foresters and warreners, sheriffs and their officers, river banks and their wardens, shall immediately by inquired into in each county by twelve sworn knights of the same county chosen by the honest men of the same county, and shall, within forty days of the said inquest, be utterly abolished, so as never to be restored, provided

always that we previously have intimation thereof, or our justiciar, if we should not be in England.

49. We will immediately restore all hostages and charters delivered to us by Englishmen, as sureties of the peace of faithful service.

50. We will entirely remove from their bailiwicks, the relations of Gerard of Athee (so that in future they shall have no bailiwick in England); namely, Engelard of Cigogne, Peter, Guy, and Andrew of Chanceaux, Guy of Cigogne, Geoffrey of Martigny with his brothers, Philip Mark with his brothers and his nephew Geoffrey, and the whole brood of the same.

51. As soon as peace is restored, we will banish from the kingdom all foreign born knights, crossbowmen, serjeants, and mercenary soldiers who have come with horses and arms to the kingdom's hurt.

52. If anyone has been dispossessed or removed by us, without the legal judgment of his peers, from his lands, castles, franchises, or from his right, we will immediately restore them to him; and if a dispute arise over this, then let it be decided by the five and twenty barons of whom mention is made below in the clause for securing the peace. Moreover, for all those possessions, from which anyone has, without the lawful judgment of his peers, been disseised or removed, by our father, King Henry, or by our brother, King Richard, and which we retain in our hand (or which as possessed by others, to whom we are bound to warrant them) we shall have respite until the usual term of crusaders; excepting those things about which a plea has been raised, or an inquest made by our order, before our taking of the cross; but as soon as we return from the expedition, we will immediately grant full justice therein.

53. We shall have, moreover, the same respite and in the same manner in rendering justice concerning the disafforestation or retention of those forests which Henry our father and Richard our brother afforested, and concerning the wardship of lands which are of the fief of another (namely, such wardships as we have hitherto had by reason of a fief which anyone held of us by knight's service), and concerning abbeys founded on other fiefs than our own, in which the lord of the fee claims to have right; and when we have returned, or if we desist from our expedition, we will immediately grant full justice to all who complain of such things.

54. No one shall be arrested or imprisoned upon the appeal of a woman, for the death of any other than her husband.

55. All fines made with us unjustly and against the law of the land, and all amercements, imposed unjustly and against the law of the land, shall be entirely remitted, or else it shall be done concerning them according to the decision of the five and twenty barons whom mention is made below in the clause for securing the pease, or according to the judgment of the majority of the same, along with the aforesaid Stephen, archbishop of Canterbury, if he can be present, and such others as he may wish to bring with him for this purpose, and if he cannot be present the business shall nevertheless proceed without him, provided always that if any one or more of the aforesaid five and twenty barons are in a similar suit, they shall be removed as far as concerns this particular judgment, others being substituted in their places after having been selected by the rest of the same five and twenty for this purpose only, and after having been sworn.

56. If we have disseised or removed Welshmen from lands or liberties, or other things, without the legal judgment of their peers in England or in Wales, they shall be immediately restored to them; and if a dispute arise over this, then let it be decided in the marches by the judgment of their peers; for the tenements in England according to the law of England, for tenements in Wales according to the law of Wales, and for tenements in the marches according to the law of the marches. Welshmen shall do the same to us and ours.

57. Further, for all those possessions from which any Welshman has, without the lawful judgment of his peers, been disseised or removed by King Henry our father, or King Richard our brother, and which we retain in our hand (or which are possessed by others, and which we ought to warrant), we will have respite until the usual term of crusaders; excepting those things about which a plea has been raised or an inquest made by our order before we took the cross; but as soon as we return (or if perchance we desist from our expedition), we will immediately grant full justice in accordance with the laws of the Welsh and in relation to the foresaid regions.

58. We will immediately give up the son of Llywelyn and all the hostages of Wales, and the charters delivered to us as security for the peace.

59. We will do towards Alexander, king of Scots, concerning the return of his sisters and his hostages, and concerning his franchises, and his right, in the same manner as we shall do towards our other barons of England, unless it ought to be otherwise according to the charters which we hold from William his father, formerly king of Scots; and this shall be according to the judgment of his peers in our court.

60. Moreover, all these aforesaid customs and liberties, the observances of which we have granted in our kingdom as far as pertains to us towards our men, shall be observed b all of our kingdom, as well clergy as laymen, as far as pertains to them towards their men.

61. Since, moveover, for God and the amendment of our kingdom and for the better allaying of the quarrel that has arisen between us and our barons, we have granted all these concessions, desirous that they should enjoy them in complete and firm endurance forever, we give and grant to them the underwritten security, namely, that the barons choose five and twenty barons of the kingdom, whomsoever they will, who shall be bound with all their might, to observe and hold, and cause to be observed, the peace and liberties we have granted and confirmed to them by this our present Charter, so that if we, or our justiciar, or our bailiffs or any one of our officers, shall in anything be at fault towards anyone, or shall have broken any one of the articles of this peace or of this security, and the offense be notified to four barons of the foresaid five and twenty, the said four barons shall repair to us (or our justiciar, if we are out of the realm) and, laying the transgression before us, petition to have that transgression redressed without delay. And if we shall not have corrected the transgression (or, in the event of our being out of the realm, if our justiciar shall not have corrected it) within forty days, reckoning from the time it has been intimated to us (or to our justiciar, if we should be out of the realm), the four barons aforesaid shall refer that matter to the rest of the five and twenty barons, and those five and twenty barons shall, together with the community of the whole realm, distrain and distress us in all possible ways, namely, by seizing our castles, lands, possessions, and in any other way they can, until redress has been obtained as they deem fit, saving harmless our own person, and the persons of our queen and children; and when redress has been obtained, they shall resume their old relations towards us. And let whoever in the country desires it, swear to obey the orders of the said five and twenty barons for the execution of all the aforesaid matters, and along with them, to molest us to the utmost of his power; and we publicly and freely grant leave to everyone who wishes to swear, and we shall never forbid anyone to swear. All those, moreover, in the land who of themselves and of their own accord are unwilling to swear to the twenty five to help them in constraining and molesting us, we shall by our command compel the same to swear to the effect foresaid. And if any one of the five and twenty barons shall have died or departed from the land, or be incapacitated in any other manner which would prevent the foresaid provisions being carried out, those of the said twenty five barons who are left shall choose another in his place according to their own judgment, and he shall be sworn in the same way as the others. Further, in all matters, the execution of which is entrusted, to these twenty five barons, if perchance these twenty five are present and disagree about anything, or if some of them, after being summoned, are unwilling or unable to be present, that which the majority of those present ordain or command shall be held as fixed and established, exactly as if the whole twenty five had concurred in this; and the said twenty five shall swear that they will faithfully observe all that is aforesaid, and cause it to be observed with all their might. And we shall procure nothing from anyone, directly or indirectly, whereby any part of these concessions and liberties might be revoked or diminished; and if any such things has been procured, let it be void and null, and we shall never use it personally or by another.

62. And all the will, hatreds, and bitterness that have arisen between us and our men, clergy and lay, from the date of the quarrel, we have completely remitted and pardoned to everyone. Moreover, all trespasses occasioned by the said quarrel, from Easter in the sixteenth year of our reign till the restoration of peace, we have fully remitted to all, both clergy and laymen, and completely forgiven, as far as pertains to us. And on this head, we have caused to be made for them letters testimonial patent of the lord Stephen, archbishop of Canterbury, of the lord Henry, archbishop of Dublin, of the bishops aforesaid, and of Master Pandulf as touching this security and the concessions aforesaid.

63. Wherefore we will and firmly order that the English Church be free, and that the men in our kingdom have and hold all the aforesaid liberties, rights, and concessions, well and peaceably, freely and quietly, fully and wholly, for themselves and their heirs, of us and our heirs, in all respects and in all places forever, as is aforesaid. An oath, moreover, has been taken, as well on our part as on the art of the barons, that all these conditions aforesaid shall be kept in good faith and without evil intent.

Given under our hand—the above named and many others being witnesses—in the meadow which is called Runnymede, between Windsor and Staines, on the fifteenth day of June, in the seventeenth year of our reign.

GLOSSARY

amerced (v): charged a financial penalty

assizes (n): periodic English courts

burage: a tenure by which houses or land are held by the tenant for yearly rent or trade and handicraft services

darrein: the previous (legal) presentation

demesne: the land attached to a manor and retained for the owner's own use

disseisin: the act of disseising, or the wrongful removal of a person from property he lawfully possess

distrained: to constrain by seizing and holding goods until a claim or pledge has been fulfilled or paid

ells: an L-shaped extension usually at the end of a building

escheat: a common law under which the property of someone who dies without an heir transfers to the crown or state

fief: a fee or piece of land held but subject to feudal obligations

kydells: fishing weirs

mort d'ancestor: death of an ancestor

pease: peas

scutage: a fee paid in lieu of military service

selvedge: a small piece of extra material left on finished fabric to prevent unraveling

serjeancy: a type of feudal land-holding in England

socage: a tenure of land held by the tenant in performance of specific services or payment of rent, without military service

stank: a small pool or cofferdam, especially one of wood made watertight with clay

trithing: one of three ancient divisions of counties in England

wainage: articles needed for farming

wapentakes: an administrative unit of an English county

Document Analysis

Though the Magna Carta is the first European document that embodies the principals of rule of law and individual rights, and though many modern constitutions refer to it, the charter was intended primarily to restrain the king's behavior toward his barons. One of the ways that King John raised money was to charge exorbitant fees when an estate changed hands through inheritance. Though technically these lands were held by vassals of the king, there was no limit on the amount that could be charged, and the fees charged by the king amounted to the seizure of estates in many cases. Scutage was another hated tax. All nobles were required to perform military service for the king in exchange for their land. Many could not offer this service and were required to pay a fee instead. John raised the rate of scutage to untenable levels.

John had also come into conflict with the English church. Like his predecessors, John sought to exercise significant authority over the church, including the right to treat them as vassals (meaning they would owe him military service or payments) and the right to reject appointments that he disliked. Meanwhile, the popes had asserted their authority over the church and had established the right to appoint and invest bishops without royal permission. John had been unable to prevent the placement of Stephen Langton as archbishop of Canterbury, the primary drafter of this charter. The Magna Carta promises that the king will respect the freedom of the church: "the English Church shall be free, and shall have her rights entire, and her liberties inviolate."

Though the English judicial system was already well established during King John's reign, he used the judges, commissioned initially by the king to ensure that regional feuds would not be reflected in the courts, to charge huge sums of money to the nobility in fines and fees. In some cases, the king refused to allow judges to hear a case unless a significant fee was paid. This is expressly prohibited in the Magna Carta. In its most famous passage, the charter promises, "To no one will we sell, to no one will we refuse or delay, right or justice." The king himself is to be restrained by the law of the land. A council of noblemen will decide whether decrees of the king, including taxes, are lawful and could be implemented.

One way that the king had been able to circumvent traditional feudal land rights was through his designation of forest lands. Designated forests had been under the king's jurisdiction for centuries, and they provided the crown with income and provisions. These royal forests had been expanded under King John, which the barons resented. The Magna Carta contains provisions returning the forests to their previous boundaries and limiting royal rights in these areas.

The Magna Carta also deals with a variety of other economic issues, from how debt will be settled upon the death of a debtor to the establishment of the rights of merchants and the removal of fishing weirs, which obstructed access to rivers. Though many of its pronouncements were changed or lifted as they became obsolete, the Magna Carta's restraint of the power of the king and its assertion of the rule of law are mainstays in many modern constitutions.

Essential Themes

The primary theme of the Magna Carta is that the ruler is not above the law. Though other charters existed in English history, the Magna Carta was the first to explicitly state that taxation could not be levied arbitrarily and without the consent of the governed. It also protected the freemen of England from being imprisoned or banished without recourse to the legal system, and it protected their property in the same way. These principles are both embodied in the US Constitution. The Magna Carta's limits on the power of royal authority paved the way for the American Revolution, as colonists demanded that the king adhere to the rule of law and not tax the colonies without their consent. They believed that liberties granted in the Magna Carta were being denied to them as English subjects, and this provided them with the justification for their disobedience to the king, and ultimately, their independence from England.

—*Bethany Groff, MA*

Bibliography and Additional Reading

Breay, Claire. *Magna Carta: Manuscripts and Myths*. London: British Library, 2003. Print.

Danziger, Danny & John Gillingham. *1215: The Year of Magna Carta*. New York: Touchstone, 2003. Print.

Howard, A. E. Dick. *Magna Carta: Text and Commentary*. Charlottesville: UP of Virginia, 1964. Print.

Loengard, Janet Senderowitz. *Magna Carta and the England of King John*. Suffolk, UK: Boydell, 2010. Print.

■ Three Summonses to the Parliament of 1295

Date: 1295
Country: England
Author: Edward I

Summary Overview

The Parliament of 1295 is known as the Model Parliament because it not only included representatives of the church and the nobility, but also required attendance from two knights from each of the counties and two citizens of each of the cities and boroughs of England; this configuration—with representation from the king, the aristocracy, and the people (or "commons")—provided the model for the future development of the English Parliament. Though this was a notable gathering called by King Edward I, it was not the first parliament to gather representatives of these three groups. In 1265, Simon de Montfort, a rebel baron who had seized control of government, held the first parliament, in which representatives of the boroughs and counties discussed matters of national importance. When Edward I became king, he maintained this model of representation, recognizing that the support of the cities, boroughs, and counties bolstered his authority, kept the nobility in check, and reinforced the popular idea that people should have a say in their government. Parliaments were summoned erratically, generally when the king needed resources, and so attendees were able to negotiate reforms and concessions from the monarch, thereby laying the foundation for representative government in England.

Defining Moment

In the thirteenth century, significant moves were made away from autocratic rule in England, beginning with the concessions made by King John in the Magna Carta of 1215. Magna Carta required the king to accept the Great Council, an assembly of barons that would advise the king. Over time, the Great Council became known as Parliament, a word that derives from the French *parler*, "to talk." By the middle of the century, in 1254, knights who represented the counties were elected to come to a council to negotiate greater taxes. This was the first time that representation was called from a broader body of the English people.

During the tumultuous reign of Henry III (Edward I's father) the concept of the right of council to the king became broadly accepted, meaning that the king could not impose extraordinary taxes without the consent of the barons. In 1258, the barons met to discuss reforms they would demand in return for agreeing to raise additional taxes for the king, who both was fighting unpopular and expensive uprisings in Wales and had agreed to help finance a papal conflict in Sicily, without the barons' consent. A group of powerful barons, most notably Montfort, issued the Provisions of Oxford, which demanded reforms from the king, including regular meetings of parliament with representation from the counties, and the establishment of a king's council that would make key administrative appointments. Though the king initially accepted the Provisions of Oxford, he failed to comply with its terms, and in 1261, he had the provisions declared void by the pope. The barons, headed by Montfort, had sworn to abide by the Provisions, and in 1264, after failed attempts at arbitration, a civil war began. In May, the barons captured Henry III and his son, the future King Edward I, and reestablished the provisions. In 1265, Montfort called a parliament that included representatives of not only counties, but also, for the first time, the boroughs, fortified towns and cities that had been granted special status in medieval England. After the death of Montfort and Henry III, Edward I became king and continued to call parliament frequently. In his thirty-five year reign, from 1272 to 1307, he convened parliament forty-six times, and official records of its decisions were kept. His first parliament, called in 1275, included the nobility and the clergy, but also asked for representation from the counties and boroughs for the purposes of raising a broad-based tax. The parliament he convened in 1295, with its representation by nobles, both secular and religious, as well as two knights from the counties and two citizens of the cities and burgesses from the boroughs, would become the standard format for future parliaments.

Author Biography and Document Information

Edward I, also known as Edward Longshanks, was born in Westminster in 1239. He was the eldest son of King Henry III and his wife, Eleanor of Provence. As a teenager, he was made the Duke of Gascony and given control of Ireland and Wales as well as several other significant titles and territories. In 1254, he married Eleanor of Castile, whose foreign retinue would antagonize the barons of England later in Edward's reign. In 1255, Edward tried to put down an uprising in Wales and was soundly defeated, partly because of a lack of support from his father, the king. This seems to have caused significant tension in their relationship, and when the rebel baron Simon de Montfort, Edward's uncle by marriage, forced reforms on Henry in 1258, Edward supported Montfort. He reconciled with his father in time to return from his continental estates in 1264 to fight against Montfort. Both Edward and his father were captured and imprisoned, but Edward escaped in May 1265 and led the royalist army to victory, killing Montfort. Edward ruled from then on, as his father was increasingly incapacitated, and he became king upon his father's death in 1272. Edward's reign was characterized by wars with France, the bloody suppression of rebellions in Wales and Scotland, and his increasing reliance on his parliament to ensure support for these military endeavors. He died in 1307 and is buried in Westminster Abbey.

HISTORICAL DOCUMENT

Summons of a Bishop to Parliament (1295)

The King to the venerable father in Christ Robert, by the same grace archbishop of Canterbury, primate of all England, greeting. As a most just law, established by the careful providence of sacred princes, exhorts and decrees that what affects all, by all should be approved, so also, very evidently should common danger be met by means provided in common. You know sufficiently well, and it is now, as we believe, divulged through all regions of the world, how the king of France fraudulently and craftily deprives us of our land of Gascony, by withholding it unjustly from us. Now, however, not satisfied with the before-mentioned fraud and injustice, having gathered together for the conquest of our kingdom a very great fleet, and an abounding multitude of warriors, with which he has made a hostile attack on our kingdom and the inhabitants of the same kingdom, he now proposes to destroy the English language altogether from the earth, if his power should correspond to the detestable proposition of the contemplated injustice, which God forbid. Because, therefore, darts seen beforehand do less injury, and your interest especially, as that of the rest of the citizens of the same realm, is concerned in this affair, we command you, strictly enjoining you in the fidelity and love in which you are bound to us, that on the Lord's day next after the feast of St. Martin, in the approaching winter, you be present in person at Westminster; citing beforehand the dean and chapter of your church, the archdeacons and all the clergy of your diocese, causing the same dean and archdeacons in their own persons, and the said chapter by one suitable proctor, and the said clergy by two, to be present along with you, having full and sufficient power from the same chapter and clergy, to consider, ordain and provide, along with us and with the rest of the prelates and principal men and other inhabitants of our kingdom, how the dangers and threatened evils of this kind are to be met. Witness the king at Wangham, the thirtieth day of September.

Summons of a Baron to Parliament (1295)

The king to his beloved and faithful relative, Edmund, Earl of Cornwall, greeting. Because we wish to have a consultation and meeting with you and with the rest of the principal men of our kingdom, as to provision for remedies against the dangers which in these days are threatening our whole kingdom; we command you, strictly enjoining you in the fidelity and love in which you are bound to us, that on the Lord's day next after the feast of St. Martin, in the approaching winter, you be present in person at Westminster, for considering, ordaining and doing along with us and with the prelates, and the rest of the principal men and other inhabitants of our kingdom, as may be necessary for meeting dangers of this kind.

Witness the king at Canterbury, the first of October.

Summons of Representatives of Shires and Towns to Parliament (1295)

The king to the sheriff of Northamptonshire. Since we intend to have a consultation and meeting with the earls, barons and other principal men of our kingdom with regard to providing remedies against the dangers which are in these days threatening the same kingdom; and on that account have commanded them to be with us on the Lord's day next after the feast of St. Martin in the approaching winter, at Westminster, to consider, ordain, and do as may be necessary for the avoidance of these dangers; we strictly require you to cause two knights from the aforesaid county, two citizens from each city in the same county, and two burgesses from each borough, of those who are especially discreet and capable of laboring, to be elected without delay, and to cause them to come to us at the aforesaid said time and place.

Moreover, the said knights are to have full and sufficient power for themselves and for the community of the aforesaid county, and the said citizens and burgesses for themselves and the communities of the aforesaid cities and boroughs separately, then and there for doing what shall then be ordained according to the common counsel in the premises; so that the aforesaid business shall not remain unfinished in any way for defect of this power. And you shall have there the names of the knights, citizens and burgesses and this writ.

Witness the king at Canterbury on the third day of October.

GLOSSARY

burgess: a freeman of a borough

prelate: a high church official

Document Analysis

These three summonses to the Model Parliament of 1295 illustrate how thoroughly the idea of representation by the governed had taken root. Though this was certainly nothing like a modern democratic government, Edward called his people to share in both the cost and the benefit of war. The idea that a proper law should not only govern but also have the input of all the citizens was new, and one that would eventually lead to the modern form of parliamentary government. King Edward I was explicit in this belief in his summonses of 1295. "Just law . . . exhorts and decrees that what affects all, by all should be approved. . . . Common danger (should) be met by means provided in common." In other words, the governed should have a say in issues that affect them, and they should also be prepared to contribute to their common defense. In Edward's letter to the archbishop of Canterbury he outlines his primary reason for calling this parliament. The French king has taken what was intended to be temporary custody of Gascony, one of Edward's territories by right, and refuses to give it back. "The king of France fraudulently and craftily deprives us of our land of Gascony, by withholding it unjustly from us." As if this outrage were not enough, the French king is making all-out war on England. A new national consciousness is in evidence as Edward invokes the threat that the French would "destroy the English language altogether from the earth." In anticipation of what Edward feels is a war of national defense, he reminds the archbishop of the "fidelity and love in which you are bound to us." He reminds the summoned nobles that they have the same duty to him. When it came time to summon the representatives of the counties, cities, and the boroughs, however, there is no mention of fidelity or love. "We strictly require you to cause two knights from the aforesaid county, two citizens from each city in the same county, and two burgesses from each borough, of those who are especially discreet and capable of laboring, to be elected without delay, and to cause them to come to us at the aforesaid said time and place." The ecclesiastical and secular nobility are bound by feudal duty to the king, but his people are bound to him by his rule alone. Still, by including them in the parliament of 1295, Edward speaks to his understanding that they bear some of the responsibility for the decisions made regarding the affairs of the country. Their inclusion is further evidence of a growing sense of national identity.

Essential Themes

These summonses to the parliament of 1295 demonstrate that the king felt that discussions of matters of national importance should include not only the nobility and the clergy, but also representatives of the counties and the boroughs. This model of representation became the parliamentary standard over the following centuries. Though this was far from a true representative government, it was a groundbreaking idea that the king had to consult with anyone for any reason other than strictly demanding taxes. This idea had a profound influence on the future government of England, as parliaments became more secure in their right to impose limits and to demand concessions from the monarchy. The inclusion of the counties, cities, and boroughs also ensured that common people, through their representatives, could regulate the activities of both the monarchy and the aristocracy. Their inclusion also ensured a strong sense of national identity, as many more people in England saw themselves represented in government.

—*Bethany Groff, MA*

Bibliography and Additional Reading

Jones, Clyve. *A Short History of Parliament: England, Great Britain, the United Kingdom, Ireland, and Scotland*. Woodbridge: Boydell, 2009. Print.

Maddicott, J. R. *The Origins of the English Parliament, 924–1327*. New York: Oxford UP, 2010. Print.

"Origins of Parliament." *Parliament.uk*. British Parliament, n.d. Web. 18 May 2015.

■ Ordinances of the Merchant Gild of Southampton

Date: ca.1300
Geographic Region: England
Author: Unknown
Translator: E. P. Cheyney

Summary Overview

Merchant gilds (or guilds) such as that of Southampton, England, were organizations of merchants that banded together for a variety of reasons, including mutual assistance and common economic and social interests. These merchants were most often involved in local wholesale and retail trade, though some large merchant guilds organized international commerce and established headquarters in other countries. The guilds had political influential in their communities, and often the heads of the most powerful guilds would also hold local office. Additionally, merchant guilds offered a measure of social security. If a guild member died, the member's children and spouse received benefits. An injured or ill guild member was also eligible for relief. Guilds enforced contracts and ensured the quality of their members' products. They also protected their members from arbitrary taxation and issued boycotts when politically expedient. Ordinances of guilds laid out the rules by which the guild would operate. Disobeying these rules could cost a merchant his livelihood and, in some cases, his freedom.

Defining Moment

Associations of skilled artisans and merchants appear in the historical record as early as the final years of the Roman Republic. Known as *collegia*, they were eventually regulated by Roman emperors, who sought to structure them to their political and financial advantage, taxing them almost out of existence. After the fall of the Roman Empire, a form of guilds continued to exist in the Byzantine Empire, where organizations of artisans and traders were tightly controlled by the emperor.

The guilds that emerged in medieval Europe had little in common with these earlier groups, who existed more or less as taxable and politically expedient units. European guilds began to emerge with the growth of permanent towns around the eleventh century. Before the establishment of commerce in medieval towns, European society was primarily feudal and agrarian. Traders would most often produce and peddle their wares, traveling from site to site and sometimes joining together for safety. As the European economy grew, merchants could leave the production and transportation of goods and to others, establishing their trade centers in one place. As settled merchants began to dominate large towns, they organized themselves into guilds. Recognized by both local and national government, they were endowed with certain rights and privileges written into their charters. These guilds protected their members by reducing competition through control of raw materials and staple goods as well as setting up funds and traditions for mutual and community aid. As these guilds grew, they were able to restrict and sometimes prohibit outsiders from trading in their town, though in many of these communities, an active black market thrived.

By the time of these ordinances to the merchants of Southampton around 1300, thanks to brisk international trade, merchants were increasingly wealthy and their guilds dominated the political life of many towns. The head of the guild was often also the head of local government and could ensure that laws were passed that favored them. Some guilds were set up to provide networks for foreign trade and would have offices in multiple ports, but most were locally based. Guild membership was not automatic, and a breach of the rules could mean expulsion and ruin; however, most guilds allowed for hereditary membership. Craft guilds often worked hand in hand with merchant guilds, each controlling some aspect of the finished product. For example, a merchant guild would control the importation of lumber, while the carpenters' or joiners' guild would control the means of production; the merchants would then sell the finished product. Aspiring guild members worked their way up through a long training process, from apprentice status, to journeyman, to master.

The guild system declined slowly as local government gave way to stronger central and national government and as their restrictions proved no match for emerging markets and technologies from the sixteenth century onward. Still, guilds contributed a great deal to the growth of the medieval economy by organizing and supporting merchants and artisans. At the height of their power, the guilds provided more infrastructure support and more social and economic benefit to their communities than any other body.

Document Information

The ordinances of the merchant guild of Southampton were originally written on vellum, or very fine sheep-skin. Like most municipal records in England, the document was held by the public records office when it was discovered, or rediscovered, by British antiquarians in the early nineteenth century. Comprehensive surveys of all the guild records available were published by the 1850s, and the Southampton records appeared in the *Archaeological Journal* in 1859 in their original French. The ordinances were traditionally kept in the guildhall in Southampton in a locked trunk. They were bound along with other important documents in the *Oak Book,* so called because its covers were made of slabs of wood. They were of particular interest to anti-industrialists, who looked to the medieval past as an ideal at odds with the capitalist and industrial Victorian reality.

HISTORICAL DOCUMENT

1. In the first place, there shall be elected from the gild merchant, and established, an alderman, a steward, a chaplain, four skevins, and an usher. And it is to be known that whosoever shall be alderman shall receive from each one entering into the gild fourpence; the steward, twopence; the chaplain, twopence; and the usher, one penny. And the gild shall meet twice a year: that is to say, on the Sunday next after St. John the Baptist's day, and on the Sunday next after St. Mary's day.

2. And when the gild shall be sitting no one of the gild is to bring in any stranger, except when required by the alderman or steward. And the alderman shall have a sergeant to serve before him, the steward another sergeant, and the chaplain shall have his clerk.

3. And when the gild shall sit, the alderman is to have, each night, so long as the gild sits, two gallons of wine and two candles, and the steward the same; and the four skevins and the chaplain, each of them one gallon of wine and one candle, and the usher one gallon of wine.

4. And when the gild shall sit, the lepers of La Madeleine shall have of the alms of the gild, two sesters (approximately eight gallons) of ale, and the sick of God's House and of St. Julian shall have two sesters of ale. And the Friars Minors shall have two sesters of ale and one sester of wine. And four sesters of ale shall be given to the poor wherever the gild shall meet.

5. And when the gild is sitting, no one who is of the gild shall go outside the town for any business, without the permission of the steward. And if any does so, let him be fined two shillings, and pay them.

6. And when the gild sits, and any gildsman is outside of the city so that he does not know when it will happen, he shall have a gallon of wine, if his servants come to get it. And if a gildsman is ill and is in the city, wine shall be sent to him, two loaves of bread and a gallon of wine and a dish from the kitchen; and two approved men of the gild shall go to visit him and look after his condition.

7. And when a gildsman dies, all those who are of the gild and are in the city shall attend the service of the dead, and the gildsmen shall bear the body and bring it to the place of burial. And whoever will not do this shall pay according to his oath, two pence, to be given to the poor. And those of the ward where the dead man shall be ought to find a man to watch over the body the night that the dead shall lie in his house. And so long as the service of the dead shall last, that is to say the vigil and the mass, there ought to burn four candles of the gild, each candle of two pounds weight or more, until the body is buried. And these four candles shall remain in the keeping of the steward of the gild.

8. The steward ought to keep the rolls and treasures of the gild under the seal of the alderman of the gild.

9. And when a gildsman dies, his eldest son or his next heir shall have the seat of his father, or of his uncle, if his father was not a gildsman, and of no other one; and he shall give nothing for his seat. No husband can have a seat in the gild by right of his wife, nor demand a seat by right of his wife's ancestors.

19. And no one of the city of Southampton shall buy anything to sell again in the same city, unless he is of the gild merchant or of the franchise. And if anyone shall do so and is convicted of it, all which he has so bought shall be forfeited to the king; and no one shall be quit of custom unless he proves that he is in the gild or in the franchise, and this from year to year.

20. And no one shall buy honey, fat, salt herrings, or any kind of oil, or millstones, or fresh hides, or any kind of fresh skins, unless he is a gildsman: nor keep a tavern for wine, nor sell cloth at retail, except in market or fair days; nor keep grain in his granary beyond five quarters, to sell at retail, if he is not a gildsman; and whoever shall do this and be convicted, shall forfeit all to the king.

22. If any gildsman falls into poverty and has not the wherewithal to live, and is not able to work or to provide for himself, he shall have one mark from the gild to relieve his condition—when the gild shall sit. No one of the gild nor of the franchise shall avow another's goods for his by which the custom of the city shall be injured. And if any one does so and is convicted, he shall lose the gild and the franchise; and the merchandise so avowed shall be forfeited to the king.

23. And no private man nor stranger shall bargain for or buy any kind of merchandise coming into the city before a burgess of the gild merchant, so long as the gildsman is present and wishes to bargain for and buy this merchandise; and if anyone does so and is convicted, that which he buys shall be forfeited to the king.

35. The common chest shall be in the house of the chief alderman or of the steward, and the three keys of it shall be lodged with three discreet men of the aforesaid twelve sworn men, or with three of the skevins, who shall loyally take care of the common seal, and the charters and of the treasure of the town, and the standards, and other muniments of the town; and no letter shall be sealed with the common seal, nor any charter taken out of the common-chest but in the presence of six or twelve sworn men, and of the alderman or steward; and nobody shall sell by any kind of measure or weight that is not sealed, under forfeiture of two shillings.

[items 37–62 are omitted in the version presented here]

63. No one shall go out to meet a ship bringing wine or other merchandise coming to the town, in order to buy anything, before the ship be arrived and come to anchor for unlading; and if any one does so and is convicted, the merchandise which he shall have bought shall be forfeited to the king.

GLOSSARY

alderman: a high-ranking member of a town's or city's governing body; the head of a guild

burgess: a representative, or sometimes an inhabitant, of a borough

muniments: documents by which rights or privileges are defended or maintained

sesters: medieval measure for liquid

skevins: wardens or officers in a guild

Document Analysis

The guild ordinances were responsible for ordering every aspect of the professional lives of a guild's members. At the same time, they served to guide members' charitable activities and regulate their social-service function. These regulations were crucial to the rights of the guild to operate and were often kept in medieval towns under lock and key. This selection is not a complete list of ordinances, which did change over time and were added to, but it gives examples of the primary functions of the guild. The leadership structure of the guild, which is described first in the document, was primary. An alderman, a steward, a chaplain, four skevins, and an usher lead the guild, each receiving a payment from new members. The meeting schedule is also set—the guild would meet twice per year.

The charitable function of the guild is established in these regulations as well. The sick, the poor, and the holy orders of the town receive ale and wine when the meeting was in session. The document also stipulates that attendance in these meetings was compulsory, and if anyone goes out of town during the meeting, that member is fined. If, however, a member is delayed beyond his control, a servant can be sent to collect a portion of the wine. If a guild member is ill during the meeting, food, wine, and the company of other guild members is provided. Guild members who fall into poverty are also granted alms from the guild. The provisions for a guild member who dies are even more thorough. Guild members attend all services, sit with the body at night, burn special guild candles, and carry the body to the burial ground. A trained son or nephew can assume the guild membership of the deceased. Because the guild is patriarchal, the ordinances also assert that no rights can be gained by marrying a guild widow, and women cannot pass on a guild seat.

The commercial restrictions that apply to guild members, but also protect them, are spelled out in the remainder of the document. It is these restrictions, and the guild members' adherence to them, that is at the heart of the guild's function. For instance, one of the ordinances declares that "no one of the city of Southampton shall buy anything to sell again in the same city, unless he is of the gild merchant or of the franchise." Raw materials and imports are tightly controlled, and there are penalties in place for anyone who tries to operate outside of guild restrictions.

Essential Themes

The primary themes of this selection are the economic, charitable, and mutual assistance functions of the medieval guilds that were established to organize and to support merchants at a crucial time when commercial trade was thriving. These ordinances spelled out the guild's responsibilities to its members, providing them with a measure of security in a time when few could count on a safety net in case of illness or injury. Guild members could expect their brethren to visit them if they fell ill. If they were injured or incapacitated to the extent that they could no longer earn an income, they were the beneficiary of relief from the guild. Their bodies were even carried to the burial ground by the guild, and its members kept watch over them, even in death.

The guild also protected—and restricted—the ability to access raw materials and sell finished goods. This ensured price stability and reduced competition, while limiting markets on behalf of members, making it impossible for nonmembers to earn a living in their field. This economic protectionism disproportionately benefitted the few guild members at the top of the hierarchy.

Guild members also supported the poor and sick in their community in addition to the monks and nuns who dispensed charity. In many towns, the guilds were the primary source of support for the poor, and they also benefitted the community by building bridges, roads, and other infrastructure.

—Bethany Groff, MA

Bibliography and Additional Reading

Epstein, Steven A. *Wage Labor and Guilds in Medieval Europe*. Chapel Hill: U of North Carolina P, 1991. Print.

Lambert, J. Malet. *Two Thousand Years of Gild Life: Or an Outline of the History and Development of the Gild System from Early Times*. Hull: Brown, 1891. Print.

Ogilvie, Sheilagh. *Institutions and European Trade: Merchant Guilds, 1000–1800*. New York: Cambridge UP, 2011. Print.

■ The Battle of Poitiers, from *The Chronicles of Froissart*

Date: 1369
Country: France
Author: Jean Froissart
Translator: John Bourchier (Lord Berners)

Summary Overview

The Battle of Poitiers was a surprising and devastating defeat for the French king John II at the hands of a much smaller English army. The English army was led by Edward, later known as the Black Prince, who was heir to the English throne. The battle was recorded in vivid detail by contemporary historian Jean Froissart in his *Chronicles*, a record of the conflicts known as the Hundred Years' War. The Battle of Poitiers was a decisive victory for the English, as they effectively utilized archers and captured the French king. As negotiations for John's ransom drew out over the years, France dissolved into a period of instability and violence. The king's release cost France nearly one-third of its territory and a colossal cash settlement, and it was ultimately unsuccessful. Froissart's *Chronicles* were written not only as a historical record but also to promote and to describe the chivalric behavior of the time.

Defining Moment

The first phase of the Hundred Years' War unfolded in favor of the English, including the decisive victory at the Battle of Crécy in 1346. The Black Prince pushed for further action, raiding the countryside of France in the late summer of 1356. These raids successfully destroyed crops and farms, and his troops sacked towns and burned villages to the ground. The Black Prince's forces halted at Tours, along the Loire River, but were not able to attack the castle because of unusually heavy rain. King John II of France, whose forces outnumbered the seven thousand knights, infantry, and archers of the English army (the exact number of French troops is not known, but estimated at around thirty-five thousand), caught up with them outside Poitiers on September 17, 1356, but a truce was called for the following day in hope that a battle could be avoided.

Despite earnest negotiations by the leading local religious figure, Cardinal Talleyrand de Perigord, the truce proved temporary. Aware that the English forces were vastly outnumbered and expecting an easy victory, King John II refused the Black Prince's offer to return everything that had been taken during raids on the countryside and maintain a seven-year truce. Meanwhile, the delay allowed the English army to secure its position in a marshy area with excellent natural defenses.

On September 19, English archers took up protected positions behind hedges along the road. French knights mounted direct assaults on the English position that exposed the unprotected backs and necks of their horses to the arrows of the skilled English archers. Most of the knights in these ill-conceived charges were killed, wounded, or taken prisoner to be ransomed later. King John himself led the last division of the army into battle on foot. The English army then mounted and charged into the French divisions. The French army broke under the assault, and King John surrendered and was taken captive along with his teenage son, Philip.

After the battle, the Black Prince reported that his forces had killed three thousand French soldiers and lost only forty men. Though the French casualties are accurate, English deaths were likely in the hundreds. The French king went into a genteel captivity in England, while France, under the rule of his eldest son, the Dauphin Charles, disintegrated into near civil war, as the people resisted efforts to continue the war and ransom the king. In 1360, nearly a third of France was relinquished to England, and King John was released in exchange for other hostages. The king found chaos and rebellion in France when he returned. In 1361, one of the replacement hostages escaped, and John voluntarily returned to captivity in London, where he died in 1364.

Author Biography

Jean Froissart was born around 1333 in Valenciennes, in the duchy of Brabant, then part of the Holy Roman Empire and now part of France. Froissart was a poet and a scholar who spent time in several European courts. He was part of the court of Queen Philippa of England, wife of King Edward III, and her sons, including the Black Prince. He later joined the household of Guy II de Chatillon, comte de Blois, and was named canon of Chimay, in present-day Belgium.

Froissart's most noted work is his *Chronicles*, documenting the conflicts between England and France that made up the Hundred Years' War. He also composed poems of courtly love, and his writing encouraged nobles to follow the rules and customs of chivalric behavior. Froissart died around 1400.

HISTORICAL DOCUMENT

OF THE GREAT HOST THAT THE FRENCH KING BROUGHT TO THE BATTLE OF POITIERS

After the taking of the castle of Romorantin and of them that were therein, the prince then and his company rode as they did before, destroying the country, approaching to Anjou and to Touraine. The French king, who was at Chartres, departed and came to Blois and there tarried two days, and then to Amboise and the next day to Loches: and then he heard how that the prince was at Touraine and how that he was returning by Poitou: ever the Englishmen were coasted by certain expert knights of France, who alway made report to the king what the Englishmen did. Then the king came to the Haye in Touraine and his men had passed the river of Loire, some at the bridge of Orleans and some at Meung, at Saumur, at Blois, and at Tours and whereas they might: they were in number a twenty thousand men of arms beside other; there were a twenty-six dukes and earls and more than sixscore banners, and the four sons of the king, who were but young, the duke Charles of Normandy, the lord Louis, that was from thenceforth duke of Anjou, and the lord John duke of Berry, and the lord Philip, who was after duke of Burgoyne. The same season, pope Innocent the sixth sent the lord Bertrand, cardinal of Perigord, and the lord Nicholas, cardinal of Urgel, into France, to treat for a peace between the French king and all his enemies, first between him and the king of Navarre, who was in prison: and these cardinals oftentimes spake to the king for his deliverance during the siege at Bretuel, but they could do nothing in that behalf. Then the cardinal of Perigord went to Tours, and there he heard how the French king hasted sore to find the Englishmen: then

he rode to Poitiers, for he heard how both the hosts drew thitherward.

The French king heard how the prince hasted greatly to return, and the king feared that he should escape him and so departed from Haye in Touraine, and all his company, and rode to Chauvigny, where he tarried that Thursday in the town and without along by the river of Creuse, and the next day the king passed the river at the bridge there, weening that the Englishmen had been before him, but they were not. Howbeit they pursued after and passed the bridge that day more than threescore thousand horses, and divers other passed at Chatelleraut, and ever as they passed they took the way to Poitiers.

On the other side the prince wist not truly where the Frenchmen were; but they supposed that they were not far off, for they could not find no more forage, whereby they had great fault in their host of victual, and some of them repented that they had destroyed so much as they had done before when they were in Berry, Anjou and Touraine, and in that they had made no better provision. The same Friday three great lords of France, the lord of Craon, the lord Raoul of Coucy and the earl of Joigny, tarried all day at the town of Chauvigny, and part of their companies. The Saturday they passed the bridge and followed the king, who was then a three leagues before, and took the way among bushes without a wood side to go to Poitiers.

The same Saturday the prince and his company dislodged from a little village thereby, and sent before him certain currours to see if they might find any adventure and to hear where the Frenchmen were. They were in number a three-score men of arms well horsed, and with them was the lord Eustace d'Aubrecicourt and the lord John of Ghistelles, and by adventure the Englishmen and

Frenchmen met together by the foresaid wood side. The Frenchmen knew anon how they were their enemies; then in haste they did on their helmets and displayed their banners and came a great pace towards the Englishmen: they were in number a two hundred men of arms. When the Englishmen saw them, and that they were so great a number, then they determined to fly and let the Frenchmen chase them, for they knew well the prince with his host was not far behind. Then they turned their horses and took the corner of the wood, and the Frenchmen after them crying their cries and made great noise. And as they chased, they came on the prince's battle or they were ware thereof themselves; the prince tarried there to have word again from them that he sent forth. The lord Raoul de Coucy with his banner went so far forward that he was under the prince's banner: there was a sore battle and the knight fought valiantly; howbeit he was there taken, and the earl of Joigny, the viscount of Brosse, the lord of Chauvigny and all the other taken or slain, but a few that scaped. And by the prisoners the prince knew how the French king followed him in such wise that he could not eschew the battle: then he assembled together all his men and commanded that no man should go before the marshals' banners. Thus the prince rode that Saturday from the morning till it was against night, so that he came within two little leagues of Poitiers. Then the captal de Buch, sir Aymenion of Pommiers, the lord Bartholomew of Burghersh and the lord Eustace d'Aubrecicourt, all these the prince sent forth to see if they might know what the Frenchmen did. These knights departed with two hundred men of arms well horsed: they rode so far that they saw the great battle of the king's, they saw all the fields covered with men of arms. These Englishmen could not forbear, but set on the tail of the French host and cast down many to the earth and took divers prisoners, so that the host began to stir, and tidings thereof came to the French king as he was entering into the city of Poitiers. Then he returned again and made all his host do the same, so that Saturday it was very late or he was lodged in the field. The English currours returned again to the prince and shewed him all that they saw and knew, and said how the French host was a great number of people. 'Well,' said the prince, 'in the name of God let us now study how we shall fight with them at our advantage.' That night the Englishmen lodged in a strong place among hedges, vines and bushes, and their host well watched, and so was the French host.

OF THE ORDER OF THE FRENCHMEN BEFORE THE BATTLE OF POITIERS

On the Sunday in the morning the French king, who had great desire to fight with the Englishmen, heard his mass in his pavilion and was houselled, and his four sons with him. After mass there came to him the duke of Orleans, the duke of Bourbon, the earl of Ponthieu, the lord Jaques of Bourbon, the duke of Athens, constable of France, the earl of Tancarville, the earl of Sarrebruck, the earl of Dammartin, the earl of Ventadour, and divers other great barons of France and of other neighbours holding of France, as the lord Clermont, the lord Arnold d'Audrehem, marshal of France, the lord of Saint-Venant, the lord John of Landas, the lord Eustace Ribemont, the lord Fiennes, the lord Geoffrey of Charny, the lord Chatillon, the lord of Sully, the lord of Nesle, sir Robert Duras and divers other; all these with the king went to counsel. Then finally it was ordained that all manner of men should draw into the field, and every lord to display his banner and to set forth in the name of God and Saint Denis: then trumpets blew up through the host and every man mounted on horseback and went into the field, where they saw the king's banner wave with the wind. There might a been seen great nobless of fair harness and rich armoury of banners and pennons; for there was all the flower of France, there was none durst abide at home without he would be shamed for ever. Then it was ordained by the advice of the constable and marshals to be made three battles, and in each ward sixteen thousand men of arms all mustered and passed for men of arms. The first battle the duke of Orleans to govern, with thirty-six banners and twice as many pennons, the second the duke of Normandy and his two brethren the lord Louis and the lord John, the third the king himself: and while that these battles were setting in array, the king called to him the lord Eustace Ribemont, the lord John of Landas and the lord Richard of Beaujeu, and said to them: 'Sirs, ride on before to see the dealing of the Englishmen and advise well what number they be and by what means we may fight with them, other afoot or a-horseback.' These three knights rode forth and the king was on a white courser and said a-high to his men: 'Sirs, among you, when ye be at Paris, at Chartres, at Rouen or at Orleans, then ye do threat the Englishmen and desire to be in arms out against them. Now ye be come thereto: I shall now shew you them: now shew forth your evil will that ye bear them and revenge your displeasures and damages that they have done you, for without doubt we shall fight with them.' Such as heard him said: 'Sir, in God's name so be it; that would we see gladly.'

Therewith the three knights returned again to the king, who demanded of them tidings. Then sir Eustace of Ribemont answered for all and said: 'Sir, we have seen the Englishmen: by estimation they be two thousand men of arms and four thousand archers and a fifteen hundred of other. Howbeit they be in a strong place, and as far as we can imagine they are in one battle; howbeit they be wisely ordered, and along the way they have fortified strongly the hedges and bushes: one part of their archers are along by the hedge, so that none can go nor ride that way, but must pass by them, and that way must ye go an ye purpose to fight with them. In this hedge there is but one entry and one issue by likelihood that four horsemen may ride afront. At the end of this hedge, whereas no man can go nor ride, there be men of arms afoot and archers afore them in manner of a herse, so that they will not be lightly discomfited.' 'Well,' said the king, 'what will ye then counsel us to do?' Sir Eustace said: 'Sir, let us all be afoot, except three hundred men of arms, well horsed, of the best in your host and most hardiest, to the intent they somewhat to break and to open the archers, and then your battles to follow on quickly afoot and so to fight with their men of arms hand to hand. This is the best advice that I can give you: if any other think any other way better, let him speak.' The king said: 'Thus shall it be done': then the two marshals rode from battle to battle and chose out a three hundred knights and squires of the most expert men of arms of all the host, every man well armed and horsed. Also it was ordained that the battles of Almains should abide still on horseback to comfort the marshals, if need were, whereof the earl of Sarrebruck, the earl of Nidau and the earl of Nassau were captains. King John of France was there armed, and twenty other in his apparel; and he did put the guiding of his eldest son to the lord of Saint-Venant, the lord of Landas and the lord Thibault

of Vaudenay; and the lord Arnold of Cervolles, called the archpriest, was armed in the armour of the young earl of Alencon.

HOW THE CARDINAL OF PERIGORD TREATED TO MAKE AGREEMENT BETWEEN THE FRENCH KING AND THE PRINCE BEFORE THE BATTLE OF POITIERS

When the French king's battles was ordered and every lord under his banner among their own men, then it was commanded that every man should cut their spears to a five foot long and every man to put off their spurs. Thus as they were ready to approach, the cardinal of Perigord came in great haste to the king. He came the same morning from Poitiers; he kneeled down to the king and held up his hands and desired him for God's sake a little to abstain setting forward till he had spoken with him: then he said: 'Sir, ye have here all the flower of your realm against a handful of Englishmen as to regard your company, and, sir, if ye may have them accorded to you without battle, it shall be more profitable and honourable to have them by that manner rather than to adventure so noble chivalry as ye have here present. Sir, I require you in the name of God and humility that I may ride to the prince and shew him what danger ye have him in.' The king said: 'It pleaseth me well, but return again shortly.' The cardinal departed and diligently he rode to the prince, who was among his men afoot: then the cardinal alighted and came to the prince, who received him courteously. Then the cardinal after his salutation made he said: 'Certainly, fair son, if you and your council advise justly the puissance of the French king, ye will suffer me to treat to make a peace between you, an I may.' The prince, who was young and lusty, said: 'Sir, the honour of me and of my people saved, I would gladly fall to any reasonable way.' Then the cardinal said: 'Sir, ye say well, and I shall accord you, an I can; for it should be great pity if so many noblemen and other as be here on both parties should come together by battle.' Then the cardinal rode again to the king and said: 'Sir, ye need not to make any great haste to fight with your enemies, for they cannot fly from you though they would, they be in such a ground: wherefore, sir, I require you forbear for this day till tomorrow the sun-rising.' The king was loath to agree thereto, for some of his council would not consent to it; but finally the cardinal shewed such reasons, that the king accorded that respite: and in the same place there was pight up a pavilion of red silk fresh and rich, and gave leave for that day every man to draw to their lodgings except the constable's and marshals' battles.

That Sunday all the day the cardinal travailed in riding from the one host to the other gladly to agree them: but the French king would not agree without he might have four of the principallest of the Englishmen at his pleasure, and the prince and all the other to yield themselves simply: howbeit there were many great offers made. The prince offered to render into the king's hands all that ever he had won in that voyage, towns and castles, and to quit all prisoners that he or any of his men had taken in that season, and also to swear not to be armed against the French king in seven year after; but the king and his council would none thereof: the uttermost that he would do was, that the prince and a hundred of his knights should yield themselves into the king's prison; otherwise he would not: the which the prince would in no wise agree unto.

In the mean season that the cardinal rode thus between the hosts in trust to do some good, certain knights of France and of England both rode forth the same Sunday, because it was truce for that day, to coast the hosts and to behold the dealing of their enemies. So it fortuned that the lord John Chandos rode the same day coasting the French host, and in like manner the lord of Clermont, one of the French marshals, had ridden forth and aviewed the state of the English host; and as these two knights returned towards their hosts, they met together: each of them bare one manner of device, a blue lady embroidered in a sunbeam above on their apparel. Then the lord Clermont said: 'Chandos, how long have ye taken on you to bear my device?' 'Nay, ye bear mine,' said Chandos, 'for it is as well mine as yours.' 'I deny that,' said Clermont, 'but an it were not for the truce this day between us, I should make it good on you incontinent that ye have no right to bear my device.' 'Ah, sir,' said Chandos, 'ye shall find me to-morrow ready to defend you and to prove by feat of arms that it is as well mine as yours.' Then Clermont said: 'Chandos, these be well the words of you Englishmen, for ye can devise nothing of new, but all that ye see is good and fair.' So they departed without any more doing, and each of them returned to their host.

The cardinal of Perigord could in no wise that Sunday make any agreement between the parties, and when it was near night he returned to Poitiers. That night the Frenchmen took their ease; they had provision enough, and the Englishmen had great default; they could get no forage, nor they could not depart thence without danger of their enemies. That Sunday the Englishmen made great dikes and hedges about their archers, to be the more stronger; and on the Monday in the morning the prince and his company were ready apparelled as they were before, and about the sun-rising in like manner were the Frenchmen. The same morning betimes the cardinal came again to the French host and thought by his preaching to pacify the parties; but then the Frenchmen said to him: 'Return whither ye will: bring hither no more words of treaty nor peace: and ye love yourself depart shortly.' When the cardinal saw that he travailed in vain, he took leave of the king and then he went to the prince and said: 'Sir, do what ye can: there is no remedy but to abide the battle, for I can find none accord in the French king.' Then the prince said: 'The same is our intent and all our people: God help the right!' So the cardinal returned to Poitiers. In his company there were certain knights and squires, men of arms, who were more favourable to the French king than to the prince: and when they saw that the parties should fight, they stale from their masters and went to the French host; and they made their captain the chatelain of Amposte, who was as then there with the cardinal, who knew nothing thereof till he was come to Poitiers.

The certainty of the order of the Englishmen was shewed to the French king, except they had ordained three hundred men a-horseback and as many archers a-horseback to coast under covert of the mountain and to strike into the battle of the duke of Normandy, who was under the mountain afoot. This ordinance they had made of new, that the Frenchmen knew not of. The prince was with his battle down among the vines and had closed in the weakest part with their carriages.

Now will I name some of the principal lords and knights that were there with the prince: the earl of Warwick, the earl of Suffolk, the earl of Salisbury, the earl of Oxford, the lord Raynold Cobham, the lord Spencer, the lord James Audley, the lord Peter his brother, the lord Berkeley, the lord Bassett, the lord Warin, the lord Delaware, the lord Manne, the lord Willoughby, the lord Bartholomew de Burghersh, the lord of Felton, the lord Richard of Pembroke, the lord Stephen of Cosington, the lord Bradetane and other Englishmen; and of Gascon there was the lord of Pommiers, the lord of Languiran, the captal of Buch, the lord John of Caumont, the lord de Lesparre, the lord of Rauzan, the lord of Condon, the lord of Montferrand, the lord of Landiras, the lord soudic of Latrau and other that I cannot name; and of Hainowes the lord Eustace d'Aubrecicourt, the lord John of Ghistelles, and two other strangers, the lord Daniel Pasele and the lord Denis of Morbeke: all the prince's company passed not an eight thousand men one and other, and the Frenchmen were a sixty thousand fighting men, whereof there were more than three thousand knights.

OF THE BATTLE OF POITIERS BETWEEN THE PRINCE OF WALES AND THE FRENCH KING

When the prince saw that he should have battle and that the cardinal was gone without any peace or truce making, and saw that the French king did set but little store by him, he said then to his men: 'Now, sirs, though we be but a small company as in regard to the puissance of our enemies, let us not be abashed therefor; for the victory lieth not in the multitude of people, but whereas God will send it. If it fortune that the journey be ours, we shall be the most honoured people of all the world; and if we die in our right quarrel, I have the king my father and brethren, and also ye have good friends and kinsmen; these shall revenge us. Therefore, sirs, for God's sake I require you do your devoirs this day; for if God be pleased and Saint George, this day ye shall see me a good knight.' These words and such other that the prince spake comforted all his people. The lord sir John Chandos that day never went from the prince, nor also the lord James Audley of a great season; but when he saw that they should needs fight, he said to the prince: 'Sir, I have served always truly my lord your father and you also, and shall do as long as I live. I say this because I made once a vow that the first battle that other the king your father or any of his children should be at, how that I would be one of the first setters on, or else to die in the pain: therefore

I require your grace, as in reward for any service that ever I did to the king your father or to you, that you will give me licence to depart from you and to set myself thereas I may accomplish my vow.' The prince accorded to his desire and said, 'Sir James, God give you this day that grace to be the best knight of all other,' and so took him by the hand. Then the knight departed from the prince and went to the foremost front of all the battles, all only accompanied with four squires, who promised not to fail him. This lord James was a right sage and a valiant knight, and by him was much of the host ordained and governed the day before. Thus sir James was in front of the battle ready to fight with the battle of the marshals of France. In like wise the lord Eustace d'Aubrecicourt did his pain to be one of the foremost to set on. When sir James Audley began to set forward to his enemies, it fortuned to sir Eustace d'Aubrecicourt as ye shall hear after. Ye have heard before how the Almains in the French host were appointed to be still a-horseback. Sir Eustace being a-horseback laid his spear in the rest and ran into the French battle, and then a knight of Almaine, called the lord Louis of Recombes, who bare a shield silver, five roses gules, and sir Eustace bare ermines, two branches of gules,—when this Almain saw the lord Eustace come from his company, he rode against him and they met so rudely, that both knights fell to the earth. The Almain was hurt in the shoulder, therefore he rose not so quickly as did sir Eustace, who when he was up and had taken his breath, he came to the other knight as he lay on the ground; but then five other knights of Almaine came on him all at once and bare him to the earth, and so perforce there he was taken prisoner and brought to the earl of Nassau, who as then took no heed of him; and I cannot say whether they sware him prisoner or no, but they tied him to a chare and there let him stand.

Then the battle began on all parts, and the battles of the marshals of France approached, and they set forth that were appointed to break the array of the archers. They entered a-horseback into the way where the great hedges were on both sides set full of archers. As soon as the men of arms entered, the archers began to shoot on both sides and did slay and hurt horses and knights, so that the horses when they felt the sharp arrows they would in no wise go forward, but drew aback and flang and took on so fiercely, that many of them fell on their masters, so that for press they could not rise again; insomuch that the marshals' battle could never come at the prince. Certain knights and squires that were well horsed passed through the archers and thought to approach to the prince, but they could not. The lord James Audley with his four squires was in the front of that battle and there did marvels in arms, and by great prowess he came and fought with sir Arnold d'Audrehem under his own banner, and there they fought long together and sir Arnold was there sore handled. The battle of the marshals began to disorder by reason of the shot of the archers with the aid of the men of arms, who came in among them and slew of them and did what they list, and there was the lord Arnold d'Audrehem taken prisoner by other men than by sir James Audley or by his four squires; for that day he never took prisoner, but always fought and went on his enemies.

Also on the French party the lord John Clermont fought under his own banner as long as he could endure: but there he was beaten down and could not be relieved nor ransomed, but was slain without mercy: some said it was because of the words that he had the day before to sir John Chandos. So within a short space the marshals' battles were discomfited, for they fell one upon another and could not go forth; and the Frenchmen that were behind and could not get forward reculed back and came on the battle of the duke of Normandy, the which was great and thick and were afoot, but anon they began to open behind; for when they knew that the marshals' battle was discomfited, they took their horses and departed, he that might best. Also they saw a rout of Englishmen coming down a little mountain a-horseback, and many archers with them, who brake in on the side of the duke's battle. True to say, the archers did their company that day great advantage; for they shot so thick that the Frenchmen wist not on what side to take heed, and little and little the Englishmen won ground on them.

And when the men of arms of England saw that the marshals' battle was discomfited and that the duke's battle began to disorder and open, they leapt then on their horses, the which they had ready by them: then they assembled together and cried, 'Saint George! Guyenne!' and the lord Chandos said to the prince: 'Sir, take your horse and ride forth; this journey is yours: God is this day in your hands: get us to the French king's battle, for

their lieth all the sore of the matter. I think verily by his valiantness he will not fly: I trust we shall have him by the grace of God and Saint George, so he be well fought withal: and, sir, I heard you say that this day I should see you a good knight.' The prince said, 'Let us go forth; ye shall not see me this day return back,' and said, 'Advance, banner, in the name of God and of Saint George.' The knight that bare it did his commandment: there was then a sore battle and a perilous, and many a man overthrown, and he that was once down could not be relieved again without great succour and aid. As the prince rode and entered in among his enemies, he saw on his right hand in a little bush lying dead the lord Robert of Duras and his banner by him, and a ten or twelve of his men about him. Then the prince said to two of his squires and to three archers: 'Sirs, take the body of this knight on a targe and bear him to Poitiers, and present him from me to the cardinal of Perigord, and say how I salute him by that token.' And this was done. The prince was informed that the cardinal's men were on the field against him, the which was not pertaining to the right order of arms, for men of the church that cometh and goeth for treaty of peace ought not by reason to bear harness nor to fight for neither of the parties; they ought to be indifferent: and because these men had done so, the prince was displeased with the cardinal, and therefore he sent unto him his nephew the lord Robert of Duras dead: and the chatelain of Amposte was taken, and the prince would have had his head stricken off because he was pertaining to the cardinal, but then the lord Chandos said: 'Sir, suffer for a season: intend to a greater matter: and peradventure the cardinal will make such excuse that ye shall be content.'

Then the prince and his company dressed them on the battle of the duke of Athens, constable of France. There was many a man slain and cast to the earth. As the Frenchmen fought in companies, they cried, 'Mountjoy! Saint Denis!' and the Englishmen, 'Saint George! Guyenne!' Anon the prince with his company met with the battle of Almains, whereof the earl of Sarrebruck, the earl Nassau and the earl Nidau were captains, but in a short space they were put to flight: the archers shot so wholly together that none durst come in their dangers: they slew many a man that could not come to no ransom: these three earls was there slain, and divers other knights and squires of their company, and there was the lord d'Aubrecicourt rescued by his own men and set on horseback, and after he did that day many feats of arms and took good prisoners. When the duke of Normandy's battle saw the prince approach, they thought to save themselves, and so the duke and the king's children, the earl of Poitiers and the earl of Touraine, who were right young, believed their governors and so departed from the field, and with them more than eight hundred spears, that strake no stroke that day. Howbeit the lord Guichard d'Angle and the lord John of Saintre, who were with the earl of Poitiers, would not fly, but entered into the thickest press of the battle. The king's three sons took the way to Chauvigny, and the lord John of Landas and the lord Thibauld of Vaudenay, who were set to await on the duke of Normandy, when they had brought the duke a long league from the battle, then they took leave of the duke and desired the lord of Saint-Venant that he should not leave the duke, but to bring him in safeguard, whereby he should win more thank of the king than to abide still in the field. Then they met also the duke of Orleans and a great company with him, who were also departed from the field with clear hands: there were many good knights and squires, though that their masters departed from the field, yet they had rather a died than to have had any reproach.

Then the king's battle came on the Englishmen: there was a sore fight and many a great stroke given and received. The king and his youngest son met with the battle of the English marshals, the earl of Warwick and the earl of Suffolk, and with them of Gascons the captal of Buch, the lord of Pommiers, the lord Amery of Tastes, the lord of Mussidan, the lord of Languiran and the lord de Latrau. To the French party there came time enough the lord John of Landas and the lord of Vaudenay; they alighted afoot and went into the king's battle, and a little beside fought the duke of Athens, constable of France, and a little above him the duke of Bourbon and many good knights of Bourbonnais and of Picardy with him, and a little on the one side there were the Poitevins, the lord de Pons, the lord of Partenay, the lord of Dammartin, the lord of Tannay-Bouton, the lord of Surgieres, the lord John Saintre, the lord Guichard d'Angle, the lord Argenton, the lord of Linieres, the lord of Montendre and divers other, also the viscount of Rochechouart and the earl of Aunay; and of Burgoyne the lord James of Beaujeu, the lord de Chateau-Vilain and other: in another part there was the earl of Ventadour and of Montpensier, the lord James of Bourbon, the lord John d'Artois and also the lord James his brother, the lord Arnold of Cervolles, called the archpriest, armed for the young earl of Alencon; and of Auvergne there was the lord of Mercoeur, the lord de la Tour, the lord of Chalencon, the lord of Montaigu, the lord of Rochfort, the lord d'Acier, the lord d'Acon; and of Limousin there was the lord de Melval, the lord of Mareuil, the lord of Pierrebuffiere; and of Picardy there was the lord William of Nesle, the lord Arnold of Rayneval, the lord Geoffrey of Saint-Dizier, the lord of Chauny, the lord of Helly, the lord of Montsault, the lord of Hangest and divers other: and also in the king's battle there was the earl Douglas of Scotland, who fought a season right valiantly, but when he saw the discomfiture, he departed and saved himself; for in no wise he would be taken of the Englishmen, he had rather been there slain. On the English part the lord James Audley with the aid of his four squires fought always in the chief of the battle: he was sore hurt in the body and in the visage: as long as his breath served him he fought; at last at the end of the battle his four squires took and brought him out of the field and laid him under a hedge side for to refresh him; and they unarmed him and bound up his wounds as well as they could. On the French party king John was that day a full right good knight: if the fourth part of his men had done their devoirs as well as he did, the journey had been his by all likelihood. Howbeit they were all slain and taken that were there, except a few that saved themselves, that were with the king. There was slain the duke Peter of Bourbon, the lord Guichard of Beaujeu, the lord of Landas, and the duke of Athens, constable of France, the bishop of Chalons in Champagne, the lord William of Nesle, the lord Eustace of Ribemont, the lord de la Tour, the lord William of Montaigu, sir Grismouton of Chambly, sir Baudrin de la Heuse, and many other, as they fought by companies; and there were taken prisoners the lord of Vaudenay, the lord of Pompadour, and the archpriest, sore hurt, the earl of Vaudimont, the earl of Mons, the earl of Joinville, the earl of Vendome, sir Louis of Melval, the lord Pierrebuffiere and the lord of Serignac: there were at that brunt, slain and taken more than two hundred knights.

OF TWO FRENCHMEN THAT FLED FROM THE BATTLE OF POITIERS AND TWO ENGLISHMEN THAT FOLLOWED THEM

Among the battles, recounterings, chases and pursuits that were made that day in the field, it fortuned so to sir Oudart of Renty that when he departed from the field because he saw the field was lost without recovery, he thought not to abide the danger of the Englishmen; wherefore he fled all alone and was gone out of the field a league, and an English knight pursued him and ever cried to him and said, 'Return again, sir knight, it is a shame to fly away thus.'

Then the knight turned, and the English knight thought to have stricken him with his spear in the targe, but he failed, for sir Oudart swerved aside from the stroke, but he failed not the English knight, for he strake him such a stroke on the helm with his sword, that he was astonied and fell from his horse to the earth and lay still. Then sir Oudart alighted and came to him or he could rise, and said, 'Yield you, rescue or no rescue, or else I shall slay you.' The Englishman yielded and went with him, and afterward was ransomed. Also it fortuned that another squire of Picardy called John de Hellenes was fled from the battle and met with his page, who delivered him a new fresh horse, whereon he rode away alone. The same season there was in the field the lord Berkeley of England, a young lusty knight, who the same day reared his banner, and he all alone pursued the said John of Hellenes. And when he had followed the space of a league, the said John turned again and laid his sword in the rest instead of a spear, and so came running toward the lord Berkeley, who lift up his sword to have stricken the squire; but when he saw the stroke come, he turned from it, so that the Englishman lost his stroke and John strake him as he passed on the arm, that the lord Berkeley's sword fell into the field. When he saw his sword down, he lighted suddenly off his horse and came to the place where his sword lay, and as he stooped down to take up his sword, the French squire did pike his sword at him, and by hap strake him through both the thighs, so that the knight fell to the earth and could not help himself. And John alighted off his horse and took the knight's sword that lay on the ground, and came to him and demanded if he would yield him or not. The knight then demanded his name. 'Sir,' said he, 'I hight John of Hellenes; but what is your name?' 'Certainly,' said the knight, 'my name is Thomas and am lord of Berkeley, a fair castle on the river of Severn in the marches of Wales.' 'Well, sir,' quoth the squire, 'then ye shall be my prisoner, and I shall bring you in safe-guard and I shall see that you shall be healed of your hurt.' 'Well,' said the knight, 'I am content to be your prisoner, for ye have by law of arms won me.' There he sware to be his prisoner, rescue or no rescue. Then the squire drew forth the sword out of the knight's thighs and the wound was open: then he wrapped and bound the wound and set him on his horse and so brought him fair and easily to Chatelleraut, and there tarried more than fifteen days for his sake and did get him remedy for his hurt: and when he was somewhat amended, then he gat him a litter and so brought him at his ease to his house in Picardy. There he was more than a year till he was perfectly whole; and when he departed he paid for his ransom six thousand nobles, and so this squire was made a knight by reason of the profit that he had of the lord Berkeley.

HOW KING JOHN WAS TAKEN PRISONER AT THE BATTLE OF POITIERS

Oftentimes the adventures of amours and of war are more fortunate and marvellous than any man can think or wish. Truly this battle, the which was near to Poitiers in the fields of Beauvoir and Maupertuis, was right great and perilous, and many deeds of arms there was done the which all came not to knowledge. The fighters on both sides endured much pain: king John with his own hands did that day marvels in arms: he had an axe in his hands wherewith he defended himself and fought in the breaking of the press. Near to the king there was taken the earl of Tancarville, sir Jaques of Bourbon earl of Ponthieu, and the lord John of Artois earl of Eu, and a little above that under the banner of the captal of Buch was taken sir Charles of Artois and divers other knights and squires. The chase endured to the gates of Poitiers: there were many slain and beaten down, horse and man, for they of Poitiers closed their gates and would suffer none to enter; wherefore in the street before the gate was horrible murder, men hurt and beaten down. The Frenchmen yielded themselves as far off as they might know an Englishman: there were divers English archers that had four, five or six prisoners: the lord of Pons, a great baron of Poitou, was there slain, and many other knights and squires; and there was taken the earl of Rochechouart, the lord of Dammartin, the lord of Partenay, and of Saintonge the lord of Montendre and the lord John of Saintre, but he was so sore hurt that he had never health after: he was reputed for one of the best knights in France. And there was left for dead among other dead men the lord Guichard d'Angle, who fought that day by the king right valiantly, and so did the lord of Chamy, on whom was great press, because he bare the sovereign banner of the king's: his own banner was also in the field, the which was of gules, three scutcheons silver. So many Englishmen and Gascons come to that part, that perforce they opened the king's battle, so that the Frenchmen were so mingled among their enemies that sometime there was five men upon one gentleman. There was taken the lord of Pompadour and the lord Bartholomew de Burghersh, and there was slain sir Geoffrey of Charny with the king's banner in his hands: also the lord Raynold Cobham slew the earl of Dammartin. Then there was a great press to take the king, and such as knew him cried, 'Sir, yield you, or else ye are but dead.' There was a knight of Saint-Omer's, retained in wages with the king of England, called sir Denis Morbeke, who had served the Englishmen five year before, because in his youth he had forfeited the realm of France for a murder that he did at Saint-Omer's. It happened so well for him, that he was next to the king when they were about to take him: he stept forth into the press, and by strength of his body and arms he came to the French king and said in good French, 'Sir, yield you.' The king beheld the knight and said: 'To whom shall I yield me? Where is my cousin the prince of Wales? If I might see him, I would speak with him.' Denis answered and said: 'Sir, he is not here; but yield you to me and I shall bring you to him. 'Who be you?' quoth the king. 'Sir,' quoth he, 'I am Denis of Morbeke, a knight of Artois; but I serve the king of England because I am banished the realm of France and I have forfeited all that I had there.' Then the king gave him his right gauntlet, saying, 'I yield me to you.' There was a great press about the king, for every man enforced him to say, 'I have taken him,' so that the king could not go forward with his young son the lord Philip with him because of the press.

The prince of Wales, who was courageous and cruel as a lion, took that day great pleasure to fight and to chase his enemies. The lord John Chandos, who was with him, of all that day never left him nor never took heed of taking of any prisoner: then at the end of the battle he said to the prince: 'Sir, it were good that you rested here and set your banner a-high in this bush, that your people may draw hither, for they be sore spread abroad, nor I can see no more banners nor pennons of the French party; wherefore, sir, rest and refresh you, for ye be sore chafed.' Then the prince's banner was set up a-high on a bush, and trumpets and clarions began to sown. Then the prince did off his bassenet, and the knights for his body and they of his chamber were ready about him, and a red pavilion pight up, and then drink was brought forth to the prince and for such lords as were about him, the which still increased as they came from the chase: there they tarried and their prisoners with them. And when the two marshals were come to the prince, he demanded of them if they knew any tiding of the French king. They answered and said: 'Sir, we hear none of certainty, but we think verily he is other dead or taken, for he is not gone out of the battles.' Then the prince said to the earl of Warwick and to sir Raynold Cobham: 'Sirs, I require you go forth and see what ye can know, that at your return ye may shew me the truth.' These two lords took their horses and departed from the prince and rode up a little hill to look about them: then they perceived a flock of men of arms coming together right wearily: there was the French king afoot in great peril, for Englishmen and Gascons were his masters; they had taken him from sir Denis Morbeke perforce, and such as were most of force said, 'I have taken him.' 'Nay,' quoth another, 'I have taken him': so they strave which should have him. Then the French king, to eschew that peril, said: 'Sirs, strive not: lead me courteously, and my son, to my cousin the prince, and strive not for my taking, for I am so great a lord to make you all rich.' The king's words somewhat appeased them; howbeit ever as they went they made riot and brawled for the taking of the king. When the two foresaid lords saw and heard that noise and strife among them, they came to them and said: 'Sirs, what is the matter that ye strive for?' 'Sirs,' said one of them, 'it is for the French king, who is here taken prisoner, and there be more than ten knights and squires that challengeth the taking of him and of his son.' Then the two lords entered into the press and caused every man to draw aback, and commanded them in the prince's name on pain of their heads to make no more noise nor to approach the king no nearer, without they were commanded. Then every man gave room to the lords, and they alighted and did their reverence to the king, and so brought him and his son in peace and rest to the prince of Wales.

OF THE GIFT THAT THE PRINCE GAVE TO THE LORD AUDLEY AFTER THE BATTLE OF POITIERS

As soon as the earl of Warwick and the lord Cobham were departed from the prince, as ye have heard before, then the prince demanded of the knights that were about him for the lord Audley, if any knew anything of him. Some knights that were there answered and said: 'Sir, he is sore hurt and lieth in a litter here beside.' 'By my faith,' said the prince, 'of his hurts I am right sorry: go and know if he may be brought hither, or else I will go and see him thereas he is.' Then two knights came to the lord Audley and said: 'Sir, the prince desireth greatly to see you, other ye must go to him or else he will come to you.' 'Ah, sir,' said the knight, 'I thank the prince when he thinketh on so poor a knight as I am.' Then he called eight of his servants and caused them to bear him in his litter to the place whereas the prince was. Then the prince took him in his arms and kissed him and made him great cheer and said: 'Sir James, I ought greatly to honour you, for by your valiance ye have this day achieved the grace and renown of us all, and ye are reputed for the most valiant of all other.' 'Ah, sir,' said the knight, 'ye say as it pleaseth you: I would it were so: and if I have this day anything advanced myself to serve you and to accomplish the vow that I made, it ought not to be reputed to me any prowess.' 'Sir James,' said the prince, 'I and all ours take you in this journey for the best doer in arms, and to the intent to furnish you the better to pursue the wars, I retain you for ever to be my knight with five hundred marks of yearly revenues, the which I shall assign you on mine heritage in England.' 'Sir,' said the knight, 'God grant me to deserve the great goodness that ye shew me': and so he took his leave of the prince, for he was right feeble, and

so his servants brought him to his lodging. And as soon as he was gone, the earl of Warwick and the lord Cobham returned to the prince and presented to him the French king. The prince made lowly reverence to the king and caused wine and spices to be brought forth, and himself served the king in sign of great love.

HOW THE ENGLISHMEN WON GREATLY AT THE BATTLE OF POITIERS

Thus, this battle was discomfited, as ye have heard, the which was in the fields of Maupertuis a two leagues from Poitiers the twenty-second day of September the year of our Lord MCCCLVI. It begun in the morning and ended at noon, but as then all the Englishmen were not returned from the chase; therefore the prince's banner stood on a bush to draw all his men together, but it was well nigh night or all came from the chase. And as it was reported, there was slain all the flower of France, and there was taken with the king and the lord Philip his son a seventeen earls, beside barons, knights and squires, and slain a five or six thousand of one and other. When every man was come from the chase, they had twice as many prisoners as they were in number in all. Then it was counselled among them because of the great charge and doubt to keep so many, that they should put many of them to ransom incontinent in the field, and so they did: and the prisoners found the Englishmen and Gascons right courteous; there were many that day put to ransom and let go all only on their promise of faith and truth to return again between that and Christmas to Bordeaux with their ransoms. Then that night they lay in the field beside whereas the battle had been: some unarmed them, but not all, and unarmed all their prisoners, and every man made good cheer to his prisoner; for that day whosoever took any prisoner, he was clear his and might quit or ransom him at his pleasure. All such as were there with the prince were all made rich with honour and goods, as well by ransoming of prisoners as by winning of gold, silver, plate, jewels, that was there found: there was no man that did set anything by rich harness, whereof there was great plenty, for the Frenchmen came thither richly beseen, weening to have had the journey for them.

HOW THE LORD JAMES AUDLEY GAVE TO HIS FOUR SQUIRES THE FIVE HUNDRED MARKS OF REVENUES THAT THE PRINCE HAD GIVEN HIM

When sir James Audley was brought to his lodging, then he sent for sir Peter Audley his brother and for the lord Bartholomew of Burghersh, the lord Stephen of Cosington, the lord of Willoughby and the lord Ralph Ferrers, all these were of his lineage, and then he called before him his four squires, that had served him that day well and truly. Then he said to the said lords: 'Sirs, it hath pleased my lord the prince to give me five hundred marks of revenues by year in heritage, for the which gift I have done him but small service with my body. Sirs, behold here these four squires, who hath always served me truly and specially this day: that honour that I have is by their valiantness. Wherefore I will reward them: I give and resign into their hands the gift that my lord the prince hath given me of five hundred marks of yearly revenues, to them and to their heirs for ever, in like manner as it was given me. I clearly disherit me thereof and inherit them without any repeal or condition.' The lords and other that ere there, every man beheld other and said among themselves: 'It cometh of a great nobleness to give this gift.' They answered him with one voice: 'Sir, be it as God will; we shall bear witness in this behalf wheresoever we be come.' Then they departed from him, and some of them went to the prince, who the same night would make a supper to the French king and to the prisoners, for they had enough to do withal, of that the Frenchmen brought with them, for the Englishmen wanted victual before, for some in three days had no bread before.

HOW THE PRINCE MADE A SUPPER TO THE FRENCH KING THE SAME DAY OF THE BATTLE

The same day of the battle at night the prince made a supper in his lodging to the French king and to the most part of the great lords that were prisoners. The prince made the king and his son, the lord James of Bourbon, the lord John d'Artois, the earl of Tancarville, the earl of Estampes, the earl Dammartin, the earl of Joinville and the lord of Partenay to sit all at one board, and other lords, knights and squires at other tables; and always the prince served before the king as humbly as he could, and would not sit at the king's board for any desire that the king could make, but he said he was not sufficient to sit at the table with so great a prince as the king was. But then he said to the king: 'Sir, for God's sake make none evil nor heavy cheer, though God this day did not consent to follow your will; for, sir, surely the king my father shall bear you as much honour and amity as he may do, and shall accord with you so reasonably that ye shall ever be friends together after. And, sir, methinks ye ought to rejoice, though the journey be not as ye would have had it, for this day ye have won the high renown of prowess and have passed this day in valiantness all other of your party. Sir, I say not this to mock you, for all that be on our party, that saw every man's deeds, are plainly accorded by true sentence to give you the prize and chaplet.' Therewith the Frenchmen began to murmur and said among themselves how the prince had spoken nobly, and that by all estimation he should prove a noble man, if God send him life and to persevere in such good fortune.

HOW THE PRINCE RETURNED TO BORDEAUX AFTER THE BATTLE OF POITIERS

When supper was done, every man went to his lodging with their prisoners. The same night they put many to ransom and believed them on their faiths and troths, and ransomed them but easily, for they said they would set no knight's ransom so high, but that he might pay at his ease and maintain still his degree. The next day, when they had heard mass and taken some repast and that everything was trussed and ready, then they took their horses and rode towards Poitiers. The same night there was come to Poitiers the lord of Roye with a hundred spears: he was not at the battle, but he met the duke of Normandy near to Chauvigny, and the duke sent him to Poitiers to keep the town till they heard other tidings. When the lord of Roye knew that the Englishmen were so near coming to the city, he caused every man to be armed and every man to go to his defence to the walls, towers and gates; and the Englishmen passed by without any approaching, for they were so laded with gold, silver and prisoners, that in their returning they assaulted no fortress; they thought it a great deed if they might bring the French king, with their other prisoners and riches that they had won, in safeguard to Bordeaux. They rode but small journeys because of their prisoners and great carriages that they had: they rode in a day no more but four or five leagues and lodged ever betimes, and rode close together in good array saving the marshals' battles, who rode ever before with five hundred men of arms to open the passages as the prince should pass; but they found no encounters, for all the country was so frayed that every man drew to the fortresses.

As the prince rode, it was shewed him how the lord Audley had given to his four squires the gift of the five hundred marks that he had given unto him: then the prince sent for him and he was brought in his litter to the prince, who received him courteously and said: 'Sir James, we have knowledge that the revenues that we gave you, as soon as ye came to your lodging, you gave the same to four squires: we would know why ye did so, and whether the gift was agreeable to you or not.' 'Sir,' said the knight, 'it is of truth I have given it to them, and I shall shew you why I did so. These four squires that be here present have a long season served me well and truly in many great businesses and, sir, in this last battle they served me in such wise that an they had never done nothing else I was bound to reward them, and before the same day they had never nothing of me in reward. Sir, I am but a man alone; but by the aid and comfort of them I took on me to accomplish my vow long before made. I had been dead in the battle an they had not been: wherefore, sir, when I considered the love that they bare unto me, I had not been courteous if I would not a rewarded them. I thank God I have had and shall have enough as long as I live: I will never be abashed for lack of good. Sir, if I have done this without your pleasure, I require you to pardon me, for, sir, both I and my squires shall serve you as well as ever we did.' Then the prince said: 'Sir James, for anything that ye have done I cannot blame you, but can you good thank therefor; and for the valiantness of these squires, whom ye praise so much, I accord to them your gift, and I will render again to you six hundred marks in like manner as ye had the other.'

Thus the prince and his company did so much that they passed through Poitou and Saintonge without damage and came to Blaye, and there passed the river of Gironde and arrived in the good city of Bordeaux. It cannot be recorded the great feast and cheer that they of the city with the clergy made to the prince, and how honour-

ably they were there received. The prince brought the French king into the abbey of Saint Andrew's, and there they lodged both, the king in one part and the prince in the other. The prince bought of the lords, knights and squires of Gascoyne the most part of the earls of the realm of France, such as were prisoners, and paid ready money for them. There was divers questions and challenges made between the knights and squires of Gascoyne for taking of the French king; howbeit Denis Morbeke by right of arms and by true tokens that he shewed challenged him for his prisoner. Another squire of Gascoyne called Bernard of Truttes said how he had right to him: there was much ado and many words before the prince and other lords that were there, and because these two challenged each other to fight in that quarrel, the prince caused the matter to rest till they came in England and that no declaration should be made but afore the king of England his father; but because the French king himself aided to sustain the challenge of Denis Morbeke, for he inclined more to him than to any other, the prince therefore privily caused to be delivered to the said sir Denis two thousand nobles to maintain withal his estate.

Anon after the prince came to Bordeaux, the cardinal of Perigord came thither, who was sent from the pope in legation, as it was said. He was there more than fifteen days or the prince would speak with him because of the chatelain of Amposte and his men, who were against him in the battle of Poitiers. The prince believed that the cardinal sent them thither, but the cardinal did so much by the means of the lord of Caumont, the lord of Montferrand and the captal of Buch, who were his cousins, they shewed so good reasons to the prince, that he was content to hear him speak. And when he was before the prince, he excused himself so sagely that the prince and his council held him excused, and so he fell again into the prince's love and redeemed out his men by reasonable ransoms; and the chatelain was set to his ransom of ten thousand franks, the which he paid after. Then the cardinal began to treat on the deliverance of the French king, but I pass it briefly because nothing was done. Thus the prince, the Gascons and Englishmen tarried still at Bordeaux till it was Lent in great mirth and revel, and spent foolishly the gold and silver that they had won. In England also there was great joy when they heard tidings of the battle of Poitiers, of the discomfiting of the Frenchmen and taking of the king: great solemnities were made in all churches and great fires and wakes throughout all England. The knights and squires, such as were come home from that journey, were much made of and praised more than other.

GLOSSARY

anon: in a short time, soon

currours: English light cavalry

devoirs: respects or compliments

gule: a tincture red

houselled: given communion

pennon: a long triangular flag, generally carried to identify a knight

puissance: power, might, force

scutcheon: a shield or similar surface on which a coat of arms is shown; also escutcheon

sixscore: six groups of twenty (a score), or 120

targe: a shield

thitherward: to or toward that place or point

troths: pledges or oaths of fidelity; loyalty

weening: thinking, supposing

Document Analysis

Froissart's *Chronicles* offers an extraordinary level of detail in his depiction of battles fought during the period called the Hundred Years' War. This selection, his description of the Battle of Poitiers, is no exception. Although Froissart was not likely an eyewitness to such battles, he interviewed numerous witnesses and compiled a record that, while not a completely accurate historical source, provides much of the detail of what is known of the chivalric battles of the Hundred Years' War. Froissart recorded chivalric war at its height, with its complex rules of behavior and its celebration of honor and ceremony.

This passage begins with a description of the chase that led to the Battle of Poitiers. The scene is set, as the French knights pursue the English, who are strategically retreating after their destructive raids across the French countryside. Froissart writes for a noble audience, and though his language is engaging and active, he pays a great deal of attention to the action and motivation of the elites, giving less space to a description of common soldiers or the French people. He glorifies the knights on both sides as they meet to set out he terms of battle: "There might a been seen great nobless of fair harness and rich armoury of banners and pennons; for there was all the flower of France, there was none durst abide at home without he would be shamed for ever." The nobility of France, in order to prove their honor, want to go into battle, and Froissart vividly describes the armor, the noise as trumpets blared, the appearance of King John II, and the banners waving in the breeze, setting the scene for the battle to follow.

Froissart describes the attempts to prevent the battle in almost as much detail as the battle itself. The cardinal of Perigord approaches the French king, who all assume would be the clear winner, and argues that it is against the laws of chivalry to attack a force that was so inferior to his own, and he should not risk his own noblemen. He persuades John to let him appeal to "the prince" (Edward). The English prince claims he will "gladly fall to any reasonable way" to avoid fighting, and so the cardinal secures a day of negotiations. However, this proves fruitless, as John demands complete surrender, while Edward offers only the return of his spoils and a promise of peace for seven years.

Froissart subtly suggests that the king's determination to go into battle leads him to act rashly, ultimately costing him the victory and the lives of many of his men. The description of the battle itself focuses in detail on the actions of particular knights, particularly their chivalric response to being taken prisoner and heroic or cowardly conduct during battle. Froissart also offers a broad description of the overall course of the battle, but the hierarchical, deeply structured performance of chivalric battle takes center stage. The capture of King John is explained in detail, as is the aftermath of the battle and the extent of the victory for the English.

Essential Themes

The conflict between the French and the English would continue despite the capture of the French king, but the Battle of Poitiers marked the end of the initial phase of the Hundred Years' War. The English would win another major victory at the Battle of Agincourt, again using archers to overcome a numerical disadvantage. However, France would regain most of its lost territory by 1453. The long conflict had a lasting effect on the formation of the modern nations of England and France.

The primary theme of this selection is the importance of behavior that followed the rules of chivalric warfare. Froissart was a chronicler not of strictly historical events, but of the nobility of France and England and, in particular, how they behaved throughout the Hundred Years' War. The chivalric conduct of battle, and all of the ceremony and tradition around it, was more important, in some sense, than the outcome of a particular engagement. He names and describes the nobility in great detail and focuses on their conduct on the battlefield and, in some cases, their capture or death. For this reason, the *Chronicles* has served as an invaluable source of information on medieval social life and etiquette as well as a somewhat flawed and biased description of actual events.

—*Bethany Groff, MA*

Bibliography and Additional Reading

Corrigan, Gordon. *A Great and Glorious Adventure: A History of the Hundred Years War and the Birth of Renaissance* England. New York: Pegasus, 2014. Print.

Given-Wilson, *Chris. Chronicles: The Writing of History in Medieval England.* New York: Hambledon, 2004. Print.

Tuchman, Barbara W. *A Distant Mirror: The Calamitous Fourteenth Century.* New York: Random, 2014. Print.

■ Excerpts from *The Book of the City of Ladies*

Date: 1405
Author: Christine de Pizan
Country: France

Summary Overview

These are two passages from the late medieval French writer Christine de Pizan's classic *The Book of the City of Ladies,* written in praise of the good qualities of women and against the misogyny common among medieval elites. In the first passage, Christine voices support for the education of women, citing classical examples and arguing against the commonly held idea that education made women less virtuous. In the second, she argues against the misogynist cliché that woman are inconstant (fickle) by pointing out that men are just as inconstant, if not more so, and much of women's inconstancy is the fault of men anyway. She employs the classical examples of two Roman emperors to demonstrate that even men in the highest stations are subject to inconstancy.

Defining Moment

The fourteenth century saw the beginning of the revival of interest in the lives and works of the ancient Greeks and Romans known as the humanist movement. Individualism, secularism, and the arts began to flourish as economic conditions improved for a larger section of the European population. This shift away from medieval traditions eventually led to the Renaissance. Italy, where Christine was born, was at the heart of humanism.

The period was also a time of refinement of court culture in northern Europe, particularly in France and Burgundy. Kings and nobles collected and displayed fine books as status symbols, helping to fuel a market for literature. Debates about women were also prominent in court culture, partly due to the continuing popularity of poem *The Romance of the Rose*, begun around 1225 by Guillaume de Lorris and continued in 1280 by Jean de Meun. It combined an allegorical presentation of a love affair with denunciations of female inconstancy. Much of Christine's early work, including *The Book of the City*

of Ladies, was in part a response to and critique of the *Romance of the Rose*.

Author Biography

Christine de Pizan was born in 1354 in Venice, where her father, Thomas de Pizan, was a physician, astrologer, and councilor in the Venetian government. Thomas encouraged his daughter's intellectual interests. He relocated to France along with Christine and the rest of his family when he was offered the position of astrologer to the French king Charles V (1338–1380). There, at the age of fifteen, Christine married a French royal official, Etienne de Castel, who supported his wife's education, despite the rarity of education for women in the Middle Ages. From what Christine wrote of the marriage later, it seems to have been happy. Despite her Italian origins, she readily adopted French life and culture.

Her husband's death ten years later left Christine with three small children. By that time, her father had also died, and she had to support herself. She may have worked copying manuscripts, as the industry of bookmaking moved out of the monasteries and into commercial scriptoria, which were among the few businesses interested in hiring educated women. By the early fifteenth century, she had become the first woman in Europe known as a professional writer, producing both poetry and prose. She worked in a patronage economy rather than writing for a public market, however, and her works were dedicated to her various noble patrons and reflect the culture of the French nobility. Many survive in richly illustrated editions meant for the wealthy.

Several of Christine's works are notable for refuting the misogyny of much late medieval culture. She joined a convent after 1415, after which she wrote little, and she died around 1430.

HISTORICAL DOCUMENT

Chapter 36.

Against those who say that it is not good for women to be educated.

Following these remarks, I, Christine, spoke, "My lady, I realise that women have accomplished many good things and that even if evil women have done evil, it seems to me, nevertheless, that the benefits accrued and still accruing because of good women—particularly the wise and literary ones and those educated in the natural sciences whom I mentioned above—outweigh the evil. Therefore, I am amazed by the opinion of some men who claim that they do not want their daughters, wives, or kinswomen to be educated because their mores would be ruined as a result."

She responded, "Here you can clearly see that not all opinions of men are based on reason and that these men are wrong. For it must not be presumed that mores necessarily grow worse from knowing the moral sciences, which teach the virtues, indeed, there is not the slightest doubt that moral education amends and ennobles them. How could anyone think or believe that whoever follows good teaching or doctrine is the worse for it? Such an opinion cannot be expressed or maintained. I do not mean that it would be good for a man or a woman to study the art of divination or those fields of learning which are forbidden—for the holy Church did not remove them from common use without good reason – but it should not be believed that women are the worse for knowing what is good. Quintus Hortensius, a great rhetorician and consummately skilled orator in Rome, did not share this opinion. He had a daughter, named Hortensia, whom he greatly loved for the subtlety of her wit. He had her learn letters and study the science of rhetoric, which she mastered so thoroughly that she resembled her father Hortensius not only in wit and lively memory but also in her excellent delivery and order of speech—in fact, he surpassed her in nothing. As for the subject discussed above, concerning the good which comes about through women, the benefits realised by this woman and her teaming were, among others, exceptionally remarkable. That is, during the time when Rome was governed by three men, this Hortensia began to support the cause of women and to undertake what no man dared to undertake. There was a question whether certain taxes should be levied on women and on their jewelry during a needy period in Rome. This woman's eloquence was so compelling that she was listened to, no less readily than her father would have been, and she won her case."

"Similarly, to speak of more recent times, without searching for examples in ancient history, Giovanni Andrea, a solemn law professor in Bologna not quite sixty years ago, was not of the opinion that it was bad for women to be educated. He had a fair and good daughter, named Novella, who was educated in the law to such an advanced degree that when he was occupied by some task and not at leisure to present his lectures to his students, he would send Novella, his daughter, in his place to lecture to the students from his chair. And to prevent her beauty from distracting the concentration of her audience, she had a little curtain drawn in front of her. In this manner she could on occasion supplement and lighten her father's occupation. He loved her so much that, to commemorate her name, he wrote a book of remarkable lectures on the law which he entitled *Novella super Decretalium*, after his daughter's name."

"Thus, not all men (and especially the wisest) share the opinion that it is bad for women to be educated. But it is very true that many foolish men have claimed this because it displeased them that women knew more than they did. Your father, who was a great scientist and philosopher, did not believe that women were worth less by knowing science; rather, as you know, he took great pleasure from seeing your inclination to learning. The feminine opinion of your mother, however, who wished to keep you busy with spinning and silly girlishness, following the common custom of women, was the major obstacle to your being more involved in the sciences. But just as the proverb already mentioned above says, 'No one can take away what Nature has given,' your mother could not hinder in you the feeling for the sciences which you, through natural inclination, had nevertheless gathered together in little droplets. I am sure that, on account of these things, you do not think you are worth less but rather that you consider it a great treasure for yourself; and you doubtless have reason to."

And I, Christine, replied to all of this, "Indeed, my lady, what you say is as true as the Lord's Prayer."

Chapter 47.

Christine speaks of evidence against what is said about the inconstancy of women, and then Lady Rectitude in her answer mentions the inconstancy and frailty of certain emperors.

"My Lady, you certainly tell me about wonderful constancy, strength and virtue and firmness of women, so can one say the same thing about men? And yet, among all the vices that men, and their books too, cry out with one voice that are in women, it is always said that they are changeable and inconstant, fickle and light and of frail spirit, darting about like children, that there is no firmness in them at all. Are men then so constant that any change of mind is entirely outside their habits, or not common to them, that they so accuse women of inconstancy? And surely, if they are not firm, it is ugly of them to accuse another of their own vice or to demand a virtue that they themselves don't possess."

Response: "Fair sweet friend, have you not yet heard the saying that the fool sees well enough a small cut in the face of his neighbour, but he disregards the great gaping one above his own eye? I will show you the great contradiction in what the men say about the changeability and inconstancy of women. It is true that they all generally insist that women are very frail by nature. And since they accuse women of frailty, one would suppose that they themselves take care to maintain a reputation for constancy, or at the very least, that the women are indeed less so than they are themselves. And yet, it is obvious that they demand of women greater constancy than they themselves have, for they who claim to be of this strong and noble condition cannot refrain from a whole number of very great defects and sins, and not out of ignorance, either, but out of pure malice, knowing well how badly they are misbehaving. But all this they excuse in themselves and say that it is in the nature of man to sin, yet if it so happens that any women stray into any misdeed (of which they themselves are the cause by their great power and longhandedness), then it's suddenly all frailty and inconstancy, they claim. But it seems to me that since they do call women frail, they should not support that frailty, and not ascribe to them as a great crime what in themselves they merely consider a little defect. For it is neither the law nor written anywhere else that if they are free to sin, women's vice is any less excusable. But in fact they claim such authority that they do not want to tolerate women, so they do and say, several have suffered much outrage and grievances, nor do they deign to call women strong and constant if they in turn endure their harsh outrages. And so in all respects the men want to be in the right and want both ends of the stick. And of that you have spoken enough in your Letter to the God of Loves.

"But regarding that which you have asked me, whether men are so strong and constant that they have grounds to accuse anyone else of inconstancy, if you look all the way from the ancient times and ages until today, I refer you to the books and to what you have seen in your own age and can see every day with your own eyes, and not among simple men and men of low standing, either. And in the greatest you can see and recognise the perfection, strength, and constancy they have, and see how widespread is for the most part the dire need of wise, constant and strong men.

"And if you want me to give you proof from this time and ancient times to see why, if in men's spirit there truly is neither inconstancy nor fickleness, they so accuse women of this vice, look at the most powerful princes and greatest men, who weigh more than others. What can I tell you about the emperors? I ask you where there was ever such frail spirit in a woman, so much weakness or meanness, or if any was ever less constant than the emperor Claudius? He was so fickle that whatever he ordered at one hour, he despised at another, and never was any firmness found in his words. He agreed with any counsel. He had his wife killed by his own folly and cruelty, and then in the evening he wanted to know why she did not come to bed. And he sent to his relatives, whose testicles he had had cut off, so that they would come and play with him. He was of so miserable courage that at times he trembled and fled for nothing. What shall I tell you? All bad things pertaining to morals and spirit were in this miserable emperor. But why am I telling you this? Was he the only one in the empire who was so full of frailty? The emperor Tiberius, how much better was he? All inconstancy, all changeability, all fickleness, was there not more of it in him than in any woman?"

GLOSSARY

longhandedness: an antiquated phrase for "talking a lot"

mores: ways of living that are accepted without question and embody the moral views of a group

Document Analysis

Christine attacks the typical literature of the day by arguing that women have an equal, if not superior, claim with men to virtue and learning. These passages do not take on religious arguments based on blaming Eve for the Fall of Man, but deal with secular arguments and claims. (Christine does deal with religious issues elsewhere in *The Book of the City of Ladies*.) In the humanist manner, Christine draws upon the examples of ancient Romans, both positive (educated women) and negative (men who exhibited the bad character traits usually ascribed to women). She respects the limitations to learning imposed by the church, but her argument is fundamentally based on observation and ancient authority rather than Christianity.

Unlike many humanist writings, her works are written in French rather than Latin. Vernacular writing was associated with women, as far fewer women than men understood Latin. Christine's work was also aimed at a lay audience, who understood less Latin than the clergy, and she employs the common medieval literary technique of using an interlocutor to avoid presenting herself, the writer, as an authority. In these passages, Christine is a character conversing with two of the Virtues, Lady Reason and Lady Rectitude; Lady Justice appears in later passages. They help construct the titular City of Ladies.

In the first passage, Christine attacks the commonly held belief that learning makes women less virtuous. She instead argues that education, particularly in morality, makes all people more moral. Christine credits her own education to her father and states that her mother wanted her restricted to traditionally feminine tasks. This suggests that men are not the only ones standing in the way of women's getting an education—sometimes other women are, too.

The learning she suggests is appropriate for women includes both studies in humanism, such as moral philosophy, and also those identified with the university, such as law. She uses the example of Novella d'Andrea, a law professor at the University of Bologna, as a woman who was not merely educated, but in turn taught men. (The idea that a woman teacher is so beautiful that she must teach behind a veil to avoid disturbing her male students is a common trope in discussions of woman teachers.) Both the women that Christine discusses at length here, Hortensia (a political activist in ancient Rome) and Novella, are not merely educated women, but women who took on public roles usually reserved for men—Hortensia as a political advocate and Novella as a teacher. Both of them also were educated by their fathers, reflecting Christine's own situation.

The second passage takes on one of the most common misogynistic accusations—that of women's inconstancy, or fickleness. This idea had roots in the ancient world and was frequently voiced in the Middle Ages. Christine turns the accusation around by pointing out the existence of a double standard, and that men are not only inconstant themselves but often the cause of inconstancy in women. They treat their own inconstancy as a minor fault, she claims, while treating women's inconstancy as a major flaw. Christine also invokes examples of men more fickle than any woman, again using humanistic learning about the ancient world. The two examples she chooses are the Roman emperors Tiberius and Claudius, showing that high station is no guard against inconstancy and weakness among men.

Essential Themes

The humanistic Renaissance of which Christine was an early representative in France continued into the sixteenth century. Educated women, frequently encouraged by their fathers as Christine was, were always a part of this movement, but the humanistic education of women did not become as fully institutionalized as that of men. Men maintained a near monopoly on university education (there were a few scattered exceptions over the next few centuries in Christine's home country of Italy, but not in her adopted country of France).

Although the misogynist arguments that Christine refuted in her works continued to be made for centuries and even into the twenty-first century, so too did her refutations. The subsequent centuries in Europe would see repeated *querelles des femmes*, "arguments over women," in which Christine's ideas would be repeated, whether or not the defenders of women were directly inspired by her works. Christine is the earliest woman's voice surviving from this debate.

Christine's many works, which included love poems, a treatise on war, and a verse tribute to Joan of Arc, were popular both in and out of France, translated into several European vernaculars. The twentieth-century feminist revival of interest in women's writing led to numerous biographies and studies of her work. *The Book of the City of Ladies* has become her best-known work, and Christine herself is often identified as the first feminist in the Western tradition.

—*William E. Burns, PhD*

Bibliography and Additional Reading

Brown-Grant, Rosalind. *Christine de Pizan and the Moral Defence of Women: Reading beyond Gender.* Cambridge: Cambridge UP, 2003. Cambridge Studies in Medieval Literature Ser.

Lloyd, Jean. "Christine de Pizan." *Women's History.* King's College, 7 Jul. 2006. Web. 9 June 2015.

Margolis, Nadia. *An Introduction to Christine de Pizan.* Gainesville: UP of Florida, 2012. Print.

Willard, Charity Cannon. *Christine de Pizan: Her Life and Works.* New York: Persea, 1990.

■ Excerpt from *The Treasure of the City of Ladies*

Date: 1405
Author: Christine de Pizan
Country: France
Translator: Sarah Lawson

Summary Overview

In this passage from the educational book *The Treasure of the City of Ladies*, medieval French writer Christine de Pizan provides advice to women of the lower ranks of the aristocracy. In language reminiscent of the description of a virtuous woman from the biblical book of Proverbs, she encourages "ordinary ladies" to take an active role in the overseeing of their households and estates, particularly when their husbands are absent due to wars or travels. Her description of the work that a lady is required to do covers many aspects of a late medieval estate and household. The lady must oversee a variety of agricultural activities, including raising crops, managing viniculture, and tending to livestock. She must also manage the budget and the legal rights and obligations of the property as well as carry out her own work of spinning and weaving. Christine emphasizes that workers need to be constantly supervised because, away from the watchful eye of the mistress, they will not work as hard or as well. She also asserts the necessity of charity to the poor.

Defining Moment

The fourteenth century saw the beginning of the revival of interest in the ancient Greeks and Romans, known as the humanist movement. Italy, where Christine was born, was at the heart of this movement, which would lead eventually into the Enlightenment as society shifted away from medieval traditions. By Christine's time, this movement was being brought to France, partly by Italian transplants like her family. As Europe grew more prosperous, secular and individualist values began to flourish and increased attention was given to art and literature. It was a period of growing interest in books among both men and women of the aristocracy, and writers served mainly noble patrons.

Christine wrote during a time of war when many French noblemen could expect protracted absences from their homes and estates in order to fight on distant battlefields, or for other reasons, such as attending court functions. The Hundred Years' War between England and France was going on, and there were also Crusades in the Middle East and other wars during lulls in the fight against England. The most notable recent Crusade, less than a decade before the publication of *The Treasure of the City of Ladies*, was the one that led to the Battle of Nicopolis in 1396, in which hundreds of French noblemen were killed or taken prisoner, often dying in captivity.

During this time, women's roles in society, no matter what the social class, were dictated by medieval traditions that viewed women as inferior to men. Women were not allowed to study at universities, though some noblewomen became highly educated with family support. Christine, who had gained such an education and supported herself as a writer, had completed *The Book of the City of Ladies* (also in 1405), a history of women and a defense of their rights. She then set out to write a sequel that would serve as a manual to women of all classes on how to live properly.

Author Biography and Document Information

Christine de Pizan was born in 1364 in Venice, but soon moved to France when her father, Thomas de Pizan, was offered the position of astrologer to the French king Charles V (1338–1380). There, at the age of fifteen, Christine married a French royal official, Etienne de Castel. The marriage seems to have been happy, but Castel died in 1390. Impoverished after the death of her father and husband and with children to support, Christine became the first woman on record in European history to support herself as a professional writer. She wrote both poetry and prose for noble patrons, and her later work often rebutted stereotypes about women. She died around 1430, after joining a convent and mostly retiring from writing.

This passage is an excerpt from *The Treasure of the City of Ladies*, also known as *The Book of the Three Virtues*, which served as a sequel to her *Book of the City of Ladies* and was dedicated to Princess Margaret of Burgundy (1393–1442). The three virtues are Reason, Rectitude, and Justice, personified as women who urged Christine to write both books. At least twenty-one copies of *The Treasure* from the fifteenth century survive, eight of which have miniature illustrations.

HISTORICAL DOCUMENT

How ladies and young women who live on their manors ought to manage their households and estates.

There is another condition of rank and of life than that of baronesses that pertains to ordinary ladies and young women living on or off their lands outside fine cities. Because barons and still more commonly knights and squires and gentlemen travel and go off to the wars, their wives should be wise and sound administrators and manage their affairs well, because most of the time they stay at home without their husbands, who are at court or abroad. They should have all the responsibility of the administration and know how to make use of their revenues and possessions. Every lady of such rank (if she is sensible) ought to know how much her annual income is and how much the revenue of her land is worth. This wise lady ought to persuade her husband if she can by kind words and sensible admonitions to agree to discuss their finances together and try to keep to such a standard of living as their income can provide and not so far above it that at the end of the year they find themselves in debt to their own people or other creditors. There is absolutely no shame in living within your income, however small it may be, but there is shame if creditors are always coming to your door to repossess their goods or if they are obliged to make nuisances of themselves to your men or your tenants or if they have to try by hook or by crook to get their payment.

It is proper for such a lady or young woman to be thoroughly knowledgeable about the laws related to fiefs, sub-fiefs, quit rents, champarts , taxes for various causes, and all those sorts of things that are within the jurisdiction of the lordship, according to the customs of the region, so that no one can deceive her about them. Since there are a great many administrators of lands and of noblemen's estates who are quite willing to deceive their masters, she ought to be well versed in all these matters and take care over them. There is nothing dishonourable about making herself familiar with the accounts. She will see them often and wish to know how they are managed in regard to her vassals so that they are not being cheated or incommoded unreasonably, for otherwise it would be a burden on the souls of her and her husband until they made amends for it. Towards poor people a lady should out of love of God, be more compassionate than strict.

In addition, she will do well to be a very good manager of the estate and to know all about the work on the land and at what time and in which season one ought to perform what operations. She should know which way is the best for the furrows to go according to the lay of the land and according to whether it is in a dry or damp region. She should see that the furrows are straight and well made and of the right depth and sown at exactly the right time with such grains as are best for the land. And likewise she should know all about the work of the vineyard if it is a wine-growing area. She ought to make sure that she has good workmen and overseers in these duties and not take people who change masters every quarter, because that is a bad sign. They should be neither too old, for they will be lazy and weak, nor too young, for they will always be larking about.

She is careful to have them get up early but she does not depend on anyone for it, if she is a skillful manager of the estate. She herself rises and puts on a houppeland and busies herself at her window so that she sees them go outside, for if they are lazy, the laziness will most likely be shown in an unwillingness to go out. She should often take time to visit the fields to see how the men are getting on with the work, for there are a good many workers who will gladly abstain from working the land and give it up for the day if they think no one is keeping an eye on them. Some of them are very accomplished at sleeping in the fields in the shade of a tree while letting their horses or oxen graze in the meadow, and then they say in the evening that they have done a day's work. The wise manager of the estate will be on the look-out for these things. Furthermore, when the wheat is ripe from the month of May, she will not wait for an unrealistically high price, but will harvest her crop, having it cut by strong and industrious fellows. She will pay them in cash or in grain, and when the time comes that they are harvesting the grain, she will be careful that they do not leave any wheat behind them or that they do not try any other tricks not mentioned before that such people are apt to get up to. The lady must likewise be attentive to these matters in the other work on the estate.

The lady should get up early in the morning, for in the establishment where the lady usually lies in bed until late it is unlikely that the household will run smoothly. She will busy herself around the house; she will find plenty of orders to give. She will have the animals brought in at the right time, take care how the shepherd looks after them and see that he is in control of them and that he is not cruel, for shepherds sometimes kill them in spite of the mistress or master. She sees that the animals are kept clean, protected from too hot a sun and from the rain and prevented from catching mange. If she is wise she will often go in the evening with one of her women to see how the sheep are being penned up, and thus the shepherd will be more careful that there is nothing for which he may be reproached. She will have him take special care at lambing time and look after the lambs well, for they often tie for lack of attention. The lady will rear the young animals carefully and be present at the shearing and ensure that it is done at the right time of year. In areas where there are broad plains and grazing lands, she will keep a large herd of cattle and grow oats for them to eat, selling a little of it. She will keep oxen in the stable, from which she will make a handsome profit when they are fat. If she has woods, she will keep a breeding stock of horses there, which is a profitable thing for whoever knows how to break and train them.

In the winter-time, she will reflect that labour is cheap, and therefore she will have her men cut her willow or hazel groves and make vine props to sell in the season. She will set her young lads to cutting wood for heating the manor house, but if the weather is too inclement she will have them thresh in the barn. She will never let them be idle, for there is nothing more wasteful in a manor than an idle staff. Likewise, she will employ her women and her chambermaids to attend to the livestock, to feed the workmen, to seed the courtyards and work in the herb garden, even getting covered in mud. She and her girls and young women will occupy themselves in making clothing. They will select the wool, putting the best quality to one side to make fine garments for her and her husband or to sell if she needs to do so. She uses the coarse wool for little children and for her women and household. She will make heavy table covers from the wool, and from the scraps she will have the linens trimmed that her chambermaids will spin and weave on winter evenings. They will also make many other things that are too long to list.

In flat, arable country there is a great need to run an estate well, and the one who is most diligent and careful about it, however great she may be, is more than wise and ought to be highly praised for it. This practice of running the household wisely sometimes renders more profit than the entire income from the land. For example, the Countess of Eu, mother of the fine young count who died on the way to Hungary, was very skilled in this. She was a wise estate manager who felt no shame in occupying herself in the perfectly respectable work of household duties, to the extent that the profit that resulted was worth more annually than all the income from her land. The praise of the virtuous woman recounted in the book of Solomon may be aptly applied to such a woman as this.

GLOSSARY

champarts: taxes in kind levied on peasants by feudal lords as a share of the crop.

GLOSSARY CONTINUED

fief: a tenure of land subject to feudal obligations

houppelande: an outer garment worn by men and women, consisting of a robe with loose, flaring sleeves.

incommoded: inconvenienced or disturbed; troubled

quit rents: rent paid by a freeholder in lieu of services that might otherwise have been required

Document Analysis

Christine's focus in this passage is resolutely practical. She concentrates on the running of the household and the estate, rather than the gathering of wisdom or the care of the soul. Much of what she discusses echoes the Old Testament's Proverbs Chapter 31, the famous description of a virtuous woman. Like the biblical virtuous woman, the woman Christine endorses is a hard worker (indeed, both do the same work of spinning and weaving), a shrewd trader, and charitable to the needy. The values reflected here are not the values of wealth and display characteristic of the high aristocracy, but those of thrift and self-restraint.

In this passage, Christine is not addressing the greatest noblewomen, but women of the lesser nobility— "ordinary ladies and young women living on or off their lands outside fine cities." She assumes that in that class the husband and wife will spend a great deal of time apart, particularly if the husband is fighting in a war or attending court. In that time, it will be necessary for the wife to be the primary administrator of the household and estate. She encourages women to establish themselves as their husband's most trusted associates and to find out the revenues and obligations of the property from their husbands so they will be prepared in his absence. She stresses that being financially literate is not dishonorable and helps one avoid being cheated. She also asserts that being constantly in debt is dishonorable, while operating on a budget, even a small one, should bring no shame.

Christine exhibits a suspicious attitude toward workers, suggesting that they will not work well unless carefully supervised. She suggests that many workers tend to be lazy and will attempt various tricks to get out of work or steal, and a lady must be aware of this and prevent it by frequently checking on them. Christine also suggests that the lady, as the estate manager, must take the responsibility to select the best workers and understand their tasks in order to ensure things run smoothly. This involves everything from hiring workers of the right age and avoiding those who change employers too often to being familiar with the land and specific agricultural techniques.

The ideal woman described in this passage will work herself in addition to supervising workers. The work Christine describes is that which European civilization considered at the time to be women's work—spinning and weaving with the female staff of the manor. Although this is primarily in a household context, to provide clothing for the family, she also mentions production for the market. Christine also puts the work of the lady in a religious context, urging ladies to show charity to the poor and pointing out that unfairness to vassals and tenants would weigh on the souls of both lord and lady.

Essential Themes

Women continued to play an important role in estate management as the Middle Ages gave way to the Renaissance, as the Hundred Years' War lasted until around 1453 and was followed by other conflicts that left many women as heads of households. The debate over women's place in society, known as the *querelle des femmes*, would last for centuries. Meanwhile, the values of thrift, self-discipline, and industry that Christine recommended to the lower nobility would eventually become identified as middle-class or "bourgeois" during the early modern period.

Christine's work was popular in the Middle Ages. Numerous French manuscripts survive, and her work was translated into other vernacular languages, such as English and Portuguese. Christine's patron Margaret of Burgundy was particularly influential in dispersing copies of it, and the work inspired other women to write books of advice for women, a genre hitherto dominated by men. The growth of interest in the history of women's writing sparked by feminism in the twentieth century has led to a renewed interest in her work. Now she is considered part of the canon of important medieval writers and often identified as the first feminist in Western history.

—*William E. Burns, PhD*

Bibliography and Additional Reading

Brown-Grant, Rosalind. *Christine de Pizan and the Moral Defence of Women: Reading beyond Gender.* Cambridge: Cambridge UP, 2003. Cambridge Studies in Medieval Literature Ser. Print.

Lloyd, Jean. "Christine de Pizan." *Women's History.* King's College, 7 July 2006. Web. 10 June 2015.

Margolis, Nadia. *An Introduction to Christine de Pizan.* Gainesville: UP of Florida, 2012. Print.

Willard, Charity Cannon. *Christine de Pizan: Her Life and Works.* New York: Persea, 1990. Print.

■ Letter to the King of England from Joan of Arc

Date: 1429
Country: France
Author: Joan of Arc
Translator: Belle Tuten

Summary Overview

Joan of Arc (Jeanne d'Arc) was a French peasant girl born during the tumultuous years of the long-running series of Anglo-French conflicts known as the Hundred Years' War. By the 1420s, around half of France, including Paris, had come under English control, and the heir to the French throne, Charles of Valois (later Charles VII), had been disinherited and his crown given to the English king. Joan of Arc was illiterate, but deeply devout and became convinced that she had been chosen by God to restore Charles to the throne and lead France to victory against England. She believed that she was the embodiment of a prophecy that a virgin would free France, and she called herself "the Maid." Dressed as a boy, Joan traveled in secret to meet Charles, and he gave her command of a French force of about six thousand. Joan of Arc led this force to the besieged city of Orléans, where she issued this ultimatum to the king of England and his envoys. Though Joan of Arc did see Charles crowned king of France and was able to lead the French to significant military victories, she was captured and burned at the stake in 1431 by the English and their allies.

Defining Moment

France and England had been engaged in a series of bloody conflicts for the better part of a century by the time Joan of Arc was born, around 1412. At issue was the right of the English king to rule in France. Since the Norman Conquest of England in 1066, English kings had held significant territory in France, and a complex web of marriages and alliances left the French throne vulnerable to rival claims. In 1337, Charles IV of France died, and Edward III of England, believing that he had a strong claim to the throne, declared himself the legitimate king of France. He was encouraged by his mother, who was the daughter of the French king Philip IV. According to French law, however, the throne could not be claimed through a maternal line, and Charles IV's first cousin, Philip, Count of Valois (Philip VI), was crowned king instead. Feudal laws required that the English king perform homage to the French king, recognizing his primacy over lands held by the English crown. Edward III agreed to pay homage for some lands and not for others, and when the French made a treaty with Scotland, which was then at war with England, the English navy sailed for France and gained control of the English Channel.

In the decades of conflict that followed, the French crown was beset by mental instability and familial conflict. In 1356, John II of France was captured by the English and died in captivity in London. His son, Charles V, was a rare and capable ruler and successfully regained much of the territory lost to England. His son, Charles VI, known as Charles the Mad, was a disastrous ruler, however, and appears to have suffered increasingly crippling bouts of mental illness beginning in 1392. In 1415, Henry V of England once again asserted the English claim on the French throne. After a series of decisive battles, he was able to force the French to name him heir to the throne in the Treaty of Troyes in 1420. The English and their French allies argued that Charles VI's young son and heir, Charles of Valois, was illegitimate, and he and his heirs were barred from rule. France was effectively split, as some provinces did not accept the English king. After the death of Charles VI in 1422, Charles of Valois was recognized as Charles VII, King of France, in the provinces of southern France. The English and their allies, including Charles VII's uncle, held the north.

By 1428, Henry V of England had died, and the Duke of Bedford was regent for his infant son. Bedford directed his forces to capture the city of Orléans, and by the end of October, the city was cut off, surrounded, and under siege. The city held out until May 1429, when Joan of Arc was able to rally its defenders and drive away the English army.

Author Biography

Joan of Arc was born into a peasant family in the village of Domrémy around 1412. She was not taught to read or write, but was given religious instruction. By early adolescence, she began hearing voices that ordered her to lead the French army to victory over the English and to bring Charles, Prince of Valois, to the city of Reims to be crowned king of France. In May 1428, Joan made her way to the town of Vaucouleurs and persuaded the local magistrate to let her disguise herself as a boy and travel to see Charles. Joan of Arc convinced him that

she could lead his men to victory, and she was outfitted as a knight and led an army of French forces against the English who were besieging Orléans. She was able to break the siege and drive the English out of Orléans—a decisive victory. She escorted Charles to Reims, where he was crowned Charles VII in July 1429 (though he had been recognized as king in southern France since 1422). The advantage was short-lived, however. Charles's support for her wavered, and Joan of Arc was captured outside the city of Compiègne in 1430. She was tried for heresy and witchcraft by the English and their Burgundian allies and was burned at the stake on May 30, 1431. She was nineteen years old. She was made a saint in the Catholic Church in 1920.

HISTORICAL DOCUMENT

JESUS, MARY

King of England, render account to the King of Heaven of your royal blood. Return the keys of all the good cities which you have seized, to the Maid. She is sent by God to reclaim the royal blood, and is fully prepared to make peace, if you will give her satisfaction; that is, you must render justice, and pay back all that you have taken.

King of England, if you do not do these things, I am the commander of the military; and in whatever place I shall find your men in France, I will make them flee the country, whether they wish to or not; and if they will not obey, the Maid will have them all killed. She comes sent by the King of Heaven, body for body, to take you out of France, and the Maid promises and certifies to you that if you do not leave France she and her troops will raise a mighty outcry as has not been heard in France in a thousand years. And believe that the King of Heaven has sent her so much power that you will not be able to harm her or her brave army.

To you, archers, noble companions in arms, and all people who are before Orleans, I say to you in God's name, go home to your own country; if you do not do so, beware of the Maid, and of the damages you will suf-

fer. Do not attempt to remain, for you have no rights in France from God, the King of Heaven, and the Son of the Virgin Mary. It is Charles, the rightful heir, to whom God has given France, who will shortly enter Paris in a grand company. If you do not believe the news written of God and the Maid, then in whatever place we may find you, we will soon see who has the better right, God or you.

William de la Pole, Count of Suffolk, Sir John Talbot, and Thomas, Lord Scales, lieutenants of the Duke of Bedford, who calls himself regent of the King of France for the King of England, make a response, if you wish to make peace over the city of Orleans! If you do not do so, you will always recall the damages which will attend you.

Duke of Bedford, who call yourself regent of France for the King of England, the Maid asks you not to make her destroy you. If you do not render her satisfaction, she and the French will perform the greatest feat ever done in the name of Christianity.

Done on the Tuesday of Holy Week (March 22, 1429). HEAR THE WORDS OF GOD AND THE MAID.

Document Analysis

This selection is a letter from Joan of Arc to the representatives of the English crown. It was dictated on March 22, 1429, to a member of the clergy when she was at Poitiers, before she left with her small army to break the siege of Orléans. Sent in April, it was the first such message from her, though others would follow.

The message begins with an invocation to Jesus and Mary, a paring that was particularly important to Joan of Arc and appeared on her battle flag and her letters. The pairing of Jesus with his mother is significant. Mary's virginity made the birth of Jesus miraculous, and Joan of Arc refers to herself repeatedly in this letter as "maid," also translated as "virgin." She demanded that the king of England, then a seven-year-old boy represented in France by his regent, Bedford, "return the keys of all the good cities which you have seized, to the Maid." She claims that she was sent by God to reclaim the throne for the rightful heir, the "royal blood," and there is no doubt how she intended to do it: "I am the commander of the military," and she believes that God will protect her and her army from harm.

She calls out the king's representatives in France and warns them that their only option is to make peace by leaving France and repaying all that had been taken during their occupation. Joan of Arc also makes a point of addressing the rank and file. "To you, archers, noble companions in arms, and all people who are before Orléans, I say to you in God's name, go home to your own country." If they refuse to leave France, their destruction is assured because God has told her that they have no right to be in France and that it is her duty to drive them out.

Joan of Arc demands a response from the commanders who lead the armies of England and their French allies. If they refuse to answer and make peace on her terms, she threatens to "perform the greatest feat ever done in the name of Christianity" and destroy them. She demands that they "hear the words of God and the Maid." Joan of Arc repeatedly uses "the Maid" as her name to emphasize her virginity and her kinship with the virgin mother of Jesus. Her conviction about her sacred mission and her willingness to go to battle to achieve it are clear.

Essential Themes

This letter from Joan of Arc to the king of England and his representatives in France demanded that the English leave France and make good on the damage they had done, or suffer the consequences. Joan of Arc believed that she was sent from God to return France to its proper king and save it from invaders, and the righteous indignation she felt was clear in this letter. Her authority was derived from her divine mission, and she repeated the message that God was speaking through her. The essential themes of this letter are the illegitimacy of the English claim to the French throne and Joan of Arc's determination to do the will of God and return Charles of Valois to his rightful place as king of all France.

—*Bethany Groff, MA*

Bibliography and Additional Reading

Corrigan, Gordon. *A Great and Glorious Adventure: A History of the Hundred Years War and the Birth of Renaissance England.* New York: Pegasus, 2014. Print.

Harrison, Kathryn. *Joan of Arc: A Life Transfigured.* New York: Doubleday, 2014. Print.

Seward, Desmond. *The Hundred Years War: The English in France 1337–1453.* New York, Penguin, 1978. Print.

Stolpe, Sven. *The Maid of Orleans: The Life and Mysticism of Joan of Arc.* New York: Pantheon, 1956. Print.

■ Excerpt from the Trial of Joan of Arc

Date: 1431
Geographic Region: Rouen, France
Authors: Thomas de Courcelles and Guillaume Manchon
Translator: W. P. Barrett

Summary Overview

The trial of Joan of Arc, heroine of the French military resurgence against the English in the late 1420s, was held in an ecclesiastical court, since the primary charge against her was heresy. This selection draws from letters defending the decision to try her in a church court rather than a military one. Joan of Arc was a French peasant girl, born around 1412 during the tumultuous years of the series of Anglo-French conflicts now known as the Hundred Years' War. In the 1420s, France was deeply divided, and the heir to the throne, Charles of Valois (later Charles VII), had been disinherited and his crown given to the English king. Joan of Arc was illiterate, but deeply devout. In her early teens, she heard voices that told her that she had been chosen by God to restore Charles to the throne and lead France to victory against England. Joan, dressed as a boy, traveled in secret to meet Charles, and he gave her command of a French force that went on to break the English siege of Orléans and revive France's flagging military fortunes. Though Joan of Arc did see Charles crowned king of France and was able to lead the French to significant military victories, she was captured and burned at the stake in 1431 by the English and their allies.

Defining Moment

The series of bloody conflicts now known as the Hundred Years' War had dragged on for the better part of a century by the time Joan of Arc was born. At issue was the right of the English king to rule in France. Since the Norman conquest of England in 1066, English kings had held significant territory in France, and a complex web of marriages and alliances left the French throne vulnerable to rival claims. In 1337, Charles IV of France died, and Edward III of England, believing that he had a strong claim to the throne, declared himself the legitimate king of France. When Charles IV's cousin, Philip of Valois, was crowned Philip VI instead and then made a treaty with Scotland, the English navy sailed for France and gained control of the English Channel.

In the decades of conflict that followed, the French crown was beset by mental instability and familial conflict. In 1356, John II of France was captured by the English and died in captivity in London. His son, Charles V, was a rare and capable ruler, who successfully regained much of the territory lost to England. His son, Charles VI, known as Charles the Mad, was a disastrous ruler, however, and appears to have suffered increasingly crippling bouts of mental illness beginning in 1392. In 1415, Henry V of England once again asserted the English claim on the French throne. After a series of decisive battles, he was able to force the French to name him heir to the throne in the Treaty of Troyes in 1420. The English and their French allies argued that Charles VI's young son and heir, Charles of Valois, was illegitimate, and he and his heirs were barred from rule. France was effectively split, as some provinces did not accept the English king. After the death of Charles VI in 1422, Charles of Valois was recognized as Charles VII, king of France, in the provinces of southern France. The English and their allies, including Charles VII's uncle, held the north.

By 1428, Henry V of England had died, and the Duke of Bedford was regent for his infant son, Henry VI. Bedford directed his forces to capture the city of Orléans, and by the end of October, the city was cut off, surrounded, and under siege. The city held out until May 1429, when Joan of Arc was able to rally its defenders and drive away the English army. Following this victory, she cleared the way to the cathedral city of Reims, where Charles VII was crowned on Sunday, July 17, 1429. A series of setbacks followed, however, and an attack on Paris in September was abandoned, and

Joan was wounded in the leg. After a winter of maddening inactivity, Joan of Arc was sent to Compiègne in the spring of 1430 to repel an attack by the Burgundians, allied with the English. During the attack, she was thrown from her horse and captured by the Burgundians, who eventually turned her over to the English. She was then brought before an ecclesiastical court in Rouen and charged with heresy. After a year of imprisonment, she was executed as a heretic on May 30, 1431.

Author Biography and Document Information

Joan of Arc was born into a peasant family in the village of Domrémy around 1412. She was not taught to read or write, but was given religious instruction. By early adolescence, she began hearing voices that ordered her to lead the French army to victory over the English, and to bring Charles, Prince of Valois, to the city of Reims to be crowned king of France. In May 1428, Joan made her way to the town of Vaucouleurs and persuaded the local magistrate to let her disguise herself as a boy and travel to see Charles. Joan of Arc convinced him that she could lead his men to victory, and she was outfitted as a knight and led an army of French forces against the English who were besieging Orléans. She was able to break the siege and drive the English out of Orléans—a decisive victory. She escorted Charles to Reims, where he was crowned Charles VII in July 1429 (though he had been recognized as king in southern France since 1422). The advantage was short-lived, however. Charles's support for her wavered, and Joan of Arc was captured outside the city of Compiègne in 1430. She was tried for heresy and witchcraft by the English and their Burgundian allies, and she was burned at the stake on May 30, 1431. She was nineteen years old. She was made a saint in the Catholic Church in 1920.

This selection is from the beginning of Joan of Arc's trial transcript, which was translated into Latin from notes taken in French. During the trial, Guillaume Manchon, the head notary, took detailed notes that he translated four years later, with the help of University of Paris master Thomas de Courcelles. A lengthy posthumous appeals process took place in the 1450s, providing additional detail, but the three copies of the original trial transcript that survive provide the most accurate details of the trial itself. This excerpt is from the first complete English translation, published by W. P. Barrett in 1932.

HISTORICAL DOCUMENT

IN THE NAME OF THE LORD, AMEN
HERE BEGIN THE PROCEEDINGS IN MATTER OF FAITH AGAINST A DEAD WOMAN, JEANNE, COMMONLY KNOWN AS THE MAID.

To all those who shall see these present letters or public instrument, Pierre, by divine mercy Bishop of Beauvais, and brother Jean Le Maistre, of the order of Preaching brothers, deputy in the diocese of Rouen, and especially appointed in this trial to the office of the pious and venerable master Jean Graverent of the same order, renowned doctor of theology, by apostolic authority Inquisitor of the Faith and of Heretical Error in all the kingdom of France: greeting in the author and consummator of the faith, Our Lord Jesus Christ.

It has pleased divine Providence that a woman of the name of Jeanne, commonly called The Maid, should be taken and apprehended by famous warriors within the boundaries and limits of our diocese and jurisdiction. The reputation of this woman had already gone forth into many parts: how, wholly forgetful of womanly honesty, and having thrown off the bonds of shame, careless of all the modesty of womankind, she wore with an astonishing and monstrous brazenness, immodest garments belonging to the male sex; how moreover, her presumptuousness had grown until she was not afraid to perform, to speak, and to disseminate many things contrary to the Catholic faith and hurtful to the articles of the orthodox belief. And by so doing, as well in our diocese as in several other districts of this kingdom, she was said to be guilty of no inconsiderable offenses. These things having come to the knowledge of our mother the University of Paris, and of brother Martin Billorin, vicar-general of the lord Inquisitor of Heretical Error, they immediately summoned the illustrious prince, the Duke of Burgundy and the noble lord Jean de Luxembourg, who at this time held the said woman in their power and authority, in the name of the vicar-general above mentioned, and under penalty of law, to surrender and dispatch to us, as ordinary judge, the woman so defamed and suspected of heresy.

We, the said Bishop, according to our pastoral office, desirous of promoting with all our might the exaltation and increase of the Christian faith, did resolve to institute a proper inquiry into these facts so commonly known, and so far as law and reason should persuade us, to proceed with mature deliberation to such further decisions as were incumbent upon us. We required the said prince and the said lord Jean also, under penalties of law, to surrender for trial the said woman to our spiritual jurisdiction; whilst the very serene and most Christian prince, our lord the King of France and England, summoned them to the same effect. Finally, the most illustrious lord Duke of Burgundy and the lord Jean de Luxembourg graciously consenting to these demands, and solicitous in their Catholic souls of the accomplishment of what appeared to them as helpful to the growth of the faith, surrendered and dispatched the woman to our lord the King and his commissioners. Thereafter the King in his providence, burning with a desire to succor the orthodox faith, surrendered this woman to us, that we might, hold a complete inquiry into her acts and sayings before proceeding further, according to the ecclesiastical laws. When that was done, we requested the distinguished and notable chapter of the church of Rouen, charged with the administration of all spiritual jurisdiction in the vacancy of the archiepiscopal seat, to grant us territory in the town of Rouen for us to make this inquiry: which was graciously and freely given. But before preferring any further charge against this woman we held it wise to consult, with prolonged and mature deliberation, the opinion of experienced authorities in canon and civil law, of which, by God's grace, the number in the town of Rouen was considerable.

January 9th (1431). The First day of the Proceedings

And on Tuesday the ninth day of January in the year of our Lord fourteen hundred and thirty-one, according to the rite and computation of the Church of France, in the fourteenth year of the most Holy Father in Christ Martin V, by divine providence Pope, we the aforesaid bishop, in the house of the King's Counsel, summoned the doctors and masters whose names follow: my lord abbots Gilles of Ste. Trinité de Fécamp, doctor of sacred theology, and Nicolas de Jumièges, doctor of canon law; Pierre, prior of Longueville, doctor of theology; Raoul Roussel, treasurer of the Cathedral of Rouen, doctor of both canon and civil law; Nicolas de Venderès, archdeacon of Eu, licentiate in canon law; Robert Le Barbier, licentiate in canon and civil law; Nicolas Couppequesne, bachelor of theology, and Nicolas Loiseleur, master of arts.

Now when these men, as numerous as famous, were gathered together at the same time and place, we demanded of their wisdom the manner and the order to be followed herein, after having shown as related above what diligence had been brought to the matter. The doctors and masters, having reached full knowledge thereof, decided that it was meet first to inquire into the acts and sayings publicly imputed to this woman; and decently deferring to their advice we declared that already certain information had been obtained at our command, and similarly decided to order more to be collected; all of which, at a certain day determined by us, should be presented to the council, that it might be more clearly informed upon the subsequent procedure necessary in the trial. And, the better and more conveniently to effect and achieve the collection of the information, it was this day decided by the aforesaid lords and masters that there was need of certain especial officers to whom this particular duty should be given. Consequently, at the counsel and deliberation of those present it was decided and decreed by us that the venerable and discreet person master Jean d'Estivet, canon of the cathedral churches of Beauvais and Bayeux, should exercise in the trial the office of Promoter or Procurator General. Master Jean de La Fontaine, master of arts and licentiate of canon law, was ordained councillor, commissary, and examiner. To the office of notaries or secretaries were designated the prudent and honest master Guillaume Colles, also called Boisguillaume, and Guillaume Manchon, priests, notaries by apostolic and imperial authority at the archiepiscopal court of Rouen; and master Jean Massieu, priest, ecclesiastical dean of Rouen, was appointed executor of the commands and convocations emanating from our authority. Further, we have had here inserted and transcribed at their order the tenor of all these letters, secret or public, that the sequence of the said acts might appear with greater clarity.

And first follows the tenor of the letter from our mother the University of Paris, addressed to the most illustrious lord Duke of Burgundy

"Most high and most puissant prince and our much feared and honored lord, we commend ourselves in all humility to your highness. Notwithstanding, most feared and honored lord, our recent letter to your highness, beseeching you in all humility that this woman known as The Maid, being by God's grace in your subjection, should be transferred into the hands of the justice of the Church that due trial might be made of her idolatries and other matters concerning our holy faith, and to repair the scandals that have arisen therefrom in our Kingdom, likewise the evils and unnumbered inconveniences which have therefrom resulted: nevertheless we have had no reply nor have we learned that any provision has been made to obtain in the affair of this woman a fitting discussion. But we greatly fear lest through the falsity and seduction of the enemy of Hell and through the malice and subtlety of evil persons, your enemies and adversaries, who put their whole might, as it is said, to effect the deliverance of this woman by subtle means, she may in some manner be taken from your subjection (which may God prevent!). For in truth in the judgment of all good informed Catholics, such a great lesion in the holy faith, such an enormous peril, obstacle or hurt to all the estate of this realm, has not occurred within human memory to compare with the escape of this woman by such damned ways without fitting reparation; but it would be in truth greatly to the prejudice of your honor and of the most Christian name of the house of France, of which you and your most noble progenitors have been and still are loyal protectors and the most noble principal members. For these reasons, most feared and sovereign lord, we beseech you again in all humility on behalf of Our Saviour's faith, and for the conservation of the Holy Church and the protection of the divine honor, and also for the great benefit of this most Christian realm, that it may please your highness to transfer this woman into the hands of the Inquisitor of the Faith, and to dispatch her safely thither, as we formerly besought, or to surrender this woman or have her surrendered to the reverend father in God my lord bishop of Beauvais in whose spiritual jurisdiction she was apprehended, that he may try her in matter of faith, as it is reasonable and fitting for him to do to the glory of God, to the exaltation of our said holy faith, and to the profit of the good and loyal Catholics and the estate of this realm, and also to the honor and praise of your highness, whom may God keep in good prosperity and in the end grant His glory. Written. . . ." [no date].

Then follows the tenor of the letter from our said mother the University of Paris, addressed to the noble and puissant lord Jean de Luxembourg

"Most noble, honored and puissant lord, we commend ourselves lovingly to your high nobility. Your noble prudence knows well and recognizes that all good Catholic knights should employ their strength and puissance first to the service of God and then to the profit of the state. And most especially the first oath of the order of chivalry is to keep and protect the honor of God, the Catholic faith and His Holy Church. This oath you well remembered when you employed your noble power and personal presence to apprehend this woman who is called The Maid, by whom God's honor has been immeasurably offended, the Catholic faith wounded and the Church much dishonored; for through her, idolatries, errors, false doctrines and other evils and inestimable hurts have spread through the realm. In truth all loyal Christians must cordially thank you for having rendered so great a service to our holy faith and to all the kingdom; and for our part we thank with our whole heart God and your prowess. But it would be a little thing to have done this if it were not followed by what is necessary to remedy the offense perpetrated by this woman against our sweet Creator, His faith and His Holy Church, with the other numberless misdeeds which have been told. And it would be a greater evil than ever, and a worse error would remain among the people; it would be an intolerable offense against the divine Majesty if it were to come to pass that this woman were set free, lost to us, which certain of our adversaries, it is said, would endeavor to obtain, setting to that end all their knowledge by the most subtle means, and what is worse, attempting it by silver or ransom. But we hope that God will not permit such a misfortune to visit His people, and that your good and noble providence will not suffer it, but will be able to meet the occasion fittingly; for if her deliverance took place, without appropriate reparation, it would be an irreparable dishonor to your nobility and to every one concerned: such a scandal must of necessity cease as soon as possible. And since in this matter delay is most perilous and prejudicial to the realm, on behalf of the divine honor, and for the conservation of the holy Catholic faith, and for the good and exaltation of the whole realm, we most humbly and heartily beseech that it may please your puissant and honored highness to dispatch this woman to the Inquisitor of the faith, who has urgently required and demanded her, in order to weigh the heavy charges which burden her, to the pleasure of God, and the proper edification of the people, according to good and sacred doctrine: or that it may please you to have her surrendered and delivered to the reverend father in God our most honored lord bishop of Beauvais who likewise has demanded her, and in whose jurisdiction, as has been said, she was apprehended. The which prelate and Inquisitor are her judges in matter of faith; and every Christian is bound to obey them whatever his estate, in this case, under great legal penalties. And by so doing you gain the grace a love of the high deity; you become the instrument of the exaltation of the holy faith, and so increase the glory of your most high and noble name, with that of the high and most puissant prince our most feared lord and your own, my lord Duke of Burgundy. And every one will be charged to pray for the prosperity of your most noble person, which may our Saviour, by His grace, lead and keep in all its doings and the end reward with an everlasting joy. Written . [at Paris, July 14th, 1431]

Then follows the tenor of the letter of the Vicar-General the Inquisitor addressed to the said lord Duke of Burgundy

"To the most high and puissant prince Philippe Duke of Burgundy, count of Flanders, of Artois, of Burgundy and Namur, and to all others concerned, Brother Martin, master sacred theology, and Vicar-General of the Inquisitor of the faith in the kingdom of France, greeting in Jesus Christ of true Saviour. Whereas all loyal and Christian princes and all other true Catholics are charged with extirpation of error arising against the faith, as well as scandals resulting there from among the private Christian folk, and whereas at this time it is reported and commonly said that through a certain woman named Jeanne, whom the adversaries of the kingdom call The Maid, at her instance in many cities, good towns and other places of this realm, many and diverse errors have been sown, uttered, published and spread abroad, and still continued to be so, whence many hurts and scandals against the divine honor and against the holy faith have resulted and do result, causing the loss of souls and of many private Christians: which cannot and must not be dissimulated nor pass without a fair and appropriate reparation. Now since it so happens that by God's grace the said Jeanne is at this time in your power and subjection, or in that of your noble and loyal vassals: for these reasons, puissant prince, we most lovingly beseech you and pray your said noble vassals to surrender the said Jeanne, through you or through them, safely and soon; and we hope that you will so do as true defenders of the faith and protectors of God's honor, and that none shall hinder or delay you (which God prevent). And with the rights of our office and the authority committed to us by the Holy See of Rome, we urgently summon and enjoin for the sake of the Catholic faith and under penalty of law all the above-said and every person of what state, condition, preëminence and authority so ever, as soon as possible with safety and fitness to send and bring captive to us the said Jeanne vehemently suspected of many crimes, and tainted with heresy, that she may appear before us against the Procurator of the Holy Inquisition, and may reply and proceed rightly according to the counsel, favor and aid of the good doctors and masters of the University of Paris, and other notable counselors therefrom. Given at Paris under our seal of office of the Holy Inquisition, the year 1430, the 26th day of May."

GLOSSARY

archiepiscopal: pertaining to an archbishop

idolatries: the worshipping of idols

licentiate: a person who has received a license, as from a university, to practice an art or profession

prelate: a high church official

puissant: powerful or influential

Document Analysis

This selection is from the beginning of the trial transcript of Joan of Arc, and it is primarily concerned with the ecclesiastical authority over the trial. The opening words of the selection identify it as a posthumous record. It is "the proceedings in matter of faith against a dead woman." Though the trial was clearly politically motivated, the court took great pains to record the reasons why they demanded that she be turned over to the English-controlled ecclesiastical court in Rouen. Since she could not be tried for being victorious in battle, the only way to obtain the desired death sentence was to find her guilty of heresy.

The first section of this selection is a summary of the jurisdictional situation that would later throw the proceedings into even more doubt. Bishop Pierre Cauchon of Beauvais, who played a prominent role in her trial, had jurisdiction in Burgundy, where Joan of Arc was captured, but should not have been able to officiate in Rouen, where she was ultimately tried. The transcript of the trial defended the decision that allowed

Cauchon to proceed, arguing that "we requested the distinguished and notable chapter of the church of Rouen, charged with the administration of all spiritual jurisdiction in the vacancy of the archiepiscopal seat, to grant us territory in the town of Rouen for us to make this inquiry: which was graciously and freely given." In other words, Rouen was granted temporarily to an outside bishop for the purposes of the trial.

The first day of court hearings, January 9, 1431, is recorded as being primarily concerned with the court's demands that Joan of Arc be turned over to them in 1430, when she was still being held by the Burgundians: "It may please your highness to transfer this woman into the hands of the Inquisitor of the Faith . . . or to surrender this woman . . . to the reverend father in God my lord bishop of Beauvais in whose spiritual jurisdiction she was apprehended, that he may try her in matter of faith." The clerics reminded the lords who held Joan of Arc that their primary loyalty was to the church, and if she was to escape and spread heresy, it would have damning consequences: "All good Catholic knights should employ their strength and puissance first to the service of God."

Essential Themes

The primary theme of this selection is the desire of the English and their clerical supporters to try Joan of Arc as a heretic in an ecclesiastical court. The fact that the court was irregular, since it was not under the authority of the Bishop of Beauvais, was an issue from the beginning of the trial, and the court argued that they had "borrowed" Rouen for the trial and therefore it was fine. The primary argument of the court was the danger to religion if Joan of Arc's heresies were to spread. If she had been treated as a military commander, she would likely have been held for ransom. The only way to dispose of her completely was to ensure her execution, and the only means of lawfully executing her was to convict her of heresy.

—*Bethany Groff Dorau, MA*

Bibliography and Additional Reading

Harrison, Kathryn. *Joan of Arc: A Life Transfigured*. New York: Doubleday, 2014. Print.

Seward, Desmond. *The Hundred Years War: The English in France 1337–1453*. New York: Penguin, 1978. Print.

Stolpe, Sven. *The Maid of Orleans: The Life and Mysticism of Joan of Arc*. New York: Pantheon, 1956. Print.

The Near East and Beyond

Following the death of Muhammad, Islam took deeper root in the eastern Mediterranean and elsewhere outside the Arabian Peninsula. During the Umayyad Caliphate (661-750), the capital of the Muslim world was Damascus, which had been part of the eastern Roman Empire and which now contained many Byzantine Christians, some of whom assisted in the building of the Great Mosque. Arabic scholars absorbed and built on Greek and Roman learning, developing a new synthesis that stood the test of time until the Enlightenment, when new paradigms emerged.

Ibn Battuta (1304-1368/69) was a medieval Arab traveler and author. After a pilgrimage to Mecca, he decided to visit as many parts of the world as he could. Over a 27-year period he covered three different continents and some 75,000 miles. His recorded reminiscences, *Rihlah* ("Journey"), became one of the world's most beloved travel books.

■ The Pact of Umar: Peace Accord to the Christians of Syria

Date: ca. seventh century
Geographic Region: Syria
Author: Umar ibn al-Khattab

Summary Overview

The Pact of Umar is an agreement that details the restrictions and obligations of non-Muslims under Muslim rule. In it, Umar ibn al-Khattab, the second caliph (Islamic leader, "successor of Muhammad"), received promises from the *dhimmi* (non-Muslim people in Muslim-conquered lands; in this case, Christians in Syria) that offered the acceptance of certain restrictions in exchange for protection. In this document, Umar accepted their offer, adding an additional rule.

The origin of this document is questioned by scholars. Some believe it was significantly altered, if not written outright, in the ninth century. Other scholars believe that the conquest of Syria and other former Byzantine states by the Muslims under Umar would have prompted this agreement; whether or not Umar was the author, the pact has traditionally been attributed to him. During a time of rapid expansion, Muslim leaders deemed it important to establish peaceful relations with non-Muslims, as the latter continued to outnumber their conquerors in many cases. Whatever its origin, the Pact of Umar has become a central part of Islamic law and has dictated relations between Muslims and non-Muslims for centuries.

Defining Moment

In 613, Muhammad began sharing the revelations that became the foundation of Islam in his home community, the Arabian city of Mecca. As the new religion spread, the leaders of the powerful Quraysh tribe of Mecca feared that it would undermine their authority, and followers of Muhammad were increasingly persecuted. In 621, Medina city officials invited Muhammad and his followers to relocate, so they left Mecca and set up a thriving community in Medina. Many of Islam's most important early leaders, including Umar, were part of the group that came from Mecca. When Muhammad died in 632, leaving no clear leadership in place, the fledgling Muslim community began to fragment, as some tribespeople claimed that their allegiance was to Muhammad only and not to his companions. Abu Bakr, Muhammad's father-in-law and a respected leader, became the first caliph, uniting the community. Umar, who had also followed Muhammad from Mecca, was chosen as Abu Bakr's successor, and he became the second caliph just two years later, in 634.

Umar is known for his dramatic expansion of the Islamic state, the stage for which was set by the military success of Muhammad's early battles. In 624, the Quraysh of Mecca sent a force of one thousand men against the Muslim community in Medina. Despite being outnumbered three to one, the Muslims won a decisive victory in what is known as the Battle of Badr, believing they had been assisted by angels. Though the Quraysh won a subsequent victory, they were never able to capture Medina, and they eventually signed a treaty with the Muslims. Muhammad and his followers were eager to spread the faith outside of the Arabian Peninsula, and they sent letters to leaders in North Africa, Persia, and the Byzantine Empire (Eastern Roman Empire). In these letters, Muhammad promised that non-pagans—Christians, Jews, and Zoroastrians—would not be forced to convert. As Muhammad and his followers consolidated control of the Arabian Peninsula, they allowed Christians and Jews to practice their religions as long as they submitted to Muslim authority, which included paying special taxes.

During his two years as caliph, Abu Bakr spent much of his energy stabilizing the young community and reining in disparate factions. When Umar succeeded him in 634, he took over a well-organized, experienced army and a strong, unified Islamic state. Umar first led campaigns against the Byzantine Empire, conquering Palestine, Lebanon, and Syria. Umar is thought to have made his pact with the Christians of conquered Syria, which continued Muhammad's policy of allowing non-Muslims to practice their religion, with additional penalties and restrictions. Umar went on to conquer much of the Middle East in subsequent years, and his treatment of non-Muslims in conquered territories was consistent with this agreement. As long as taxes were paid and Jews and Christians obeyed these restrictions, they were not forced to convert.

Author Biography

Umar ibn al-Khattab was born in Mecca, Arabia (now Saudi Arabia), around 586. He was part of an influential tribe in Mecca, and he learned to read and write. As a young man, Umar likely traveled to Persia and Rome. When he met the prophet Muhammad, he was initially hostile, believing that the fragile peace between the polytheistic tribesmen on the Arabian Peninsula was threatened. Around 615, Umar became a Muslim and one of Muhammad's closest advisors, a relationship made closer when Muhammad married Umar's daughter in 625. After Muhammad's death in 632, Umar prevented a rift between groups from Mecca and Medina, persuading them to accept Abu Bakr as the first caliph. Abu Bakr named Umar his successor and died two years after becoming caliph, leaving Umar to govern the rapidly expanding Islamic state until his death. Umar was assassinated by a Persian slave in 644. He is buried in Medina, in present-day Saudi Arabia.

HISTORICAL DOCUMENT

We heard from 'Abd al-Rahman ibn Ghanam as follows: When Umar ibn al-Khattab, may God be pleased with him, accorded a peace to the Christians of Syria, we wrote to him as follows:

In the name of God, the Merciful and Compassionate. This is a letter to the servant of God Umar, Commander of the Faithful, from the Christians of such-and-such a city. When you came against us, we asked you for safe-conduct (aman) for ourselves, our descendants, our property, and the people of our community, and we undertook the following obligations toward you:

We shall not build, in our cities or in their neighborhood, new monasteries, Churches, convents, or monks' cells, nor shall we repair, by day or by night, such of them as fall in ruins or are situated in the quarters of the Muslims.

We shall keep our gates wide open for passersby and travelers. We shall give board and lodging to all Muslims who pass our way for three days.

We shall not give shelter in our churches or in our dwellings to any spy, nor bide him from the Muslims.

We shall not teach the Qur'an to our children.

We shall not manifest our religion publicly nor convert anyone to it. We shall not prevent any of our kin from entering Islam if they wish it.

We shall show respect toward the Muslims, and we shall rise from our seats when they wish to sit.

We shall not seek to resemble the Muslims by imitating any of their garments, the qalansuwa, the turban, footwear, or the parting of the hair. We shall not speak as they do, nor shall we adopt their kunyas.

We shall not mount on saddles, nor shall we gird swords nor bear any kind of arms nor carry them on our persons.

We shall not engrave Arabic inscriptions on our seals.

We shall not sell fermented drinks.

We shall clip the fronts of our heads.

We shall always dress in the same way wherever we may be, and we shall bind the zunar round our waists

We shall not display our crosses or our books in the roads or markets of the Muslims. We shall use only clappers in our churches very softly. We shall not raise our voices when following our dead. We shall not show lights on any of the roads of the Muslims or in their markets. We shall not bury our dead near the Muslims.

We shall not take slaves who have been allotted to Muslims.

We shall not build houses overtopping the houses of the Muslims.

(When I brought the letter to Umar, may God be pleased with him, he added, "We shall not strike a Muslim.")

We accept these conditions for ourselves and for the people of our community, and in return we receive safe-conduct.

If we in any way violate these undertakings for which we ourselves stand surety, we forfeit our covenant, and we become liable to the penalties for contumacy and sedition.

Umar ibn al-Khittab replied: Sign what they ask, but add two clauses and impose them in addition to those which they have undertaken. They are: "They shall not buy anyone made prisoner by the Muslims," and "Whoever strikes a Muslim with deliberate intent shall forfeit the protection of this pact."

GLOSSARY

kunya: an honorable name given to the mother or father of an Arabic child

qalansuwa: a borderless hat worn with a turban

Qur'an: the central scripture of Islam

zunar: a wide yellow belt required to be worn by non-Muslims

Document Analysis

Structured as a request for protection from the Christians of Syria to the Caliph Umar, the Pact of Umar is rooted in an oral tradition that established Islamic customs by referencing the sayings or works of its founding leaders. This pact is said to have been told to the author by a Syrian Christian who recorded the terms of the agreement. In this document, the Syrian Christians ask for protection and offer to accept certain restrictions in exchange "for safe-conduct (aman) for ourselves, our descendants, our property, and the people of our community."

The obligations were designed to ensure that non-Muslim beliefs were not spread, that non-Muslims were able to be clearly identified, and that Muslims had both symbolic and practical supremacy over non-Muslims. The petitioners agree not to build any new houses of worship or to stand in the way of family members who wish to convert to Islam. In addition, traditional customs are prohibited or altered, including ringing of bells and wearing or carrying religious symbols or books. In other versions of this agreement, Syrian Christians agree not to parade or to sing.

The petitioners offer both practical and symbolic gestures of submission. For example, the Syrian Christians are restricted from speaking Arabic. By limiting access to the Arabic language to themselves, Muslim conquerors would increase their own security and the privacy of their conversations. Symbolically, the language restriction delineated status. As another concession, the Syrian Christians agree not to arm themselves or protect a traitor or spy from the Muslims. Furthermore, the petitioners must give Muslim travelers lodging in their houses for up to three days and agree not to sell alcohol. Also, non-Muslims agree not to wear traditional Islamic dress, to cut their hair in a distinctive way, and to give up their seat to Muslims who wish to sit.

Umar agrees to these restrictions but adds one more: non-Muslims could not hit Muslims. Though this document granted certain protections for the petitioners, and on terms that compared favorably to how nonbelievers were treated in other lands (non-Christians in the Byzantine Empire, for example, or Christians in the earlier Roman Empire), the protection came at a cost. The Muslims levied special taxes, limited access to positions in the government or civil service, and vowed to remove all of the agreement's protections if Syrian Christians violated the pact.

Essential Themes

The Pact of Umar is an agreement between Muslim conquerors and the peoples of conquered lands, the latter of whom submitted to certain restrictions in exchange for the right to keep their property and practice their religion. As the Islamic state spread across the Middle East, North Africa, and as far north as Armenia, vast numbers of people came under Muslim rule. Although this agreement is harshly lopsided by modern civil rights standards, the comparative religious tolerance practiced by the Muslims of this time contributed to their success as a conquering people. The Pact of Umar is a foundational document from a respected leader, outlining acceptable relationships with non-Muslims in conquered territory. As such, it became the basis for centuries of Islamic legal thought and continues to influence Islamic law.

—Bethany Groff, MA

Bibliography and Additional Reading

Calder, Norman, Jawid Mojaddedi, & Andrew Rippin, ed. *Classical Islam: A Sourcebook of Religious Literature.* 2nd ed. New York: Routledge. 2012. Print.

Cohen, Mark. "What Was the Pact of 'Umar? A Literary-Historical Study." *Jerusalem Studies in Arabic and Islam* 23 (1999): 100–157. Print.

Emon, Anver M. *Religious Pluralism and Islamic Law: Dhimmīs and Others in the Empire of Law.* Oxford: Oxford UP, 2012. Print.

■ Ibn Battuta Makes the Pilgrimage to Mecca and Travels to Baghdad

Date: 1326
Geographic Region: present-day Syria, Saudi Arabia, Iran
Author: Ibn Battuta

Summary Overview

The hajj, or sacred pilgrimage to Mecca, was the impetus for Ibn Battuta's travels, and was his duty as a devout Muslim. Battuta was a legal scholar from Tangier, in what is today Morocco. The Muslim world at the time was referred to as Dar al-Islam and stretched from the West African coast to Southeast Asia. In his almost thirty years of travel, he ultimately saw nearly all of it, as well as important Muslim communities outside its borders. He logged over seventy-five thousand miles in that time. When he finally retired from his travels in 1354 and settled back in Morocco, a local sultan commissioned a record of Ibn Battuta's journey, recorded by a young scholar. Battuta's adventures were recorded in a traditional Arabic form called a *rihla*, a record of travels in search of divine knowledge.

Defining Moment

Pilgrimages to Mecca predate the prophet Muhammad by thousands of years, to an Old Testament story about Ishmael, the son of Abraham (called Ibrahim in the Muslim tradition). Ishmael and his mother, Hagar, were stranded in the desert, and dying of thirst. Hagar ran back and forth between two hills looking for water until an angel performed a miracle and made a well in the desert to save the baby's life. This is known as the Well of Zamzam. To honor the preservation of Ishmael's life, a monument was built at the site of the spring. This monument, known as the Kaaba, was visited by pilgrims of many faiths for centuries, until Muhammad led the first hajj to Mecca in 630 CE. He dedicated the city to Allah, and removed the idols and images set up by other religious groups. The black cube that marks the Kaaba is the center of the Muslim world.

The hajj re-creates both important elements of the story of Ishmael and moments in the life of the prophet Muhammad. The performing of the sacred rituals is believed to guarantee a place in heaven and also brings great honor in the Muslim community. Pilgrims from all over the world come to complete this journey. The hajj was established as a duty of the devout during Muhammad's lifetime and was well established by the time Ibn Battuta visited Mecca in 1326. Pilgrims would gather in major cities by the thousands and make their way from there to Mecca. Overland trade and pilgrimage routes were well traveled and protected, though pilgrims like Ibn Battuta often traveled together to ensure their safety.

By the time of Ibn Battuta's travels, the Dar al-Islam covered Arabia, Syria, Palestine, Persia, Turkey, South and Southeast Asia, areas of the Mediterranean, eastern Europe, and much of north and central Africa. Islam had advanced as far north as France, but had been blocked from advancing further into Western Europe. Jews, Christians, and Zoroastrians in Muslim lands enjoyed fairly cordial treatment and were allowed to practice their religion, but they had to pay a special tax.

The relative longevity and stability of the medieval Islamic world produced a remarkable flourishing of cultural and scientific endeavor. The willingness of Islamic leaders to blend the traditions of the lands that they conquered and converted with their own contributed to a period when traditions from Asia, Europe, and even ancient Greece, Rome, and Egypt combined to produce advances in medicine, mathematics, art, and literature. Islamic rulers supported scholars and teachers financially, and such professions held a respected position in society. Trade was crucial to this cultural flowering, as ideas and books could be spread throughout the Islamic world. Developments in navigation were critical to the establishment of overseas trade, and Muslims were the first to use a sextant and sail a three-masted ship. The tradition of travel ran deep in Muslim culture. In addition to the hajj, visits to other sacred sites, particularly

Medina (where Muhammed and the other fathers of early Islam are buried), were encouraged. Ibn Battuta's three decades of adventuring is an extreme example, but many Muslims who could afford it traveled extensively throughout the Dar al-Islam.

Author Biography and Document Information

Ibn Battuta was born Abu Abdullah Muhammad ibn Abdullah al Lawati al Tanji ibn Battuta in 1304 in Tangier, a port in northern Morocco. He was born into a Berber family of legal scholars and was educated in a local school. In 1325, Ibn Battuta set off in search of further education and to perform the hajj, the traditional Muslim pilgrimage to Mecca. Though he did visit Mecca, his travels eventually took him as far as India, China, and Spain. He traveled for a total of twenty-nine years before returning to Fez, Morocco, where his travels were recorded for posterity. Ibn Battuta worked as a judge in Fez, and little is known of his later life. He died in 1368 or 1369.

The *Rihla* of Ibn Battuta was unknown in the Western world until German explorer Ulrich Jasper Seetzen found and purchased a copy in the early nineteenth century. The work was first published in 1818 in German and French journals. Excerpts were translated into English in 1829, and during the French occupation of Algeria, five more manuscripts were acquired by the Bibliothèque Nationale in Paris. During the twentieth century, Battuta's complete work has been translated into English and published in four volumes, the last one in 1994.

HISTORICAL DOCUMENT

Leaving Damascus with the annual pilgrim caravan

When the new moon of the month Shawwal appeared in the same year, the Hijaz caravan left Damascus and I set off along with it. At Bosra the caravans usually halt for four days so that any who have been detained at Damascus by business affairs may make up on them. Thence they go to the Pool of Ziza, where they stop for a day, and then through al-Lajjun to the Castle of Karak. Karak, which is also called "The Castle of the Raven," is one of the most marvellous, impregnable, and celebrated of fortresses. It is surrounded on all sides by the river-bed, and has but one gate, the entrance to which is hewn in the living rock, as also is the approach to its vestibule. This fortress is used by kings as a place of refuge in times of calamity, as the sultan an-Nasir did when his mamluke Salar seized the supreme authority. The caravan stopped for four days at a place called ath-Thaniya outside Karak, where preparations were made for entering the desert.

Thence we Journeyed to Ma'an, which is the last town in Syria, and from 'Aqabat as-Sawan entered the desert, of which the saying goes: "He who enters it is lost, and he who leaves it is born."

Crossing the desert from Syria to Medina

After a march of two days we halted at Dhat Hajj, where there are subterranean waterbeds but no habitations, and then went on to Wadi Baldah (in which there is no water) and to Tabuk, which is the place to which the Prophet led an expedition. The great caravan halts at Tabuk for four days to rest and to water the camels and lay in water for the terrible desert between Tabuk and al-Ula. The custom of the watercarriers is to camp beside the spring, and they have tanks made of buffalo hides, like great cisterns, from which they water the camels and fill the waterskins. Each amir or person of rank has a special tank for the needs of his own camels and personnel; the other people make private agreements with the watercarriers to water their camels and fill their waterskins for a fixed sum of money.

From Tabuk the caravan travels with great speed night and day, for fear of this desert. Halfway through is the valley of al-Ukhaydir, which might well be the valley of Hell (may God preserve us from it). One year the pilgrims suffered terribly here from the samoom-wind; the water-supplies dried up and the price of a single drink rose to a thousand dinars, but both seller and buyer perished. Their story is written on a rock in the valley.

Five days after leaving Tabuk they reach the well of al-Hijr, which has an abundance of water, but not a soul draws water there, however violent his thirst, following the example of the Prophet, who passed it on his expedition to Tabuk and drove on his camel, giving orders that none should drink of its waters. Here, in some hills of red rock, are the dwellings of Thamud. They are cut in the rock and have carved thresholds. Anyone seeing them would take them to be of recent construction. [The] decayed bones are to be seen inside these houses.

Al-Ula, a large and pleasant village with palm-gardens and water-springs, lies half a day's journey or less from al-Hijr. The pilgrims halt there four days to provision themselves and wash their clothes. They leave behind them here any surplus of provisions they may have, taking with them nothing but what is strictly necessary. The people of the village are very trustworthy. The Christian merchants of Syria may come as far as this and no further, and they trade in provisions and other goods with the pilgrims here. On the third day after leaving al-Ula the caravan halts in the outskirts of the holy city of Medina.

Visiting the holy sites of Medina

That same evening we entered the holy sanctuary and reached the illustrious mosque, halting in salutation at the Gate of Peace; then we prayed in the illustrious "garden" between the tomb of the Prophet and the noble pulpit, and reverently touched the fragment that remains of the palm-trunk against which the Prophet stood when he preached. Having paid our meed of salutation to the lord of men from first to last, the intercessor for sinners, the Prophet of Mecca, Muhammad, as well as to his two companions who share his grave, Abu Bakr and 'Omar, we returned to our camp, rejoicing at this great favour bestowed upon us, praising God for our having reached the former abodes and the magnificent sanctuaries of His holy Prophet, and praying Him to grant that this visit should not be our last and that we might be of those whose pilgrimage is accepted.

On this journey, our stay at Medina lasted four days. We used to spend every night in the illustrious mosque, where the people, after forming circles in the courtyard and, lighting large numbers of candles, would pass the time either in reciting the Koran from volumes set on rests in front of them, or in intoning litanies, or in visiting the sanctuaries of the holy tomb.

From Medina to Mecca through a final desert, the vale of Bazwa

We then set out from Medina towards Mecca, and halted near the mosque of Dhu'l-Hulayfa, five miles away. It was at this point that the Prophet assumed the pilgrim garb and obligations, and here too I divested myself of my tailored clothes, bathed, and putting on the pilgrim's garment I prayed and dedicated myself to the pilgrimage. Our fourth halt from here was at Badr, where God aided His Prophet and performed His promise. It is a village containing a series of palm-gardens and a bubbling spring with a stream flowing from it. Our way lay thence through a frightful desert called the Vale of Bazwa for three days to the valley of Rabigh where the rainwater forms pools which lie stagnant for a long time. From this point (which is just before Juhfa) the pilgrims from Egypt and Northwest Africa put on the pilgrim garment. Three days after leaving Rabigh we reached the pool of Khulays which lies in a plain and has many palm-gardens. The Bedouin of that neighbourhood hold a market there, to which they bring sheep, fruits, and condiments. Thence we travelled through 'Usfan to the Bottom of Marr, a fertile valley with numerous palms and a spring supplying a stream from which the district is irrigated. From this valley fruit and vegetables are transported to Mecca.

We set out at night from this blessed valley, with hearts full of joy at reaching the goal of our hopes, and in the morning arrived at the City of Surety, Mecca (may God ennoble her!), where we immediately entered the holy sanctuary and began the rites of pilgrimage.

The pious kindness of the people of Mecca

The inhabitants of Mecca are distinguished by many excellent and noble activities and qualities, by their beneficence to the humble and weak, and by their kindness to strangers. When any of them makes a feast, he begins by giving food to the religious devotees who are poor and without resources, inviting them first with kindness and delicacy. The majority of these unfortunates are to be found by the public bakehouses, and when anyone has his bread baked and takes it away to his house, they follow him and he gives each one of them some share of it, sending away none disappointed. Even if he has but a single loaf, he gives away a third or a half of it, cheerfully and without any grudgingness.

Another good habit of theirs is this. The orphan children sit in the bazaar, each with two baskets, one large and one small. When one of the townspeople comes to the bazaar and buys cereals, meat and vegetables, he hands them to one of these boys, who puts the cereals in one basket and the meat and vegetables in the other and takes them to the man's house, so that his meal may be prepared. Meanwhile the man goes about his devotions and his business. There is no instance of any of the boys having ever abused their trust in this matter, and they are given a fixed fee of a few coppers.

The cleanliness of the people of Mecca

The Meccans are very elegant and clean in their dress, and most of them wear white garments, which you always see fresh and snowy. They use a great deal of perfume and kohl and make free use of toothpicks of green arak-wood. The Meccan women are extraordinarily beautiful and very pious and modest. They too make great use of perfumes to such a degree that they will spend the night hungry in order to buy perfumes with the price of their food. They visit the mosque every Thursday night, wearing their finest apparel; and the whole sanctuary is saturated with the smell of their perfume. When one of these women goes away the odour of the perfume clings to the place after she has gone.

On the caravan route to Basra

Three days' march through this district brought us to the town of Wisit. Its inhabitants are among the best people in Iraq—indeed, the very best of them without qualification. All the Iraqis who wish to learn how to recite the Koran come here, and our caravan contained a number of students who had come for that purpose.

The customs of the Ahmadi dervishes at Umm 'Ubayda

As the caravan stayed here three days, I had an opportunity of visiting the grave of ar-Rifai which is at a village called Umm 'Ubayda, one day's journey from there. I reached the establishment at noon the next day and found it to be an enormous monastery containing thousands of darwishes. After the mid-afternoon prayer drums and kettledrums were beaten and the darwishes began to dance. After this they prayed the sunset prayer and brought in the meal, consisting of rice-bread, fish, milk and dates. After the night prayer they began to recite their litany. A number of loads of wood had been brought in and kindled into a flame, and they went into the fire dancing; some of them rolled in it and others ate it in their mouths until they had extinguished it entirely. This is the peculiar custom of the Ahmadi darwishes. Some of them take large snakes and bite their heads with their teeth until they bite them clean through.

Arrival in Basra

After visiting ar-Rifai's tomb I returned to Wasit and found that the caravan had already started, but overtook them on the way, and accompanied them to Basra. As we approached the city I had remarked at a distance of some two miles from it a lofty building resembling a fortress. I asked about it and was told that it was the mosque of 'Ali. Basra was in former times a city so vast that this mosque stood in the centre of the town, whereas now it is two miles outside it. Two miles beyond it again is the old wall that encircled the town, so that it stands midway between the old wall and the present city.

Basra is one of the metropolitan cities of Iraq and no place on earth excels it in quantity of palm-groves. The current price of dates in its market is fourteen pounds to an Iraqi dirham, which is one-third of a nuqra. The qadi sent me a hamper of dates that a man could scarcely carry; I sold them and received nine dirhams, and three of those were taken by the porter for carrying the basket from the house to the market.

The kindness and ignorance of the inhabitants

The inhabitants of Basra possess many excellent qualities; they are affable to strangers and give them their due, so that no stranger ever feels lonely amongst them. They hold the Friday service in the mosque of 'Ali mentioned above, but for the rest of the week it is closed. I was present once at the Friday service in this mosque and when the preacher rose to deliver his discourse he committed many gross errors of grammar. In astonishment at this I spoke of it to the qadi and this is what he said to me: "In this town there is not a man left who knows anything of the science of grammar." Here is a lesson for those who will reflect on it—Magnified be He who changes all things! This Basra, in whose people the mastery of grammar reached its height, from whose soil sprang its trunk and its branches, amongst whose inhabitants is numbered the leader whose primacy is undisputed—the preacher in this town cannot deliver a discourse without breaking its rules!

Leaving Basra by boat

At Basra I embarked in a sumbuq, that is a small boat, for Ubulla, which lies ten miles distant. One travels between a constant succession of orchards and palm-groves both to right and left, with merchants sitting in the shade of the trees selling bread, fish, dates, milk and fruit. Ubulla was formerly a large town, frequented by merchants from India and Firs, but it fell into decay and is now a village.

The city of Baghdad

Thence we travelled to Baghdad, the Abode of Peace and Capital of Islam. Here there are two bridges like that at Hilla on which the people promenade night and day, both men and women. The town has eleven cathedral mosques, eight on the right bank and three on the left, together with very many other mosques and madrasas, only the latter are all in ruins.

The baths at Baghdad are numerous and excellently constructed, most of them being painted with pitch, which has the appearance of black marble. This pitch is brought from a spring between Kufa and Basra, from which it flows continually. It gathers at the sides of the spring like clay and is shovelled up and brought to Baghdad. Each establishment has a large number of private bathrooms, every one of which has also a wash-basin in the corner, with two taps supplying hot and cold water.

Every bather is given three towels, one to wear round his waist when he goes in, another to wear round his waist when he comes out, and the third to dry himself with. In no town other than Baghdad have I seen all this elaborate arrangement, though some other towns approach it in this respect.

The western part of Baghdad was the earliest to be built, but it is now for the most part in ruins. In spite of that there remain in it still thirteen quarters, each like a city in itself and possessing two or three baths. The hospital (maristan) is a vast ruined edifice, of which only vestiges remain.

The eastern part has an abundance of bazaars, the largest of which is called the Tuesday bazaar. On this side there are no fruit trees, but all the fruit is brought from the western side, where there are orchards and gardens.

Leaving Baghdad for Persia and the city of Tabriz

I left Baghdad with the mahalla of Sultan Abu Sa'id, on purpose to see the way in which the king's marches are conducted and travelled with it for ten days, thereafter accompanying one of the amirs to the town of Tabriz.

Journey to Tabriz

I left Baghdad with the mahalla of Sultan Abu Sa'id, on purpose to see the way in which the king's marches are conducted, and travelled with it for ten days, thereafter accompanying one of the amirs to the town of Tabriz. We reached the town after ten days' travelling, and encamped outside it in a place called ash-Sham. Here there is a fine hospice, where travellers are supplied with food, consisting of bread, meat, rice cooked in butter, and sweetmeats.

GLOSSARY

Bedouin: a nomadic tribe from the Arabian Desert

darwish: a status title for a Sufi holy man; alternate spelling of darvish or dervish

litanies: religious recitations

mahalla: an Islamic congregation or parish, typically with one mosque

mamluke: Arabic word meaning "slave of the king" (also spelled "mamluk")

Prophet: the prophet Muhammad, founder of Islam

GLOSSARY CONTINUED

qadi: a judge in a Muslim community, whose bases decisions on Islamic religious law

vestibule: a passage, hall, or antechamber between the outer door and the interior of the building

Document Analysis

This selection of Ibn Battuta's *Rihla* covers his hajj, or trip to Mecca, his primary reason for undertaking his travels in the first place. He also visited the holy city of Medina, where the Prophet and several other founders of Islam were buried. The details of his travels were not written down at the time, but were dictated to a student after his return to Morocco later in his life. Though some scholars question the veracity of his memory, these impressions form one of the most complete pictures of the medieval Islamic world.

At the start of the selection, Battuta leaves Damascus in Syria with a caravan of pilgrims. Damascus, like the other major cities of the Dar al-Islam, was a gathering and departure point for hajj pilgrims numbering in the thousands. Because of this, most cities and holy sites along the route were well equipped to meet the needs of travelers, and Battuta documents not only the people and places he visits, but also the services they provide to travelers. The route through Syria had several stops, the first for four days, so business travelers from Damascus could catch up, and the last a crucial stop where the caravan prepared for the most arduous leg of its journey. They stopped at a town called ath-Thaniya, "where preparations were made for entering the desert."

Even in modern times, the journey from Syria to Mecca that these pilgrims undertook is a dangerous one, but Battuta counts on the completion of his pilgrimage through the desert to transform him, recalling an old saying: "He who enters it is lost, and he who leaves it is born." Battuta is not blind to the dangers of the journey, and he recounts cautionary tales and known dangers from past travelers. At the last stop before Medina, Battuta makes note that this is the farthest that Christians can travel on the Arabian Peninsula, as the notable Muslim tolerance did not extend to Islam's holiest sites. The group then enters Medina, the second-holiest site in Islam, where the prophet Muhammad and his companions Omar and Abu Bakr

are buried. After leaving Medina, the pilgrims change into the ceremonial garb required of pilgrims and make their way to Mecca.

Battuta describes his visit to Mecca in detail, taking pains to praise the people of the city for their cleanliness and hospitality, but he does not describe the rituals of the hajj in detail, perhaps counting on his reader to know what would have been done. Upon entering Mecca, Battuta and his fellow pilgrims "immediately entered the holy sanctuary and began the rites of pilgrimage." After his departure from Mecca, Battuta continues to describe the people and places he encounters with the same zest as when he visited Mecca.

Essential Themes

The primary theme of this selection is the importance of the hajj and the more general observations of a traveler in the Muslim world of the fourteenth century. Ibn Battuta is a detailed observer, though others have questioned his ability to recall so much detail from his travels, about which he did not write himself, but only dictated to a scribe decades later. Still, they are a unique window into the everyday life of a traveler in parts of the world that remained mysterious to the West for centuries. Ibn Battuta saw the world from the perspective of a Muslim and observed customs and institutions that were meaningful to him. He commented in detail on charitable institutions, for example, and noted scholars and mystics. He was joined by many thousands in his completion of the hajj, but is one of only two narrators from this time whose records of further travels in the Dar al-Islam survived. As flawed as his recollections may be, his experience provides a picture that would have been lost to history otherwise.

—*Bethany Groff, MA*

Bibliography and Additional Reading

Dunn, Ross E. *The Adventures of Ibn Battuta, a Muslim Traveler of the Fourteenth Century.* Berkeley: U of California P, 1986. Print.

Ezzati, A. *The Spread of Islam: The Contributing Factors.* London: Saqi, 2002. Print.

Waines, David. *The Odyssey of Ibn Battuta: Uncommon Tales of a Medieval Adventurer.* Chicago: U of Chicago P, 2010. Print.

Ibn Battuta's Travels in Cairo, Damascus, and Jerusalem

Date: 1326
Geographic Region: present-day Egypt, Syria, Israel
Author: Ibn Battuta

Summary Overview

Ibn Battuta was a legal scholar from Tangier, in what is today Morocco. As a young man, he found his opportunities for further education limited and set out to visit the best libraries and foremost scholars in the Muslim world, which then stretched from the West African coast to Southeast Asia. He was also a personally devout man and wanted to make the hajj, the sacred pilgrimage to Mecca. In his nearly three decades of travel, he saw nearly all of the Dar al-Islam—the Muslim world—as well as important Muslim communities outside its borders. He logged over seventy-five thousand miles in that time. When he finally retired from his travels in 1354 and settled back in Morocco, a local sultan commissioned a record of Ibn Battuta's journey, recorded by a young scholar. Battuta's adventures were recorded in a traditional Arabic form called a *rihla*, a travelogue recounting a search for divine knowledge.

Defining Moment

Islam spread very rapidly during the lifetime of the prophet Muhammad and immediately after his death in 632. Early Islamic leaders, starting with Muhammad himself, were extremely successful in converting conquered communities to Islam, beginning on the Arabian Peninsula and moving quickly into Syria. The instability of the Persian and Byzantine empires contributed to the successful spread of Islam, as it was preferable to many to live under the far more stable Muslim rule. By 636, Syria was conquered, followed by Iraq and Persia. Most of Egypt was brought under Islamic rule in 640, and the rest followed soon after.

Islam spread along trade routes into Africa, Asia Minor, the Balkans, and the Indian subcontinent; by the time of Ibn Battuta's travels, the Dar al-Islam, the area governed by Islam, covered Arabia, Syria, Palestine, Persia, Turkey, South and Southeast Asia, areas of the Mediterranean, eastern Europe, and much of north and central Africa. Islam had advanced as far north as France, but had been blocked from advancing further into Western Europe. Jews, Christians, and Zoroastrians in Muslim lands enjoyed fairly cordial treatment, and they were allowed to practice their religion, but they had to pay a special tax.

The relative longevity and stability of the medieval Islamic world produced a remarkable flourishing of cultural and scientific endeavor. The willingness of Islamic leaders to blend the traditions of the lands that they conquered and converted with their own contributed to a period when traditions from Asia, Europe, and even ancient Greece, Rome, and Egypt combined to produce advances in medicine, mathematics, art, and literature. Islamic rulers supported scholars and teachers financially, and such professions held a respected position in society. Trade was crucial to this cultural flowering, as ideas and books could be spread throughout the Islamic world. Developments in navigation were critical to the establishment of overseas trade, and Muslims were the first to use a sextant and sail a three-masted ship. Overland trade and pilgrimage routes were well-established and protected, though pilgrims like Ibn Battuta often traveled together to ensure their safety.

Though Ibn Battuta is an extreme example, Muslim culture also valued the tradition of travel, as the hajj, the visit to the birthplace of the prophet Muhammad in Arabia, was the duty of every able-bodied Muslim. By the fourteenth century, pilgrims would gather in major cities by the thousands and make their way to Mecca by well-established roads. It was his desire to perform this religious duty that sent Ibn Battuta on his twenty-nine year journey.

Author Biography and Document Information

Ibn Battuta was born Abu Abdullah Muhammad ibn Abdullah al Lawati al Tanji ibn Battuta in 1304 in Tangier, a port in northern Morocco. He was born into a Berber family of legal scholars and was educated in a local school. In 1325, Ibn Battuta set off in search of further education and to perform the hajj, the traditional Muslim pilgrimage to Mecca. Though he did visit Mecca, his travels eventually took him as far as India, China, and Spain. He traveled for a total of twenty-nine years before returning to Fez, Morocco, where his travels were recorded for posterity. Ibn Battuta worked as a judge in Fez, and little is known of his later life. He died in 1368 or 1369.

The *Rihla* of Ibn Battuta was unknown in the Western world until German explorer Ulrich Jasper Seetzen found and purchased a copy in the early nineteenth century. The work was first published in 1818 in German and French journals. Excerpts were translated into English in 1829, and during the French occupation of Algeria, five more manuscripts were acquired by the Bibliothèque Nationale in Paris. During the twentieth century, Battuta's complete work has been translated into English and published in four volumes, the last one in 1994.

HISTORICAL DOCUMENT

Arrival in Cairo

I arrived at length at Cairo, mother of cities and seat of Pharaoh the tyrant, mistress of broad regions and fruitful lands, boundless in multitude of buildings, peerless in beauty and splendour, the meeting-place of comer and goer, the halting-place of feeble and mighty, whose throngs surge as the waves of the sea, and can scarce be contained in her for all her size and capacity. It is said that in Cairo there are twelve thousand water-carriers who transport water on camels, and thirty thousand hirers of mules and donkeys, and that on the Nile there are thirty-six thousand boats belonging to the Sultan and his subjects which sail upstream to Upper Egypt and downstream to Alexandria and Damietta, laden with goods and profitable merchandise of all kinds.

A pleasure garden

On the bank of the Nile opposite Old Cairo is the place known as The Garden, which is a pleasure park and promenade, containing many beautiful gardens, for the people of Cairo are given to pleasure and amusements. I witnessed a fete once in Cairo for the sultan's recovery from a fractured hand; all the merchants decorated their bazaars and had rich stuffs, ornaments and silken fabrics hanging in their shops for several days.

Religious institutions

The mosque of 'Amr is highly venerated and widely celebrated. The Friday service is held in it and the road runs through it from east to west. The madrasas of Cairo cannot be counted for multitude. As for the Maristan, which lies "between the two castles" near the mausoleum of Sultan Qala'un, no description is adequate to its beauties. It contains an innumerable quantity of appliances and medicaments, and its daily revenue is put as high as a thousand dinars.

There are a large number of religious establishments which they call khanqahs, and the nobles vie with one another in building them. Each of these is set apart for a separate school of darwishes, mostly Persians, who are men of good education and adepts in the mystical doctrines. Each has a superior and a doorkeeper and their affairs are admirably organized. They have many special customs one of which has to do with their food. The steward of the house comes in the morning to the darwishes, each of whom indicates what food he desires, and when they assemble for meals, each person is given his bread and soup in a separate dish, none sharing with another. They eat twice a day. They are each given winter clothes and summer clothes, and a monthly allowance of from twenty to thirty dirhams. Every Thursday night they receive sugar cakes, soap to wash their clothes, the price of a bath, and oil for their lamps. These men are celibate; the married men have separate convents.

At Cairo too is the great cemetery of al-Qarafa, which is a place of peculiar sanctity and contains the graves of innumerable scholars and pious believers. In the Qarafa the people build beautiful pavilions surrounded by walls, so that they look like houses. They also build chambers and hire Koran-readers who recite night and day in agreeable voices. Some of them build religious houses and madrasas beside the mausoleums and on Thursday nights they go out to spend the night there with their children and women-folk, and make a circuit of the famous tombs. They go out to spend the night there also on the "Night of midSha'ban," and the market-people take out all kinds of eatables. Among the many celebrated sanctuaries is the holy shrine where there reposes the head of alHusayn. Beside it is a vast monastery of striking construction, on the doors of which there are silver rings and plates of the same metal.

The great river Nile

The Egyptian Nile surpasses all rivers of the earth in sweetness of taste, length of course, and utility. No other river in the world can show such a continuous series of towns and villages along its banks, or a basin so intensely cultivated. Its course is from South to North, contrary to all the other great rivers. One extraordinary thing about it is that it begins to rise in the extreme hot weather at the time when rivers generally diminish and dry up, and begins to subside just when rivers begin to increase and overflow. The river Indus resembles it in this feature. The Nile is one of the five great rivers of the world, which are the Nile, Euphrates, Tigris, Syr Darya and Amu Darya; five other rivers resemble these, the Indus, which is called Panj Ab, the river of India which is called Gang—it is to it that the Hindus go on pilgrimage, and when they burn their dead they throw the ashes into it, and they say that it comes from Paradise—the river Jun in India, the river Itil in the Qipchaq steppes, on the banks of which is the city of Sara, and the river Saru in the land of Cathay. All these will be mentioned in their proper places, if God will. Some distance below Cairo the Nile divides into three streams, none of which can be crossed except by boat, winter or summer. The inhabitants of every township have canals led off the Nile; these are filled when the river is in flood and carry the water over the fields.

Upriver

From Cairo I travelled into Upper Egypt, with the intention of crossing to the Hijaz. On the first night I stayed at the monastery of Dayr at-Tin, which was built to house certain illustrious relics—a fragment of the Prophet's wooden basin and the pencil with which he used to apply kohl, the awl he used for sewing his sandals, and the Koran belonging to the Caliph Ali written in his own hand. These were bought, it is said, for a hundred thousand dirhams by the builder of the monastery, who also established funds to supply food to all comers and to maintain the guardians of the sacred relics.

Thence my way lay through a number of towns and villages to Munyat Ibn Khasib, a large town which is built on the bank of the Nile, and most emphatically excels all the other towns of Upper Egypt. I went on through Manfalut, Asyut, Ikhmim, where there is a berba with sculptures and inscriptions which no one can now read—another of these berbas there was pulled down and its stones used to build a madrasa—Qina, Qus, where the governor of Upper Egypt resides, Luxor, a pretty little town containing the tomb of the pious ascetic Abu'l-Hajjaj, Esna, and thence a day and a night's journey through desert country to Edfu.

Camels, hyenas, and Bejas

Here we crossed the Nile and, hiring camels, journeyed with a party of Arabs through a desert, totally devoid of settlements but quite safe for travelling. One of our halts was at Humaythira, a place infested with hyenas. All night long we kept driving them away, and indeed one got at my baggage, tore open one of the sacks, pulled out a bag of dates, and made off with it. We found the bag next morning, torn to pieces and with most of the contents eaten. After fifteen days' travelling we reached the town of Aydhab, a large town, well supplied with milk and fish; dates and grain are imported from Upper Egypt. Its inhabitants are Bejas. These people are black-skinned; they wrap themselves in yellow blankets and tie headbands about a fingerbreadth wide round their heads. They do not give their daughters any share in their inheritance. They live on camels milk and they ride on Meharis. One-third of the city belongs to the Sultan of Egypt and two-thirds to the King of the Bejas, who is called al-Hudrubi. On reaching Aydhab we found that al-Hudrubi was engaged in warfare with the Turks, that he had sunk the ships and that the Turks had fled before him. It was impossible for us to attempt the sea-crossing, so we sold the provisions that we had made ready for it, and returned to Qus with the Arabs from whom we had hired the camels.

Back downriver to Cairo; from Cairo to Syria and Jerusalem

We sailed thence down the Nile (it was at the flood time) and after an eight days' journey reached Cairo, where I stayed only one night, and immediately set out for Syria. This was in the middle of July, 1326. My route lay through Bilbays and as-Salihiya, after which we entered the sands and halted at a number of stations. At each of these there was a hostelry which they call a khan, where travellers alight with their beasts. Each khan has a water wheel supplying a fountain and a shop at which the traveller buys what he requires for himself and his beast.

Crossing the border into Syria

At the station of Qatya customs-dues are collected from the merchants, and their goods and baggage are thoroughly examined and searched. There are offices here, with officers, clerks, and notaries, and the daily revenue is a thousand gold dinars. No one is allowed to pass into Syria without a passport from Egypt, nor into Egypt without a passport from Syria, for the protection of the property of the subjects and as a measure of precaution against spies from Iraq. The responsibility of guarding this road has been entrusted to the Badawin. At nightfall they smooth down the sand so that no track is left on it, then in the morning the governor comes and looks at the sand. If he finds any track on it he commands the Arabs to bring the person who made it, and they set out in pursuit and never fail to catch him. He is then brought to the governor, who punishes him as he sees fit. The governor at the time of my passage treated me as a guest and showed me great kindness, and allowed all those who were with me to pass. From here we went on to Gaza, which is the first city of Syria on the side next the Egyptian frontier.

On the road to Jerusalem: Hebron and Bethlehem

From Gaza I travelled to the city of Abraham, the mosque of which is of elegant, but substantial construction, imposing and lofty, and built of squared stones. At one angle of it there is a stone, one of whose faces measures twenty-seven spans. It is said that Solomon commanded the jinn to build it. Inside it is the sacred cave containing the graves of Abraham, Isaac, and Jacob, opposite which are three graves, which are those of their wives. I questioned the imam, a man of great piety and learning, on the authenticity of these graves, and he replied: "All the scholars whom I have met hold these graves to be the very graves of Abraham, Isaac, Jacob and their wives. No one questions this except introducers of false doctrines; it is a tradition which has passed from father to son for generations and admits of no doubt." This mosque contains also the grave of Joseph, and somewhat to the east of it lies the tomb of Lot, which is surmounted by an elegant building. In the neighbourhood is Lot's lake, which is brackish and is said to cover the site of the settlements of Lot's people.

On the way from Hebron to Jerusalem, I visited Bethlehem, the birthplace of Jesus. The site is covered by a large building; the Christians regard it with intense veneration and hospitably entertain all who alight at it.

Jerusalem and its holy sites

We then reached Jerusalem (may God ennoble her!), third in excellence after the two holy shrines of Mecca and Medina and the place whence the Prophet was caught up into heaven. Its walls were destroyed by the illustrious King Saladin and his Successors, for fear lest the Christians should seize it and fortify themselves in it. The sacred mosque is a most beautiful building, and is said to be the largest mosque in the world. Its length from east to west is put at 752 "royal" cubits and its breadth at 435. On three sides it has many entrances, but on the south side I know of one only, which is that by which the imam enters. The entire mosque is an open court and unroofed, except the mosque al-Aqsa, which has a roof of most excellent workmanship, embellished with gold and brilliant colours. Some other parts of the mosque are roofed as well. The Dome of the Rock is a building of extraordinary beauty, solidity, elegance, and singularity of shape. It stands on an elevation in the centre of the mosque and is reached by a flight of marble steps. It has four doors. The space round it is also paved with marble, excellently done, and the interior likewise. Both outside and inside the decoration is so magnificent and the workmanship so surpassing as to defy description. The greater part is covered with gold so that the eyes of one who gazes on its beauties are dazzled by its brilliance, now glowing like a mass of light, now flashing like lightning. In the centre of the Dome is the blessed rock from which the Prophet ascended to heaven, a great rock projecting about a man's height, and underneath it there is a cave the size of a small room, also of a man's height, with steps leading down to it. Encircling the rock are two railings of excellent workmanship, the one nearer the rock being artistically constructed in iron and the other of wood.

The Christian holy places

Among the grace-bestowing sanctuaries of Jerusalem is a building, situated on the farther side of the valley called the valley of Jahannam to the east of the town, on a high hill. This building is said to mark the place whence Jesus ascended to heaven. In the bottom of the same valley is a church venerated by the Christians, who say that it contains the grave of Mary. In the same place there is another church which the Christians venerate and to which they come on pilgrimage. This is the church of which they are falsely persuaded to believe that it contains the grave of Jesus. All who come on pilgrimage to visit it pay a stipulated tax to the Muslims, and suffer very unwillingly various humiliations. Thereabouts also is the place of the cradle of Jesus which is visited in order to obtain blessing.

Arrival in Damascus

I entered Damascus on Thursday 9th Ramadan 726, and lodged at the Malikite college called ash-Sharabishiya. Damascus surpasses all other cities in beauty, and no description, however full, can do justice to its charms.

The Ummayad Mosque

The Cathedral Mosque, known as the Umayyad Mosque, is the most magnificent mosque in the world, the finest in construction and noblest in beauty, grace and perfection; it is matchless and unequalled. The person who undertook its construction was the Caliph Walid I. He applied to the Roman Emperor at Constantinople, ordering him to send craftsmen to him, and the Emperor sent him twelve thousand of them. The site of the mosque was a church, and when the Muslims captured Damascus, one of their commanders entered from one side by the sword and reached as far as the middle of the church, while the other entered peaceably from the eastern side and reached the middle also. So the Muslims made the half of the church which they had entered by force into a mosque and the half which they had entered by peaceful agreement remained as a church. When Walid decided to extend the mosque over the entire church he asked the Greeks to sell him their church for whatsoever equivalent they desired, but they refused, so he seized it. The Christians used to say that whoever destroyed the church would be stricken with madness and they told that to Walid. But he replied "I shall be the first to be stricken by madness in the service of God," and seizing an axe, he set to work to knock it down with his own hands. The Muslims on seeing that followed his example, and God proved false the assertion of the Christians.

This mosque has four doors. The southern door, called the "Door of Increase," is approached by a spacious passage where the dealers in second-hand goods and other commodities have their shops. Through it lies the way to the Cavalry House, and on the left as one emerges from it is the coppersmiths' gallery, a large bazaar, one of the finest in Damascus, extending along the south wall of the mosque. This bazaar occupies the site of the palace of the Caliph Mu'awiya I, which was called al Khadri; the Abbasids pulled it down and a bazaar took its place.

The eastern door, called the Jayrun door, is the largest of the doors of the mosque. It also has a large passage, leading out to a large and extensive colonnade which is entered through a quintuple gateway between six tall columns. Along both sides of this passage are pillars, supporting circular galleries, where the cloth merchants amongst others have their shops; above these again are long galleries in which are the shops of the jewellers and booksellers and makers of admirable glass-ware. In the square adjoining the first door are the stalls of the principal notaries, in each of which there may be five or six witnesses in attendance and a person authorized by the qadi to perform marriage-ceremonies. The other notaries are scattered throughout the city. Near these stalls is the bazaar of the stationers who sell paper, pens, and ink. In the middle of the passage there is a large round marble basin, surrounded by a pavilion supported on marble columns but lacking a roof. In the centre of the basin is a copper pipe which forces out water under pressure so that it rises into the air more than a man's height. They call it "The Waterspout" and it is a fine sight. To the right as one comes out of the Jayrun door, which is called also the "Door of the Hours," is an upper gallery shaped like a large arch, within which there are small open arches furnished with doors, to the number of the hours of the day. These doors are painted green on the inside and yellow on the outside, and as each hour of the day passes the green inner side of the door is turned to the outside, and vice versa. They say that inside the gallery there is a person in the room who is responsible for turning them by hand as the hours pass.

The western door is called the "Door of the Post"; the passage outside it contains the shops of the candlemakers and a gallery for the sale of fruit.

The northern door is called the "Door of the Confectioners"; it too has a large passageway, and on the right as one leaves it is a khanqah, which has a large basin of water in the centre and lavatories supplied with running water. At each of the four doors of the mosque is a building for ritual ablutions, containing about a hundred rooms abundantly supplied with running water.

A controversial theologian

One of the principal Hanbalite doctors at Damascus was Taqi ad-Din Ibn Taymiya, a man of great ability and wide learning, but with some kink in his brain. The people of Damascus idolized him. He used to preach to them from the pulpit, and one day he made some statement that the other theologians disapproved; they carried the case to the sultan and in consequence Ibn Taymiya was imprisoned for some years. While he was in prison he wrote a commentary on the Koran, which he called "The Ocean," in about forty volumes. Later on his mother presented herself before the sultan and interceded for him, so he was set at liberty, until he did the same thing again. I was in Damascus at the time and attended the service which he was conducting one Friday, as he was addressing and admonishing the people from the pulpit. In the midst of his discourse he said "Verily God descends to the sky over our world in the same bodily fashion that I make this descent," and stepped down one step of the pulpit. A Malikite doctor present contradicted him and objected to his statement, but the common people rose up against this doctor and beat him with their hands and their shoes so severely that his turban fell off and disclosed a silken skull-cap on his head. Inveighing against

him for wearing this, they haled him before the qadi of the Hanbalites, who ordered him to be imprisoned and afterwards had him beaten. The other doctors objected to this treatment and carried the matter before the principal amir, who wrote to the sultan about the matter and at the same time drew up a legal attestation against Ibn Taymiya for various heretical pronouncements. This deed was sent on to the sultan, who gave orders that Ibn Taymiya should be imprisoned in the citadel, and there he remained until his death.

The Plague of 1348

One of the celebrated sanctuaries at Damascus is the Mosque of the Footprints (al-Aqdam), which lies two miles south of the city, alongside the main highway which leads to the Hijaz, Jerusalem, and Egypt. It is a large mosque, very blessed, richly endowed, and very highly venerated by the Damascenes. The footprints from which it derives its name are certain footprints impressed upon a rock there, which are said to be the mark of Moses' foot. In this mosque there is a small chamber containing a stone with the following inscription "A certain pious man saw in his sleep the Chosen One, who said to him 'Here is the grave of my brother Moses.'"

I saw a remarkable instance of the veneration in which the Damascenes hold this mosque during the great pestilence on my return journey through Damascus, in the latter part of July 1348. The viceroy Arghun Shah ordered a crier to proclaim through Damascus that all the people should fast for three days and that no one should cook anything eatable in the market during the daytime. For most of the people there eat no food but what has been prepared in the market. So the people fasted for three successive days, the last of which was a Thursday, then they assembled in the Great Mosque, amirs, sharifs, qadis, theologians, and all the other classes of the people, until the place was filled to overflowing, and there they spent the Thursday night in prayers and litanies. After the dawn prayer next morning they all went out together on foot, holding Korans in their hands, and the amirs barefooted. The procession was joined by the entire population of the town, men and women, small and large; the Jews came with their Book of the Law and the Christians with their Gospel, all of them with their women and children. The whole concourse, weeping and supplicating and seeking the favour of God through His Books and His Prophets, made their way to the Mosque of the Footprints, and there they remained in supplication and invocation until near midday. They then returned to the city and held the Friday service, and God lightened their affliction; for the number of deaths in a single day at Damascus did not attain two thousand, while in Cairo and Old Cairo it reached the figure of twenty-four thousand a day.

The good and pious works of the Damascenes

The variety and expenditure of the religious endowments at Damascus are beyond computation. There are endowments in aid of persons who cannot undertake the pilgrimage to Mecca, out of which are paid the expenses of those who go in their stead. There are other endowments for supplying wedding outfits to girls whose families are unable to provide them, and others for the freeing of prisoners. There are endowments for travellers, out of the revenues of which they are given food, clothing, and the expenses of conveyance to their countries. Then there are endowments for the improvement and paving of the streets, because all the lanes in Damascus have pavements on either side, on which the foot passengers walk, while those who ride use the roadway in the centre.

The story of a slave who broke a valuable dish

Besides these there are endowments for other charitable purposes. One day as I went along a lane in Damascus I saw a small slave who had dropped a Chinese porcelain dish, which was broken to bits. A number of people collected round him and one of them said to him, "Gather up the pieces and take them to the custodian of the endowments for utensils." He did so, and the man went with him to the custodian, where the slave showed the broken pieces and received a sum sufficient to buy a similar dish. This is an excellent institution, for the master of the slave would undoubtedly have beaten him, or at least scolded him, for breaking the dish, and the slave would have been heartbroken and upset at the accident. This benefaction is indeed a mender of hearts—may

God richly reward him whose zeal for good works rose to such heights!

Hospitality and friendship received

The people of Damascus vie with one another in building mosques, religious houses, colleges and mausoleums. They have a high opinion of the North Africans, and freely entrust them with the care of their moneys, wives, and children. All strangers amongst them are handsomely treated and care is taken that they are not forced to any action that might injure their self-respect.

When I came to Damascus a firm friendship sprang up between the Malikite professor Nur ad-Din Sakhawi and me, and he besought me to breakfast at his house during the nights of Ramadan. After I had visited him for four nights I had a stroke of fever and absented myself. He sent in search of me, and although I pleaded my illness in excuse he refused to accept it. I went back to his house and spent the night there, and when I desired to take my leave the next morning he would not hear of it, but said to me "Consider my house as your own or as your father's or brother's." He then had a doctor sent for, and gave orders that all the medicines and dishes that the doctor prescribed were to be made for me in his house. I stayed thus with him until the Fast-breaking when I went to the festival prayers and God healed me of what had befallen me. Meanwhile, all the money I had for my expenses was exhausted. Nur ad-Din, learning this, hired camels for me and gave me travelling and other provisions, and money in addition, saying "It will come in for any serious matter that may land you in difficulties"— may God reward him!

Funeral customs

The Damascenes observe an admirable order in funeral processions. They walk in front of the bier while reciters intone the Koran in beautiful and affecting voices, and pray over it in the Cathedral mosque. When the reading is completed the muezzins rise and say "Reflect on your prayer for so-and-so, the pious and learned," describing him with good epithets, and having prayed over him they take him to his grave.

GLOSSARY

amir: also emir, a chieftan or commander in some Islamic countries

caliph: the spiritual and at times political head of the Islamic world, considered a successor to the prophet Muhammad; in Battuta's day, based in Cairo under the Mamluk Sultanate

darwish: honorary name of a Sufi holy man, also called a dervish

fete: also fête; a day of celebration, holiday, a festive celebration

Hijaz: a sacred Islamic region in what is today western Saudi Arabia, where the holy cities of Mecca and Medina are located

khanqah: a Sufi hostel or spiritual retreat center

madrasa: an Islamic religious school

medicament: a healing substance; medicine

mosque: an Islamic house of worship

qadi: a judge in a Muslim community who makes decisions based on Islamic religious law

sharif: a governor of Mecca descended from Muhammad; an Arab chief, prince or ruler

viceroy: a person appointed to rule a country or province as the deputy of a sovereign

Document Analysis

This selection of Ibn Battuta's *Rihla* covers an early stage of his journey when he traveled to Cairo and on through the Middle East. The details of his travels were not written down at the time but were dictated to a student after his return to Morocco later in his life. Though some scholars question the veracity of his memory, these impressions form one of the most complete pictures of the medieval Islamic world.

Battuta found Cairo magnificent, crowded and teeming with life. He notes the animals that worked in the city, and the thousands of boats used for trade up and down the Nile River. He makes note of the city's many religious buildings and also the abundant evidence of charitable work, including hospitals and convents for the poor. Charity, as one of the five pillars of Islam, was a requirement of the faithful, and so many elites competed with one another to provide relief to the poor. He describes the wide variety and copious quantity of goods for sale, and comments extensively on the vendors and merchants throughout the city. He

also describes the Nile as a sacred river, central to the life and livelihood of all of Egypt.

After his stay in Cairo, Battuta relates his attempt to continue on to Mecca by traveling up the Nile and then to the port town of Aydhab on the Red Sea. On his way there, he stayed at the homes of local scholars and holy men, and a monastery housing Islamic relics such as a bowl and pencil said to have belonged to Muhammad. Because of local military hostilities, Battuta was not able to sail from Aydhab, but turned around and returned to Cairo. Once there, he set out for Damascus, Syria, where he would be easily able to find a group of pilgrims to accompany on the hajj.

Battuta kept up a tourist's pace through Syria, stopping at hostels centered on water wheels, and then at cities with strong religious meaning along the way. He comments on Gaza, Bethlehem, Hebron, and particularly on Jerusalem, whose ownership had been contested for centuries (as it remains in the twenty-first century). He makes a note of the destruction of the walls of Jerusalem: "Its walls were destroyed by the illustrious King Saladin and his Successors, for fear lest the Christians should seize it and fortify themselves in it." He lists the sites of Christian pilgrimage, acknowledging that they "suffer very unwillingly various humiliations" at the hands of the Muslim authorities in order to be allowed to pray at their holy sites. When he finally entered Damascus, it was the month of Ramadan, when all Muslims fast during daylight hours. He was impressed with the city and comments at length about its fine mosques, its renowned scholars, and its customs. During his time in Damascus, he fell ill, and it is notable that he concludes this section with a description of a funeral.

Essential Themes

The primary theme of this selection is the observations of a traveler in the Muslim world of the fourteenth century. Ibn Battuta was a detailed observer, though others have questioned his ability to recall so much detail from travels that took place decades before he recorded them. Still, they are a unique window into everyday life of a traveler in parts of the world that remained mysterious to the West for centuries. Ibn Battuta saw the world from the perspective of a Muslim and observed customs and institutions that were meaningful to him. He commented in detail on charitable institutions, for example, and noted scholars and mystics. He was joined by many thousands in his completion of the hajj, but is one of only two narrators whose records of further travels in the Dar al-Islam survived. His experience, as flawed as his recollections may be, provides a perspective that would have been lost to history otherwise.

—Bethany Groff, MA

Bibliography and Additional Reading

Dunn, Ross E. *The Adventures of Ibn Battuta, a Muslim Traveler of the Fourteenth Century.* Berkeley: U of California P, 1986. Print.

Ezzati, A. *The Spread of Islam: The Contributing Factors.* London: Saqi, 2002. Print.

Waines, David. *The Odyssey of Ibn Battuta: Uncommon Tales of a Medieval Adventurer.* Chicago: U of Chicago P, 2010. Print.

■ Ibn Battuta's Travels to Mali

Date: 1352
Geographic Region: Mali
Author: Ibn Battuta

Summary Overview

Ibn Battuta traveled across the Sahara Desert to Mali near the end of his travels, which had begun nearly three decades earlier. Ibn Battuta was a legal scholar from Tangier, in present-day Morocco. As a young man, he found his opportunities for further education limited. In 1325, he set out to visit the best libraries and foremost scholars in the Muslim world, which then stretched from the West African coast to Southeast Asia. He was also a personally devout man and wanted to make the hajj, the sacred pilgrimage to Mecca. The Muslim world at the time was called the Dar al-Islam, and in his twenty-nine years of travel, Ibn Battuta saw nearly all of it, as well as important Muslim communities outside its borders. He logged over seventy-five thousand miles in that time. When he finally retired from his travels in 1354 and settled back in Morocco, a local sultan commissioned a record of Ibn Battuta's journey, recorded by a young scholar. Battuta's adventures were recorded in a traditional Arabic form called a *rihla*, a travelogue recounting a search for divine knowledge.

Defining Moment

Ibn Battuta's is one of a small number of first-person accounts by travelers of the African land he called "Mali," known to historians as the Mali Empire, which lasted from around 1230 CE to around 1600. It was at perhaps its greatest extent in Ibn Battuta's day, centered on the Niger River and stretching from the city of Gao to the Atlantic Ocean, across large swaths of the present-day countries of Mali, Mauritania, and Senegal. It was part of the Dar al-Islam. Africans were introduced to Islam around 800 CE by Arab traders enticed to the inhospitable region by rumors of vast quantities of gold south of the Sahara Desert. Most of the merchants and traders in the cities along the borders of Mali adopted Islam, and it became the official religion of all of Mali around 1200.

Islam spread along trade routes into not just Africa but also Asia Minor, the Balkans, and the Indian subcontinent; by the time of Ibn Battuta's travels, the Dar al-Islam covered Arabia, Syria, Palestine, Persia, Turkey, South and Southeast Asia, areas of the Mediterranean, eastern Europe, and much of north and central Africa. Islam had advanced as far north as France, but had been blocked from advancing further into Western Europe. Jews, Christians, and Zoroastrians in Muslim lands enjoyed fairly cordial treatment, and they were allowed to practice their religion, but they had to pay a special tax.

The relative longevity and stability of the medieval Islamic world produced a remarkable flourishing of cultural and scientific endeavor. The willingness of Islamic leaders to blend the traditions of the lands that they conquered and converted with their own contributed to a period when traditions from Asia, Europe, and even ancient Greece, Rome, and Egypt combined to produce advances in medicine, mathematics, art, and literature. Islamic rulers supported scholars and teachers financially, and such professions held a respected position in society. Trade was crucial to this cultural flowering, as ideas and books could be spread throughout the Islamic world. Developments in navigation were critical to the establishment of overseas trade, and Muslims were the first to use a sextant and sail a three-masted ship. Overland trade and pilgrimage routes were well-established and protected, though pilgrims like Ibn Battuta often traveled together to ensure their safety.

Though Ibn Battuta is an extreme example, Muslim culture also valued the tradition of travel, as the hajj, the pilgrimage to the birthplace of the prophet Muhammad in Arabia, was the duty of every able-bodied Muslim. By the fourteenth century, pilgrims would gather in major cities by the thousands and make their way to Mecca by well-established roads. It was his desire to perform this religious duty that sent Ibn Battuta on his twenty-nine year journey.

Author Biography and Document Information

Ibn Battuta was born Abu Abdullah Muhammad ibn Abdullah al Lawati al Tanji ibn Battuta in 1304 in Tangier, a port in northern Morocco. He was born into a Berber family of legal scholars and was educated in a local school. In 1325, Ibn Battuta set off in search of further education and to perform the hajj, the traditional Muslim pilgrimage to Mecca. Though he did visit Mecca, his travels eventually took him as far as India, China, and Spain. He traveled for a total of twenty-nine years before returning to Fez, Morocco, where his travels were recorded for posterity. Ibn Battuta worked as a judge in Fez, and little is known of his later life. He died in 1368 or 1369.

The *Rihla* of Ibn Battuta was unknown in the Western world until German explorer Ulrich Jasper Seetzen found and purchased a copy in the early nineteenth century. The work was first published in 1818 in German and French journals. Excerpts were translated into English in 1829, and during the French occupation of Algeria, five more manuscripts were acquired by the Bibliothèque Nationale in Paris. During the twentieth century, Battuta's complete work was translated into English and published in four volumes, the last one in 1994.

HISTORICAL DOCUMENT

From Walata to the river Niger

When I decided to make the journey to Malli, which is reached in twenty-four days from Iwalatan if the traveller pushes on rapidly, I hired a guide from the Massufa—for there is no necessity to travel in a company on account of the safety of that road—and set out with three of my companions.

On the way there are many trees, and these trees are of great age and girth; a whole caravan may shelter in the shade of one of them. There are trees which have neither branches nor leaves, yet the shade cast by their trunks is sufficient to shelter a man. Some of these trees are rotted in the interior and the rain-water collects in them, so that they serve as wells and the people drink of the water inside them. In others there are bees and honey, which is collected by the people. I was surprised to find inside one tree, by which I passed, a man, a weaver, who had set up his loom in it and was actually weaving.

A traveller in this country carries no provisions, whether plain food or seasonings, and neither gold nor silver. He takes nothing but pieces of salt and glass ornaments, which the people call beads, and some aromatic goods. When he comes to a village the womenfolk of the blacks bring out millet, milk, chickens, pulped lotus fruit, rice, "funi" (a grain resembling mustard seed, from which "kuskusu" and gruel are made), and pounded haricot beans. The traveller buys what of these he wants, but their rice causes sickness to whites when it is eaten, and the funi is preferable to it.

Reaching the Niger river [identified as the Nile]

The Nile flows from there down to Kabara, and thence to Zagha. In both Kabara and Zagha there are sultans who owe allegiance to the king of Malli. The inhabitants of Zagha are of old standing in Islam; they show great devotion and zeal for study.

Thence the Nile descends to Tumbuktu and Gawgaw, both of which will be described later; then to the town of Muli in the land of the Limis, which is the frontier province of Malli; thence to Yufi, one of the largest towns of the negroes, whose ruler is one of the most considerable of the negro rulers. It cannot be visited by any white man because they would kill him before he got there.

A crocodile

I saw a crocodile in this part of the Nile, close to the bank; it looked just like a small boat. One day I went down to the river to satisfy a need, and lo, one of the blacks came and stood between me and the river. I was amazed at such lack of manners and decency on his part, and spoke of it to someone or other. [That person] answered. "His purpose in doing that was solely to protect you from the crocodile, by placing himself between you and it."

The city of Mali, capital of the kingdom of Mali

Thus I reached the city of Malli, the capital of the king of the blacks. I stopped at the cemetery and went to the quarter occupied by the whites, where I asked for Muhammad ibn al-Faqih. I found that he had hired a house for me and went there. His son-in-law brought me candles and food, and next day Ibn al-Faqih himself came to visit me, with other prominent residents. I met the qadi of Malli, 'Abd ar-Rahman, who came to see me; he is a negro, a pilgrim, and a man of fine character. I met also the interpreter Dugha, who is one of the principal men among the blacks. All these persons sent me hospitality-gifts of food and treated me with the utmost generosity—may God reward them for their kindnesses!

Ten days after our arrival we ate a gruel made of a root resembling colocasia, which is preferred by them to all other dishes. We all fell ill—there were six of us—and one of our number died. I for my part went to the morning prayer and fainted there. I asked a certain Egyptian for a loosening remedy and he gave me a thing called "baydar," made of vegetable roots, which he mixed with aniseed and sugar, and stirred in water. I drank it off and vomited what I had eaten, together with a large quantity of bile. God preserved me from death but I was ill for two months.

Meeting the king of Mali

The sultan of Malli is Mansa Sulayman, "mansa" meaning sultan, and Sulayman being his proper name. He is a miserly king, not a man from whom one might hope for a rich present. It happened that I spent these two months without seeing him, on account of my illness. Later on he held a banquet in commemoration of our master Abu'l-Hasan, to which the commanders, doctors, qadi and preacher were invited, and I went along with them. Reading-desks were brought in, and the Koran was read through, then they prayed for our master Abu'l-Hasan and also for Mansa Sulayman.

When the ceremony was over I went forward and saluted Mansa Sulayman. The qadi, the preacher, and Ibn al-Faqih told him who I was, and he answered them in their tongue. They said to me, "The sultan says to you 'Give thanks to God,'" so I said, "Praise be to God and thanks under all circumstances." When I withdrew the hospitality gift was sent to me. It was taken first to the qadi's house, and the qadi sent it on with his men to Ibn al-Faqih's house. Ibn al-Faqih came hurrying out of his house barefooted, and entered my room saying, "Stand up; here comes the sultan's stuff and gift to you." So I stood up thinking—since he had called it "stuff"—that it consisted of robes of honour and money, and lo!, it was three cakes of bread, and a piece of beef fried in native oil, and a calabash of sour curds. When I saw this I burst out laughing, and thought it a most amazing thing that they could be so foolish and make so much of such a paltry matter.

The court ceremonial of king Sulayman of Mali

On certain days the sultan holds audiences in the palace yard, where there is a platform under a tree, with three steps; this they call the "pempi." It is carpeted with silk and has cushions placed on it. [Over it] is raised the umbrella, which is a sort of pavilion made of silk, surmounted by a bird in gold, about the size of a falcon. The sultan comes out of a door in a corner of the palace, carrying a bow in his hand and a quiver on his back. On his head he has a golden skull-cap, bound with a gold band which has narrow ends shaped like knives, more than a span in length. His usual dress is a velvety red tunic, made of the European fabrics called "mutanfas." The sultan is preceded by his musicians, who carry gold and silver guimbris, and behind him come three hundred armed slaves. He walks in a leisurely fashion, affecting a very slow movement, and even stops from time to time. On reaching the pempi he stops and looks round the assembly, then ascends it in the sedate manner of a preacher ascending a mosque-pulpit. As he takes his seat the drums, trumpets, and bugles are sounded. Three slaves go out at a run to summon the sovereign's deputy and the military commanders, who enter and sit down. Two saddled and bridled horses are brought, along with two goats, which they hold to serve as a protection against the evil eye. Dugha stands at the gate and the rest of the people remain in the street, under the trees.

The negroes are of all people the most submissive to their king and the most abject in their behaviour before him. They swear by his name, saying "Mansa Sulayman ki". If he summons any of them while he is holding an audience in his pavilion, the person summoned takes off his clothes and puts on worn garments, removes his turban and dons a dirty skullcap, and enters with his garments and trousers raised knee-high. He goes forward in an attitude of humility and dejection and knocks the ground hard with his elbows, then stands with bowed head and bent back listening to what he says. If anyone addresses the king and receives a reply from him, he uncovers his back and throws dust over his head and back, for all the world like a bather splashing himself with water. I used to wonder how it was they did not blind themselves. If the sultan delivers any remarks during his audience, those present take off their turbans and put them down, and listen in silence to what he says.

Sometimes one of them stands up before him and recalls his deeds in the sultan's service, saying, "I did so-and-so on such a day," or, "I killed so-and-so on such a day." Those who have knowledge of this confirm his words, which they do by plucking the cord of the bow and releasing it, just as an archer does when shooting an arrow. If the sultan says, "Truly spoken," or thanks him, he removes his clothes and "dusts." That is their idea of good manners.

Festival ceremonial

I was at Malli during the two festivals of the sacrifice and the fast-breaking. On these days the sultan takes his seat on the pempi after the midafternoon prayer. The armour-bearers bring in magnificent arms--quivers of gold and silver, swords ornamented with gold and with golden scabbards, gold and silver lances, and crystal maces. At his head stand four amirs driving off the flies, having in their hands silver ornaments resembling saddle-stirrups. The commanders, qadi and preacher sit in their usual places.

The interpreter Dugha comes with his four wives and his slave-girls, who are about a hundred in number. They are wearing beautiful robes, and on their heads they have gold and silver fillets, with gold and silver balls attached. A chair is placed for Dugha to sit on. He plays on an instrument made of reeds, with some small calabashes at its lower end, and chants a poem in praise of the sultan, recalling his battles and deeds of valour. The women and girls sing along with him and play with bows. Accompanying them are about thirty youths, wearing red woollen tunics and white skull-caps; each of them has his drum slung from his shoulder and beats it. Afterwards come

his boy pupils who play and turn wheels in the air, like the natives of Sind. They show a marvellous nimbleness and agility in these exercises and play most cleverly with swords. Dugha also makes a fine play with the sword. Thereupon the sultan orders a gift to be presented to Dugha and he is given a purse containing two hundred mithqals of gold dust and is informed of the contents of the purse before all the people. The commanders rise and twang their bows in thanks to the sultan. The next day each one of them gives Dugha a gift, every man according to his rank. Every Friday after the 'asr prayer, Dugha carries out a similar ceremony to this that we have described.

On feast-days after Dugha has finished his display, the poets come in. Each of them is inside a figure resembling a thrush, made of feathers, and provided with a wooden head with a red beak, to look like a thrush's head. They stand in front of the sultan in this ridiculous make-up and recite their poems. I was told that their poetry is a kind of sermonizing in which they say to the sultan: "This pempi which you occupy was that whereon sat this king and that king, and such and such were this one's noble actions and such and such the other's. So do you too do good deeds whose memory will outlive you." After that the chief of the poets mounts the steps of the pempi and lays his head on the sultan's lap, then climbs to the top of the pempi and lays his head first on the sultan's right shoulder and then on his left, speaking all the while in their tongue, and finally he comes down again. I was told that this practice is a very old custom amongst them, prior to the introduction of Islam, and that they have kept it Up.

The people of Mali

The negroes possess some admirable qualities. They are seldom unjust, and have a greater abhorrence of injustice than any other people. Their sultan shows no mercy to anyone who is guilty of the least act of it. There is complete security in their country. Neither traveller nor inhabitant in it has anything to fear from robbers or men of violence. They do not confiscate the property of any white man who dies in their country, even if it be uncounted wealth. On the contrary, they give it into the charge of some trustworthy person among the whites, until the rightful heir takes possession of it. They are careful to observe the hours of prayer, and assiduous in attending them in congregations, and in bringing up their children to them.

Their piety

On Fridays, if a man does not go early to the mosque, he cannot find a corner to pray in, on account of the crowd. It is a custom of theirs to send each man his boy with his prayer-mat; the boy spreads it out for his master in a place befitting him until he comes to the mosque. Their prayer-mats are made of the leaves of a tree resembling a date-palm, but without fruit.

Another of their good qualities is their habit of wearing clean white garments on Fridays. Even if a man has nothing but an old worn shirt, he washes it and cleans it, and wears it to the Friday service. Yet another is their zeal for learning the Koran by heart. They put their children in chains if they show any backwardness in memorizing it, and they are not set free until they have it by heart. I visited the qadi in his house on the day of the festival. His children were chained up, so I said to him, "Will you not let them loose?" He replied, "I shall not do so until they learn the Koran by heart."

The nakedness of their women

Among their bad qualities are the following. The women servants, slave-girls, and young girls go about in front of everyone naked, without a stitch of clothing on them. Women go into the sultan's presence naked and without coverings, and his daughters also go about naked. Then there is their custom of putting dust and ashes on their heads, as a mark of respect, and the grotesque ceremonies we have described when the poets recite their verses. Another reprehensible practice among many of them is the eating of carrion, dogs, and asses.

Leaving Mali

The date of my arrival at Malli was 14th Jumada I, 53, and of my departure from it 22nd Muharram of the year 54.

The hippos of the river Niger

I was accompanied by a merchant called Abu Bakr ibn Ya'qub. We took the Mima road. I had a camel which I was riding, because horses are expensive, and cost a hundred mithqals each. We came to a wide channel which flows out of the Nile and can only be crossed in boats. The place is infested with mosquitoes, and no one can pass that way except by night. We reached the channel three or four hours after nightfall on a moonlit night.

On reaching it I saw sixteen beasts with enormous bodies, and marvelled at them, taking them to be elephants, of which there are many in that country. Afterwards I saw that they had gone into the river, so I said to Abu Bakr, "What kind of animals are these?" He replied, "They are hippopotami which have come out to pasture ashore." They are bulkier than horses, have manes and tails, and their heads are like horses' heads, but their feet like elephants' feet. I saw these hippopotami again when we sailed down the Nile from Tumbuktu to Gawgaw. They were swimming in the water, and lifting their heads and blowing. The men in the boat were afraid of them and kept close to the bank in case the hippopotami should sink them.

They have a cunning method of catching these hippopotami. They use spears with a hole bored in them, through which strong cords are passed. The spear is thrown at one of the animals, and if it strikes its leg or neck it goes right through it. Then they pull on the rope until the beast is brought to the bank, kill it and eat its flesh. Along the bank there are quantities of hippopotamus bones.

Cannibals

We halted near this channel at a large village, which had as governor a negro, a pilgrim, and man of fine character named Farba Magha. He was one of the negroes who made the pilgrimage in the company of Sultan Mansa Musa. Farba Magha told me that when Mansa Musa came to this channel, he had with him a qadi, a white man. This qadi attempted to make away with four thousand mithqals and the sultan, on learning of it, was enraged at him and exiled him to the country of the heathen cannibals. He lived among them for four years, at the end of which the sultan sent him back to his own country. The reason why the heathens did not eat him was that he was white, for they say that the white is indigestible because he is not "ripe," whereas the black man is "ripe" in their opinion.

Sultan Mansa Sulayman was visited by a party of these negro cannibals, including one of their amirs. They have a custom of wearing in their ears large pendants, each pendant having an opening of half a span. They wrap themselves in silk mantles, and in their country there is a gold mine. The sultan received them with honour, and gave them as his hospitality-gift a servant, a negress. They killed and ate her, and having smeared their faces and hands with her blood came to the sultan to thank him. I was informed that this is their regular custom whenever they visit his court. Someone told me about them that they say that the choicest parts of women's flesh are the palm of the hand and the breast.

Arrival in Timbuktoo

Thence we went on to Tumbuktu, which stands four miles from the river. Most of its inhabitants are of the Massufa tribe, wearers of the face-veil. Its governor is called Farba Musa. I was present with him one day when he had just appointed one of the Massufa to be amir of a section. He assigned to him a robe, a turban, and trousers, all of them of dyed cloth, and bade him sit upon a shield, and the chiefs of his tribe raised him on their heads. In this town is the grave of the meritorious poet Abu Ishaq as-Sahili, of Gharnata, who is known in his own land as at-Tuwayjin.

Leaving Timbuktoo for Gogo

From Tumbuktu I sailed down the Nile on a small boat, hollowed out of a single piece of wood.

I went on . . . to Gawgaw, which is a large city on the Nile, and one of the finest towns in the Negrolands. It is also one of their biggest and best-provisioned towns, with rice in plenty, milk, and fish, and there is a species of cucumber there called "inani" which has no equal. The buying and selling of its inhabitants is done with cowry-shells, and the same is the case at Malli. I stayed there about a month, and then set out in the direction of Tagadda by land with a large caravan of merchants from Ghadamas.

GLOSSARY

amir: a title of nobility in Arabic, referring to a prince or other high ranking official; also spelled "emir"

calabash: a hollowed-out gourd used as a container

colocasia: a type of flowering plant from southeastern Asia and India

guimbri: a stringed instrument similar to a guitar, used in West Africa

mithqal: a gold coin used for centuries across much of the Islamic world

qadi: a judge in a Muslim community who makes decisions based on Islamic religious law

Document Analysis

This selection of Ibn Battuta's *Rihla* covers the last stage in his journey, when he traveled to Mali (often spelled "Malli" in the text) and its major trading center, Timbuktu. The details of this period of his adventures may be among the most reliable, since they were recorded by a student soon after his return from Mali. Battuta started off from Fez, in his home country of Morocco, in 1351, and came to the northern border of the Sahara Desert in February 1352.

Ibn Battuta expresses fascination with the landscape and the people of Mali, whom he refers to as "the blacks." He makes note of the size and use of massive trees along the route (identifiable as baobabs, though not named as such in the text)—so massive that "a whole caravan may shelter in the shade of one of them." Some of these trees were hollow inside, and in one the space was so large that a man had set up a loom inside and was weaving. Battuta also describes scenes along the Niger River, which he mistook for the Nile. He relates an amusing instance when he went to the river to "fulfill a need" (presumably urination), and one of the locals came and stood between him and the river, which seemed to Ibn Battuta quite rude. In fact, the man was protecting him from large crocodiles in the river. Ibn Battuta traveled southwest along the Niger until he reached the capital of Mali—also called Mali—and was met with a warm reception from notable men in the city, though he was not able to meet the king for two months because Ibn Battuta had a terrific case of food poisoning.

When Battuta finally did meet Mansa Sulayman, the ruler of Mali, he was unimpressed with his welcome. After a traditional meeting, he was sent a gift from the king, which was attended with great anticipation and pomp. When the gift turned out to be a meager meal, Battuta was amused, "thinking that it consisted of robes of honour and money, and lo!, it was three cakes of bread, and a piece of beef fried in native oil, and a calabash of sour curds. When I saw this I burst out laughing, and thought it a most amazing thing that they could be so foolish and make so much of such a paltry matter." He contrasted this pitiful gift with the reverence and abject servitude shown to the king by his subjects, who put on dirty clothes and threw dirt on themselves in his presence. Battuta observed a festival where poets sang the praises of the kings, and he noted that this was a holdover from pre-Islamic times. He gave a thorough review of the people of Mali, laying out their good points, chiefly their honesty, hospitality, and piety. He did not approve of the nakedness of Mali women, however, and he thought their rituals were "grotesque."

Ibn Mattuta left the Mali capital and traveled by camel to Timbuktu, and he comments on first seeing a hippopotamus, which he describes in fascinated detail. This selection ends with his trip down the Niger River to Gao (rendered in the text as "Gogo" or "Gawgaw"), another important commercial city.

Essential Themes

This selection is one of a very small number of first-person traveler accounts of the Mali Empire of the fourteenth century, making it a crucial source for this part of African history. Ibn Battuta's observations, though flawed by the limits of his memory and colored by his own biases, are a unique window into everyday life by a Muslim traveler in parts of the world that remained mysterious to the West for centuries. Ibn Battuta saw the world from the perspective of a Muslim, and he observed customs and institutions that were meaningful to him. He commented in detail on charitable institutions, for example, and noted scholars and mystics. He was joined by many thousands in his completion of the hajj, but is one of only two narrators whose records of further travels in the Dar al-Islam survived. His experience, as flawed as his recollections may be, provides a perspective that would have been lost to history otherwise.

—*Bethany Groff, MA*

Bibliography and Additional Reading

Dunn, Ross E. *The Adventures of Ibn Battuta, a Muslim Traveler of the Fourteenth Century.* Berkeley: U of California P, 1986. Print.

Ezzati, A. *The Spread of Islam: The Contributing Factors.* London: Saqi, 2002. Print.

Waines, David. *The Odyssey of Ibn Battuta: Uncommon Tales of a Medieval Adventurer.* Chicago: U of Chicago P, 2010. Print.

PHILOSOPHY, RELIGION, AND SCIENCE

Through most of the Middle Ages, education was an ad hoc affair. The majority of the populace received no formal education; the focus, instead, was on learning a trade through an apprenticeship or from a family member. Every Catholic diocese was supposed to operate a school, but there is little evidence that such was the case. Many monasteries seem to have run schools, but these were attended primarily by adepts within the monastery, not young people from the surrounding area. Royalty and other elites could afford private tutors, and for the serious student a wealthy family might arrange to have him or her become a pupil under a master at a university.

By the late 1100s, the university system of higher education had begun to take shape. The university setting featured an established curriculum, standardized texts (most of which had to be certified by the church), and different levels of achievement, with their associated degrees. The method of questioning, dialectical reasoning, between student and master was one advanced by Thomas Aquinas in Paris during the 13th century, though it was based on classical precedents. Called scholasticism, the school of thought to which Aquinas belonged encouraged questioning to gain a better understanding of Christian doctrine. One understood that religious belief—faith—transcended logic and reasoning, however. Saint Anselm, for example, an Italian who served as prior in a Norman abbey before becoming Archbishop of Canterbury, held that faith was paramount but that reason could stimulate or reinforce faith.

The men who built up scholasticism in the High Middle Ages, then, were not just university masters but officials or representatives of the church. In general, people in the Middle Ages did not think of religion or faith as something apart from earthly life; rather, the two interpenetrated each other and made every thought and action part of a larger calculus about god and man in the universe.

■ On Fate and Providence, from *The Consolation of Philosophy*

Date: 523
Geographic Region: Rome
Author: Boethius
Translator: Richard Hooker

Summary Overview

The Consolation of Philosophy (originally titled *De consolatione philosophiae* and translated into English in the late ninth century) is a work that married Greek Neoplatonist dialogue with a Christian view of a providential God. Its author, Boethius, was born around the end of the Western Roman Empire, and his life and work are a bridge between classical philosophy and the Middle Ages. Boethius was from an elite Roman family. He was well educated in Greek philosophy, and he translated, wrote, and studied mathematics, logic and philosophy, and theology. He wrote *The Consolation of Philosophy*—an imagined dialogue between him and philosophy personified as a woman—while in prison in northern Italy, awaiting execution after being arrested on charges of treason.

Defining Moment

The Rome that Boethius was born into was a world in transition. Three hundred years earlier, the Roman Empire stretched from Turkey to the Atlantic Ocean. The empire was a patchwork of languages and traditions, generally tolerated by the central Roman government, whose primary interest was in collecting taxes and gaining territory. Historians debate the causes of the decline of the Roman Empire, but by the third century, the empire was divided by civil war, plague, and threatened invasion from Germanic tribes. The seat of the empire moved east to the city of Byzantium in 330 CE and was renamed Constantinople, while corulers were, at times, established to administer the eastern and western halves of the empire. Rome and the rest of modern-day Italy remained part of the empire, but were under increasing threat from invaders. The final rulers of the Western Roman Empire were controlled by tribal warlords, and the capital was moved in 402 from Rome to Ravenna. In 476, Odoacer, a Germanic tribesman, deposed the last Western Roman emperor and declared himself king of Rome, though nominally he still paid symbolic tribute to the Eastern Roman emperor in Constantinople.

Though Boethius was born in Rome during this period of turmoil, his family was allowed to maintain their customs and privileged position during the reign of Odoacer. In 493, however, Odoacer was defeated and killed by Theodoric, leader of the Ostrogoths, who set up a new kingdom in Italy. Theodoric had been raised and educated as a hostage at the court of Constantinople, and maintained a tenuous relationship with the Eastern emperor. He had been given a Roman education and understood the value of preserving Roman institutions, and he promoted capable Roman aristocrats to powerful positions in his government, including Boethius, his sons, and his adopted father. Theodoric valued the education and experience of Boethius, who was widely known for his knowledge on a variety of subjects.

After a period of peace, tensions grew between Theodoric and the new Eastern emperor, Justin I. When Boethius came to the defense of a former consul accused of treason for his correspondence with Justin I, Boethius was himself charged with treason. During his subsequent imprisonment, he produced *The Consolation of Philosophy*.

Author Biography

Boethius (Anicius Manlius Severinus) was born in Rome around 480 CE to an aristocratic family. His father was a consul, but died when Boethius was a child; Boethius was adopted and raised by another patrician and scholar, Quintus Aurelius Memmius Symmachus, from whom Boethius learned philosophy and mastered Greek, increasingly uncommon in Christianized Rome. Boethius wrote extensively on logic, philosophy, mathematics, and theology. Around 510, he was brought into the service of Theodoric, the Ostrogoth king, and in 522, both of his sons were made consuls and he was appointed to the position of *magister officiorum*, essentially the head of civil services. In this office, he investigated charges of corruption and alienated many former allies in court. He also defended a former consul against charges of treason and was then accused

himself of treason. He was taken to a country estate far from Rome, where he was eventually executed around 524. Although steeped in Greek philosophy as well as Christian theology, Boethius was revered as a Christian martyr. In 1883, he was declared a saint by the Catholic Church, which noted his insight into the nature of providence.

HISTORICAL DOCUMENT

Fate and Providence 1 (Book IV, Prose 6)

"It remains," I said, "for you to explain this apparent injustice I'm suffering now [that is, Boethius' imprisonment, torture, and impending execution]."

"The question you're asking," Lady Philosophy replied with a smile, "is the grandest of all mysteries, one which can never be explained completely to the human intellect, for, when one problem is removed, many more arise to take its place, and arise and arise unless the mind is keen and awake. For the problem you raise touches on a number of difficult questions: the simplicity of Providence, the nature of Fate, the unpredictability of Chance, divine and human knowledge, predestination, and free will. You know the difficulty involved in these questions; nevertheless, I will try to answer them in the short space allotted us."

Then, as though she were beginning for the first time, Philosophy said, "The coming-into-being of all things, and the entire course that changeable things take, derive their causes, their order, and their forms from the unchanging mind of God. The mind of God set down all the various rules by which all things are governed while still remaining unchanged in its own simplicity. When the government of all things is seen as belonging to the simplicity and purity of the divine mind, we call it 'Providence.' When this government of all things is seen from the point of view of the things that change and move, that is, all things which are governed, from the very beginning of time we have called this 'Fate.' We can easily see that Providence and Fate are different if we think over the power of discernment each has. Providence is the divine reason, the divine logos, and only belongs to the highest ruler of all things: it is the perspective of the divine mind. 'Fate,' on the other hand, belongs to the things that

change and is the way in which Providence joins things together in their proper order. Providence views all things equally and at the same time, despite their diversity and seemingly infinite magnitude. Fate sets individual things in motion once their proper order and form has been established. In other words, Providence is the vision of the divine mind as it sees the unfolding in time of all things, and sees all these things all at once, whereas the unfolding of these events in time, seen as they unfold in time, is called Fate. Even though the two are different, the one depends on the other, for the complex unfolding of Fate derives from the unity of Providence. Think of it this way: a craftsman imagines in his mind the form of whatever thing he intends to make before he sets about making it; he makes it by producing in time through a succession of acts that thing that he originally conceived of in his mind. God, in his Providence, in a unified and simple way, orders all things that are to be done in time; Fate is the unfolding in time through a succession of acts in the order God has conceived. Therefore, whether or not Fate is worked out by angelic spirits serving God, or by some "soul," or nature, or the motions of the stars, or the devil himself, or by none or all of these, one thing you can be certain of: Providence is the unchangeable, simple, and unified form of all things which come into and pass out of existence, while Fate is the connection and temporal order of all those things which the divine mind decided to bring into existence. This leads to the conclusion that all things subject to Fate are in turn subject to Providence; therefore, Fate itself is subject to Providence.

"However, some things subject to Providence are not in turn subject to Fate. For example: consider the example of spheres orbiting around a central point. The sphere closest to the center inscribes a motion very much like the center itself, since its orbit is very small, whereas the outermost sphere circles about in a massively wide orbit which increases in size the farther the sphere retreats from the center. If any of these spheres were to occupy the center, it would become simple like the center and cease to move in space. In this very same way are things related to the divine mind: whatever is at the greatest distance from the divine mind is the most entangled in the nets of Fate; whatever is nearest to the divine mind approaches the center of everything. If anything should adhere directly to the divine mind, it ceases to move and frees itself from the necessities of Fate. We conclude that the changing course of Fate is to the immovable unity of Providence as reasoning is to intellect, as that which comes into and passes from existence is to that which always exists, as time is to eternity, as a circle to its center. Fate moves the heavens and all the stars, governs the basic elements and their combinations, and transforms these mixtures and combinations of elements in reciprocal change. Fate renews all mortal things by allowing them to reproduce into similar creatures. This same power, this Fate, connects all the actions and fortunes of humanity into an unbreakable chain of causation; these causes have their origin in unchangeable Providence, therefore, these causes, too, must be unchangeable. This is how things of the world are governed: all things are produced and affected by an unchangeable order of causes that originate in the unity and simplicity of the divine mind, and this unchangeable order of causes, because it never changes, controls the changeable things which would, without this governance, fall into chaos and disorder. Therefore, even though to you, since you do not understand the unchanging order that governs all things, the changeable things of this world may seem to be chaotic and disordered, still everything is governed by a set and proper order which directs everything in existence towards the Good. Nothing whatsoever is ever done or created for the sake of evil, which includes the actions of evil men, which also are directed towards the good even though their perverted and wretched wills do not conceive this. The order which derives from the center of all things does not turn anyone from their proper course.

"Now, your original question concerns the apparent confusion and disorder which seems to be manifestly shown forth when good men both prosper and suffer, and evil men both prosper and suffer and get both what they want and what they do not want. First, is human judgement so perfect that it can discern who is truly good and who is truly evil? If that were true, why do humans disagree so often, so that the same person is thought by one group to deserve the highest rewards and is thought by another group to deserve the most miserable punishments? Even if I were to grant that some people can somehow distinguish between good and evil people, would that person also be able to look inside the soul and, like a doctor examining a body, discern the inner condition of the person? . . . Now the health of the soul is virtue, and the sickness of the soul is vice. Now, who else is the physician of the soul but God, who preserves and rewards the good and punishes the wicked, and who sees in the great panorama of Providence what is best for everyone? Here is the great conclusion about Fate we have been tending to: divine wisdom understands and does what humanity, in their ignorance, never can understand.

"Because of this ignorance, I will confine myself to explaining what your limited intellect can understand about the divine mind. You may see a man and judge him to be just and good; Providence, which sees all things including the inner condition of the man, may view the man completely otherwise. Thus the poet Lucan wrote that even though Cato was on the side of the conquered, the gods were on the side of the conquerors. Therefore, when something happens which appears contrary to your opinion of right and wrong, it is your opinion which is wrong and confused, while the order of things is right. Let me give you an example. Suppose we have a man who is so fortunate that he seems to be the beloved of God and men. This man may be so weak that were he to suffer any adversity at all, even the slightest, he would buckle and collapse and forsake all virtue and goodness if he did not feel it brought him any profit. Therefore, God in his wise governance spares this poor man any adversity that might ruin his virtue, so that he who cannot bear suffering need not suffer. Suppose we have another man, perfectly virtuous, saintly, and truly beloved of God; this man may also be kept free from illness because it is not right for him to suffer any adversity at all. . . . To other people, Providence mixes both prosperity and adversity according to the condition of their souls; Providence gives suffering to those who would be ruined by too much prosperity, and tests others with sufferings and difficulties who would strengthen their virtue and patience with such sufferings. Most humans are of two types: some are terrified of burdens they can easily bear, while others dismiss burdens they are, in fact, unable to bear. Providence leads both these types through various trials to self-knowledge. Some people earn fame through glorious death or by not breaking down under the most horrific torture; these people prove that evil cannot overcome goodness: it is beyond doubt that these adversities were good, just, and beneficial to the ones who suffered them.

"Let us look at evil men. Sometime their lives are easy and sometimes painful; the source of both of these effects is the divine mind and both of these effects are wrought for the same reasons. Of course, no-one marvels when wicked people suffer, since everyone believes they deserve what they get, for such suffering and punishment prevents others from committing crimes and urges those who are suffering to reform their ways. Yet, evil men who prosper are an extremely powerful argument for good people, for they see, in the prosperity of the wicked, how they should judge the good fortune the wicked often enjoy. The prosperity of the wicked lead to another good, for if it is in the nature of a particular wicked man to be driven to violence and crime if he suffer poverty, Providence prevents this by granting him great wealth. Such a man might compare his evil nature to the good fortune he is enjoying and grow terrified at the possibility of losing his good fortune; he may then reform and behave uprightly as long as he fears losing his wealth. Some evil men who undeservedly enjoy worldly prosperity are driven to ruin by their reprobate character; some evil men have been given the right to heap adversity on the good so that the latter may be tested and strengthened. You see, there is just as much disagreement between evil men and other evil men as there is between evil and good men, because such evil men are frequently in conflict with themselves and their consciences, and are frequently wracked with guilt and self-hatred at their foolishness. From this Providence works the great mystery in which the evil make other evil men good. For when an evil man finds himself unjustly

suffering because of other evil men, that man flares with anger and loathing for those evil men and returns to virtue because he cannot stand to be like the men he hates. To the divine mind alone are all evil things good, because the divine mind brings about good effects from these seemingly evil causes. All things are part of a predetermined order, so that when something moves from the place it has been assigned, it moves into a new order of things. As far as Providence is concerned, there is nothing, nothing whatsoever, that is left to Chance. . . .

"It is sufficient for humans to understand one and only one thing: God, who has created everything in nature, also governs all things and directs them towards good. Since God preserves all things, which are, after all, in his image, God also excludes necessarily, all evil from the boundaries of his government. If you consider only Providence as the governor of all things, you will conclude that evil, which seems to exist all over the universe, does not exist.

Providence and Free Will (Book V, Prose 4 and 6)
If it is granted that Providence sees everything, (past, present, and future), that means that God, from the perspective of Providence, knows in advance everything we are going to do. If that were true, it implies that human beings really don't have any choice in the matter, that our actions have been "predestined" before we even decide to act. Boethius is now convinced that there is no evil in the world, but is now puzzled by this problem of the relation between God's Providence and human "free will," for if all things are predestined, how can we be responsible for our actions? How can we be punished or rewarded if we are not responsible for our actions? The question hinges on the notion of "necessity," which simply defined, means that things happen because of some extrinsic rule either enforced from above or implanted in the very nature of things. Boethius is asking, is the universe "mechanistic"? If God knows things in the future, have their outcomes already been "determined"? Philosophy will answer the question by redefining "necessity." Pay close attention; this rather obtuse and high-falutin' argument will form one of the cornerstones in the development of Enlightenment rationality and science of which we are the heirs.

Prose 4

Philosophy replied, "This is an old enigma about Providence and has occupied your mind for much of your life; no-one, however, has ever really thought about the problem carefully. The reason the problem is so enigmatic is because human reason can never really understand the unity and simplicity of the divine mind. If human beings could understand the divine mind, the problem would disappear. . . .

"Let us start with the following supposition: foreknowledge exists but does not impose necessity on the things it has foreknowledge of. If this were true, the will of human beings would still be independent and absolutely free. Your answer to this would be: even if foreknowledge does not impose necessity, it still indicates that the things it has foreknowledge of will necessarily happen, so that, even if there were no foreknowledge, the possible existence of such foreknowledge would show that the future outcome of all things is somehow necessary. In order to prove that foreknowledge can exist, we first need to prove that all things happen through necessity, since foreknowledge indicates such a necessity. If necessity did not govern things, then no foreknowledge could exist. All proofs depend not on outside arguments, but on deduction from proper and necessary causes. How can it happen, then, that the things which are foreseen will not happen? However, we are not arguing that the things which are foreseen will not happen, only that they have nothing in their natures which make it necessary that they should happen, that is, that there can be divine foreknowledge without necessity. Look now, we see things happening around us all the time . . . do you think these things are happening out of necessity just because you see them happening?" "No," I replied. . . . "Then, since these things happen without necessity, these very same things are not determined by necessity before they happen. Therefore, some things are destined to occur at some future time which are not determined by necessity. . . . For just as knowledge of things which are occurring right now before our eyes does not imply that they are happening out of necessity, so also divine foreknowledge of the things of the future imposes no necessity on those things or their outcomes. "But you'll answer that the question concerns the existence of divine foreknowledge, that there can be no foreknowledge of things which do not occur by necessity. These two things, you'll say, are utterly incompatible: things foreseen must necessarily happen, and if this necessity were not there, those things could not be foreseen. You will say that any knowledge, including foreknowledge, qualifies as knowledge only if it knows things that are certain; so that if uncertain things (anything not governed by necessity) are known as certain (such as divine foreknowledge), this knowledge is, in reality, opinion, not knowledge. . . . The origin of your error in these matters is your assumption that whatever is known is known by the nature of the thing known. However, this assumption is false. Everything which is known is known not according to its own nature and power, but by the capacity and power of the knower. "Confused? Let me give you an example: a body that is round is known to be round in one way through touch and in another way through vision. The vision, which remains at a distance from the round body, takes in the entire body all at once by means of reflected light, but the touch must make contact with the body and understand it in parts by moving about the surface. A human being is understood in different ways by the senses, the imagination, the reason, and the intellect: the senses understand the form as it is constituted in matter; the imagination understand the form without the matter; the reason goes far beyond this in comprehending the universal form of the species which inheres in particular things; the intellect is higher than all these, and passes beyond the universe and sees clearly with the mind the pure Form itself.

Prose 6

"Since we have shown that knowledge is not based on the thing known but on the nature of the knower, let us consider the nature of the Divine Being and what sort of knowledge it has. All rational creatures judge the Divine Being to be eternal, so we should start by explaining the nature of eternity, for this will reveal to us the nature of the Divine Being and the capacity of divine knowledge.

Eternity is the entire and perfect possession of endless life at a single instant. This becomes clear when we consider temporal things: whatever lives in time lives only in the present, which passes from the past into the future, and no temporal thing has such a nature that it can simultaneously embrace its entire existence, for it has not yet arrived at tomorrow and no longer exists in yesterday. Even one's life today exists only in each and every transient moment. Therefore, anything which exists in time . . . cannot properly be considered eternal, for anything in time does not embrace the infinity of life all at once, since it does not embrace the future or the past. Only that which understands and possesses the infinity of endless life, that lacks no future nor has lost any past, can properly be considered eternal. Such an eternal thing fully possesses itself, is always present to itself, and possesses all the infinity of changing time before itself. . . . God should not be thought of as older than creation, but rather prior to it in terms of simplicity and unity. For the endless motion of the things in time imitate the single present of God's changeless intellect. . . . Since every intellect understands according to its own nature, and since God lives in an eternal present, with no past or future, His knowledge transcends the movement of time and exists only in a single, simple, unified present. This knowledge encompasses all things, the endless course of the past and the future, in one single vision as if the infinity of things past and present were occurring in a single instant. Therefore, if you consider the divine foreknowledge through which God knows all things, you will conclude that it is not a knowledge of things in the future but a knowledge of an unchanging present. That is why it is called Providence rather than "prevision," because it sees everything not from their inferior perspective but from above, as it were. Why then, do you think that the things which Providence sees in its eternal present are governed by necessity whereas the things which you see in your present you don't regard as being governed by necessity? Does your vision of things impose necessity on the things which are present before you?" "Not at all," I replied. Lady Philosophy continued, "If we may properly compare God's vision to human vision, He sees all things in an eternal present just as humans see things in a non-eternal present. If you consider divine vision in this light, it follows that divine foreknowledge does not change the nature or the properties of individual things: it simply sees those things as present which we would regard as future. The intellect of God is not confused or changeable: He knows all things intuitively, whether these things happen of necessity or not. Think of it this way: you may happen to see at one and the same time

a man walking down the street and the sun shining in the sky; even though you see both of these at one and the same time, you recognize that one action is a voluntary action, the man walking down the street, and the other is necessary, the shining of the sun. In this manner, the divine mind looks down on all things and, without intervening and changing the nature of the things it is viewing, sees things as eternally present but which, in respect to us, belong to the future. Therefore, when God knows that something is going to happen in the future, he may know a thing which will not happen out of necessity, but voluntarily; God's foreknowledge does not impose necessity on things. "But you might answer that whatever God foresees as happening must necessarily be happening. Now, if we were to be absolutely precise about this word, "necessity," I would have to agree with your objection. But I would answer that a future event may be necessary as regards God's knowledge or vision of it, but voluntary and undetermined in regards to its own nature. How can I say this? There are two types of necessity. One is simple, as when we say that all humans are necessarily mortal. The other is conditional, as when you see a man walking, it is necessary that he's walking, or else you wouldn't see him walking. For whenever a thing is known, it is known as it is and as it must be. This conditional necessity, however, does not imply simple necessity, for it is not caused by the particular nature of the thing, but on some condition added to the thing. No necessity forces the walking man to walk: he has voluntarily chosen to move himself forward using his feet. However, as long as he's walking, he is necessarily moving himself forward using his feet. In the same manner, if Providence sees anything in its eternal present, it follows that this thing exists necessarily in the way Providence sees it, but it may not exist the way it does out of some necessity in its nature. So God sees future things that are the result of human free will; these things, then, are necessary, on the condition that they are known by God, but, considered only in themselves, they are still free in their own natures. . . . Since all this is true, we can conclude that the freedom of human will remains completely independent of God's foreknowledge, and the laws which prescribe rewards and punishments are just since they provide rewards and punishments for the free actions of the human will rather than reward or punish things that happen of necessity. God sees us from above and knows all things in his eternal present and judges our future, free actions, justly distributing rewards and punishments . . .

Document Analysis

The Consolation of Philosophy is Boethius's philosophical examination of his sudden change in status from one of privilege and respect to that of a condemned prisoner. Though he does not explicitly reference Christianity, this work became a foundational text for religious scholars of the Middle Ages, who relied on its discussion of "the simplicity of Providence, the nature of Fate, the unpredictability of Chance, divine and human knowledge, predestination, and free will." In this selection, Boethius carries on a dialogue with "Philosophy" addressing the question of why good people suffer and evil people prosper, and how events are known by God and yet left to the agency of individuals.

Providence is "the government of all things . . . belonging to the simplicity and purity of the divine mind." This is essential to an understanding of fate, which is the governance of "things that change and move," while "providence is the divine reason . . . the highest ruler of all things." This difference allows God to know all and yet to allow events to unfold in complex ways, based on the actions of "angelic spirits serving God, or by some 'soul,' or nature, or the motions of the stars, or the devil himself, or by none or all of these." Providence is God's unchanging view of the course of events over time. Everything, even suffering and punishment, serves a divine purpose, even if the purpose is not readily apparent. Good people may be made better by being tested, and evil people may be turned to good by the evil deeds of others. The nature of good and evil is beyond the comprehension of the human mind, and those who live virtuous lives but suffer can be comforted in the knowledge that there is a purpose to their suffering: "Everything is governed by a set and proper order which directs everything in existence towards the Good."

Boethius also tackles the question of whether or not humans have free will or choice, given that God knows everything. His answer is complicated but hinges on the argument that God experiences time totally differently than humans do; therefore, God does not dictate what is done in the future, but experiences and knows it as it is done. God is at the center of time and knowledge and, therefore, sees future actions the way humans experience the present. Future events, including those that are the result of free will, happen because they are known by God. "God sees us from above and knows all things in his eternal present and judges our future, free actions, justly distributing rewards and punishments."

Essential Themes

Boethius addressed the question of why good people suffer and evil people prosper in a complex dialogue that took its form and tone from Greek philosophy but, nevertheless, became a foundational text for Christian scholars in the Middle Ages. He concluded that there is no true evil; circumstances that appear evil serve purposes not known at the time. Suffering has a deeper meaning, either to reward the just, to cause repentance, or to test resolve. While imprisoned, Boethius also wrestled with the notions of free will and predestination. If God knows everything and what will happen is already set, what is the motivation for good behavior? Boethius argued that time is different for God, who knows the past, present, and future in one unified moment. Because of this, God knows what will happen but does not control its happening in a way that humans can comprehend.

—*Bethany Groff, MA*

Bibliography and Additional Reading

Böhm, Thomas, Thomas Jürgasch, & Andreas Kirchner. *Boethius as a Paradigm of Late Ancient Thought*. Berlin: De Gruyter, 2014. Print.

Chadwick, Henry. *Boethius: The Consolations of Music, Logic, Theology and Philosophy*. Oxford: Clarendon, 1990. Print.

Gottlieb, Anthony. *The Dream of Reason: A History of Philosophy from the Greeks to the Renaissance*. New York: Norton, 2000. Print.

Kaylor, Noel Harold, & Phillip Edward Phillips. *A Companion to Boethius in the Middle Ages*. Leiden: Brill, 2012. Print.

■ Excerpt from St. Anselm's *Proslogium,* or Discourse on the Existence of God

Date: 1077
Geographic Region: Europe
Author: Saint Anselm
Translator: Sidney Norton Deane

Summary Overview

Anselm was a Benedictine monk, philosopher, and Christian scholar, who served as the archbishop of Canterbury from 1093 to 1109. During Anselm's time as archbishop, he became embroiled in the Investiture Controversy and was exiled several times for refusing to allow the English kings William II and Henry I to control the selection of bishops. His refusal to submit to the authority of the state enhanced the power and prestige of the church in England, as he and other prelates throughout Europe changed the relationship between secular and religious leaders. Anselm wrote extensively throughout his life. He is best known for his meditations on the nature of faith and his treatises on the rational proof of the existence of God. His ontological argument for the existence of God, which declares that since the idea of God can exist in the mind, he must exist in reality, has been studied for centuries. This excerpt, from his *Proslogium* of 1077, highlights his commitment to faith despite the challenges in understanding God.

Defining Moment

During the eleventh and twelfth centuries there was extraordinary upheaval in the church in Europe and in England. In 1066, England was conquered by the Duke of Normandy (a region of northern France), who became King William I. He defeated the Anglo-Saxon King Harold and established a new dynasty. William began a wholesale redistribution of land and power, transferring traditional estates and titles to Norman lords. He employed this strategy with both church positions and land, replacing English-born church leaders with his own advisors and friends. He installed Anselm's close friend and advisor Lanfranc as archbishop of Canterbury, and the king and archbishop worked closely together to restructure the English church. Bishops of the church were part of the feudal military structure and were expected to contribute men and money to the king's military adventures. The king sat on church councils, could overrule a church court, and appointed bishops and other church leaders to their positions, ensuring that their primary loyalty was to him. Though the pope and the king clashed over William's refusal to acknowledge the pope as his superior, the conflict never came to a head.

After the death of William I in 1087, Lanfranc supported William's younger son, William II, in a bid for the combined crowns of England and Normandy, which had been split between William II and his older brother Robert. Lanfranc died in 1089, in the midst of this struggle, and William II delayed appointing a new archbishop of Canterbury for four years, redirecting church revenues to his own coffers. When he became seriously ill in 1093, he feared that he was being punished for this behavior and nominated Lanfranc's closest Norman colleague, Anselm, as archbishop. Though Lanfranc and Anselm were closely connected as theologians and had both contributed to the rise of Bec Abbey in Normandy as a Scholastic center in Europe, Anselm was much more interested in reforming the church than his predecessor. Throughout Europe at this time, the Investiture Controversy pitted kings and emperors against the pope, as each side struggled to determine which rulers—secular or religious—were supreme in Christendom. At the heart of the issue was who had the right to appoint bishops and other church leaders, and the conflict was most vitriolic in the Holy Roman Empire, where Pope Gregory VII at one point excommunicated the emperor and was, in turn, driven out of Rome.

Papal assertions of power were no more popular with the English king, and William II and Anselm (whose first loyalty as archbishop was to the pope) immediately came into conflict over questions of church finances and hierarchy. The English clergy, torn between its spiritual duty to the pope and Anselm, but dependent on the king for its position, refused to publicly support the archbishop, and Anselm was given the choice between submission to the king or exile. Choosing the latter, he left for Rome in 1097. William died in a hunting accident in 1100, with Anselm still in Rome, and was succeeded by his younger brother, Henry I. Henry was embroiled in several dynastic conflicts and needed the support of a strong archbishop of Canterbury. He recalled Anselm with a promise that he would work with him on church reform. In 1103, after Henry refused to comply with the promised reforms, Anselm went into exile again. In 1107, Henry and the church settled the controversy with a compromise: Henry gave up his right to choose his bishops and invest them with the symbols of their spiritual office, but he reserved the right to have bishops swear allegiance to him for their secular positions and land.

Author Biography

Anselm was born in 1033 to an aristocratic family in Aosta, Burgundy (in present-day northern Italy).

Though little is known of his education, it is likely that he was privately educated. His later life demonstrated that he was well read and a talented writer and thinker who was also fluent in several languages. Anselm was drawn to a monastic life, and he attempted to enter a monastery without his parents' permission when he was fifteen years old. After he was declined, he traveled widely, until at age twenty-seven, he joined the prominent Benedictine monastery of Bec, in Normandy. He became the prior (a high-ranking monk) of Bec three years later, and then abbot (head monk) in 1078. During his years at Bec, Anselm wrote some of his best-known meditations and treatises, and he was regarded as one of the foremost spiritual teachers of his time. He carried on a lively correspondence with rulers and nobles all over Europe. In 1093, he was made archbishop of Canterbury under William II of England, with whom he came into constant conflict over church finances and reform, and in 1097, he was exiled to Rome. He was recalled in 1100 by the new king, Henry I, who subsequently also forced him into exile from 1103 to 1107. He died in 1109 in Canterbury and was declared a saint in 1494.

HISTORICAL DOCUMENT

CHAPTER I.

Exhortation of the mind to the contemplation of God.—It casts aside cares, and excludes all thoughts save that of God, that it may seek Him. Man was created to see God. Man by sin lost the blessedness for which he was made, and found the misery for which he was not made. He did not keep this good when he could keep it easily. Without God it is ill with us. Our labors and attempts are in vain without God. Man cannot seek God, unless God himself teaches him; nor find him, unless he reveals himself. God created man in his image, that he might be mindful of him, think of him, and love him. The believer does not seek to understand, that he may believe, but he believes that he may understand: for unless he believed he would not understand.

Up now, slight man! flee, for a little while, your occupations; hide yourself, for a time, from your disturbing thoughts. Cast aside, now, your burdensome cares, and put away your toilsome business. Yield room for some little time to God; and rest for a little time in him. Enter the inner chamber of your mind; shut out all thoughts save that of God, and such as can aid you in seeking him; close your door and seek him. Speak now, my whole heart! speak now to God, saying, I seek your face; your face, Lord, will I seek (Psalms xxvii. 8). And come you now, O Lord my God, teach my heart where and how it may seek you, where and how it may find you.

Lord, if you are not here, where shall I seek you, being absent? But if you are everywhere, why do I not see you present? Truly you dwell in unapproachable light. But where is unapproachable light, or how shall I come to it? Or who shall lead me to that light and into it, that I may see you in it? Again, by what marks, under what form, shall I seek you? I have never seen you, O Lord, my God; I do not know your form. What, O most high Lord, shall this man do, an exile far from you? What shall your servant do, anxious in his love of you, and cast out afar from your face? He pants to see you, and your face is too far from him. He longs to come to you, and your dwelling-place is inaccessible. He is eager to find you, and knows not your place. He desires to seek you, and does not know your face. Lord, you are my God, and you are my Lord, and never have I seen you. It is you that hast made me, and has made me anew, and has bestowed upon me all the blessing I enjoy; and not yet do I know you. Finally, I was created to see you, and not yet have I done that for which I was made.

O wretched lot of man, when he has lost that for which he was made! O hard and terrible fate! Alas, what has he lost, and what has he found? What has departed, and what remains? He has lost the blessedness for which he was made, and has found the misery for which he was not made. That has departed without which nothing is happy, and that remains which, in itself, is only miserable. Man once did eat the bread of angels, for which he hungers now; he eateth now the bread of sorrows, of which he knew not then. Alas! for the mourning of all mankind, for the universal lamentation of the sons of Hades! He choked with satiety, we sigh with hunger. He abounded, we beg. He possessed in happiness, and miserably forsook his possession; we suffer want in unhappiness, and feel a miserable longing, and alas! we remain empty.

Why did he not keep for us, when he could so easily, that whose lack we should feel so heavily? Why did he shut us away from the light, and cover us over with darkness? With what purpose did he rob us of life, and inflict death upon us? Wretches that we are, whence have we been driven out; whither are we driven on? Whence hurled? Whither consigned to ruin? From a native country into exile, from the vision of God into our present blindness, from the joy of immortality into the bitterness and horror of death. Miserable exchange of how great a good, for how great an evil! Heavy loss, heavy grief heavy all our fate!

But alas! wretched that I am, one of the sons of Eve, far removed from God! What have I undertaken? What have I accomplished? Whither was I striving? How far have I come? To what did I aspire? Amid what thoughts am I sighing? I sought blessings, and lo! confusion. I strove toward God, and I stumbled on myself. I sought calm in privacy, and I found tribulation and grief, in my inmost thoughts. I wished to smile in the joy of my mind, and I am compelled to frown by the sorrow of my heart. Gladness was hoped for, and lo! a source of frequent sighs!

And you too, O Lord, how long? How long, O Lord, do you forget us; how long do you turn your face from us? When will you look upon us, and hear us? When will you enlighten our eyes, and show us your face? When will you restore yourself to us? Look upon us, Lord; hear us, enlighten us, reveal yourself to us. Restore yourself to us, that it may be well with us,—yourself, without whom it is so ill with us. Pity our toilings and strivings toward you since we can do nothing without you. You do invite us; do you help us. I beseech you, O Lord, that I may not lose hope in sighs, but may breathe anew in hope. Lord, my heart is made bitter by its desolation; sweeten you it, I beseech you, with your consolation. Lord, in hunger I began to seek you; I beseech you that I may not cease to hunger for you. In hunger I have come to you; let me not go unfed. I have come in poverty to the Rich, in misery to the Compassionate; let me not return empty and despised. And if, before I eat, I sigh, grant, even after sighs, that which I may eat. Lord, I am bowed down and can only look downward; raise me up that I may look upward. My iniquities have gone over my head; they overwhelm me; and, like a heavy load, they weigh me down. Free me from them; unburden me, that the pit of iniquities may not close over me.

Be it mine to look up to your light, even from afar, even from the depths. Teach me to seek you, and reveal yourself to me, when I seek you, for I cannot seek you, except you teach me, nor find you, except you reveal yourself. Let me seek you in longing, let me long for you in seeking; let me find you in love, and love you in finding. Lord, I acknowledge and I thank you that you has created me in this your image, in order that I may be mindful of you, may conceive of you, and love you; but that image has been so consumed and wasted away by vices, and obscured by the smoke of wrong-doing, that it cannot achieve that for which it was made, except you renew it, and create it anew. I do not endeavor, O Lord, to penetrate your sublimity, for in no wise do I compare my understanding with that; but I long to understand in some degree your truth, which my heart believes and loves. For I do not seek to understand that I may believe, but I believe in order to understand. For this also I believe, --that unless I believed, I should not understand.

GLOSSARY

iniquities: serious grievances or wickedness; a sin

suffragans: a bishop who is subordinate to a metropolitan or diocesan bishop

Document Analysis

The *Proslogium* (also published under the Greek title *Proslogion* and commonly rendered in English as Discourse on the Existence of God) is written as a meditation, or prayer. It reflects on the nature of God, and endeavors to explain his existence and reconcile his seemingly contradictory attributes. The *Proslogium* is the first work that laid out the ontological argument for the existence of God, an argument that has been studied for centuries by Western theologians and philosophers. The argument is complex, but centers on the idea that if the human mind can conceive of the notion of the greatest possible being or entity (God), then such a being must exist in reality. This argument is put out most strongly in the second chapter of the *Proslogium*. In this first chapter, Anselm seeks to prepare his mind for the contemplation of God. He speaks to his own state of mind, asking God to reveal himself. This type of meditation on the sinfulness of the man seeking God's revelation, and the desire to understand the nature of God, were common forms of prayer, as the penitent sought to rid him- or herself of earthly barriers to communion with God.

Anselm identifies the qualities of his own mind that are obstacles to revelation from God. First, he needs to rid himself of all distractions, as the penitent mind "excludes all thoughts save that of God, that it may seek Him." It is in people's nature, he argues, to seek God; they were made in God's image so that they "might be mindful of him, think of him, and love him." In order to seek understanding of God, a person must also begin with belief. The obstacles to seeking God are present in everyday life. Anselm identifies "occupations . . . disturbing thoughts . . . burdensome cares, and . . . toilsome business" as interfering with the desire to communicate with God. With distractions put away, the penitent is able to seek God with the "whole heart."

The remainder of the chapter expresses the desire to know God, the frustration that comes with not knowing how best to seek him, and the sinfulness that has driven humankind away from the divine purpose for which they were made: "From a native country into exile, from the vision of God into our present blindness, from the joy of immortality into the bitterness and horror of death." Anselm pleads to God to reveal himself and asks that his own sinfulness be forgiven, since only through God's grace and love can people understand him.

Essential Themes

The primary theme of this selection is the obstacles that face the faithful in their pursuit of an understanding of God. Anselm asked that he be forgiven for his sinfulness and that he be allowed to communicate with God. He lays out the obstacles as twofold. One, his own life is filled with distractions, and he must focus himself on the divine. Two, people were driven away from God by their sinfulness, and must ask God for forgiveness and revelation. Since people's purpose is to seek a greater understanding of God, Anselm asks God for forgiveness and help in knowing how to find him. It is only through God's help, and true belief, that the seeker can hope to understand the nature of God.

—*Bethany Groff, MA*

Bibliography and Additional Reading

Blumenthal, Uta-Renate. *The Investiture Controversy: Church and Monarchy from the Ninth to the Twelfth Century.* Philadelphia: U of Pennsylvania P, 2010. Print.

Miller, Maureen C. *Power and the Holy in the Age of the Investiture Conflict: A Brief History with Documents.* New York: Palgrave, 2005. Print.

Visser, Sandra & Thomas Williams. *Anselm.* Oxford: Oxford UP, 2009. Print.

■ "In Behalf of the Fool": A Response to St. Anslem

Date: 1078
Geographic Region: France
Author: Gaunilo
Translator: Sidney Norton Deane

Summary Overview

Gaunilo was a Benedictine monk of the Marmoutier Abbey in France. Little is known of his life outside of his legendary rebuttal to Saint Anselm's ontological argument for the existence of God. Anselm was a Benedictine monk, philosopher, and Christian scholar, who served as the archbishop of Canterbury from 1093 to 1109. He is best known for his meditations on the nature of faith and his treatises on the rational proof of the existence of God. His ontological argument for the existence of God, which declares that since God can exist in the mind, he must exist in reality, was taken to task by Gaunilo, who argued that it was unsound because this logic would prove the existence of every perfect thing. He used the analogy of a perfect island to demonstrate that people would not accept the existence of an island so perfect that human beings could not conceive of a better one based only on the mind's ability to imagine its perfection. Gaunilo's disagreement with Anselm has been studied for centuries, as this debate voiced the fundamental question that continues to be at the heart of Christian philosophy—how people can truly know that God exists.

Defining Moment

Gaunilo and Anselm were both part of the Benedictine order that was at the height of its power in the eleventh century. Both were adherents of the Rule of Saint Benedict, a sixth-century Italian abbot whose regulations for his own monastery were adopted by others across Europe, until it had supplanted most other religious orders. At the heart of the Benedictine rule was the daily order of work (this came to include teaching and writing), prayer, and study, a routine that was conducive to the written meditations that form the bulk of medieval Christian philosophy.

When Anselm wrote his meditation on the nature of God, or *Proslogium*, he was the prior and then the abbot of Bec Abbey in Normandy. The two men may have known each other—their abbeys were linked by their common order, though they operated independently of each other. Under the leadership of Lanfranc, Anselm's predecessor and mentor, Bec had become one of the preeminent centers of scholarship and intellectual life; it continued to flourish under Anselm's leadership. At the same time, Marmoutier was one of the richest monasteries in Christendom, with properties in England after the Norman Conquest and the patronage of the influential Counts of Blois. The monasteries were both powerful and influential and were in competition with one another for patronage and influence. Given these circumstances, it is not surprising that the rebuttal to the work of Anselm of Bec came from a brother at Marmoutier.

Anselm's *Proslogium* was the first to offer the ontological argument for the existence of God. According to this argument, God is "that than which nothing greater can be thought." He is so great that human beings cannot imagine a being who would be greater than he is. Anselm's argument is directed at a biblical fool, who, in the book of Psalms, says, "there is no God." Anselm wished to convince the fool, and this fool is the key to understanding the title of Gaunilo's rebuttal. Anselm argued that the fool could be convinced if he just understood the rational way to think about God. Since the fool understands the idea of God as "that than which nothing greater can be thought," this is the premise of the argument. Anselm stated that if something exists in the mind, it must also exist in reality, which is even greater. If that than which nothing greater can be thought existed only in the mind, it would not be that than which nothing greater can be thought. Since this is contradictory, Anselm declared that God must exist in reality, not just in the understanding mind.

Author Biography

Gaunilo was a monk at the Marmoutier Abbey near Tours, France, in the eleventh century. Nothing is known of his life outside of his response to Anselm's *Proslogium*, and he produced no other written work that survives. The Marmoutier Abbey in which he lived and worked was established in 372 by Saint Martin, bishop of Tours. At the time of Gaunilo's writing, the abbey was under the leadership of Bartholomew of Tours, who extended the abbey's holdings into England. His monks were considered so well disciplined and educated that they were in demand during the establishment of new monasteries or the reformation of old ones throughout England and France. Bartholomew himself fought for the autonomy of the abbey.

HISTORICAL DOCUMENT

1. If one doubts or denies the existence of a being of such a nature that nothing greater than it can be conceived, he receives this answer:

The existence of this being is proved, in the first place, by the fact that he himself, in his doubt or denial regarding this being, already has it in his understanding; for in hearing it spoken of he understands what is spoken of. It is proved, therefore, by the fact that what he understands must exist not only in his understanding, but in reality also.

And the proof of this is as follows.—It is a greater thing to exist both in the understanding and in reality than to be in the understanding alone. And if this being is in the understanding alone, whatever has even in the past existed in reality will be greater than this being. And so that which was greater than all beings will be less than some being, and will not be greater than all: which is a manifest contradiction.

And hence, that which is greater than all, already proved to be in the understanding, must exist not only in the understanding, but also in reality: for otherwise it will not be greater than all other beings.

2. The fool might make this reply:

This being is said to be in my understanding already, only because I understand what is said. Now could it not with equal justice be said that I have in my understanding all manner of unreal objects, having absolutely no existence in themselves, because I understand these things if one speaks of them, whatever they may be?

Unless indeed it is shown that this being is of such a character that it cannot be held in concept like all unreal objects, or objects whose existence is uncertain: and hence I am not able to conceive of it when I hear of it, or to hold it in concept; but I must understand it and have it in my understanding; because, it seems, I cannot conceive of it in any other way than by understanding it, that is, by comprehending in my knowledge its existence in reality.

But if this is the case, in the first place there will be no distinction between what has precedence in time—namely, the having of an object in the understanding—and what is subsequent in time—namely, the understanding that an object exists; as in the example of the picture, which exists first in the mind of the painter, and afterwards in his work.

Moreover, the following assertion can hardly be accepted: that this being, when it is spoken of and heard of, cannot be conceived not to exist in the way in which even God can be conceived not to exist. For if this is impossible, what was the object of this argument against one who doubts or denies the existence of such a being?

Finally, that this being so exists that it cannot be perceived by an understanding convinced of its own indubitable existence, unless this being is afterwards conceived of—this should be proved to me by an indisputable argument, but not by that which you have advanced: namely, that what I understand, when I hear it, already is in my understanding. For thus in my understanding, as I still think, could be all sorts of things whose existence is uncertain, or which do not exist at all, if some one whose words I should understand mentioned them. And so much the more if I should be deceived, as often happens, and believe in them: though I do not yet believe in the being whose existence you would prove.

3. Hence, your example of the painter who already has in his understanding what he is to paint cannot agree with this argument. For the picture, before it is made, is contained in the artificer's art itself; and any such thing, existing in the art of an artificer, is nothing but a part of his understanding itself. A joiner, St. Augustine says, when he is about to make a box in fact, first has it in his art. The box which is made in fact is not life; but the box which exists in his art is life. For the artificer's soul lives, in which all these things are, before they are produced. Why, then, are these things life in the living soul of the artificer, unless because they are nothing else than the knowledge or understanding of the soul itself?

With the exception, however, of those facts which are known to pertain to the mental nature, whatever, on being heard and thought out by the understanding, is perceived to be real, undoubtedly that real object is one thing, and the understanding itself, by which the object is grasped, is another. Hence, even if it were true that there is a being than which a greater is inconceivable: yet to this being, when heard of and understood, the not yet created picture in the mind of the painter is not analogous.

4. Let us notice also the point touched on above, with regard to this being which is greater than all which can be conceived, and which, it is said, can be none other than God himself. I, so far as actual knowledge of the object, either from its specific or general character, is concerned, am as little able to conceive of this being when I hear of it, or to have it in my understanding, as I am to conceive of or understand God himself: whom, indeed, for this very reason I can conceive not to exist. For I do not know that reality itself which God is, nor can I form a conjecture of that reality from some other like reality. For you yourself assert that that reality is such that there can be nothing else like it.

For, suppose that I should hear something said of a man absolutely unknown to me, of whose very existence I was unaware. Through that special or general knowledge by which I know what man is, or what men are, I could conceive of him also, according to the reality itself, which man is. And yet it would be possible, if the person who told me of him deceived me, that the man himself, of whom I conceived, did not exist; since that reality according to which I conceived of him, though a no less indisputable fact, was not that man, but any man.

Hence, I am not able, in the way in which I should have this unreal being in concept or in understanding, to have that being of which you speak in concept or in understanding, when I hear the word God or the words, a being greater than all other beings. For I can conceive of the man according to a fact that is real and familiar to me: but of God, or a being greater than all others, I could not conceive at all, except merely according to the word. And an object can hardly or never be conceived according to the word alone.

For when it is so conceived, it is not so much the word itself (which is, indeed, a real thing—that is, the sound of the letters and syllables) as the signification of the word, when heard, that is conceived. But it is not conceived as by one who knows what is generally signified by the word; by whom, that is, it is conceived according to a reality and in true conception alone. It is conceived as by a man who does not know the object, and conceives of it only in accordance with the movement of his mind produced by hearing the word, the mind attempting to image for itself the signification of the word that is heard. And it would be surprising if in the reality of fact it could ever attain to this.

Thus, it appears, and in no other way, this being is also in my understanding, when I hear and understand a person who says that there is a being greater than all conceivable beings. So much for the assertion that this supreme nature already is in my understanding.

5. But that this being must exist, not only in the understanding but also in reality, is thus proved to me:

If it did not so exist, whatever exists in reality would be greater than it. And so the being which has been already proved to exist in my understanding, will not be greater than all other beings.

I still answer: if it should be said that a being which cannot be even conceived in terms of any fact, is in the understanding, I do not deny that this being is, accordingly, in my understanding. But since through this fact it can in no wise attain to real existence also, I do not yet concede to it that existence at all, until some certain proof of it shall be given.

For he who says that this being exists, because otherwise the being which is greater than all will not be greater than all, does not attend strictly enough to what he is saying. For I do not yet say, no, I even deny or doubt that this being is greater than any real object. Nor do I concede to it any other existence than this (if it should be called existence) which it has when the mind, according to a word merely heard, tries to form the image of an object absolutely unknown to it.

How, then, is the veritable existence of that being proved to me from the assumption, by hypothesis, that it is greater than all other beings? For I should still deny this, or doubt your demonstration of it, to this extent, that I should not admit that this being is in my understanding and concept even in the way in which many objects whose real existence is uncertain and doubtful, are in my understanding and concept. For it should be proved first that this being itself really exists somewhere; and then, from the fact that it is greater than all, we shall not hesitate to infer that it also subsists in itself.

6. For example: it is said that somewhere in the ocean is an island, which, because of the difficulty, or rather the impossibility, of discovering what does not exist, is called the lost island. And they say that this island has an inestimable wealth of all manner of riches and delicacies in greater abundance than is told of the Islands of the Blest; and that having no owner or inhabitant, it is more excellent than all other countries, which are inhabited by mankind, in the abundance with which it is stored.

Now if some one should tell me that there is such an island, I should easily understand his words, in which there is no difficulty. But suppose that he went on to say, as if by a logical inference: "You can no longer doubt that this island which is more excellent than all lands exists somewhere, since you have no doubt that it is in your understanding. And since it is more excellent not to be in the understanding alone, but to exist both in the understanding and in reality, for this reason it must exist. For if it does not exist, any land which really exists will be more excellent than it; and so the island already understood by you to be more excellent will not be more excellent."

If a man should try to prove to me by such reasoning that this island truly exists, and that its existence should no longer be doubted, either I should believe that he was jesting, or I know not which I ought to regard as the greater fool: myself, supposing that I should allow this proof; or him, if he should suppose that he had established with any certainty the existence of this island. For he ought to show first that the hypothetical excellence of this island exists as a real and indubitable fact, and in no wise as any unreal object, or one whose existence is uncertain, in my understanding.

7. This, in the mean time, is the answer the fool could make to the arguments urged against him. When he is assured in the first place that this being is so great that its non-existence is not even conceivable, and that this in turn is proved on no other ground than the fact that otherwise it will not be greater than all things, the fool may make the same answer, and say:

When did I say that any such being exists in reality, that is, a being greater than all others?—that on this ground it should be proved to me that it also exists in reality to such a degree that it cannot even be conceived not to exist? Whereas in the first place it should be in some way proved that a nature which is higher, that is, greater and better, than all other natures, exists; in order that from this we may then be able to prove all attributes which necessarily the being that is greater and better than all possesses.

Moreover, it is said that the non-existence of this being is inconceivable. It might better be said, perhaps, that its non-existence, or the possibility of its non-existence, is unintelligible. For according to the true meaning of the word, unreal objects are unintelligible. Yet their existence is conceivable in the way in which the fool conceived of the non-existence of God. I am most certainly aware of my own existence; but I know, nevertheless, that my non-existence is possible. As to that supreme being, moreover, which God is, I understand without any doubt both his existence, and the impossibility of his non-existence. Whether, however, so long as I am most positively aware of my existence, I can conceive of my non-existence, I am not sure. But if I can, why can I not conceive of the non-existence of whatever else I know with the same certainty? If, however, I cannot, God will not be the only being of which it can be said, it is impossible to conceive of his non-existence.

8. The other parts of this book are argued with such truth, such brilliancy, such grandeur; and are so replete with usefulness, so fragrant with a certain perfume of devout and holy feeling, that though there are matters in the beginning which, however rightly sensed, are weakly presented, the rest of the work should not be rejected on this account. The rather ought these earlier matters to be reasoned more cogently, and the whole to be received with great respect and honor.

Document Analysis

In his *Proslogium*, Anselm of Bec made reference to the fools in the book of Psalms who doubted the existence of God and formulated a solution that he believed even they could understand. God exists, he said, because you can conceive of him.

Gaunilo of Marmoutier's rebuttal points out the weaknesses of that argument. He does not attack the whole of Anselm's *Proslogium*, however, since "parts of this book are argued with such truth . . . that though there are matters in the beginning which, however rightly sensed, are weakly presented, the rest of the work should not be rejected on this account." His logical argument against Anselm's proof of God's existence, based on the analogy of the conception of a perfect island, is one that has been carried forward for centuries by various philosophers. Although Gaunilo's argument is complex, it focuses on the idea that Anselm's proof of the existence of God relies on a verbal trick, itself based on inadequate human understanding. Unless some perfect thing could be proven to exist in the first place, humans could not truly conceive of anything not as great as that object. How could human understanding be such that it could adequately conceive of God? Gaunilo describes this conceptual limitation when he writes, "I do not know that reality itself which God is, nor can I form a conjecture of that reality from some other like reality."

The crux of his argument is that Anselm's proof could be applied to anything perfect. The argument could be made to prove that anything could exist that could be imagined and has nothing greater than it, even things that are obviously false or absurd. He uses the example of an uninhabited island filled with riches. If this island could be conceived of that was greater than any other, then that fact would serve as proof that this island exists in reality. According to Gaunilo, this argument is clearly not enough evidence for a person to simply accept the existence of this island.

Essential Themes

The primary theme of this passage is the weakness of Anselm of Bec's ontological proof of the existence of God. Since his proof was based on the human ability to conceive of the idea of the thing that is greater than all, that thing, called God, must exist in reality. Gaunilo was not arguing against the existence of God, but against Anselm's reasoning. He denied that human understanding could adequately conceive of God, and therefore, it was not possible to subject their understanding to this proof. If the only standard for proving existence was that something must be thought of that is greater than anything else, then he argued that any perfect thing could be claimed to exist. His example of a perfect island is evidence of that. Imagining a perfect island does not make it exist in reality, or at least the idea of it would not be accepted as proof of its existence.

Gaunilo's objection to Anselm's ontological argument inspired a significant debate regarding this argument for God's existence that has continued into the twenty-first century. Anselm issued a response to Gaunilo's challenge, claiming that his original argument only applies to things that have a necessary, rather than contingent, existence, such as God. Over the years, philosophers, including David Hume and Immanuel Kant, have revisited Anselm's argument and the question of God's existence.

—*Bethany Groff, MA*

Bibliography and Additional Reading

Daniel, David Mills. *Briefly: Anselm's Proslogion with the Replies of Gaunilo and Anselm.* London: SCM, 2006. Print.

Smith, A. D. *Anselm's Other Argument.* Cambridge: Harvard UP, 2014. Print.

Visser, Sandra & Thomas Williams. *Anselm.* New York: Oxford UP, 2009. Print.

■ Prologue to *Sic et non*

Date: 1120
Country: France
Author: Peter Abelard
Translator: James Harvey Robinson

Summary Overview

The French theologian and philosopher Peter Abelard wrote *Sic et non* (*Yes and no*) after encountering what he saw as contradictions or opposing concepts in the teachings of the church fathers (early and highly influential Christian theologians). These were unresolved in the teachings of the foremost scholars of his day, and Abelard sought to reconcile them through the application of rigorous logic. Around 1118, an ill-fated romance with a brilliant student, Héloïse d'Argenteuil, resulted in Abelard's castration. He then withdrew to live as a monk at the Abbey of Saint Denis, near Paris. While there, Abelard employed his formidable skill in Latin, Greek, and Hebrew to closely examine the Bible and the writings of the early Christian theologians. He was well-versed in philosophy and theology and assembled a collection of seeming inconsistencies in Christian teachings. In the prologue to *Sic et non*, Abelard laid out methods for resolving these questions, based on logic and deep understanding of the use of language. He encouraged his readers to understand how words could have multiple meanings over time and how the audience, for which a work was intended, could dictate how language was used. Abelard encouraged students to find truth through the "questioning spirit" championed by Aristotle.

Defining Moment

By the end of the eleventh century, the schools and monasteries of France were in a period of ascendancy. After a period of relative fragmentation and instability, the monarchies of Europe were consolidating their power, providing the resources and stability to foster intellectual growth. Monastic estates had grown in wealth and prestige, and gifted teachers became akin to celebrities in scholarly circles. Monumental cathedrals were constructed, classics of Greek and Roman philosophy were rediscovered, and the first great European universities were established. This fertile new intellectual ground gave rise to Scholastic philosophy and new ways of examining questions of theology.

Sic et non is an excellent example of Scholastic inquiry, which would become the predominant method of teaching and intellectual inquiry in high medieval Europe. Scholasticism embodies the fundamental principal that seemingly contradictory teachings can often be resolved by close study and a deeper understanding of how words are used. Scholasticism found its full flowering as the Greek and Latin classics were being recovered in Europe, and scholars sought to reconcile the rational tradition of classical thinkers, such as Plato and Aristotle, with Christian dogma. *Sic et non* is a textbook for how the Scholastic method could be used to resolve such apparent contradictions. To apply the method, a document was read thoroughly, along with relevant glosses by other respected teachers and any works that the document references. Next, the Scholastic laid out all the disagreements within and among these documents, in the form of a philosophical dialogue or dialectic. Key words and phrases were then closely examined to find multiple meanings, obscure uses, or possible transcription errors. Lastly, logical study was applied to identify areas where apparent contradictions are problems of human understanding or the limitations of language, rather than errors in the actual meaning of the text.

Abelard also contributed to philosophical inquiry by his work on the problem of universals. Even before much of Aristotle's work had been recovered, Abelard promoted Aristotle's philosophy as superior to that of Plato. In particular, he agreed with Aristotle that universal attributes, such as color, exist only in the mind, and that language, which seeks to provide a universal word for attributes, is inherently inexact. The problem of universals was a hotly debated concept among Abelard's peers. Abelard argued that people know universals only through their experience with individual things, and universals have no existence apart from them. Texts, particularly theological works, required rigorous study and the application of logical reasoning in order to be understood and to have their apparent contradictions resolved.

Author Biography

Peter Abelard was born around 1097 in La Pallet in Brittany, in northwestern France. He was the eldest son in a family of minor nobility and showed an early gift for learning, leaving home at age thirteen to study with a series of philosopher-theologians. By 1100, Abelard was in Paris, studying under William of Champeaux at the cathedral school at Notre Dame. He and William eventually became rivals, and Abelard began to lecture on his own, becoming popular at schools he set up in the Paris area. After an ill-fated romance with his student Héloïse (for which he is most popularly known today), he retreated to the Abbey of Saint Denis, where he continued to study and to teach. In 1121, his teachings were condemned at a synod held at Soissons, and he was forced to burn his own theological lectures. After 1122, Abelard built a rustic retreat with a chapel for himself in Champagne, and he began to teach there, later giving this retreat to Héloïse, now a nun, and her sisters. In the late 1130s, Abelard's teachings were again questioned, and in 1141, he was briefly excommunicated and then ordered into silence by the pope. He died in 1142, and his body was eventually interred at Père Lachaise Cemetery in Paris, next to Héloïse's. He left a significant body of theological work and also composed poetry and hymns.

HISTORICAL DOCUMENT

There are many seeming contradictions and even obscurities in the innumerable writings of the church fathers. Our respect for their authority should not stand in the way of an effort on our part to come at the truth. The obscurity and contradictions in ancient writings may be explained upon many grounds, and may be discussed without impugning the good faith and insight of the fathers. A writer may use different terms to mean the same thing, in order to avoid a monotonous repetition of the same word. Common, vague words may be employed in order that the common people may understand; and sometimes a writer sacrifices perfect accuracy in the interest of a clear general statement. Poetical, figurative language is often obscure and vague.

Not infrequently apocryphal works are attributed to the saints. Then, even the best authors often introduce the erroneous views of others and leave the reader to distinguish between the true and the false. Sometimes, as Augustine confesses in his own case, the fathers ventured to rely upon the opinions of others.

Doubtless the fathers might err; even Peter, the prince of the apostles, fell into error: what wonder that the saints do not always show themselves inspired? The fathers did not themselves believe that they, or their companions, were always right. Augustine found himself mistaken in some cases and did not hesitate to retract his errors. He warns his admirers not to look upon his letters as they would upon the Scriptures, but to accept only those things which, upon examination, they find to be true.

All writings belonging to this class are to be read with full freedom to criticize, and with no obligation to accept unquestioningly; otherwise they way would be blocked to all discussion, and posterity be deprived of the excellent intellectual exercise of debating difficult questions of language and presentation. But an explicit exception must be made in the case of the Old and New Testaments. In the Scriptures, when anything strikes us as absurd, we may not say that the writer erred, but that the scribe made a blunder in copying the manuscripts, or that there is an error in interpretation, or that the passage is not understood. The fathers make a very careful distinction between the Scriptures and later works. They advocate a discriminating, not to say suspicious, use of the writings of their own contemporaries.

In view of these considerations, I have ventured to bring together various dicta of the holy fathers, as they came to mind, and to formulate certain questions which were suggested by the seeming contradictions in the statements. These questions ought to serve to excite tender readers to a zealous inquiry into truth and so sharpen their wits. The master key of knowledge is, indeed, a persistent and frequent questioning. Aristotle, the most clear-sighted of all the philosophers, was desirous above all things else to arouse this questioning spirit, for in his

Categories he exhorts a student as follows: "It may well be difficult to reach a positive conclusion in these matters unless they be frequently discussed. It is by no means fruitless to be doubtful on particular points." By doubting we come to examine, and by examining we reach the truth.

GLOSSARY

apocryphal: likely untrue; false

Augustine: fifth-century bishop of Hippo, Christian church father and theologian

***Categories*:** Greek philosophical text by Aristotle that introduced his larger work on logic

dicta: plural, from "dictum": an authoritative statement

Document Analysis

This selection from *Sic et non* highlights the foundational principals of Abelard's methods of inquiry. He argues first that everything should be questioned and examined, that works by humans, even saints, may contain errors, and that even if texts do not contain errors, the inexact nature of language means that there are shades of meaning that may mislead the reader unless greater understanding is methodically pursued. This is not an insult to the writer, just an earnest inquiry into the deeper meaning of their words, with attention to the frailty and imperfection of the human mind and the limits of language. Abelard draws the line at the Bible, however, declaring that this does not contain errors, although it may have been subject to erroneous transcription.

Abelard was skating dangerously close to heretical writing in this work, arguing as he did that there was room for error in the foundational interpretive texts of Christian theology. Because of this, he is eager to point out that his is simply a search for truth and meaning: "Our respect for their authority should not stand in the way of an effort on our part to come at the truth." Things that seem to be errors in ancient texts can often be explained by obscure or archaic uses of language, and these may be debated without "impugning the good faith and insight of the fathers." In addition, sometimes the authors of these texts relied on others whose opin-

ions may have been erroneous. If error was found, Abelard argued, this was simply because of their human frailty—which they themselves recognized: "The fathers did not themselves believe that they, or their companions, were always right." He uses the example of Augustine of Hippo, who urged his readers to examine his words and "accept only those things which, upon examination, they find to be true." Questioning is, after all, the only pathway to truth, he argues, and quotes from Aristotle on this point. With the exception of the Old and New Testaments, which are not subject to error, only to misunderstanding, all foundational theology should be approached with questions and doubt: "By doubting we come to examine, and by examining we reach the truth."

Essential Themes

The theme of this selection from *Sic et non* is the essential principal of Scholasticism. Questioning and close, rational analysis, Abelard concludes, are the chief paths to wisdom. Abelard believed that logic could be employed in the search for truth in cases where religious texts seemed to be confusing or contradictory. He also argued for a thorough understanding of language and its uses and changing meaning over time. Though the Bible did not contain errors, the humans who tried to understand its words and the humans who transcribed them, were fallible, and therefore, even if the message were true, the words were worth examining. Words, after all, are limited and flawed, and so the search for the reality and truth they try to capture must be ongoing.

—Bethany Groff, MA

Bibliography and Additional Reading

Bredero, Adriaan H. *Christendom and Christianity in the Middle Ages.* Grand Rapids: Eerdmans, 1987. Print.

Duignan, Brian. *Medieval Philosophy: From 500 to 1500 CE.* New York: Britannica Educational, 2011. Print.

Marenbon, John. *The Philosophy of Peter Abelard.* New York: Cambridge UP, 1997. Print.

■ "Of the Perils of His Abbey," from Abelard's *Historia Calamitatum*

Date: ca. 1132
Country: France
Author: Peter Abelard
Translator: Henry Adams Bellows

Summary Overview

Peter Abelard wrote his *Historia Calamitatum* (*The Story of His Misfortunes*) ostensibly to a friend, encouraging him to take comfort in the fact that his troubles are insignificant compared to Abelard's woes. The resulting work, filled with sorrow as it is, offers an original and significant medieval autobiography and gives extraordinary insight not only into Abelard's experience, but into the world he inhabited. Abelard was a philosopher, a teacher, a monk, and eventually an abbot. He was also a famous lover, who was castrated by the angry uncle of his paramour, Héloïse.

In the course of his life, Abelard repeatedly ran into trouble with envious rivals, drawing particular censure for his firm belief in the Aristotelian form of inquiry— that everything, including Christian texts, could and should be questioned and subjected to rational inquiry. He also loudly criticized the behavior of the monks and abbots he lived with. The abbey of Saint-Gildas-de-Rhuys, where he was appointed abbot around 1125, was so unhappy with his reforming zeal that he claimed they routinely tried to murder him.

Defining Moment

Abelard began his career as a teacher and leading intellectual in a time of significant social and economic change in Europe. By the end of the eleventh century, the schools and monasteries of France were in a period of ascendancy. After a period of relative fragmentation and instability, the monarchies of Europe were consolidating their power, providing the resources and stability in which intellectual growth flourished. Monumental cathedrals were constructed, monasteries grew into wealthy, semiautonomous estates, classics of Greek and Roman philosophy were rediscovered, and the first great European universities were established. Charis-matic teachers like Peter Abelard were celebrities and founded schools that competed with one another for the patronage of well-heeled students. Because these schools dealt with issues of philosophy and theology, disagreements sometimes spilled over into accusations of heresy.

Abelard's first major conflict was with his teacher William of Champeaux. William was at the peak of his intellectual power, but Abelard challenged his authority in debates about the concept of universals. Even before much of Aristotle's work had been recovered, Abelard promoted his philosophy as superior to that of Plato. In particular, he agreed with Aristotle that properties of universal attributes such as color exist only in the mind, and language, which seeks to provide a universal word for attributes, is inherently inexact. William believed that universal attributes existed in reality, while Abelard argued that people only know universals through their experience with individual things, and universals have no existence apart from them. In his *Historia Calamitatum*, Abelard claimed that his argument had overwhelmed William, who left Paris in shame.

Though most of Abelard's conflicts with other teachers came from jealousy at his success or anger at his attracting students away from established schools, he also got himself into serious trouble over his questioning of the nature of the Holy Trinity. Abelard believed in the rigorous application of logic to any text, and made a significant enemy in Bernard of Clairvaux. Bernard believed that foundational spiritual mysteries should not be subjected to questioning, and he orchestrated two councils that condemned Abelard's work. Abelard was excommunicated, although the sentence was later lifted. Though he suffered for his writing, Abelard is one of the most important early contributors to Scholasticism. This school of thought's rigorous application of Aristotelian logic would become the main system of philosophy taught in European universities for centuries to come.

Author Biography and Document Information

Peter Abelard was born in 1097 in Le Pallet, Brittany. He was the eldest son in a family of minor nobility and showed an early gift for learning. Eschewing a career as a knight, he decided in his youth to pursue scholarly interests instead, leaving home to study with a series of philosopher-theologians. By 1100, Abelard was in Paris, studying under William of Champeaux at the cathedral school at Notre Dame. He and William became rivals, and Abelard began to lecture at Melun and then at Corbeil.

After an ill-fated romance with his student Héloïse, Abelard retreated to the monastery of Saint Denis, where he continued to teach. In 1121, his teachings were condemned at a synod held at Soissons, and he was forced to burn his theological lectures. Subsequently, Abelard built a rustic retreat with an oratory for himself in Champagne, and he began to teach there; he later gave the property to Héloïse, now a nun, and her companions. He was also made the abbot of the monastery of Saint-Gildas-de-Rhuys.

In the late 1130s, Abelard's teachings were again questioned, and in 1141 he was excommunicated by Pope Innocent II and ordered to be silent. His excommunication was lifted before his death on April 21, 1142, and his body was initially interred at the Paraclete, the home of Héloïse's order of nuns. His remains were moved in the early nineteenth century to Père Lachaise Cemetery in Paris, where he is buried with Héloïse.

HISTORICAL DOCUMENT

CHAPTER XV
OF THE PERILS OF HIS ABBEY AND OF THE REASONS FOR THE WRITING OF THIS HIS LETTER

REFLECTING often upon all these things, I determined to make provision for those sisters and to undertake their care in every way I could. Furthermore, in order that they might have the greater reverence for me, I arranged to watch over them in person. And since now the persecution carried on by my sons was greater and more incessant than that which I formerly suffered at the hands of my brethren, I returned frequently to the nuns, fleeing the rage of the tempest as to a haven of peace. There, indeed, could I draw breath for a little in quiet, and among them my labours were fruitful, as they never were among the monks. All this was of the utmost benefit to me in body and soul, and it was equally essential for them by reason of their weakness.

But now has Satan beset me to such an extent that I no longer know where I may find rest, or even so much as live. I am driven hither and yon, a fugitive and a vagabond, even as the accursed Cain (Gen. iv. 14). I have already said that "without were fightings, within were fears" (II Cor. vii. 5), and these torture me ceaselessly, the fears being indeed without as well as within, and the fightings wheresoever there are fears. Nay, the persecution carried on by my sons rages against me more perilously and continuously than that of my open enemies, for my sons I have always with me, and I am ever exposed to their treacheries. The violence of my enemies I see in the danger to my body if I leave the cloister; but within it I am compelled incessantly to endure the crafty machinations as well as the open violence of those monks who are called my sons, and who are entrusted to me as their abbot, which is to say their father.

Oh how often have they tried to kill me with poison, even as the monks sought to slay St. Benedict! Methinks the same reason which led the saint to abandon his wicked sons might encourage me to follow the example of so great a father, lest, in thus exposing myself to certain peril, I might be deemed a rash tempter of God rather than a lover of Him, nay, lest it might even be judged that I had thereby taken my own life. When I had safeguarded myself to the best of my ability, so far as my food and drink were concerned, against their daily plottings, they sought to destroy me in the very ceremony of the altar by putting poison in the chalice. One day, when I had gone to Nantes to visit the count, who was then sick, and while I was sojourning awhile in the house of one of my brothers in the flesh, they arranged to poison me with the connivance of one of my attendants believing that I would take no precautions to escape such a plot. But divine providence so ordered matters that I had no desire for the food which was set before me; one of the monks whom I had brought with me ate thereof, not knowing that which had been done, and straightway fell dead. As for the attendant who had dared to undertake this crime, he fled in terror alike of his own conscience and of the clear evidence of his guilt.

After this, as their wickedness was manifest to every one, I began openly in every way I could to avoid the danger with which their plots threatened me, even to the extent of leaving the abbey and dwelling with a few others apart in little cells. If the monks knew beforehand that I was going anywhere on a journey, they bribed bandits to waylay me on the road and kill me. And while I was struggling in the midst of these dangers, it chanced one day that the hand of the Lord smote me a heavy blow, for I fell from my horse, breaking a bone in my neck, the injury causing me greater pain and weakness than my former wound.

Using excommunication as my weapon to coerce the untamed rebelliousness of the monks, I forced certain ones among them whom I particularly feared to promise me publicly, pledging their faith or swearing upon the sacrament, that they would thereafter depart from the abbey and no longer trouble me in any way. Shamelessly and openly did they violate the pledges they had given and their sacramental oaths, but finally they were compelled to give this and many other promises under oath, in the presence of the count and the bishops, by the authority of the Pontiff of Rome, Innocent, who sent his own legate for this special purpose. And yet even this did not bring me peace. For when I returned to the abbey after the expulsion of those whom I have just mentioned, and entrusted myself to the remaining brethren, of whom I felt less suspicion, I found them even worse than the others. I barely succeeded in escaping them, with the aid of a certain nobleman of the district, for they were planning, not to poison me indeed, but to cut my throat with a sword. Even to the present time I stand face to face with this danger, fearing the sword which threatens my neck so that I can scarcely draw a free breath between one meal and the next. Even so do we read of him who, reckoning the power and heaped-up wealth of the tyrant Dionysius as a great blessing, beheld the sword secretly hanging by a hair above his head, and so learned what kind of happiness comes as the result of worldly power (Cicer. 5, Tusc.) Thus did I too learn by constant experience, I who had been exalted from the condition of a poor monk to the dignity of an abbot, that my wretchedness increased with my wealth; and I would that the ambition of those who voluntarily seek such power might be curbed by my example.

And now, most dear brother in Christ and comrade closest to me in the intimacy of speech, it should suffice for your sorrows and the hardships you have endured that I have written this story of my own misfortunes, amid which I have toiled almost from the cradle. For so, as I said in the beginning of this letter, shall you come to regard your tribulation as nought, or at any rate as little, in comparison with mine, and so shall you bear it more lightly in measure as you regard it as less. Take comfort ever in the saying of Our Lord, what he foretold for his followers at the hands of the followers of the devil: "If they have persecuted me, they will also persecute you (John xv. 20). If the world hate you, ye know that it hated me before it hated you. If ye were of the world, the world would love his own" (ib. 18-19). And the apostle says: "All that will live godly in Christ Jesus shall suffer persecution" (II Tim. iii. 12). And elsewhere he says: "I do not seek to please men. For if I yet pleased men I should not be the servant of Christ" (Galat. i. 10). And the Psalmist says: "They who have been pleasing to men have been confounded, for that God hath despised them."

Commenting on this, St. Jerome, whose heir methinks I am in the endurance of foul slander, says in his letter to Nepotanius: "The apostle says: 'If I yet pleased men, I should not be the servant of Christ.' He no longer seeks to please men, and so is made Christ's servant" (Epist. 2). And again, in his letter to Asella regarding those whom he was falsely accused of loving: "I give thanks to my God that I am worthy to be one whom the world hates" (Epist. 99). And to the monk Heliodorus he writes: "You are wrong, brother. You are wrong if you think there is ever a time when the Christian does not suffer persecution. For our adversary goes about as a roaring lion seeking what he may devour, and do you still think of peace? Nay, he lieth in ambush among the rich."

Inspired by those records and examples, we should endure our persecutions all the more steadfastly the more bitterly they harm us. We should not doubt that even if they are not according to our deserts, at least they serve for the purifying of our souls. And since all things are done in accordance with the divine ordering, let every one of true faith console himself amid all his afflictions with the thought that the great goodness of God permits nothing to be done without reason, and brings to a good end whatsoever may seem to happen wrongfully. Wherefore rightly do all men say: "Thy will be done." And great is the consolation to all lovers of God in the word of the Apostle when he says: "We know that all things work together for good to them that love God" (Rom. viii. 28). The wise man of old had this in mind when he said in his Proverbs: "There shall no evil happen to the just" (Prov. xii. 21). By this he clearly shows that whosoever grows wrathful for any reason against his sufferings has therein departed from the way of the just, because he may not doubt that these things have happened to him by divine dispensation. Even such are those who yield to their own rather than to the divine purpose, and with hidden desires resist the spirit which echoes in the words, "Thy will be done," thus placing their own will ahead of the will of God. Farewell.

GLOSSARY

Pontiff of Rome: the Catholic pope

St. Benedict: a fifth-century monk who established a monastic rule, that of the Benedictines

Document Analysis

This selection of Abelard's *Historia Calamitatum* deals with his time spent as the abbot of the monastery at Saint-Gildas-de-Rhuys, a period that coincided with his leadership of Héloïse's order of nuns. Abelard had been invited to lead the brothers at the monastery, based on his celebrity and reputation, but soon found himself hated by the men he was supposed to lead. To their dismay, the charismatic teacher was also a strict reformer. The only place where Abelard can find peace, he claims, is with his former lover, Héloïse, and her order, now living at the site of his former oratory. "I returned frequently to the nuns, fleeing the rage of the tempest as to a haven of peace." It is a stark contrast to his life with his monastic brothers, where he feels beset on all sides by treachery. This is worse for him than enemies who hate him openly, because "my sons I have always with me, and I am ever exposed to their treacheries."

Abelard is particularly afraid that he is being poisoned, lays out how he believes this is to be achieved, and the proof he has that it has been attempted. When Abelard was wise to attempts to poison his food, his enemies poisoned the communion wine. When this also failed, they sent emissaries to attempt to poison him while he was away visiting a sick noble. When the scheme killed another monk by mistake, the perpetrator fled.

Attempts on Abelard's life are not limited to poisoning, however. Although he seeks protection by living in isolation, whenever he is forced to journey out, he is attacked. "They bribed bandits to waylay me on the road and kill me," he writes. In one of these attacks, Abelard fell from his horse, breaking his neck, which was more painful than his "former wound," his castration years earlier. Finally, Abelard is forced to threaten excommunication against his monks if they do not reform, and he demanded and received the expulsion of some of the worst troublemakers. He returned to the abbey only to find that other monks had risen against him and were planning to slit his throat. He realizes that "my wretchedness increased with my wealth"; power creates enemies, and he urges others to avoid positions of power.

This selection is the last in Abelard's autobiography, and he closes by admonishing the friend to whom this entire work is addressed to take comfort in the fact that Abelard has suffered so much more: "regard your tribulation as nought, or at any rate as little, in comparison with mine, and so shall you bear it more lightly in measure as you regard it as less."

Essential Themes

The primary theme of this selection is the suffering that Abelard endured at the hands of his monastic brothers. A secondary theme is how comparing one's experience to that of another who has suffered more can actually bring comfort, as Abelard assures the friend who is the recipient of this work. Abelard's strict reforms made him extremely unpopular as the abbot of Saint-Gildas-de-Rhuys, and numerous attempts were made on his life. His enemies tried to poison him, arranged to have him attacked by bandits when he travelled, and conspired to cut his throat. Still, Abelard compares his suffering to that of the saints, who are rewarded in heaven.

Abelard's writings would go on to become highly influential in the development of Scholasticism and, therefore, in much of Western philosophy. His full *Historia Calamitatum* would become a key account of me-dieval life, particularly regarding scholarly and religious traditions. Its references to Héloïse, along with surviving correspondence between the two lovers, would establish their affair as one of the most famous love stories of all time.

—*Bethany Groff, MA*

Bibliography and Additional Reading

Bredero, Adriaan H. *Christendom and Christianity in the Middle Ages: The Relations between Religion, Church, and Society.* 2nd ed. Grand Rapids: Eerdmans, 1994. Print.

Duignan, Brian. *Medieval Philosophy: From 500 to 1500 CE.* New York: Britannica Educational, 2011. Print.

Marenbon, John. *The Philosophy of Peter Abelard.* Cambridge: Cambridge UP, 1999. Print.

■ Testament of St. Francis

Date: ca. 1226 CE
Geographic Region: Assisi (in present-day Umbria, Italy)
Author: Saint Francis of Assisi
Translator: David Burr

Summary Overview

Saint Francis was a major religious figure in the thirteenth century. He founded a religious order known as the Order of Friars Minor (more commonly known as the Franciscans) that prioritized the vow of poverty over all else. This order represented one thread of a revival of the apostolic way of life, which emphasized evangelical itinerant preaching, simplicity, and poverty. Saint Francis's followers quickly multiplied, and Saint Francis soon wrote a simple rule of life for his followers (known simply as "the rule": "to observe the holy gospel of our Lord Jesus Christ, living in obedience without anything of our own and in chastity"). The pope approved this rule, likely in part because of Francis's fierce obedience to the church and its priests. Francis died still a relatively young man, but before he passed away, he left a document to his followers which became known as the Testament of Saint Francis.

Defining Moment

The Catholic Church in the thirteenth century was often preoccupied with the Crusades, begun in 1096, which was focused on fighting wars against Muslims, pagans, and Christian sects deemed heretical by the pope. Against this military backdrop, another, far less aggressive, religious movement emerged. This was the founding of the mendicant orders, the Order of Friars Minor (Franciscans) and the Order of Preachers (Dominicans). These religious orders were different from others in many ways. Instead of calling themselves monks and living in remote monasteries, members of these orders called themselves friars and lived among the local population in towns and villages. Both orders valued preaching the gospel and living in poverty over all other attributes.

The Franciscans were known as itinerant mendicants, which meant that they traveled widely to preach the gospel and that they made their living by begging for the charity of others. Franciscans at first did not even hold communal property, but their needs soon forced them into accepting this. This was a constant source of friction within the order between those who felt that poverty should be extreme and those who felt that the practicalities of their lives and duties to the church should allow them to own communal property.

The followers of Saint Francis grew quickly; many men who heard the Franciscans' preaching joined the order, and women were also attracted to the movement. Not only single people joined the movement. Many married people thought that a simple life lived in poverty and in service to God was a noble way of life. For them and for people who did not want to take public vows, Francis formed a Third Order so that they could follow the principles of poverty and service to God, remain married if they wished, and keep living normal lives in their communities. These "tertiaries" soon desired to live together in communities as well. People of any social level could join the Third Order and did.

Author Biography

Saint Francis of Assisi was born around 1181 as Francesco di Pietro di Bernardone, the son of an affluent cloth merchant in the town of Assisi, in modern-day Italy. During his youth, he acted much like others of his age and status, dressing in fine clothes and carousing at parties. He initially wanted to be a knight, but after an ill-fated battle, he was imprisoned for a year before being ransomed by his father. After this, he began his conversion to a man of God. The process was slow, but when he fully committed, he had a great impact on the Catholic Church. As his movement grew, he provided common guidelines on how to live the life he preached, called "the rule." Francis's health declined after many years of living in poverty and traveling to preach, and he died on October 3, 1226. Less than two years later, he was proclaimed a saint.

HISTORICAL DOCUMENT

This is how the Lord gave me, brother Francis, the power to do penance. When I was in sin the sight of lepers was too bitter for me. And the Lord himself led me among them, and I pitied and helped them. And when I left them I discovered that what had seemed bitter to me was changed into sweetness in my soul and body. And shortly afterward I rose and left the world.

And the Lord gave me such faith in churches that I prayed simply, saying, "I adore you, Lord Jesus Christ, with all your churches throughout the world, and we bless you because you redeemed the world through your holy cross. Later God gave me and still gives me such faith in priests who live according to the form of the Holy Roman Church that even if they persecuted me I would still run back to them, because of their position. And if I had all the wisdom of Solomon and came upon some poor little priests in their parishes, I would preach there only if they wished me to do so. And I want to fear, love and honor these and all others as my lords. And I do not even want to think about there being any sin in them, because I see the son of God in them and they are my lords. And I do this because in this world I physically see the most high Son of God only in his most holy body and blood, which they receive and they alone administer to others. And I want this holy mystery to be honored above all things, venerated, and kept in costly containers. Whenever I find his holy names or words in improper places I pick them up and ask that they be collected and stored in a proper place. And we ought to honor and venerate all theologians and those who administer the holy divine word, for they administer to us spirit and life.

And when God gave me brothers, no one showed me what I should do, but the Most high revealed to me that I should live according to the form of the holy gospel. I had it written in few words and simply, and the lord pope confirmed it for me. And those who came to receive life gave all that they had to the poor and were content with one tunic patched inside and out, with a cord and trousers. And we did not wish to have more.

We who were clerics said the office life other clerics, and the laymen said the "Our Father," and we gladly stayed in churches. And we were ignorant and subject to all. And I worked with my hands, and want to do so still. And I definitely want all the other brothers to work at some honest job. Those who don't know how should learn, not because they want to receive wages but as an example and to avoid idleness. And when our wages are withheld from us, let us return to the Lord's table, begging alms from door to door. The Lord revealed what greeting we should use: "The Lord give you peace."

The brothers must be careful not to accept any churches, poor dwellings, or anything else constructed for them unless these buildings reflect the holy poverty promised by us in the rule. We should always live in these places as strangers and pilgrims. I firmly command all the brothers, by the obedience they owe me, that wherever they are they should not dare to ask either directly or through an intermediary for any letter from the Roman court to secure a church or any other place, to protect their preaching, or to prevent persecution of their bodies; but wherever they are not received, they should flee into another land and do penance with God's blessing.

And I firmly wish to obey the minister general of this brotherhood, and any other guardian the minister should want to give me. And I want to be such a captive in his hands that I cannot go anywhere or do anything without his desire and command, because he is my lord. And although I am simple and ill, I always want to have a cleric who can perform the office for me, as the rule states. And all the other brothers are thus bound to obey their guardians and perform the office according to the rule. And whenever some are found who do not wish to perform the office according to the rule and want to change it, or who are not Catholic in their beliefs, then all the brothers wherever they may be are bound by obedience to turn such people over to the custodian nearest the place where they found them. The custodian in turn is bound by obedience to guard him strongly life a man in chains, day and night, so that he cannot possibly escape from his hands until he personally places him in the hands of his minister. And the minister is bound by obedience to place him in the care of brothers who will guard him night and day like a man in chains until they turn him over to our lord bishop of Ostia, who is the lord protector and corrector of the whole brotherhood.

And the brothers must not say, "This is another rule," for it is a recollection, admonition, exhortation and my testament which I, poor brother Francis, make for you my brothers, so that we may observe the rule we have promised to God in a more Catholic manner. And the general minister and all other ministers and custodians are bound by obedience not to add or subtract from these words. And they must always have this writing with them in addition to the rule. And in all chapter meetings held by them, when they read the rule, they must also read these words.

And I firmly forbid my brothers, both clerics and laymen, to place glasses on the rule or say, "This is what it means." But just as the Lord gave me the power to compose and write both the rule and these words simply and purely, so you must understand them simply and without gloss and observe them by holy action until the end.

And whoever observes them will be filled in heaven with a blessing of the most high Father and on earth he will be filled with the blessing of his beloved Son, with the Holy Spirit the Comforter and all the powers of heaven and all the saints. And, I brother Francis, your servant insofar as I can be, internally and externally confirm for you this holy blessing.

GLOSSARY

gospel: an account of the life, death, and resurrection of Jesus Christ, especially the four gospels of the New Testament

leper: an individual who has leprosy, a disease that eats away at the extremities

testament: a will; a general statement of witness

Document Analysis

The Testament of Saint Francis was written by Saint Francis shortly before his death in 1226. The document has been passed down as his final words of wisdom to his followers. In it, Francis wanted to reinforce certain ideals and guidelines that he believed important for his followers to carry forward—in particular, living in strict poverty and obedience to priests and the religious order's leadership.

He begins his testament with a reminder of his own conversion. This began when he was returning from war and saw some lepers, and instead of running away, he stayed and helped them. He explains that instead of feeling "bitter," he felt "sweetness" in their presence. He then discusses his love of churches and the priesthood that serves within them. He speaks here of being obedient to all priests, as not all of his followers were priests at this time.

Francis also provides a reminder of the history of how his order came to be. He states that when he began to attract followers, he had no plan, but knew he wanted to live according to the gospel. Therefore, he wrote down a rule of life that the pope then authorized for his followers. He provides advice to his followers on how to keep to his dearest principle, poverty. It is here that he makes some of his most controversial comments. He states that his brothers should not ask the Roman court, meaning the pope, for any kind of communal property or protection.

Francis again turns to obedience when he discusses the minister general, who is the leader of the order, and the custodians, who are in charge of a geographic area where the Franciscans are active, known as a province. The performance of the divine office by his followers is also of concern to Francis, as is how to deal with a brother who is disobedient.

Finally, Francis confirms that although his testament is binding on his followers, it is not to be viewed as a new or separate rule of life, but rather as an addition to it, which is a somewhat contradictory statement. He is particularly concerned that no one analyzes and comments on ("glosses") his rule of life and that the brothers simply follow his words as given to them.

Essential Themes

Francis's testament was a cause of friction among his followers for centuries. In the immediate aftermath of his death, there were those who wanted to follow this document to the letter, and those who wished it interpreted by higher church authorities. The matter made its way to the pope himself, who was asked in 1230 if this document was legally binding on the growing order. He ruled that it was not, as Francis had already resigned the leadership of his order and was a simple brother at the time he wrote it. This decreased some of the immediate tension.

As the thirteenth century progressed, the order fractured into Spirituals, who wanted to strictly follow Francis's words, and Conventuals, who were increasingly becoming part of the church hierarchy. Originally, Franciscans were allowed to come from the general population (the laity) or from the church (priests, deacons, bishops). The Conventuals were less enthusiastic in welcoming laymen into the order and were more and more becoming key agents of the Catholic Church. This led to their moving farther away from Francis's key tenet of poverty, as the church was one of the most affluent organizations in European society at this time.

Throughout the next several centuries, various reform movements within the Franciscans occurred. The Order of Friars Minor Conventual (Greyfriars) split into a separate branch in the sixteenth century, as did the Recollects, who were mainly active in Spain and France. The more austere Capuchins developed in the seventeenth century. These orders, as well as the Order of Saint Clare, continued to exist into the twenty-first century. Although a somewhat splintered community due to these schisms, some 50,000 individuals worldwide follow some form of the Franciscan way of life. Through their nongovernmental organization, Franciscans International, the Franciscans have general consultative status within the United Nations. The fact that Pope Francis, though himself a Jesuit, took the name of Saint Francis as his papal name is testament to the enduring influence of this man and his ideals.

—*Lee Tunstall, PhD*

Bibliography and Additional Reading

Acocella, Joan. "Rich Man, Poor Man: The Radical Visions of St. Francis." *New Yorker. Condé Nast,* 14 Jan. 2013. Web. 1 May 2015.

Robinson, Paschal. "St. Francis of Assisi." *Catholic Encyclopedia.* Vol. 6. Ed. Charles G. Herbermann, et al. New York: Appleton, 1909. 221–30. Print.

Saint Francis of Assisi. *Francis and Clare: The Complete Works.* Trans. Regis J. Armstrong and Ignatius Brady. New York: Paulist, 1982. Print.

■ On the Principles of Nature

Date: ca. 1252–6
Geographic Region: France
Author: Thomas Aquinas
Translator: Gyula Klima

Summary Overview

Written early in his career, Thomas Aquinas's *De principiis naturae* (*On the Principles of Nature*) was one of the philosopher and theologian's first attempts to reconcile faith and reason. Much of his later work and influence rested upon the philosophical outlook and foundation that he laid in this essay. In it, Aquinas relies upon the ideas of the Greek philosopher Aristotle to explain the relationship between matter and form in the natural world. Aquinas saw philosophy as providing the context for theology, meaning that reason could serve as a complement to faith; his philosophical thought would always coexist with his greater concern for Christian theology, as demonstrated in his later works. Therefore, his earlier works were important to the development of philosophy in the Middle Ages, as they helped bring classical philosophy to bear on Christian theology.

Defining Moment

During the early Middle Ages in Europe (before about 1100), philosophy and Christian theology were largely indistinguishable. There were exceptions to this rule, but for the most part, Christian theologians and philosophers were not as interested in factoring classical thought—such as that from the Greek or Arabic world—into their beliefs. Most educated people turned to the works of the authoritative theologians of the day, such as those written by Saint Augustine or Saint Anselm, to understand scripture and dogma. By the time of Aquinas, however, this traditional approach had begun to change. During the early twelfth century, French philosopher Peter Abelard began integrating dialectical reasoning and logic into the study of theology, setting the stage for the reintroduction of classical philosophy.

At the same time, theology and philosophy became more distinct from one another. Scholars began to develop separate conceptual vocabulary for each discipline, rendering them more inaccessible to the average educated person. Philosophy became a more academic discipline, which was studied mainly by those in an academic vocation. Academic vocations became more feasible as cathedral schools transformed into universities. This was the case with the University of Paris, where Aquinas studied. With the rise of universities across Europe, scholars with the skill to translate Aristotle's works from Greek and the works of Muslim philosophers from Arabic increased the propagation of such classical works.

By the time Aquinas began to study and write in the 1240s, Aristotle's works had become fairly well known in academic circles. This revolution in Western European thought both influenced and was influenced by the young Aquinas. Although not everything the Greek and Arab philosophers taught readily squared with Christian dogma, the systematic and logical nature of their thought heavily impacted scholars such as Aquinas working and writing in the thirteenth century. Philosophy, according to Aquinas, could no longer be confined to simply expounding on the works of earlier church fathers.

In his early works, written in Paris, Aquinas took the ideas of Aristotle and the Muslim philosophers out of the faculty of arts—where philosophy had traditionally been housed—and into the faculty of theology, which was considered the highest of the four faculties at Paris. By bringing these rediscovered philosophical ideas to bear on his theological thought, Aquinas produced a revolution of his own that would have a long-term impact on the shape of Christian theology and Western thought as a whole.

Author Biography

Thomas Aquinas was born in Roccasecca, Italy, around 1225, the youngest son of a noble family. His early education occurred at the nearby abbey at Monte Cassino, which was where Saint Benedict himself had lived. However, political struggles within the Roman Catholic Church led Aquinas to leave Monte Cassino for the University of Naples, where he was first exposed to Greek and Arabic philosophy. The reconciliation of those philosophies with Christian thought would take up much of Aquinas's life's work. While in Naples, Aquinas joined the newly formed Order of Preachers,

known as the Dominicans, which emphasized study and teaching. In 1245, Aquinas continued his studies at the University of Paris, where he wrote his earliest works, including "On the Principles of Nature." After completing these early works, he wrote the two works for which he would be best known, *Summa contra gentiles* (ca. 1259–64) and his unfinished *Summa theologica* (ca. 1265–74). He died in 1274 and was canonized in 1323.

HISTORICAL DOCUMENT

Note that something can be, even if it is not, while something is. That which only can be is said to be in potentiality; that which already is is said to be in actuality. But there are two kinds of being, namely the essential, or substantial being of the thing, as for a man to be, and this is just to be, without any qualification. The other kind of being is accidental being, such as for a man to be white, and this is to be somehow.

And it is with respect to both kinds of being that something is in potentiality. For something is in potentiality toward being a man, as the sperm and the menstrual blood; and something is in potentiality toward being white, as a man. Both that which is in potentiality in respect of substantial being and that which is in potentiality in respect of accidental being can be said to be matter, as the sperm can be said to be the matter of man and the man the matter of whiteness. But they differ in that the matter that is in potentiality in respect of substantial being is called matter from which, while that which is in potentiality in respect of accidental being is called matter of which.

Again, properly speaking, what is in potentiality toward accidental being is called a subject, while that which is in potentiality toward substantial being is properly called matter. And it is significant that what is in potentiality toward accidental being is called a subject, for we say that an accident is in a subject, while of substantial form we do not say that it is in a subject.

So matter differs from subject in that a subject does not have being from what comes to it, as it has complete being in itself. For example, a man does not have being from whiteness; but matter has being from what comes to it, for matter in itself does not have complete being,

indeed, it does not have any being, as the Commentator says in the second book of *On the Soul*. And so, absolutely speaking, form gives being to matter, but the subject gives being to the accident, even if sometimes the one term is taken for the other, i.e. "matter" for "subject", and vice versa.

Just as everything that is in potentiality can be called matter, so everything from which something has being, whether accidental or substantial being, can be called a form; just as a man, who is white in potentiality, will be actually white by whiteness, and the sperm, which is a man in potentiality, will be actually a man by the soul. And since form makes something actual, form is also called actuality. That which makes something actual in accidental being is accidental form, and that which makes something actual in substantial being is substantial form.

Since generation is motion towards form, to these two kinds of form there correspond two kinds of generation: to substantial form there corresponds generation absolutely speaking, while to accidental form there corresponds generation with qualification. For when the substantial form is introduced, something is said to come to be, without further qualification. But when an accidental form is introduced, we do not say that something comes to be, without qualification, but that something comes to be this; just as when a man becomes white, we do not say that he comes to be, absolutely speaking, but that he comes to be white. And to these two kinds of generation there correspond two kinds of corruption, namely corruption in an absolute sense, and corruption with qualification. Generation and corruption absolutely speaking are only in the category of substance, while those with qualification are in the other categories.

And since generation is a kind of mutation from non-being into being, and corruption, conversely, should be from being to non-being, generation starts not from just any kind of non-being, but from a non-being that is a being in potentiality: for example, a statue is generated from bronze, which can be a statue, but is not actually a statue.

So for generation three things are required: a being in potentiality, which is matter, non-being in actuality, which is privation, and that by which the thing will be actual, namely form. Just as when from bronze a statue is formed, the bronze, which is in potentiality toward the form of the statue, is matter; its being amorphous is called privation; and its shape, on account of which it is called a statue is its form, though not its substantial form, for the bronze was already actual even before the introduction of this form or shape, and its existence does not depend on this shape, but is an accidental form. For all artificial forms are accidental, because art works only on what is supplied by nature already in complete existence.

So there are three principles of nature, namely matter, form and privation; of which one is that to which generation proceeds, namely form, and the other two are those from which generation proceeds. Therefore, matter and privation are the same in their subject, but differ in their concepts. For the very same thing that is bronze is amorphous before the advent of the form; but it is for different reasons that it is called bronze and amorphous.

Therefore privation is called a principle not per se but per accidens, namely because it coincides with matter, just as we say that this is per accidens: the doctor builds a house, for he builds not insofar as a doctor, but insofar as a builder, who happens to be a doctor.

But there are two kinds of accidents: namely necessary, which is not separated from its subject, as risibility from man, and not necessary, for example, whiteness, which can be separated from man. Therefore, though privation is a per accidens principle, it does not follow that it is not required for generation, because matter is never stripped of privation; for insofar as it is under one form, it has the privation of another, and conversely, as in fire there is the privation of the form of air.

We should know that even if generation proceeds from non-being, we do not say that its principle is negation, but that it is privation, for a negation does not determine its subject. For that it does not see can be said also of non-beings, as a chimera does not see, and also of beings which are naturally inept to have sight, as of stones. But a privation can be said only of a determinate subject, in which the opposite habit is naturally apt to occur, for example, only those can be said to be blind that are naturally apt to see.

And since generation does not proceed from non-being absolutely speaking, but from a non-being in some subject, and not in just any kind of subject, but in a determinate subject (for it is not from just any kind of non-being that fire is generated, but from that kind of non-fire in which the form of fire is apt to come to be), we say that privation is a principle.

But it differs from the others in that the other two are principles both of being and of coming to be. For in order that a statue is generated there has to be bronze, and in the end there has to be the form of the statue, and further when the statue already exists, these two also have to exist. However, privation is only the principle of coming to be, but not of being, for while the statue is still coming to be, it is necessary that the statue does not yet exist. For if it already existed, it would not be coming to be, for what is still coming to be does not yet exist, apart from processes. But when the statue already exists, there is no privation of the shape of the statue, for affirmation and negation cannot stand together, and similarly neither can privation and habit.

Again, privation is a principle per accidens, as was explained above, and the other two are principles per se. From what has been said it is clear, then, that matter differs from form and privation in its concept. For matter is that in which form and privation are thought to be, as it is in the bronze that form and formlessness are thought to be.

Sometimes matter is named with privation, and sometimes without it. For example, the concept of bronze, when it is the matter of the statue, does not imply privation: for when I call something bronze, this does not imply that it is amorphous or formless. On the other hand, the concept of flour does imply the privation of the form of bread, for when I call something flour, this does signify an amorphousness or formlessness opposite to the form of bread.

And since in the process of generation matter or the subject remains, but privation or what is composed of matter and privation does not, that matter which does not imply privation in its concept is permanent, while that matter which does is transient.

We should know that some matter has some form, for example, the bronze, which is matter in respect of the statue, but bronze itself is composed of matter and form; wherefore bronze is not called prime matter, for it has matter. But that matter which is thought of without any kind of form or privation as subject to all forms and privations is called prime matter, because there is no other matter before it. And this is also called hyle.

Now, since definition and cognition is by form, prime matter cannot be cognized or defined in itself, only by comparison, as when we say that prime matter is that which is to all forms and privations as bronze is to the form of the statue and to the lack of this form. And this matter is called prime matter without qualification.

For something can be called prime matter in respect of a genus, as water is the prime matter of all liquids. But it is notprime matter without qualification, for it is composed of matter and form, so it has matter prior to it.

We have to know that prime matter, and even form, is not generated, nor corrupted, for every generation proceeds to something from something. That from which generation proceeds is matter, and that to which generation proceeds is form. Therefore, if either matter or form were generated, then matter would have matter and form would have form, and so on, in infinitum. So properly speaking only the composite substance is generated.

We also have to know that matter is said to be numerically one in all things. But something is said to be numerically one in two ways. First, that is said to be numerically one which has one determinate form, e.g., Socrates; but prime matter is not said to be numerically one in this way, for in itself it does not have any form. Second, a thing can also be said to be numerically one because it lacks those dispositions which make things numerically different, and it is in this way that matter is said to be numerically one.

We should know that although matter does not have in its nature some form or privation, as in the concept of bronze neither shape nor the lack of some shape is included; nevertheless, matter is never stripped of form or privation, for sometimes it is under one form, while sometimes it is under another. But in itself it can never exist, since, as in its concept it does not have any form, it does not have actual existence—for something can have actual existence only by its form, but it is only potentially. So nothing in actual existence can be called prime matter.

From what has been said it is clear, then, that there are three principles of nature, namely matter, form and privation. But these three are insufficient for generation, for nothing drives itself into actuality, e.g., a chunk of bronze, which is in potentiality to become a statue, does not make itself into an actual statue, but it needs a sculptor, who brings out the form of the statue from potentiality to actuality. Neither would the form bring out itself from potentiality to actuality (and I am speaking here about the form of the thing being generated, which we call the end of the generation), for the form does not exist until it has come to be, but what is acting is already existing during the process of generation. So it is necessary to have another principle beside matter and form that acts, and this is called the efficient or moving cause, or the agent or the principle of motion. And since, as Aristotle says in the second book of his *Metaphysics*, whatever acts does so only with intending something, there has to be also a fourth, namely that which is intended by the agent, and this is called the end.

We have to know, however, that every agent, natural as well as voluntary, intends some end. But from this it does not follow that all agents recognize this end, or deliberate about the end. For to recognize the end is necessary only for those agents whose acts are not determined, but which can have alternatives for action, namely, voluntary agents; and so they have to recognize their ends by which they determine their actions. However, the actions of natural agents are determined, so it is not necessary that they elect the means to an end. And this is what Avicenna illustrates with his example of the guitar player, who need not deliberate any plucking of the strings, because these are determined for him, for otherwise there would be delays between the single sounds, which would result in dissonance.

Now a voluntary agent rather appears to deliberate than a natural agent. Whence by locus a maiori it follows that it is possible for a natural agent to intend some end without deliberation. And this kind of intending an end is nothing, but to have a natural inclination towards it.

From what has been said, then, it is clear that there are four kinds of causes, namely material, efficient, formal and final. And although the terms "principle" and "cause" can be used interchangeably, as is said in the fifth book of the *Metaphysics*, in the *Physics* Aristotle distinguished four causes and three principles. For he took causes to comprise both extrinsic and intrinsic ones. Now matter and form are said to be intrinsic to the thing, for they are constituent parts of the thing; but the efficient and the final cause are said to be extrinsic, for they are outside of the thing. But he took only the intrinsic causes to be principles. On the other hand, privation is not counted among the causes, for privation is a per accidens principle, as we said. So when we speak about the four causes, we mean the per se causes, but also the per accidens causes are reduced to the per se ones, for whatever is per accidens is reduced to what is per se.

But even if in the first book of his *Physics* Aristotle calls the intrinsic causes principles, as he says in the eleventh book of his *Metaphysics*, properly speaking the extrinsic causes are principles and the intrinsic causes that are parts of the thing are elements, and both can be called causes. But sometimes these terms are used interchangeably. For every cause can be called a principle and every principle can be called a cause, though the concept of a cause seems to add something to that of principle in its ordinary sense, for whatever is first can be called a principle, whether there results some existence from it or not. For example, a craftsman can be called the principle of a knife, as from his work there results the being of the knife. But when something turns from black to white, we can say that blackness is the principle of this change—and generally speaking everything from which some change begins can be called a principle—still, from this blackness there did not result the being of whiteness. But only that is called a cause from which there follows the being of a posterior thing; so we say that a cause is from the being of which there results the being of something else.

And so that first from which the motion starts cannot be called a cause per se, even if it is a principle, wherefore privation is posited among principles, though not among causes, for privation is that from which generation starts. But can also be called a cause per accidens, insofar as it coincides with matter, as was said above. However, only those things are called properly elements that are causes of which the thing is composed, which are properly material, and not just any material causes, but only those of which the thing is primarily composed. We do not say, for example, that his members are the elements of a man, for the members themselves are also composed of others; but we do say that earth and water are elements, for these are not composed of other bodies, but it is from them that all natural bodies are primarily composed. Therefore Aristotle in the fifth book of the *Metaphysics* says that an element is something from which a thing is primarily composed, is in the thing, and is not divided according to form.

The first particle of this definition, namely, "something from which a thing is primarily composed", is evident from what has been just said. The second particle, namely, "is in the thing", is put here to distinguish elements from that kind of matter which is totally corrupted in generation. For example, bread is the matter of blood, but blood is not generated, unless the bread from which it is generated passes away; so the bread does not remain in the blood, whence bread cannot be said to be an element of blood. But elements somehow have to remain, since they do not pass away, as it is said in the book *On Coming to Be and Passing Away*. The third particle, namely, that an element is not divided according to form, is meant to distinguish an element from those things that have parts different in form, i.e., in species, as, for example, a hand, the parts of which are flesh and bones, which are different in species. But an element is not divided into parts that differ in species, as water, of which every part is water. For it is not required for something to be an element that it should be indivisible in quantity, but it is sufficient, if it is not divisible according to species; but if something is indivisible also in this way, then it is also called an element, as letters are called the elements of expressions. So it is clear that "principle" covers more than "cause", and "cause" more than "element". And this is what the Commentator says in the fifth book of the *Metaphysics*.

Now having seen that there are four genera of causes, we have to know that it is not impossible for the same thing to have several causes: like a statue, the causes of which are both the bronze and the sculptor, but the sculptor as efficient, while the bronze as its matter. Neither is it impossible for the same thing to be the cause of contraries. For example, the pilot can be the cause both of the salvation and of the sinking of the ship, but of the one by his presence, while of the other by his absence. We also have to know that it is possible that something be both cause and effect in respect of the same thing, but not in the same way: for walking is the cause of health as its efficient, but health is the cause of walking as its end: for we take a walk sometimes for the sake of our health. Again, the body is the matter of the soul, while the soul is the form of the body. Also, the efficient is said to be the cause of the end, for the end comes to be by the operation of the agent, but the end is the cause of the efficient, insofar as the agent operates only for the sake of the end. Whence the efficient is the cause of the thing that is the end, say, health; but it does not cause the end to be the end; as the doctor causes health, but he does not cause health to be the end. On the other hand, the end is not the cause of the thing that is the efficient, but is the cause for the efficient to be efficient: for health does not cause the doctor to be a doctor (and I am speaking about the health that is produced by the operation of the doctor), but it causes the doctor to be efficient, so the end is the cause of the causality of the efficient, for it causes the efficient to be efficient, and similarly, it causes matter to be matter and form to be form, for matter does not receive form, except by the end, and form does not perfect matter, except by the end. Whence it is said that the end is the cause of all causes, for it is the cause of the causality of all causes. For matter is said to be the cause of form, insofar as the form exists only in matter; and similarly, form is the cause of matter, insofar as matter has actual existence only by the form. For matter and form are correlatives, as is said in the second book of *Physics*. They are related to the composite substance, however, as parts and as simple to the composite.

But since every cause is naturally prior to its effect, we should know that something is called "prior" in two ways, as Aristotle says in the sixteenth book of his on Animals [*Historia Animalium*]. And by this difference something can be called both prior and posterior in respect of the same thing, and both cause and effect. For something is said to be prior to something else in respect of generation and time, and again, in respect of substance and completion. Now since the operation of nature proceeds from what is imperfect to what is perfect and from what is incomplete to what is complete, what is imperfect is prior to what is perfect in respect of generation and time, but what is perfect is prior in completion. So we can say that a man is prior to a boy in substance and perfection, but the boy is prior to the man in generation and time. But although among generable things that which is imperfect is prior to what is perfect, and potentiality is prior to act (considering the same thing that is imperfect prior to becoming perfect, and is in potentiality, prior to becoming actual), nevertheless, absolutely speaking, what is actual and perfect is necessarily prior: for what reduces that which is in potentiality to actuality is in actuality, and what perfects the imperfect, is itself perfect. Now matter is prior to form in generation and time: for that to which something is coming is prior to what is coming to it. Form, however, is prior to matter in perfection, since matter has no complete existence, except by the form. Similarly, the efficient is prior to the end in generation and time, for it is from the efficient that motion starts toward the end. But the end is prior to the efficient, insofar as it is efficient, in substance and completion, for the action of the efficient is completed only by the end. So these two causes, namely, matter and the efficient, are prior in generation; but the form and the end are prior in perfection.

And we should note that there are two kinds of necessity: absolute necessity and conditional necessity. Absolute necessity proceeds from those causes that are prior in generation, which are matter and the efficient: for example, the necessity of death derives from matter and the disposition of the contrary components of the body; and this is called absolute, because it cannot be impeded. And this type of necessity is also called the necessity of matter. Conditional necessity, on the other hand, proceeds from those causes that are posterior in generation, namely, form and the end. For example, we say that conception is necessary, if a man is to be generated; and this is conditional, for it is not necessary for this woman to conceive, unless under this condition, namely, that if a man is to be generated. And this is called the necessity of the end.

We should also know that three causes can coincide, namely the form, the end and the efficient, as is clear in the generation of fire. For fire generates fire, so fire is the efficient, insofar as it generates; again, fire is form, insofar as it makes actual that was previously potential, and again, it is the end, insofar as it is intended by the agent, and insofar as the operation of the agent is terminated in it. But there are two kinds of ends, namely the end of generation and the end of the thing generated, as is clear in the generation of a knife. For the form of the knife is the end of its generation; but cutting, which is the operation of the knife, is the end of the thing generated, namely of the knife. Now the end of generation sometimes coincides with two of the above-mentioned causes, when something is generated by something of the same species, as when man generates man, and olive generates olive. But this may not be understood for the end of the thing generated.

We should know, however, that the end coincides with the form numerically, for it is numerically the same item that is the form of the generated thing and that is the end of generation. But with the efficient it does not coincide numerically, but can coincide specifically. For example, when a man generates a man, then the generating man and the generated man are numerically different, but are specifically the same. But matter does not coincide with the others, because matter, since it is a being in potentiality, is by its very nature imperfect, while the other causes, since they are actual, are by their nature actual; but what is perfect and what is imperfect never coincide.

Now having seen that there are four kinds of causes, namely, efficient, material, formal and final, we have to know that any of these kinds is divided in various ways. For some causes are called prior and some are called posterior, as when we say that the art of medicine and the doctor are both causes of health, but the art is the prior, while the doctor is the posterior cause; and similarly in the case of formal and the other kinds of causes.

Note here that in our inquiry we always have to go back to the first cause, as when we ask: Why is he healthy? The answer is: because the doctor cured him. And then, further: How did he cure him? The answer is: by his knowledge of medicine. And we should know that it is the same thing to say that a cause is posterior and that it is proximate, or that a cause is prior and that it is remote. So these two divisions of causes, namely, into prior vs. posterior and into proximate vs. remote, signify the same. But we should know that the more universal cause is always called the remote cause and the more specific cause is called the proximate cause. For example, we say that the proximate form of man is what his definition signifies, namely rational, mortal animal, but his more remote form is animal and the even more remote one is substance. For all superiors are forms of the inferiors. Similarly, the proximate matter of the statue is bronze, while the more remote is metal and the even more remote one is body.

Again, some causes are per se, others are per accidens. A per se cause of a thing is its cause insofar as such, as the builder is the cause of the house, or the wood is the matter of the bench. A cause per accidens is one that coincides with the cause per se, as when we say that the doctor is building. For the doctor is a cause per accidens of the building, because he is building not insofar as a doctor, but insofar as coincides with the builder. And the situation is similar in all other cases.

Again, some causes are simple, some are composite. Something is called a simple cause, when it is named only by the name of the per se cause, or only by the name of the per accidens cause, as when we say that the builder is the cause of the building, and similarly when we say that the doctor is the cause of the building. But a cause is called composite, when we name it by the name of both, as when we say that the builder-doctor is the cause of the building.

But also that can be called a simple cause, according to Avicenna's exposition, which is a cause without the addition of anything else, as the bronze of the statue, for the statue is made of bronze, without the addition of any other matter; or when we say that the doctor causes health, or the fire causes heat. We have a composite cause, however, when the cooperation of many things is needed for causation; e.g. one man cannot move a ship, but many can, or one stone does not make a house, but many stones do.

Again, some causes are actual, some are potential. An actual cause is one that is actually causing the thing, as when the builder is actually building, or the bronze, while the statue is actually being made of it. A potential cause, on the other hand, is what is not actually causing the thing, but can cause it, like the builder, when he is actually not building. And we should know that the actual cause and its effect should exist at the same time, so that if one of them exists, also the other is necessarily exists. For if the builder is actually working, then he has to be building, and if the act of building actually takes place, it is necessary that the builder be actually working. But this is not necessary in the case of merely potential causes.

We should know further that a universal cause is compared to a universal effect and a singular cause is compared to a singular effect. For example, we say that a builder is the cause of a building in general, but also that this builder is the cause of this building in particular.

We should also know that we can speak about the agreements and differences of the principles in terms of the agreements and differences of what they are the principles of. For some things are numerically identical, as Socrates and this man, pointing to Socrates; some things are numerically different, and specifically the same, as Socrates and Plato, who, although are both humans, are nevertheless numerically distinct. Again, some things differ specifically, but are generically the same, as a man and a donkey both belong to the genus of animals; still others are the same only analogically, as substance and quantity, which do not agree in some genus, but agree only analogically: for they agree only in that they are beings. But being is not a genus, because it is not predicated univocally, but analogically.

To understand this better, we have to know that it is in three ways that something can be predicated of several things: univocally, equivocally and analogically. Something is predicated univocally, if it is predicated by the same name and according to the same concept or definition, as "animal" is predicated of a man and a donkey. For both of them are said to be animals, and both are animated sensible substances, which is the definition of animal. Something is predicated equivocally, if it is predicated of several things by the same name, but according to different concepts, as "dog" is predicated both of

the barking animal and of the constellation, which agree only in this name but not in the definition or signification of this name: for what is signified by a name is its definition, as is said in the fourth book of the *Metaphysics*. Finally, something is predicated analogically, if it is predicated of several things, the concepts of which are different, yet are related to the same thing. For example, "healthy" is said of the body of animals and of urine and of food, but it does not signify the same in all these cases. For it is said of urine, insofar as it is a sign of health, of the body, insofar as it is the subject of health, and of the food, insofar as it is the cause of health; but all of these concepts are related to one and the same end, namely, health. For sometimes those that agree analogically, i.e., proportionally, are related to the same end, as is clear in the above example, but sometimes they are related to the same agent, as when "healer" is said of someone who operates by the art of medicine, as a doctor, or without it, as a midwife, or even of the instruments, but always in relation to the same agent, namely the art of medicine. Again, sometimes they are related to the same subject, as when "being" is predicated of substance, of quality, of quantity and of the other categories. For it is not wholly the same concept according to which a substance is said to be a being, and a quantity and the rest, but all these are said to be beings only in relation to substance, which is the subject of all of them. So "being" is said primarily of substance, and only secondarily of the rest. Whence "being" is not a genus, for no genus is predicated primarily and secondarily of its species, but "being" is predicated analogically. And this is what we said, namely, that substance and quantity differ generically, but they are the same analogically.

Now of those that are numerically the same, also the form and matter is numerically the same, as Tully's and Cicero's. Of those, however, that are specifically the same, but numerically distinct, also the matter and form are numerically distinct, but specifically the same, like Socrates's and Plato's. Similarly, of those that are generically the same, also the principles are generically the same: like the soul and the body of a donkey and of a horse differ specifically, but are the same generically. Again, in a similar manner, of those that agree only analogically, also the principles agree only analogically. For matter and form or potentiality and actuality are the principles both of substance and of the other catego-ries. Now the matter of substance and that of quantity, and, similarly, their forms differ generically, and agree only analogically or proportionally in that the matter of

substance is to substance as the matter of quantity is to quantity. But just as substance is the cause of other cat-egories, so are the principles of substance the principles of the rest.

GLOSSARY

amorphous: without shape or form

genera: types

locus a maiori: the proof concluding from the greater to the smaller

per accidens: by chance; indirectly

privation: lack of the usual comforts or necessities of life

univocally: having only one meaning; unambiguous

Document Analysis

"On the Principles of Nature" was written by Aquinas early in his career and reflects his studies of Aristotelian philosophy and its relationship to Christian concep-tions of being in the natural world. Written primarily for his fellow students and mentors at the University of Paris, the treatise expounds upon the rational Aristote-lian view of the nature of existence as matter and form. Aquinas rooted much of his ideology for this essay in Aristotle's *Physics* and *Metaphysics* (both composed around 350 BCE). Like Aristotle, Aquinas concerns himself with distinctions as to the nature of the exis-tence of things. In this analysis, he differentiates be-tween that which exists in reality and that which could potentially exist. Things that exist can be broken down further into things that are classified as the "substantial being" of a thing—the essential nature of something, such as a human being—and the "accidental being"—the aspects of a person that refine their identity, such as being a man or being elderly.

For Aquinas, this distinction between substantial and accidental carries over into potential existence of any form of matter as well. Further, matter can change, and those changes can be classified as substantial and accidental. Three factors can account for change, or the process by which something acquires a form that it presently does not have: matter, form, and privation. If something that comes to be was not in existence

before, the change is moving toward a state of being from a state of nonbeing. This concept allows Aqui-nas to explain how things are created without creating something out of nothing—things are generated out of things that potentially are. Matter, in its primary form, is thus eternal, as are the forms that matter takes. How-ever, matter that has taken a form can lose that form through corruption, such as what happens to a human body when the person has died.

All matter in the world, according to Aquinas, takes different forms—but those forms are changing. The na-ture of those changes might be simple, such as a fire changing the form of wood, or complex, such as the healing of a person by a physician, which is only made possible by the education of the physician and all of the factors that caused him to become a physician.

Essential Themes

Especially early in his career, the distinction between philosophy and theology in Aquinas's writing was quite clear. Concerning himself with the philosophical con-tent of Aristotle's *Physics* and *Metaphysics*, Aquinas ap-propriated the terms of Aristotle's philosophy, which would carry through to his later theological works. Though his theology was thoroughly Christian, he fit it into Aristotle's explanations of the world as being made up of matter and form. He viewed Aristotle's analysis of the physical world as proof of his Christian views of the world and how it works.

In Aquinas's later works, *Summa contra gentiles* and *Summa theologica*, he takes the philosophical ideas from "On the Principles of Nature" and applies them specifically to the divine. It is one thing to talk about the ideas of matter, form, and change, and another to delve into the theological discussions of where those things originate. In "On the Principles of Nature," he sidestepped the issue by talking of potential, but in his later works he would make clear that the order of determination of those things begins with God. Further, the nature of the physical world can be seen as analogous to the nature of the spiritual, as Aquinas later brings in discussions of human perception and thought and the nature and interplay between the human body and the human soul.

In his later theological works, Aquinas built on the ideas presented in "On the Principles of Nature," taking the ideas of ancient Greek philosophy and the Muslim elaborations upon that philosophy and using them to understand the universe within a particularly Christian context. While this more radical integration of non-Christian philosophical thought was initially frowned upon by the Catholic Church, it would eventually come to characterize the works of many scholars and theologians throughout the late Middle Ages and the Renaissance.

—*Steven L. Danver, PhD*

Bibliography and Additional Reading

Bobik, Joseph. *Aquinas on Matter and Form and the Elements: A Translation and Interpretation of the De Principiis Naturae and the De Mixtione Elementorum of St. Thomas Aquinas.* Notre Dame: U of Notre Dame P, 1998. Print.

Davies, Brian. *The Thought of Thomas Aquinas.* New York: Oxford UP, 1992. Print.

Feser, Edward. *Aquinas.* Oxford: Oneworld, 2009. Print.

Gracia, Jorge J. E. & Timothy B. Noone, eds. *A Companion to Philosophy in the Middle Ages.* Malden: Blackwell, 2003. Print.

Wippel, John F. *The Metaphysical Thought of Thomas Aquinas: From Finite Being to Uncreated Being.* Washington: Catholic U of America P, 2000. Print.

■ Excerpt from *Summa Theologica*

Dates: ca. 1265–74
Geographic Region: Italy and France
Author: Thomas Aquinas
Translator: David Burr

Summary Overview

The *Summa theologica*, Thomas Aquinas's major work addressing the principal elements of Christian theology, employs the Scholastic method of argumentation to examine questions involving the nature of God, God's presence in the world, and God's involvement in human history. The document represents a summation of medieval thought on these matters and is notable for its reliance on human reason and classical philosophy as ways one can know something about God alongside what God has revealed through sacred scripture. Before launching into his systematic examination of theological issues, Aquinas begins by explaining why theology should be considered a discipline complementary to, but separate from, other branches of philosophy.

Defining Moment

For several centuries after the fall of the Western Roman Empire in 476 CE, Christian theological study, which at that time meant Roman Catholic theology, was preserved in Western Europe in monasteries and cathedral schools. Most scholars placed great weight on authority to justify interpretations of scripture, address matters of doctrine, or combat heresies. The writings of the church fathers—early influential theologians, such as Augustine of Hippo—were the most common authorities used to expound on the fine points of dogma; classical authors were either unknown or ignored. By the twelfth century, however, theologians in the West were reintroduced to the works of classical philosophers, mainly through the writings of theologians in the Eastern Church, which had maintained its links to and interest in the Greek and Roman writers of the pre-Christian era.

The integration of classical philosophy into the study of Christian theology transformed the method by which medieval theologians practiced their craft. In addition to consulting traditional authorities, scholars began to make extensive use of dialectical reasoning, a methodology employed by classical philosophers in which reasoned arguments and the tools of logic are used to arrive at conclusions regarding the matter under study. (The term should not be confused with the dialectic developed by later secular philosophers, such as G. F. W. Hegel and Karl Marx.) Known as Scholasticism, this new approach to investigating matters of theology spurred learning and led to the production of a number of important new works.

Perhaps the most distinguished of the Scholastics, as these scholars have come to be known, Thomas Aquinas devoted his life to exploring issues involving the nature and attributes of God and the tenets of Christianity. A student of classical authors, Aquinas cites them as frequently as he does church fathers in his writings. Among his chief interests was the reconciliation of classical philosophy with church doctrine on matters involving the existence of God. From his reading of Aristotle, Aquinas was convinced that the Greek philosopher had demonstrated the existence of God through rational analysis. Furthermore, Aquinas did not hold that the God that Aristotle intuited through reason was different from the God revealed in sacred scripture. However, he felt that Aristotle's proof of God's existence did not obviate the need for the study of theology because any of the truths about God were simply unknowable to humans through their rational powers alone. Only divine revelation makes it possible to understand (even in a limited way) the nature of God and God's plan for every individual.

Author Biography

Tommaso D'Aquino, the man known in later centuries as Saint Thomas Aquinas, was born in Roccasecca, Italy, in 1225. He was sent at age six to study at the Benedictine monastery at Monte Cassino and later continued his studies in Naples. In 1244, against his family's wishes, he joined the relatively new Order of Preachers, known commonly as Dominicans after their founder, Saint Dominic. Aquinas's life was devoted to study and teaching. For four years, he studied in Cologne, Germany, under the renowned philosopher and theologian Albertus Magnus. Ordained in 1250, he continued his studies and eventually taught in Paris. He also began

writing philosophical and theological treatises, many inspired by his reading of the Greek philosopher Aristotle; chief among his works are the *Summa contra gentiles* (1259–64), a text explaining Christianity to people of other faiths, and the *Summa theologica*, a systematic exposition of the elements of Christian theology that combines the thought of Christian church fathers and numerous classical philosophers. He died in 1274 and was canonized in 1323.

HISTORICAL DOCUMENT

Article 1: Whether it is necessary to have another doctrine besides the philosophical disciplines.

Let us proceed to the first point. It seems that there is no necessity for any doctrine beyond the philosophical disciplines. Man should not strive after that which is beyond his reason. As Ecclesiastics says, "Do not be curious about what is above you" (Ecclus. 3:22). The things which can be investigated by reason are sufficiently covered in the philosophical disciplines, however. Thus it seems superfluous to have some doctrine beyond the philosophical disciplines.

Furthermore, any doctrine can deal only with that which is; for nothing can be known except that which is true, and that which is true is identical with that which is. Yet everything other signification, through which the things signified by the words signify something else in turn, is called the spiritual sense. It is based on the literal sense and presupposes it.

But on the contrary Paul says, "All divinely-inspired scripture is useful for teaching, arguing, correcting and instructing in justice" (II Tim. 3:16). Divinely-inspired scripture does not pertain to philosophical disciplines, however, for they are discovered by human reason. Thus it is useful to have another, divinely-inspired doctrine besides the philosophical disciplines.

Response: It must be said that, besides the philosophical disciplines which are investigated by human reason, another doctrine based on revelation was necessary for human well-being. Such is true, in the first place, because man is ordered by God to a certain end which exceeds the grasp of reason. As Isaiah says, "Eye has not seen, God, without you, what you have prepared

for those who love you" (Isa. 64:4). The end must be fore known to man, however, since he must order his intentions and actions to that end. Thus it was necessary to human well-being that certain things exceeding human reason be made known to man through divine revelation.

Even in the case of those things which can be investigated by human reason, it was necessary for man to be instructed by divine revelation. The truth concerning God, if left to human reason alone, would have appeared only to a few, and only after a long search, and even then mixed with many errors; yet all of man's well-being, which is in God, depends on knowledge of this truth. Thus, in order that this well-being should become known to men more commonly and more securely, it was necessary that they be instructed by divine revelation.

Thus it was necessary that, besides the philosophical doctrines which can be investigated by reason, there be a sacred doctrine known through revelation.

To the first argument, therefore, it must be said that, although what is above human knowledge should not be investigated by reason, once revealed by God it should be accepted through faith. Thus it is added in the same chapter of Ecclesiasticus, "Many things above human understanding are shown to you" (Ecclus. 3:25). Sacred doctrine consists of these things.

To the second argument it must be said that there are diverse sciences because things can be known in various ways. For example, the astronomer and the natural philosopher both demonstrate the same conclusion, such as that the world is round; yet the astronomer does so through mathematics, while the natural philosopher does so in a way that takes matter into account. Thus there is no reason why those things treated by the philosophical disciplines through natural reason should not also be treated by another science insofar as they are known by the light of divine revelation. Thus the theol- ogy which pertains to sacred doctrine differs from that theology which is a part of philosophy.

GLOSSARY

natural philosopher: in the Middle Ages, a scholar who studies the natural world; a precursor of the modern scientist

Document Analysis

Thomas Aquinas's *Summa theologica*, or "summary" of Christian theology, is a multivolume work in three major parts and was left unfinished at his death. Part one deals with God as creator and ruler of all creation; part two considers God as the end toward which all human actions should aim; part three considers the nature of Christ as humankind's savior. The extant parts each contain a hundred questions or more, and each question is further subdivided into articles that address elements of the question. Each article is further divided into sections. In the first, Aquinas states the specific problem he wishes to address. The second contains a list of objections that might be made to the answer he will propose. In the third section, Aquinas provides what theological scholars call a "contrary," essentially an objection to these objections; often this is in the form of a quotation from an authority. In the fourth section, Aquinas offers his own response to these objections and provides his own answer to the question he has posed. In the fifth section he gives further answers to the specific objections raised in the second section.

This excerpt is the first of ten articles that Aquinas addresses in his first question, "Sacred Doctrine, what it is and what it includes." His aim is to demonstrate that theology is, and ought to be, a discipline separate from, but informed by, philosophy. Theology is complementary, but not in competition with, the traditional method of arriving at knowledge through human reasoning. Aquinas begins by stating the point he wishes to disprove, that "there is no necessity for any doctrine beyond the philosophical disciplines." In Aquinas's day, the "philosophical disciplines" included logic (the way humans reason), epistemology (the way humans know), ethics (questions of human behavior), natural philosophy (questions about the natural world, what in modern times would become the sciences), and metaphys-

ics (the study of first principles of being, the abstract qualities of existence that transcend individual beings). For centuries, philosophers had argued that all that is knowable can be discovered through the study of one of these branches of knowledge.

Aquinas begins his objection to this position by citing Saint Paul, who calls for the study of divinely inspired scripture. Human reason is incapable of coming to an understanding of what has been revealed by God, and thus, Aquinas says, it is "useful to have another, divinely inspired doctrine besides the philosophical disciplines." By "doctrine" Aquinas implies the development of a body of knowledge elucidating sacred scripture; that doctrine, he goes on to explain, is "sacred doctrine," known not through human intellect but "through revelation."

The importance of belief is made clear in Aquinas's answer to the argument that philosophy can reveal all that can be known. What is revealed by God is "above human knowledge," and "should not be investigated by reason"; it must be "accepted through faith." Just as there are different ways of examining the world through various philosophical disciplines, so there ought to be a method of examining revealed truth. That is the function of theology as Aquinas sees it.

What is clear from this introductory argument in the Summa is Aquinas's unquestioning acceptance of the scripture as divinely inspired. How we can know of God's existence and what God's plan is for humankind is the subject of the rest of this remarkable tour de force of reasoning, argumentation, and careful, reverent analysis of the word of God.

Essential Themes

Ironically, shortly after Aquinas died, his works were banned in Paris, a center of theological study. The Catholic Church was not yet ready to accept what was then a radical notion: that classical philosophy (especially that of Aristotle) was reconcilable with the truths of sacred scripture. Fifty years later, the restrictions on Aquinas's teachings were lifted, and his work soon became the centerpiece of theological study throughout Europe. He became recognized as one of the leading medieval scholars, and he was named a doctor of the Church, an important contributor to theology or doctrine.

The most important contribution Aquinas made to the study of theology is his insistence that reason and revelation are not incompatible. Aquinas placed reason in the service of faith: as a preparation for faith (the acceptance of divine revelation), as a means of explaining the truths of faith, and as a discipline for defending faith. His insistence that reason can lead humans to recognize that God exists transformed the study of theology in Christendom and remained, even after the Protestant Reformation, the bedrock of Roman Catholic theological study. For Catholics, the study of Thomistic theology was an integral part of higher education well into the twentieth century.

—*Laurence W. Mazzeno, PhD*

Bibliography and Additional Reading

Bourke, Vernon. *Aquinas' Search for Wisdom*. Milwaukee: Bruce, 1965. Print.

Jenkins, John. *Knowledge and Faith in Thomas Aquinas*. Cambridge: Cambridge UP, 1997. Print.

McInerny, Ralph. *St. Thomas Aquinas*. Boston: Twayne, 1977. Print.

O'Meara, Thomas Franklin. *Thomas Aquinas, Theologian*. Notre Dame: U of Notre Dame P, 1997. Print.

Van Nieuwenhove, Rik & Joseph Wawrykow, eds. *The Theology of Thomas Aquinas*. Notre Dame: U of Notre Dame P, 2005. Print.

■ "On Experimental Science"

Date: 1268
Country: England
Author: Roger Bacon

Summary Overview

This excerpt comes from the sixth book of Roger Bacon's eight-part *Opus Majus* (1267; *Greater Work*), both a systematic exposition of the major branches of learning and a call for intellectual and religious reform addressed to Pope Clement IV, who had requested the treatise. In it, Bacon called for a greater use of experience as a way of gaining knowledge, as opposed to deductive logic (i.e., "reason"). Bacon affirmed the authority of ancient writers, in particular Aristotle, for this program and pointed to a few specific examples of how experiment adds to knowledge or refutes false beliefs. However, he also emphasizes the importance of personal virtue and divine illumination in acquiring knowledge and wisdom.

Defining Moment

In the thirteenth century, there was a continuing revival of classical learning, particularly the works of the ancient Greek philosopher Aristotle and his Greek and Arab commentators. A related phenomenon was the establishment of the university system. Both original Greek works and the scientific studies of Arabic writers became available in Latin and were widely read and circulated among intellectuals and professors, nearly all of whom were affiliated with the clergy. Also in this period, however, the Latin Christian world came under pressure from the Mongols, who launched a brief but successful invasion in the thirteenth century, and Muslims, who were on the offensive in the Middle East against the surviving crusader states. Given these security threats, many scholars, including Bacon, thought either the Christian church had become corrupt and was in need of reform or even that the end of the world was near.

The period also saw the meteoric rise of the new religious orders of men known as friars, and particularly the Friars Minor, or Franciscans, the order that Bacon joined. Friars took vows of poverty and chastity similar to those of monks, but they were more mobile, not weighed down with the lands and buildings that established monastic orders had accumulated. Franciscans were more ambivalent about the new philosophy of knowledge and its possible implications for Christianity than were one of the other major orders, the Dominicans. Although there had been no role for learning in the original Franciscan order, as founded by Francis of Assisi (1182–1226), by the middle of the thirteenth century Franciscans were an increasing presence in the universities despite the resistance of the "secular" masters, so called because they were not part of a religious order. This was particularly true in England, where Oxford University was rising into prominence as a challenger for intellectual preeminence to the established University of Paris, where the Dominicans were the dominant order. Much of Oxford's rise had to do with a quantitative and experimental approach to natural philosophy, embodied in figures who influenced Bacon, such as Robert Grosseteste. The dominant tradition in Western natural philosophy since the rediscovery of the works of Aristotle and the establishment of the university system had been textual and deductive, based on a logical structure known as the syllogism, rather than based on observation.

Author Biography and Document Information

Roger Bacon was born circa 1220 into an established Anglo-Norman family. He studied and taught at Oxford University and the University of Paris, the leading universities of Western Europe. After teaching in Paris, he returned to Oxford, England, to conduct independent research. Bacon joined the Franciscan order in the 1250s. Unlike many medieval European scholars, he was familiar with Greek, Arabic, and Hebrew as well as Latin. Bacon was a pioneer in teaching Aristotle's works on natural philosophy. Bacon was certain that the church of his time was undergoing a crisis, one caused by a bad system of education that produced poor preachers. Much of his career was devoted to church reform. He did not exempt the Franciscans from his critique, and he sometimes had a difficult time with the superiors of his order. In addition to the sciences, Bacon was interested in such diverse areas as alchemy,

moral philosophy, and the recovery of an accurate text of the Bible through study of the original languages. The *Opus Majus* was sent to Pope Clement IV, and several manuscripts of its parts survive in Roman and English libraries. Bacon died around 1292.

HISTORICAL DOCUMENT

Having laid down the main points of the wisdom of the Latins as regards language, mathematics and optics, I wish now to review the principles of wisdom from the point of view of experimental science, because without experiment it is impossible to know anything thoroughly.

There are two ways of acquiring knowledge, one through reason, the other by experiment. Argument reaches a conclusion and compels us to admit it, but it neither makes us certain nor so annihilates doubt that the mind rests calm in the intuition of truth, unless it finds this certitude by way of experience. Thus many have arguments toward attainable facts, but because they have not experienced them, they overlook them and neither avoid a harmful nor follow a beneficial course. Even if a man that has never seen fire, proves by good reasoning that fire burns, and devours and destroys things, nevertheless the mind of one hearing his arguments would never be convinced, nor would he avoid fire until he puts his hand or some combustible thing into it in order to prove by experiment what the argument taught. But after the fact of combustion is experienced, the mind is satisfied and lies calm in the certainty of truth. Hence argument is not enough, but experience is.

This is evident even in mathematics, where demonstration is the surest. The mind of a man that receives that clearest of demonstrations concerning the equilateral triangle without experiment will never stick to the conclusion nor act upon it till confirmed by experiment by means of the intersection of two circles from either section of which two lines are drawn to the ends of a given line. Then one receives the conclusion without doubt. What Aristotle says of the demonstration by the syllogism being able to give knowledge, can be understood if it is accompanied by experience, but not of the bare demonstration. What he says in the first book of the *Metaphysics*, that those knowing the reason and cause

are wiser than the experienced, he speaks concerning the experienced who know the bare fact only without the cause. But I speak here of the experienced that know the reason and cause through their experience. And such are perfect in their knowledge, as Aristotle wishes to be in the sixth book of the Ethics [*Nicomachean Ethics*], whose simple statements are to be believed as if they carried demonstration, as he says in that very place.

Whoever wishes without proof to revel in the truths of things need only know how to neglect experience. This is evident from examples. Authors write many things and the people cling to them through arguments which they make without experiment, that are utterly false. It is commonly believed among all classes that one can break adamant only with the blood of a goat, and philosophers and theologians strengthen this myth. But it is not yet proved by adamant being broken by blood of this kind, as much as it is argued to this conclusion. And yet, even without the blood it can be broken with ease. I have seen this with my eyes; and this must needs be because gems cannot be cut out save by the breaking of the stone. Similarly it is commonly believed that the secretions of the beaver that the doctors use are the testicles of the male, but this is not so, as the beaver has this secretion beneath its breast and even the male as well as the female produces a secretion of this kind. In addition also to this secretion the male has its testicles in the natural place and thus again it is a horrible lie that, since hunters chase the beaver for this secretion, the beaver knowing what they are after, tears out his testicles with his teeth and throws them away. Again it is popularly said that cold water in a vase freezes more quickly than hot; and the argument for this is that contrary is excited by the contrary, like enemies running together. They even impute this to Aristotle in the second book of *Meteorology*, but he certainly did not say this, but says something like it by which they have been deceived, that if both cold and hot water are poured into a cold place as on ice, the cold freezes quicker (which is true), but if they are placed in two vases, the hot will freeze quicker. It is necessary, then, to prove everything by experience.

Experience is of two kinds. One is through the external senses: such are the experiments that are made upon the heaven through instruments in regard to facts there, and the facts on earth that we prove in various ways to be certain in our own sight. And facts that are not true in places where we are, we know through other wise men that have experienced them. Thus Aristotle with the authority of Alexander, sent 2,000 men throughout various parts of the earth in order to learn at first hand everything on the surface of the world, as Pliny says in his *Natural History*. And this experience is human and philosophical just as far as a man is able to make use of the beneficent grace given to him, but such experience is not enough for man, because it does not give full certainty as regards corporeal things because of their complexity and touches the spiritual not at all. Hence man's intellect must be aided in another way, and thus the patriarchs and prophets who first gave science to the world secured inner light and did not rest entirely on the senses. So also many of the faithful since Christ. For grace makes many things clear to the faithful, and there is divine inspiration not alone concerning spiritual but even about corporeal things. In accordance with which Ptolemy says in the *Centilogium* that there is a double way of coming to the knowledge of things, one through the experiments of science, the other through divine inspiration, which latter is far the better as he says.

Of this inner experience there are seven degrees, one through spiritual illumination in regard to scientific things. The second grade consists of virtue, for evil is ignorance as Aristotle says in the second book of the Ethics. And Algazel says in the logic that the mind is disturbed by faults, just as a rusty mirror in which the images of things cannot be clearly seen, but the mind is prepared by virtue like a well polished mirror in which the images of things show clearly. On account of this, true philosophers have accomplished more in ethics in proportion to the soundness of their virtue, denying to one another that they can discover the cause of things unless they have minds free from faults. Augustine relates this

fact concerning Socrates in Book VIII, chapter III, of the *City of God*: to the same purpose Scripture says, to an evil mind, etc., for it is impossible that the mind should lie calm in the sunlight of truth while it is spotted with evil, but like a parrot or magpie it will repeat words foreign to it which it has learned through long practice. And this is our experience, because a known truth draws men into its light for love of it, but the proof of this love is the sight of the result. And indeed he that is busy against truth must necessarily ignore this, that it is permitted him to know how to fashion many high sounding words and to write sentences not his own, just as the brute that imitates the human voice or an ape that attempts to carry out the works of men, although he does not understand their purpose. Virtue, then, clears the mind so that one can better understand not only ethical, but even scientific things. I have carefully proved this in the case of many pure youths who, on account of their innocent minds, have gone further in knowledge than I dare to say, because they have had correct teaching in religious doctrine, to which class the bearer of this treatise belongs, to whose knowledge of principles but few of the Latins rise. Since he is so young (about twenty years old) and poor besides, not able to have masters nor the length of any one year to learn all the great things he knows, and since he neither has great genius or a wonderful memory, there can be no other cause, save the grace of God, which, on account of the clearness of his mind, has granted to him these things which it has refused to almost all students, for a pure man, he has received pure things from me. Nor have I been able to find in him any kind of a mortal fault, although I have searched diligently, and he has a mind so clear and far seeing that he receives less from instruction than can be supposed. And I have tried to lend my aid to the purpose that these two youths may be useful implements for the Church of God, inasmuch as they have with the Grace of God examined the whole learning of the Latins.

The third degree of spiritual experience is the gift of the Holy Spirit, which Isaiah describes. The fourth lies in the beatitudes which our Lord enumerates in the Gospels. The fifth is the spiritual sensibility. The sixth is in such fruits as the peace of God, which passes all understanding. The seventh lies in states of rapture and in the methods of those also, various ones of whom receive it in various ways, that they may see many things which it is not permitted to speak of to man. And whoever is thoroughly practiced in these experiences or in many of them, is able to assure himself and others, not only concerning spiritual things, but all human knowledge. And indeed, since all speculative thought proceeds through arguments which either proceed through a proposition by authority or through other propositions of argument, in accordance with this which I am now investigating, there is a science that is necessary to us, which is called experimental. I wish to explain this, not only as useful to philosophy, but to the knowledge of God and the understanding of the whole world: as in a former book I followed language and science to their end, which is the Divine wisdom by which all things are ordered.

And because this experimental science is a study entirely unknown by the common people, I cannot convince them of its utility, unless its virtue and characteristics are shown. This alone enables us to find out surely what can be done through nature, what through the application of art, what through fraud, what is the purport and what is mere dream in chance, conjuration, invocations, imprecations, magical sacrifices and what there is in them; so that all falsity may be lifted and the truths we alone of the art retained. This alone teaches us to examine all the insane ideas of the magicians in order not to confirm but to avoid them, just as logic criticizes the art of sophistry. This science has three great purposes in regard to the other sciences: the first is that one may criticize by experiment the noble conclusions of all the other sciences, for the other sciences know that their principles come from experiment, but the conclusions through arguments drawn from the principles discovered, if they care to have the result of their conclusions precise and complete. It is necessary that they have this through the aid of this noble science. It is true that mathematics reaches conclusions in accordance with universal experience about figures and numbers, which indeed apply to all sciences and to this experience, because no science can be known without mathematics. If we would attain to experiments precise, complete and made certain in accordance with the proper method, it is necessary to undertake an examination of the science itself, which is called experimental on our authority. I find an example in the rainbow and in like phenomena, of which nature are

the circles about the sun and stars, also the halo beginning from the side of the sun or of a star which seems to be visible in straight lines and is called by Aristotle in the third book of the *Meteorology* a perpendicular, but by Seneca a halo, and is also called a circular corona, which have many of the colors of the rainbow. Now the natural philosopher discusses these things, and in regard to perspective has many facts to add which are concerned with the operation of seeing which is pertinent in this place. But neither Aristotle or Avicenna have given us knowledge of these things in their books upon Nature, nor Seneca, who wrote a special book concerning them. But experimental science analyzes such things.

The experimenter considers whether among visible things, he can find colors formed and arranged as given in the rainbow. He finds that there are hexagonal crystals from Ireland or India which are called rainbow-hued in Solinus Concerning the Wonders of the World and he holds these in a ray of sunlight falling through the window, and finds all the colors of the rainbow, arranged as in it in the shaded part next the ray. Moreover, the same experimenter places himself in a somewhat shady place and puts the stone up to his eye when it is almost closed, and beholds the colors of the rainbow clearly arranged, as in the bow. And because many persons making use of these stones think that it is on account of some special property of the stones and because of their hexagonal shape the investigator proceeds further and finds this in a crystal, properly shaped, and in other transparent stones. And not only are these Irish crystals in white, but also black, so that the phenomenon occurs in smoky crystal and also in all stones of similar transparency. Moreover, in stones not shaped hexagonally, provided the surfaces are rough, the same as those of the Irish crystals, not entirely smooth and yet not rougher than those—the surfaces have the same quality as nature has given the Irish crystals, for the difference of roughness makes the difference of color. He watches, also, rowers and in the drops falling from the raised oars he finds the same colors, whenever the rays of the sun penetrate the drops.

The case is the same with water falling from the paddles of a water-wheel. And when the investigator looks in a summer morning at the drops of dew clinging to the grass in the field or plane, he sees the same colors. And, likewise, when it rains, if he stands in a shady place and the sun's rays beyond him shine through the falling drops, then in some rather dark place the same colors appear, and they can often be seen at night about a candle. In the summer time, as soon as he rises from sleep while his eyes are not yet fully opened, if he suddenly looks at a window through which the light of the sun is streaming, he will see the colors. Again, sitting outside of the sunlight, if he holds his head covering beyond his eyes, or, likewise, if he closes his eyes, the same thing happens in the shade at the edges, and it also takes place through a glass vase filled with water, sitting in the sunlight. Similarly, if any one holding water in his mouth suddenly sprinkles the water in jets and stands at the side of them; or if through a lamp of oil hanging in the air the rays shine in the proper way, or the light shines upon the surface of the oil, the colors again appear. Thus, in an infinite number of ways, natural as well as artificial, colors of this kind are to be seen, if only the diligent investigator knows how to find them.

Experimental science is also that which alone, as the mistress of the speculative sciences, can discover magnificent truths in the fields of the other sciences, to which these other sciences can in no way attain. And these truths are not of the nature of former truths, but they may be even outside of them, in the fields of things where there are neither as yet conclusions or principles, and good examples may be given of this, but in everything which follows it is not necessary for the inexperienced to seek a reason in order to understand at the beginning, but rather he will never have a reason before he has tried the experiment. Whence in the first place there should be credulity until experiment follows, in order that the reason may be found. If one who has never seen that a magnet draws iron nor heard from others that it attracts, seeks the reason before experimenting, he will never find it. Indeed, in the first place, he ought to believe those who have experimented or who have it from investigators, nor ought he to doubt the truth of it because he himself is ignorant of it and because he has no reason for it.

The third value of this science is this—it is on account of the prerogatives through which it looks, not only to the other sciences, but by its own power investigates the secrets of nature, and this takes place in two ways—in the knowledge of future and present events, and in those wonderful works by which it surpasses astronomy commonly so-called in the power of its conclusions. For Ptolemy in the introduction of the *Almagest*, says that there is another and surer way than the ordinary astronomy; that is, the experimental method which follows after the course of nature, to which many faithful philosophers, such as Aristotle and a vast crowd of the authors of predictions from the stars, are favorable, as he himself says, and we ourselves know through our own experience, which cannot be denied. This wisdom has been found as a natural remedy for human ignorance or imprudence; for it is difficult to have astronomical implements sufficiently exact and more difficult to have tables absolutely verified, especially when the motion of the planets is involved in them. The use of these tables is difficult, but the use of the instruments more so.

This science has found definitions and ways through which it quickly comes to the answer of a whole question, as far as the nature of a single science can do so, and through which it shows us the outlines of the virtues of the skies and the influence of the sky upon this earth, without the difficulty of astronomy. This part so-called has four principal laws as the secret of the science, and some bear witness that a use of this science, which illustrates its nature, is in the change of a region in order that the customs of the people may be changed. In connection with which Aristotle, the most learned of philosophers, when Alexander asked of him concerning some tribes that he had found, whether he should kill them on account of their barbarity or let them live, responded in the *Book of Secrets* [*Secretum secretorum*] if you can change their air let them live; if not, kill them. He wished that their air could be altered usefully, so that the complexion of their bodies could be changed, and finally the mind aroused through the complexion should absorb good customs from the liberty of their environment; this is one use of this science.

GLOSSARY

Algazel: Muslim philosopher and theologian Al-Ghazālī

Avicenna: Spanish Muslim philosopher and physician Ibn Sīnā

Seneca: ancient Roman author of *Natural Questions*

Solinus: Gaius Julius Solinus, third-century CE Roman author of a book on wonders

syllogism: a form of deductive reasoning; a subtle, sophisticated (or deceptive) argument

Document Analysis

This section of the *Opus Majus* deals with one part of Bacon's program for intellectual reform: greater emphasis on experience as a way of gaining knowledge of the natural world. The term "experiment" refers not only to controlled experiments that would later be common in the sciences, but also to the close observation of nature. Bacon's experimentalism is not a rejection of Aristotelianism, but a call for the revival of interest in Aristotle's experience-based work, as opposed to the one-sided emphasis on Aristotelian logic. He does not argue that deductive truth is invalid, but that true certainty comes from experience rather than argument or proof, even in mathematics, a discipline Bacon valued highly. (The longest section of the *Opus Majus* is devoted to mathematics.)

Bacon is careful, however, not to describe experience as the source of all certain knowledge of truth, a philosophical position that could be interpreted as denying God's role in giving wisdom. In particular, he emphasizes that there is a superior religious road to truth through divine inspiration. Natural knowledge is also tied to morality, in that an evil person is unable to attain it. However, Bacon does not restrict this morality to Christians; in fact, he cites the revered pagan Socrates as an example of the connection of virtue and knowledge. (Although he does not specifically make this point, his references to Muslim authorities, such as Avicenna, suggest he believed that they too were capable of reaching the appropriate moral level for the discovery of natural truth.) The higher degrees of spiritual illumination, however, are reserved for Christians.

Bacon presents an example of the discovery of the causes of rainbows to illustrate the benefits of experiment. (Optics was a particular interest of Bacon and the subject of a whole book of the *Opus Majus*.) Astrol-ogy, the influence of the stars upon earth, is another subject that can be fruitfully approached through experiment, he claims. Bacon also uses experiments to demonstrate the falsity of some commonly held beliefs about nature, such as the idea that adamant (a very hard substance) can only be broken with the blood of a goat. The neglect of experiment had enabled these false ideas to circulate for a long time, both among the common people (for whom Bacon has little intellectual respect) and "philosophers and theologians."

Essential Themes

The emphasis on experience in "On Experimental Science" helped lay the groundwork for the scientific revolution of the sixteenth and seventeenth centuries, although early modern experimentalism had origins other than Bacon's work. The early modern approach was also different in that Bacon believed in experimentalism as compatible with the Aristotelian program, while early modern empiricists would frame their experimentalism as a rejection of Aristotle and even ancient philosophy generally. English Protestants emphasized Bacon's difficulty with the Franciscans to view him as a forerunner of Protestantism. The idea of Bacon as a neglected scientific pioneer continued in popular literature on the history of science. Popular writers also have often exaggerated the hostility Bacon received from the leaders of the church and the Franciscan order to fit a distorted view of the medieval church as being opposed to science in general.

In popular culture, Bacon was commonly remembered as a great wizard, to whom magical legends were attached, as, for example, in the Robert Greene's Elizabethan play *The Honorable Historie of Frier Bacon and Frier Bungay* (1594). He has also been associated, on very little evidence, with the mysterious Voynich manuscript. He has gained a somewhat exaggerated reputation as a rebel against medieval Scholasticism and even as the first modern scientist. Modern scholars read Bacon more in the medieval context as a champion of church reform and a somewhat innovative Scholastic philosopher influenced by Grosseteste.

—*William E. Burns, PhD*

Bibliography and Additional Reading
Clegg, Brian. *The First Scientist: A Life of Roger Bacon.* New York: Carroll, 2003. Print.

Grant, Edward. *The Foundations of Modern Science in the Middle Ages: Their Religious, Institutional, and Intellectual Contexts.* New York: Cambridge UP, 1996. Print.
Hackett, Jeremiah, ed. *Roger Bacon and the Sciences.* New York: Brill, 1997. Print.
Power, Amanda. *Roger Bacon and the Defense of Christendom.* Cambridge: Cambridge UP, 2013. Print.

Excerpt from *The Love of Books*

Date: ca.1345
Country: England
Author: Richard de Bury
Translator: Ernest C. Thomas

Summary Overview

Richard de Bury was a priest, a scholar, a diplomat, and an important political figure during the reign of Edward III of England. He served as tutor for Prince Edward before his ascension to the throne, and he rose to prominence as the bishop of Durham, high chancellor, and treasurer of England. He was an important emissary for the king, who sent him on several diplomatic missions to France, where he met the famed poet Petrarch. However, De Bury is best known as a collector of books and the writer of the first treatise on library management. His *Philobiblon,* or *The Love of Books,* was intended both to encourage the clergy to value the books in their possession and to justify his own significant collection. It also provided instructions on how to manage his library, which he intended to bequeath to Durham College, Oxford. Accounts differ as to what eventually became of his beloved books, but they were scattered when Henry VIII dispersed the ancient libraries of religious orders during the English Reformation of the sixteenth century. All of De Bury's books were in manuscript form, as printing had not yet been invented. The *Philobiblon* was first printed in Germany in 1473.

Defining Moment

Richard de Bury was intimately involved in the intrigues of the English court that led to the dethroning and murder of Edward II and the crowning of the latter's son. He saw the beginning of the conflicts that would lead to the Hundred Years' War between England and France, and he had a significant, if ultimately unsuccessful, diplomatic career.

Edward II was king when De Bury was hired to tutor his young son, Prince Edward. Edward II was deeply unpopular, as he tended to fall under the influence of charismatic favorites and ignored the demands of his barons. He also had failed to protect English lands in Scotland and the border areas, and many saw him as weak-willed and cowardly. When his son and presumptive heir, Edward, was born in 1312, he inherited lands in France and Wales. In 1325, when Prince Edward was only thirteen years old, he was sent as an emissary by his father to pay homage to the French king for their lands in Aquitaine. He was accompanied by his mother, Queen Isabella, and his tutor, De Bury, who were charged with negotiating a new peace treaty with France. Instead, Isabella became the mistress of the exiled English lord Roger Mortimer, and together they planned an invasion of England, with the goal of unseating the king and crowning the prince as Edward III. De Bury helped to finance this rebellion and was temporarily exiled in France while Edward II unsuccessfully sought his arrest. Meanwhile, the queen and Mortimer led a successful invasion of England.

On January 25, 1327, Edward II was forced to abdicate in favor of his son, Edward III, who was crowned on February 1, at age fourteen. On September 21, 1327, the imprisoned king was murdered at Berkeley Castle. Mortimer, the real ruler in England, signed an unpopular peace treaty with the Scots and was reviled for his lavish spending. In 1330, after the birth of his son and heir, Edward III had Mortimer arrested and executed for treason. His mother was allowed to retain her titles and position. Edward III rewarded De Bury's loyalty to him by sending him as ambassador to the exiled papal court in Avignon, making him treasurer and chancellor of England in 1327 and 1329 and convincing the pope to appoint him bishop of Durham in 1333. De Bury retired from public life in the early 1340s to focus on amassing his library. He died in 1345, just after completing the *Philobiblon.*

Author Biography and Document Information

Richard de Bury was born around 1287 near Bury St. Edmunds, in Suffolk, England. He was from a family of minor nobility and was raised by his maternal uncle after the death of his father. He attended Oxford University, where he studied theology and philosophy. Some scholars believe he became a Benedictine monk, though many others believe he took religious vows as a priest and not as a monk. De Bury was made tutor to the future King Edward III and spent some time in France avoiding censure from King Edward II, who abdicated in 1327 in favor of his son. De Bury returned to England, where he served as bishop of Durham. He also served the king as chancellor and treasurer of England. De Bury amassed a significant library and wrote a series of essays, later published as *Philobiblon*, on the care and importance of books. He died in 1345 in Durham.

Philobiblon was written in Latin and first printed in that language in Cologne, Germany, in 1473. The first edition in England was printed in 1598, and the first English translation appeared in 1832. The most complete volume was compiled and translated in 1888 by Ernest C. Thomas.

HISTORICAL DOCUMENT

CHAPTER I:

THAT THE TREASURE OF WISDOM IS CHIEFLY CONTAINED IN BOOKS

The desirable treasure of wisdom and science, which all men desire by an instinct of nature, infinitely surpasses all the riches of the world; in respect of which precious stones are worthless; in comparison with which silver is as clay and pure gold is as a little sand; at whose splendour the sun and moon are dark to look upon; compared with whose marvellous sweetness honey and manna are bitter to the taste. O value of wisdom that fadeth not away with time, virtue ever flourishing, that cleanseth its possessor from all venom! O heavenly gift of the divine bounty, descending from the Father of lights, that thou mayest exalt the rational soul to the very heavens! Thou art the celestial nourishment of the intellect, which those who eat shall still hunger and those who drink shall still thirst, and the gladdening harmony of the languishing soul which he that hears shall never be confounded. Thou art the moderator and rule of morals, which he who follows shall not sin. By thee kings reign and princes decree justice. By thee, rid of their native rudeness, their minds and tongues being polished, the thorns of vice being torn up by the roots, those men attain high places of honour, and become fathers of their country, and companions of princes, who without thee would have melted their spears into pruning-hooks and ploughshares, or would perhaps be feeding swine with the prodigal.

Where dost thou chiefly lie hidden, O most elect treasure! and where shall thirsting souls discover thee?

Certes, thou hast placed thy tabernacle in books, where the Most High, the Light of lights, the Book of Life, has established thee. There everyone who asks receiveth thee, and everyone who seeks finds thee, and to everyone that knocketh boldly it is speedily opened. Therein the cherubim spread out their wings, that the intellect of the students may ascend and look from pole to pole, from the east and west, from the north and from the south. Therein the mighty and incomprehensible God Himself is apprehensibly contained and worshipped; therein is revealed the nature of things celestial, terrestrial, and infernal; therein are discerned the laws by which every state is administered, the offices of the celestial hierarchy are distinguished, and the tyrannies of demons described, such as neither the ideas of Plato transcend, nor the chair of Crato contained.

In books I find the dead as if they were alive; in books I foresee things to come; in books warlike affairs are set forth; from books come forth the laws of peace. All things are corrupted and decay in time; Saturn ceases not to devour the children that he generates; all the glory of the world would be buried in oblivion, unless God had provided mortals with the remedy of books.

Alexander, the conqueror of the earth, Julius, the invader of Rome and of the world, who, the first in war and arts, assumed universal empire under his single rule, faithful Fabricius and stern Cato, would now have been unknown to fame, if the aid of books had been wanting. Towers have been razed to the ground; cities have been overthrown; triumphal arches have perished from decay; nor can either pope or king find any means of more easily conferring the privilege of perpetuity than by books. The book that he has made renders its author this service in return, that so long as the book survives its author remains immortal and cannot die, as Ptolemy declares in the Prologue to his *Almagest*: He is not dead, he says, who has given life to science.

Who therefore will limit by anything of another kind the price of the infinite treasure of books, from which the scribe who is instructed bringeth forth things new and old? Truth that triumphs over all things, which overcomes the king, wine, and women, which it is reckoned holy to honour before friendship, which is the way without turning and the life without end, which holy Boethius considers to be threefold in thought, speech, and writing, seems to remain more usefully and to fructify to greater profit in books. For the meaning of the voice perishes with the sound; truth latent in the mind is wisdom that is hid and treasure that is not seen; but truth which shines forth in books desires to manifest itself to every impressionable sense. It commends itself to the sight when it is read, to the hearing when it is heard, and moreover in a manner to the touch, when it suffers itself to be transcribed, bound, corrected, and preserved. The undisclosed truth of the mind, although it is the possession of the noble soul, yet because it lacks a companion, is not certainly known to be delightful, while neither sight nor hearing takes account of it. Further the truth of the voice is patent only to the ear and eludes the sight, which reveals to us more of the qualities of things, and linked with the subtlest of motions begins and perishes as it were in a breath. But the written truth of books, not transient but permanent, plainly offers itself to be observed, and by means of the pervious spherules of the eyes, passing through the vestibule of perception and the courts of imagination, enters the chamber of intellect, taking its place in the couch of memory, where it engenders the eternal truth of the mind.

Finally we must consider what pleasantness of teaching there is in books, how easy, how secret! How safely we lay bare the poverty of human ignorance to books without feeling any shame! They are masters who instruct us without rod or ferule, without angry words, without clothes or money. If you come to them they are not asleep; if you ask and inquire of them they do not withdraw themselves; they do not chide if you make mistakes; they do not laugh at you if you are ignorant. O books, who alone are liberal and free, who give to all who ask of you and enfranchise all who serve you faithfully! By how many thousand types are ye commended to learned men in the Scriptures given us by inspiration of God! For ye are the minds of profoundest wisdom, to which the wise man sends his son that he may dig out treasures: Prov. ii. Ye are the wells of living waters, which father Abraham first digged, Isaac digged again, and which the Philistines strive to fill up: Gen. xxvi. Ye are indeed the most delightful ears of corn, full of grain, to be rubbed only by apostolic hands, that the sweetest food may be produced for hungry souls: Matt. xii. Ye are the golden pots in which manna is stored, and rocks flowing with honey, nay, combs of honey, most plenteous udders of the milk of life, garners ever full; ye are the tree of life and the fourfold river of Paradise, by which the human mind is nourished, and the thirsty intellect is watered and refreshed. Ye are the ark of Noah and the ladder of Jacob, and the troughs by which the young of those who look therein are coloured; ye are the stones of testimony and the pitchers holding the lamps of Gideon, the scrip of David, from which the smoothest stones are taken for the slaying of Goliath. Ye are the golden vessels of the temple, the arms of the soldiers of the Church with which to quench all the fiery darts of the wicked, fruitful olives, vines of Engadi, fig-trees that are never barren, burning lamps always to be held in readiness—and all the noblest comparisons of Scripture may be applied to books, if we choose to speak in figures.

CHAPTER II:
THE DEGREE OF AFFECTION THAT IS PROPERLY DUE TO BOOKS

Since the degree of affection a thing deserves depends upon the degree of its value, and the previous chapter shows that the value of books is unspeakable, it is quite clear to the reader what is the probable conclusion from this. I say probable, for in moral science we do not insist upon demonstration, remembering that the educated man seeks such degree of certainty as he perceives the subject-matter will bear, as Aristotle testifies in the first book of his Ethics. For Tully does not appeal to Euclid, nor does Euclid rely upon Tully. This at all events we endeavour to prove, whether by logic or rhetoric, that all riches and all delights whatsoever yield place to books in the spiritual mind, wherein the Spirit which is charity ordereth charity. Now in the first place, because wisdom is contained in books more than all mortals understand, and wisdom thinks lightly of riches, as the foregoing chapter declares. Furthermore, Aristotle, in his *Problems*, determines the question, why the ancients proposed prizes to the stronger in gymnastic and corporeal contests, but never awarded any prize for wisdom. This question he solves as follows: In gymnastic exercises the prize is better and more desirable than that for which it is bestowed; but it is certain that nothing is better than wisdom: wherefore no prize could be assigned for wisdom. And therefore neither riches nor delights are more excellent than wisdom. Again, only the fool will deny that friendship is to be preferred to riches, since the wisest of men testifies this; but the chief of philosophers honours truth before friendship, and the truthful Zorobabel prefers it to all things. Riches, then, are less than truth. Now truth is chiefly maintained and contained in holy books—nay, they are written truth itself, since by books we do not now mean the materials of which they are made. Wherefore riches are less than books, especially as the most precious of all riches are friends, as Boethius testifies in the second book of his Consolation; to whom the truth of books according to Aristotle is to be preferred. Moreover, since we know that riches first and chiefly appertain to the support of the body only, while the virtue of books is the perfection of reason, which is properly speaking the happiness of man, it appears that books to the man who uses his reason are dearer than riches. Furthermore, that by which the faith is more easily defended, more widely spread, more clearly preached, ought to be more desirable to the faithful. But this is the truth written in books, which our Saviour plainly showed, when he was about to contend stoutly against the Tempter, girding himself with the shield of truth and indeed of written truth, declaring "it is written" of what he was about to utter with his voice.

And, again, no one doubts that happiness is to be preferred to riches. But happiness consists in the operation of the noblest and diviner of the faculties that we possess—when the whole mind is occupied in contemplating the truth of wisdom, which is the most delectable of all our virtuous activities, as the prince of philosophers declares in the tenth book of the Ethics, on which account it is that philosophy is held to have wondrous pleasures in respect of purity and solidity, as he goes on to say. But the contemplation of truth is never more perfect than in books, where the act of imagination perpetuated by books does not suffer the operation of the intellect upon the truths that it has seen to suffer interruption. Wherefore books appear to be the most immediate instruments of speculative delight, and therefore Aristotle, the sun of philosophic truth, in considering the principles of choice, teaches that in itself to philosophize is more desirable than to be rich, although in certain cases, as where for instance one is in need of necessaries, it may be more desirable to be rich than to philosophize.

Moreover, since books are the aptest teachers, as the previous chapter assumes, it is fitting to bestow on them the honour and the affection that we owe to our teachers. In fine, since all men naturally desire to know, and since by means of books we can attain the knowledge of the ancients, which is to be desired beyond all riches, what man living according to nature would not feel the desire of books? And although we know that swine trample pearls under foot, the wise man will not therefore be deterred from gathering the pearls that lie before him. A library of wisdom, then, is more precious than all wealth, and all things that are desirable cannot be compared to it. Whoever therefore claims to be zealous of truth, of happiness, of wisdom or knowledge, aye, even of the faith, must needs become a lover of books.

GLOSSARY

apostolic: relating to the apostles, the original followers of Jesus

cherubim: plural of cherib, a member of the second order of angels, often depicted as having a chubby, rosy-cheeked face and wings

GLOSSARY CONTINUED

ferule: a rod, cane, or flat piece of wood for striking, often on the hand

manna: miraculous food provided to the Israelites in the Bible

spherules: a small sphere

Zorobabel: a governor of the province of Judah in the Bible

Document Analysis

This selection is from the beginning of *The Love of Books,* in which De Bury makes the case for why books are worthy of reverence and are the chief source of wisdom. He makes an impassioned plea for the value of the written word, arguing that books are immortal and contain revelations from God. God had created books for the advancement of humanity. Without them, all knowledge and understanding would die out as people died. "All things are corrupted and decay in time; Saturn ceases not to devour the children that he generates; all the glory of the world would be buried in oblivion, unless God had provided mortals with the remedy of books." De Bury asserts that if there were no books, humankind would not know of the feats of great leaders or thinkers. However, when their achievements are written down, they gain eternal life. "The book that he has made renders its author this service in return, that so long as the book survives its author remains immortal and cannot die."

Books contain truth, De Bury argues, and because this truth is recorded and not subject to distracting whims or false beliefs, they are vital to the formation of truth in the mind. "The written truth of books, not transient but permanent, plainly offers itself to be observed . . . it engenders the eternal truth of the mind." Books are also wonderful teachers—not harsh or judgmental—offering their truth to all who can read them and offering the chance for all to acquire knowledge. They are available at all times, never asleep or too tired to teach. De Bury waxes poetic in his praise of the richness that books have to offer. They are "wells of living waters . . . delightful ears of corn . . . most plenteous udders of the milk of life."

It is important to De Bury that books are given the reverence they deserve, and he makes a strong case that their treatment should align with their value. "It is certain that nothing is better than wisdom: wherefore no prize could be assigned for wisdom." Philosophers argued that friendship is more valuable than riches. If this is true, said De Bury, then happiness is more valuable even than friendship, and the most reliable source of happiness is the wisdom, particularly the sacred truths, that can be found in books. If there is any question of the importance of the written word, De Bury points out that Christ himself made the declaration "It is written" to underscore the truth of his statements. Who, then, could avoid desiring books above all else? "Whoever therefore claims to be zealous of truth, of happiness, of wisdom or knowledge, aye, even of the faith, must needs become a lover of books."

Essential Themes

The primary theme of this selection is Richard de Bury's impassioned argument for the value of books and his belief that they should be treated with reverence, as they are the most wonderful teacher available to mankind. De Bury wrote in an era before printing, when each manuscript was laboriously copied and often illustrated by hand. Books were extremely valuable to those who could read them, and even a very learned man would often own only one or two books. Other manuscripts would be kept in the libraries of monasteries or universities, and so their care and protection was dependent on the reverence in which they were held by their caretakers. De Bury argued that books were valuable beyond riches, beyond friendships, since they contained eternal truths and conferred immortality on their authors.

—Bethany Groff, MA

Bibliography and Additional Reading

Bothwell, James. *The Age of Edward III*. York, UK: York Medieval, 2001. Print.

Harris, Michael H. *History of Libraries in the Western World*. 4th ed. Lanham, MD: Scarecrow, 1999. Print.

Waugh, Scott L. *England in the Reign of Edward III*. New York: Cambridge UP, 1991. Print.

APPENDIXES

Chronological List

Web Resources

besthistorysites.net/medieval-history/

Handy list of selected websites devoted to many aspects of medieval history.

blogs.commons.georgetown.edu/labyrinth/

The Labyrinth, sponsored by Georgetown University, offers resources for Medieval Studies organized by category.

cumbavac.org/middle_ages.htm#websites

A more extensive list of websites, ranging from the very specific to the more general.

deremilitari.org/

De Re Militari is a portal to scholarly information on warfare in the Middle Ages.

medieval-life-and-times.info/

Medieval Life and Times allows the user to access an array of categories and drill down to specific topics.

medievalmap.org/

Maps of the medieval era displayed by selected decade and indicating the location of peoples, castles, and battles.

themiddleages.net/

The Middle Ages.net provides info on a variety of topics within Medieval Studies.

Bibliography

Abulafia, David. *Frederick II: A Medieval Emperor*. Oxford: Oxford UP, 1998. Print.

Acocella, Joan. "Rich Man, Poor Man: The Radical Visions of St. Francis." *New Yorker. Condé Nast*, 14 Jan. 2013. Web. 1 May 2015.

Albert, Edoardo & Katie Tucker. *In Search of Alfred the Great: The King, the Grave, the Legend*. Stroud: Amberley, 2014. Print.

"Alfred First King of the English, 'Known as the Great.'" *England and English History*. EnglandAndEnglishHistory.com, 2012. Web. 12 May 2015.

"Alfred 'The Great' (r. 871–899)." *The British Monarchy*. Royal Household, n.d. Web. 12 May 2015.

Amt, Emilie. *The Accession of Henry II in England: Royal Government Restored, 1149–1159*. Woodbridge: Boydell, 1993. Print.

Angold, Michael. *The Fourth Crusade: Event and Context*. New York: Longman, 2003. Print.

Bennett, Judith. *Medieval Europe: A Short History*. New York: McGraw Hill, 2010.

Blumenthal, Uta-Renate. *The Investiture Controversy: Church and Monarchy from the Ninth to the Twelfth Century*. Philadelphia: U of Pennsylvania P, 2010. Print.

Blumenthal, Ute-Renate. *The Investiture Controversy: Church and Monarchy from the Ninth to the Twelfth Century*. Philadelphia: U of Pennsylvania P, 1988. Print.

Bobik, Joseph. *Aquinas on Matter and Form and the Elements: A Translation and Interpretation of the De Principiis Naturae and the De Mixtione Elementorum of St. Thomas Aquinas*. Notre Dame: U of Notre Dame P, 1998. Print.

Böhm, Thomas, Thomas Jürgasch, & Andreas Kirchner. *Boethius as a Paradigm of Late Ancient Thought*. Berlin: De Gruyter, 2014. Print.

Bothwell, James. *The Age of Edward III*. York, UK: York Medieval, 2001. Print.

Bourke, Vernon. *Aquinas' Search for Wisdom*. Milwaukee: Bruce, 1965. Print.

Bradbury, Jim. *Stephen and Matilda: The Civil War of 1139–53*. Charleston, SC: History Press, 2012. Print.

Breay, Claire. *Magna Carta: Manuscripts and Myths*. London: British Library, 2003. Print.

Bredero, Adriaan. *Christendom and Christianity in the Middle Ages*. Grand Rapids: Eerdmans, 1987. Print.

Bredero, Adriaan H. *Christendom and Christianity in the Middle Ages*. Grand Rapids: Eerdmans, 1987. Print.

Bredero, Adriaan H. *Christendom and Christianity in the Middle Ages: The Relations between Religion, Church, and Society*. 2nd ed. Grand Rapids: Eerdmans, 1994. Print.

Brooks, Sarah. "The Byzantine State under Justinian I (Justinian the Great)." *Heilbrunn Timeline of Art History*. Metropolitan Museum of Art, 2000. Web. 13 Mar. 2015.

Brown-Grant, Rosalind. *Christine de Pizan and the Moral Defence of Women: Reading beyond Gender*. Cambridge: Cambridge UP, 2003. Cambridge Studies in Medieval Literature Ser. Print.

Brummett, Palmira J., et al. *Civilizations Past and Present*. Vol. 1. 11th ed. London: Longman, 2005. Print.

Calder, Norman, Jawid Mojaddedi, & Andrew Rippin, ed. *Classical Islam: A Sourcebook of Religious Literature*. 2nd ed. New York: Routledge. 2012. Print.

Carr, Raymond, ed. Spain: A History. Oxford. Oxford UP, 2000. Print.

Catherine of Siena. *The Letters of St. Catherine of Siena*. Trans. Susan Noffke. Tempe: Arizona Ctr. for Medieval and Early Renaissance Studies, 2012. Medieval & Renaissance Texts & Studies Ser. Print.

Cavallo, Guglielmo. *The Byzantines*. Chicago: U of Chicago P, 1997. Print.

Chadwick, Henry. *Boethius: The Consolations of Music, Logic, Theology and Philosophy*. Oxford: Clarendon, 1990. Print.

Chazan, Robert. *In the Year 1096: The First Crusade and the Jews*. Philadelphia: Jewish Publication Soc., 1996. Print.

Claster, Jill N. *Sacred Violence: The European Crusades to the Middle East, 1095–1396*. Toronto: U of Toronto P, 2009. Digital file.

Claster, Jill N. *Sacred Violence: The European Crusades to the Middle East, 1095–1396*. Toronto: U of Toronto P, 2009. Print.

Clegg, Brian. *The First Scientist: A Life of Roger Bacon*. New York: Carroll, 2003. Print.

Cohen, Mark. "What Was the Pact of 'Umar? A Literary-Historical Study." *Jerusalem Studies in Arabic and Islam* 23 (1999): 100–157. Print.

Collins, Roger. *Visigothic Spain, 409–711*. Hoboken: Wiley, 2008. Print.

Corrigan, Gordon. *A Great and Glorious Adventure: A History of the Hundred Years War and the Birth of Renaissance England.* New York: Pegasus, 2014. Print.

Cotts, John D. *The Clerical Dilemma: Peter of Blois and Literate Culture in the Twelfth Century.* Washington: Catholic U of America P, 2009. Print.

Coy, Jason Philip, Benjamin Marschke, & David Warren Sabean. *The Holy Roman Empire, Reconsidered.* New York: Berghahn, 2010. Print.

Curtayne, Alice. *Saint Catherine of Siena.* Devon: Augustine, 1981. Print.

Daniel, David Mills. *Briefly: Anselm's Proslogion with the Replies of Gaunilo and Anselm.* London: SCM, 2006. Print.

Danziger, Danny & John Gillingham. *1215: The Year of Magna Carta.* New York: Touchstone, 2003. Print.

Davies, Brian. *The Thought of Thomas Aquinas.* New York: Oxford UP, 1992. Print.

Davis, Jennifer R. & Michael McCormick, eds. *The Long Morning of Medieval Europe: New Directions in Early Medieval Studies.* Burlington: Ashgate, 2008. Print.

Dawson, Christopher, ed. *The Mongol Mission: Narratives and Letters of the Franciscan Missionaries in Mongolia and China in the Thirteenth and Fourteenth Centuries.* New York, Sheed, 1955. Print.

Duignan, Brian. *Medieval Philosophy: From 500 to 1500 CE.* New York: Britannica Educational, 2011. Print.

Dunn, Ross E. *The Adventures of Ibn Battuta, a Muslim Traveler of the Fourteenth Century.* Berkeley: U of California P, 1986. Print.

Emon, Anver M. *Religious Pluralism and Islamic Law: Dhimmīs and Others in the Empire of Law.* Oxford: Oxford UP, 2012. Print.

Epstein, Steven A. *Wage Labor and Guilds in Medieval Europe.* Chapel Hill: U of North Carolina P, 1991. Print.

Evans, James Allan. *The Emperor Justinian and the Byzantine Empire.* Westport: Greenwood, 2005. Print.

Ezzati, A. *The Spread of Islam: The Contributing Factors.* London: Saqi, 2002. Print.

Feser, Edward. *Aquinas.* Oxford: Oneworld, 2009. Print.

Fichtenau, Heinrich. *Living in the Tenth Century: Mentalities and Social Order.* Chicago: U of Chicago P, 1991. Print.

Fine, Steven, ed. *Sacred Realm: The Emergence of the Synagogue in the Ancient World.* New York: Oxford UP, 1996. Print.

Fleming, Robin. *Domesday Book and the Law: Society and Legal Custom in Early Medieval England.* New York: Cambridge UP, 2003. Print

Fried, Johannes. *The Middle Ages.* Cambridge, MA: Belknap Press, 2015.

Frugoni, Chiara. *A Day in a Medieval City.* Chicago: University of Chicago Press, 2005.

Given-Wilson, Chris. *Chronicles: The Writing of History in Medieval England.* New York: Hambledon, 2004. Print.

Gobbitt, Thom. "Treaty of Alfred and Guthrum." *Early English Laws.* University of London, n.d. Web. 12 May 2015.

Gorecki, Danuta M. "The Heraclian Land Tax Reform: Objectives and Consequences." *Byzantine Studies* 4 (1977): 127–46. Print.

Gottlieb, Anthony. *The Dream of Reason: A History of Philosophy from the Greeks to the Renaissance.* New York: Norton, 2000. Print.

Grabar, André. *The Golden Age of Justinian· From the Death of Theodosius to the Rise of Islam.* New York: Odyssey, 1967. Print.

Gracia, Jorge J. E. & Timothy B. Noone, eds. *A Companion to Philosophy in the Middle Ages.* Malden: Blackwell, 2003. Print.

Grant, Edward. *The Foundations of Modern Science in the Middle Ages: Their Religious, Institutional, and Intellectual Contexts.* New York: Cambridge UP, 1996. Print.

Hackett, Jeremiah, ed. *Roger Bacon and the Sciences.* New York: Brill, 1997. Print.

Harris, Michael H. *History of Libraries in the Western World.* 4th ed. Lanham, MD: Scarecrow, 1999. Print.

Harrison, Kathryn. *Joan of Arc: A Life Transfigured.* New York: Doubleday, 2014. Print.

Harris, Sara. "Ancestral Neologisms in Richard Fitz Nigel's Dialogue of the Exchequer." *Journal of Medieval History* 39.4 (2013): 416–30. Print.

Head, Thomas F., & Richard Allen Landes, eds. *The Peace of God: Social Violence and Religious Response in France around the Year 1000.* Ithaca: Cornell UP, 1992. Print.

Herlihy, David V., ed. *Medieval Culture and Society.* Prospect Heights, IL: Waveland Press, 1993.

Hollister, C. Warren & John W. Baldwin. "The Rise of Administrative Kingship: Henry I and Philip Augustus." *American Historical Review* 83.4 (1978): 867–905. Print.

Howard, A. E. Dick. *Magna Carta: Text and Commentary.* Charlottesville: UP of Virginia, 1964. Print.

Hudson, John. "Administration, Family and Perceptions of the Past in Late Twelfth-Century England: Richard FitzNigel and the Dialogue of the Exchequer." *The Perception of the Past in Twelfth-Century Europe.* Ed. Paul Magdalino. London: Hambledon, 1992. 75–98. Print.

Jackson, Peter. *The Mongols and the West: 1221–1410.* New York: Routledge, 2014. Print.

James, Edward, ed. *Visigothic Spain: New Approaches.* Oxford: Oxford UP, 1980. Print.

Jenkins, John. *Knowledge and Faith in Thomas Aquinas.* Cambridge: Cambridge UP, 1997. Print.

Jones, Clyve. *A Short History of Parliament: England, Great Britain, the United Kingdom, Ireland, and Scotland.* Woodbridge: Boydell, 2009. Print.

Jones, Michael John. "The Dialogus de Scaccario (c. 1179): The First Western Book on Accounting?" *Abacus* 44.4 (2008): 443–74. Print.

Jordan William Chester. *Europe in the High Middle Ages.* New York: Viking, 2001.

Kantorowicz, Ernst Hartwig. *The King's Two Bodies: A Study in Mediaeval Political Theology.* Princeton, NJ: Princeton UP, 1957. Print.

Kaylor, Noel Harold, & Phillip Edward Phillips. *A Companion to Boethius in the Middle Ages.* Leiden: Brill, 2012. Print.

Kramer, Ann. *Eleanor of Aquitaine: The Queen Who Rode Off to Battle.* Washington: National Geographic, 2006. Print.

Laiou, Angeliki E. & Cécile Morrisson. *The Byzantine Economy.* New York: Cambridge UP, 2007. Print.

Lambert, J. Malet. *Two Thousand Years of Gild Life: Or an Outline of the History and Development of the Gild System from Early Times.* Hull: Brown, 1891. Print.

Law, Timothy Michael, and Alison Salvesen, eds. *Greek Scripture and the Rabbis.* Leuven: Peeters, 2012. Print.

Lear, Floyd Seyward. "The Public Law of the Visigothic Code." *Speculum: A Journal of Medieval Studies* 26.1 (1951): 1–23. Print.

Lloyd, Jean. "Christine de Pizan." *Women's History.* King's College, 7 Jul. 2006. Web. 9 June 2015.

Lloyd, Jean. "Christine de Pizan." *Women's History.* King's College, 7 July 2006. Web. 10 June 2015.

Loengard, Janet Senderowitz. *Magna Carta and the England of King John.* Suffolk, UK: Boydell, 2010. Print.

Lyon, Bryce D., ed. *The High Middle Ages.* New York: Free Press, 1984.

Maddicott, J. R. *The Origins of the English Parliament, 924–1327.* New York: Oxford UP, 2010. Print.

Marenbon, John. *The Philosophy of Peter Abelard.* Cambridge: Cambridge UP, 1999. Print.

Marenbon, John. *The Philosophy of Peter Abelard.* New York: Cambridge UP, 1997. Print.

Margolis, Nadia. *An Introduction to Christine de Pizan.* Gainesville: UP of Florida, 2012. Print.

McInerny, Ralph. *St. Thomas Aquinas.* Boston: Twayne, 1977. Print.

Miller, Maureen C. *Power and the Holy in the Age of the Investiture Conflict: A Brief History with Documents.* New York: Palgrave, 2005. Print.

Ogilvie, Sheilagh. *Institutions and European Trade: Merchant Guilds, 1000–1800.* New York: Cambridge UP, 2011. Print.

O'Meara, Thomas Franklin. *Thomas Aquinas, Theologian.* Notre Dame: U of Notre Dame P, 1997. Print.

"Origins of Parliament." Parliament.uk. British Parliament, n.d. Web. 18 May 2015.

Perry, David M. *Sacred Plunder: Venice and the Aftermath of the Fourth Crusade.* Philadelphia: U of Pennsylvania P, 2015. Print.

Peters, Edward. *The First Crusade: "The Chronicle of Fulcher of Chartres" and Other Source Materials.* 2nd ed. Philadelphia: U of Pennsylvania P, 1998. The Middle Ages Ser. Print.

Peters, Edward. *The First Crusade: The Chronicle of Fulcher of Chartres and Other Source Materials.* Philadelphia: U of Pennsylvania P, 2011. Print.

Poole, Reginald L. *The Exchequer in the Twelfth Century: The Ford Lectures Delivered in the University of Oxford in Michaelmas Term, 1911.* Clark: Lawbook Exchange, 2006. Print.

Porter, Pamela. *Courtly Love in Medieval Manuscripts.* Toronto: U of Toronto P, 2003. Print.

Power, Amanda. *Roger Bacon and the Defense of Christendom.* Cambridge: Cambridge UP, 2013. Print.

Preston, Todd. *King Alfred's Book of Laws: A Study of the Domboc and Its Influence on English Identity, with a Complete Translation.* Jefferson: McFarland, 2012. Print.

Raymond of Capua. *The Life of St. Catherine of Siena: The Classic on Her Life and Accomplishments as Recorded by Her Spiritual Director.* Charlotte: Tan, 2011. Print.

Robinson, I. S. *Henry IV of Germany, 1056–1106*. New York: Cambridge UP, 1999. Print.

Robinson, Paschal. "St. Francis of Assisi." *Catholic Encyclopedia*. Vol. 6. Ed. Charles G. Herbermann, et al. New York: Appleton, 1909. 221–30. Print.

Robson, Michael J. P. *The Franciscans in the Middle Ages*. Woodbridge: Boydell, 2009. Print.

Saint Francis of Assisi. *Francis and Clare: The Complete Works*. Trans. Regis J. Armstrong and Ignatius Brady. New York: Paulist, 1982. Print.

Scott, S. P., ed. "The Visigothic Code (Forum Judicum)." *Library of Iberian Resources Online*. U of Central Arkansas, 2015. Web. 2 Apr. 2015.

Seward, Desmond. *Eleanor of Aquitaine: The Mother Queen of the Middle Ages*. New York: Pegasus, 1978. Print.

Seward, Desmond. *Eleanor of Aquitaine: The Mother Queen of the Middle Ages*. New York: Pegasus, 2014. Print.

Seward, Desmond. *The Hundred Years War: The English in France 1337–1453*. New York, Penguin, 1978. Print.

Smith, A. D. *Anselm's Other Argument*. Cambridge: Harvard UP, 2014. Print.

Stolpe, Sven. *The Maid of Orleans: The Life and Mysticism of Joan of Arc*. New York: Pantheon, 1956. Print.

Swietek, Francis R. "Gunther of Pairis and the Historia Constantinopolitana." *Speculum* 53.1 (1978): 49–79. Humanities and Social Sciences Index Retrospective: 1907–1984 (H.W. Wilson). Web. 14 May 2015.

Thibault, Paul R. *Pope Gregory XI: The Failure of Tradition*. Lanham: UP of America, 1986. Print.

Thorpe, Benjamin. *Ancient Laws and Institutes of England: Comprising Laws Enacted under the Anglo-Saxon Kings from Aethelbirht to Cnut*. Cambridge: Cambridge UP, 1840. Print.

Tuchman, Barbara W. *A Distant Mirror: The Calamitous Fourteenth Century*. New York: Random, 2014. Print.

Turner, Ralph V. *Judges, Administrators, and the Common Law in Angevin England*. Rio Grande: Hambledon, 1994. Print.

Tyerman, Christopher. *God's War: A New History of the Crusades*. Cambridge: Belknap P of Harvard UP, 2006. Print.

Van Nieuwenhove, Rik & Joseph Wawrykow, eds. *The Theology of Thomas Aquinas*. Notre Dame: U of Notre Dame P, 2005. Print.

Visser, Sandra & Thomas Williams. *Anselm*. New York: Oxford UP, 2009. Print.

Waines, David. *The Odyssey of Ibn Battuta: Uncommon Tales of a Medieval Adventurer*. Chicago: U of Chicago P, 2010. Print.

Waugh, Scott L. *England in the Reign of Edward III*. New York: Cambridge UP, 1991. Print.

Weir, Alison. *Eleanor of Aquitaine: By the Wrath of God, Queen of England*. London: Vintage, 2008. Print.

Willard, Charity Cannon. *Christine de Pizan: Her Life and Works*. New York: Persea, 1990.

Willard, Charity Cannon. *Christine de Pizan: Her Life and Works*. New York: Persea, 1990. Print.

Wippel, John F. *The Metaphysical Thought of Thomas Aquinas: From Finite Being to Uncreated Being*. Washington: Catholic U of America P, 2000. Print.

Wollock, Jennifer G. *Rethinking Chivalry and Courtly Love*. Santa Barbara: Praeger, 2011. Print.

Wormald, Patrick. *The Making of English Law: King Alfred to the Twelfth Century; Legislation and Its Limits*. Vol 1. Malden: Blackwell, 1999. Print.

Yule, Henry, ed. *Cathay and the Way Thither*. London: Hakluyt Soc., 1914. Print.

Index